**Systems of Care for
Children's Mental Health**

Series Editors:

Beth A. Stroul, M.Ed

Robert M. Friedman, Ph.D

Social & Emotional
Health in Early Childhood

Other Volumes in This Series

*Transition to Adulthood: A Resource for Assisting
Young People with Emotional or Behavioral Difficulties*
edited by Hewitt B. "Rusty" Clark, Ph.D.,
and Maryanne Davis, Ph.D.

Developing Outcome Strategies in Children's Mental Health
edited by Mario Hernandez, Ph.D.,
and Sharon Hodges, Ph.D.

Social & Emotional Health in Early Childhood

Building Bridges Between Services & Systems

edited by

Deborah F. Perry, Ph.D.

Women's and Children's Health Policy Center

Johns Hopkins Bloomberg School of Public Health

Roxane F. Kaufmann, M.A.

Center for Child and Human Development

Georgetown University

and

Jane Knitzer, Ed.D.

National Center for Children in Poverty

·P A U L·H·
BROOKES
PUBLISHING CO.®

Baltimore · London · Sydney

Paul H. Brookes Publishing Co.
Post Office Box 10624
Baltimore, Maryland 21285-0624

www.brookespublishing.com

Typeset by Graphic World, Maryland Heights, Missouri.
Manufactured in the United States of America by
Versa Press, Inc., East Peoria, Illinois.

The case studies appearing in this book are composites based on the authors'
experiences; these case studies do not represent the lives or experiences of
specific individuals, and no implications should be inferred.

Library of Congress Cataloging-in-Publication Data

Social and emotional health in early childhood : building bridges between
services and systems / edited by Deborah F. Perry, Roxane K. Kaufmann, and
Jane Knitzer.
    p.   cm.—(Systems of care for children's mental health)
Includes bibliographical references and index.
ISBN-13: 978-1-55766-782-3 (pbk.)
ISBN-10: 1-55766-782-9 (pbk.)
    1. Child health services—United States.   2. Child mental health services—
United States.   I. Perry, Deborah F.   II. Kaufmann, Roxane K.
III. Knitzer, Jane.   IV. Title.   V. Series.
[DNLM: 1. Mental Disorders Diagnosed in Childhood.   2. Child.
3. Developmental Disabilities—prevention & control.   4. Health Promotion.
5. Infant.   6. Mental Health Services.   WS 350 S6776 2007]
RJ102.S63 2007
618.92'89—dc22   2006101731

British Library Cataloguing in Publication data are available from the British
Library.

Contents

Series Preface

In 1982, Knitzer's seminal study, *Unclaimed Children,* was published by the Children's Defense Fund. At that time, the field of children's mental health was characterized by a lack of federal or state leadership, few community-based services, little collaboration among child-serving systems, negligible parent involvement, and little or no advocacy on behalf of youngsters with emotional disorders. Since that time, substantial gains have been realized in both the conceptualization and the implementation of comprehensive, community-based systems of care for children and adolescents with serious emotional disorders and their families.

A vast amount of information has emanated from the system-building experiences of states and communities and from research and technical assistance efforts. Many of the trends and philosophies emergent in recent years have now become widely accepted as "state of the art" for conceptualizing and providing services to youngsters with emotional disorders and their families. There is now broad agreement surrounding the need to create community-based systems of care throughout the United States of America for children and their families, and the development of these systems has become a national goal. Such systems of care are based on the premises of proving services in the most normative environments, creating effective interagency relationships among the key child-serving systems, involving families in all phases of the planning and delivery of services, and creating service systems that are designed to respond to the needs of culturally diverse populations.

A major need is to incorporate these concepts and trends into the published literature. This need stems from the critical shortage of staff who are appropriately trained to serve youngsters in community-based systems of care, with new philosophies and new service delivery approaches. Of utmost importance is the need to provide state-of-the-art information to institutions of higher education for use in the preservice education of professionals across disciplines, including the social work, counseling, psychology, and psychiatry fields. Similarly, there is an equally vital need for resources in the in-service training of staff in mental health, child welfare, education, health, and juvenile justice agencies to assist staff in working more effectively with youngsters with emotional disorders and their families.

   This book series, *Systems of Care for Children's Mental Health*, is designed to fulfill these needs by addressing current trends in children's mental health service delivery. The series has several broad goals:

- To increase awareness of the system-of-care concept and philosophy among current and future mental health professionals who will be providing services to children, adolescents, and their families

- To broaden the mental health field's understanding of treatment and services delivery beyond traditional approaches to include innovative, state-of-the-art approaches

- To provide practical information that will assist the mental health field to implement and apply the philosophy, services, and approaches embodied in the system-of-care concept

Each volume in the continuing series addresses a major issue or topic related to the development of systems of care. The books contain information useful to planners, program managers, policy makers, practitioners, parents, teachers, researchers, and others who are interested in and involved in improving systems of care for children with emotional disorders and their families. As the series editors, it is our goal for the series to provide an ongoing vehicle and forum for exploring critical aspects of systems of care as they continue to evolve.

Beth A. Stroul   Robert M. Friedman

REFERENCE

Knitzer, J. (1982). *Unclaimed children: The failure of public responsibility to children and adolescents in need of mental health services.* Washington, DC: Children's Defense Fund.

Editorial Advisory Board

About the Editors

Deborah F. Perry, Ph.D., Director, Women's and Children's Health Policy Center, Department of Population, Family and Reproductive Health, Johns Hopkins Bloomberg School of Public Health, 615 N Wolfe Street, Room E4144, Baltimore, Maryland 21205

Dr. Perry's research concerns women and children who are at risk for mental health disorders. She is the co-principal investigator of a research grant testing a preventive intervention for post-partum depression in Latina women. As Director of Research at the Georgetown University Center for Child and Human Development, she served as project director for an urban mental health grant focusing on maternal depression in low-income families of color. She has worked with states and counties to develop and evaluate systems of care for young children under the age of 6 with or at risk for special needs. Dr. Perry has conducted research into the effectiveness of mental health consultation to early care and education providers. She has a doctoral degree in maternal and child health from Johns Hopkins University and a master's degree in psychology from the New School for Social Research. She is also the mother of an 11-year-old daughter, Grace.

Roxane K. Kaufmann, M.A., Director, Early Childhood Policy, Georgetown University Center for Child and Human Development, 3300 Whitehaven Street, NW, Suite 3300, Post Office Box 57485, Washington, D.C. 20057

Since joining the faculty at Georgetown University in the early 1980s, Ms. Kaufmann has been a strong advocate for the development of integrated services, supports, and systems for young children and their families. As part of the National Technical Assistance Center for Children's Mental Health, she plays a leadership role in supporting the work of states and communities in developing early childhood mental health systems of care through the facilitation of strategic planning, targeted technical assistance, and the development of materials. Ms. Kaufmann has directed projects providing training and technical assistance to agencies such as Head Start and to programs such as child care, mental health, education, public health, and special education. She has written manuscripts, articles, and training materials on early intervention in the context of systems development. In addition, she developed curricula and provided training and technical assistance to twenty-eight countries from Eastern Europe and Central Asia in support of their education reform efforts.

Jane Knitzer, Ed.D., Executive Director, National Center for Children in Poverty, 215 West 125th Street, New York, New York 10027

In addition to her work with the National Center for Children in Poverty, Dr. Knitzer is also a Clinical Professor of Population and Family Health at the Mailman School of Public Health. As a psychologist, Dr. Knitzer has focused her own research on improving public policies related to children's mental health, child welfare, and early childhood. Her work on mental health includes the ground-breaking policy report, *Unclaimed Children: The Failure of Public Responsibility to Children and Adolescents in Need of Mental Health Services* (Children's Defense Fund, 1982). Most recently, she has been a leader in calling attention to the importance of addressing social and emotional issues in young children. Dr. Knitzer has been on the faculty at Cornell University, New York University, and Bank Street College of Education. She is a member of the New York State Permanent Judicial Commission on Justice for Children and a past president of Division 37: Child, Youth, and Family Services of the American Psychological Association, and of the American Association of Orthopsychiatry. She was the first recipient of the Nicolas Hobbs Award for Distinguished Service in the Cause of Child Advocacy from the American Psychological Association.

About the Contributors

Brenda J. Bean, M.A.C.P., Director, Early Childhood Mental Health Programs, State of Vermont Child Development Division, 203 North Building, 103 South Main Street, Waterbury, Vermont 05671. In 1997, Ms. Bean authored the successful Children's UPstream Services grant application to the federal Center for Mental Health Services. She has extensive experience administering federal and state grant awards for community-based services. Her professional and personal focus is the prevention of emotional and behavioral problems in children, youth, and families.

Charles A. Biss, M.S.W., Director, Children's Mental Health, Vermont Department of Health, 108 Cherry Street, Burlington, Vermont 05402. Since 1972, Mr. Bliss has been working in the field of mental health as a practioner, program administrator, and state administrator. He is especially committed to the principles of consumer-driven care, community-based care, and early intervention. He is married with four children.

Jennifer Boss, M.S.W., Assistant Director, Early Head Start National Resource Center, ZERO TO THREE, 2000 M Street, NW, Suite 200, Washington, D.C. 20036. In her position as assistant director, Ms. Boss is responsible for supervising and supporting the staff and working closely with the project director to ensure that all contract activities are carried out in a high-quality manner. She received her master's degree in social work from Howard University, completed postgraduate clinical training at the Yale University Child Study Center, and received a certificate in infant/young child mental heath at the Washington School of Psychiatry.

Elena P. Cohen, M.Ed., Director, Safe Start Center, JBS International, Inc., 8630 Fenton Street, Suite 1200, Silver Spring, Maryland 20910. Prior to holding her current position, Ms. Cohen worked with the Center for the Study of Social Policy. She has devoted her professional life to child welfare and has authored several articles and book chapters.

Paul J. Donahue, Ph.D., Director, Child Development Associates, 6 Palmer Avenue, Scarsdale, New York 10583. Dr. Donahue is the author of the forthcoming book *Parenting without Fear* (St. Martin's Press, in press) and the co-author of *Mental Health Consultation in Early Childhood Settings* (Paul H. Brookes Publishing Co., 2000) with Beth Falk and Anne Gersony Provet. He is a frequent lecturer to parents, teachers, and community groups throughout the country. To learn more about his work, visit http://www.drpauldonahue.com.

Glen Dunlap, Ph.D., Research Professor, University of South Florida, Department of Child and Family Services, 2778 Mayberry Drive, Reno, Nevada 89509. Dr. Dunlap has been involved with people with disabilities and their families since the mid-1970s. His research and training activities have been focused on positive behavior support, early intervention, family support, developmental disabilities, and child protection.

Beth Falk, Ph.D., Licensed Psychologist and Certified School Psychologist, 185 Kisco Avenue, Suite 6, Room 3, Mt. Kisco, New York 10549. Dr. Falk is in private practice, providing therapy to children and adolescents and providing consultation to schools and families. She previously worked in a variety of school and community mental health settings. She is the co-author of *Mental Health Consultation in Early Childhood Settings* (Paul H. Brookes Publishing Co., 2000) with Paul J. Donahue and Anne Gersony Provet.

Sally Farwell, M.Ed., Director of Programs, Achievement Centers for Children, 4255 Northfield Road, Highland Hills, Ohio 44128. The Achievement Centers for Children is a nonprofit organization that provides comprehensive services to children with disabilities and their families. Ms. Farwell has worked in the field of early intervention since the mid-1970s. She was the co-chair of the Cuyahoga County Help Me Grow Early Childhood Mental Health Committee from its inception in January of 1999 until June 2005.

Lise Fox, Ph.D., Professor, Department of Child and Family Services, University of South Florida, 13301 Bruce B. Downs Boulevard, Tampa, Florida 33612. Dr. Fox conducts research and develops intervention models for young children with disabilities and/or challenging behavior and their families. Her research interests include positive behavior support, family support, and instructional strategies.

Linette M. Fraga, Ph.D., Director of Military Projects, ZERO TO THREE, 2000 M Street, NW, Suite 200, Washington, D.C. 20036. Dr. Fraga has been involved in research, administration, training, and practice in early childhood and mental heath as an early childhood teacher, parent educator, trainer, and administrator in family support and child care settings. She received her bachelor's degree education from the University of

Arizona, her master's degree in human relations fro the University of Oklahoma, and her doctoral degree in family studies from Kansas State University.

Kathy S. Hepburn, M.S., Senior Policy Associate, Georgetown University Center for Child and Human Development, 3300 Whitehaven Street, NW, Suite 3300, Washington, D.C. 20057. Ms. Hepburn's work focuses on young children and their families in settings that include mental health services, specialty health care, and early education. As senior policy associate, she has been involved in multiple local, state, and national progress supporting the early childhood and mental health services communities through training, technical assistance, and research. She has also authored several publications related to early childhood, mental health, staff development, and service integration.

Larke N. Huang, Ph.D., Senior Advisor to the Administrator, Substance Abuse and Mental Health Services Administration, U.S. Department of Health and Human Services, 1 Choke Cherry Road, Room 8-1051, Rockville, Maryland 20857. Dr. Huang is a clinical psychologist specializing in children and families. In her past experiences, she has been a clinical practitioner, researcher, and university faculty member. She is currently engaged in national policy for children's health and mental health.

Mareasa R. Isaacs, Ph.D., Executive Director, National Alliance of Multi-Ethnic Behavioral Health Associations, 1875 Eye Street, NW, Suite 500, Washington, D.C. 20006. Prior to holding her current position, Dr. Issacs was an associate professor at the School of Social Work at Howard University. She also held the position of senior program associate for mental health at the Annie E. Casey Foundation for over 6 years.

Margot Kaplan-Sanoff, Ed.D., Associate Professor, Pediatrics, Boston University School of Medicine, Maternity Building, 91 E Concord Street, 5th Floor, Boston Medical Center, 1 Boston Medical Center Place, Boston, Massachusetts 02118. Dr. Kaplan-Sanoff trains pediatric residents and fellows in infant, child, and family development, directs clinical programs, and serves on a multidisciplinary team for a maternal depression research project. She is also director of the Healthy Steps Initiative, where she directed the transdisciplinary team who developed and implemented the Healthy Steps Program.

Tammy L. Mann, Ph.D., Deputy Executive Director, ZERO TO THREE, 2000 M Street, NW, Suite 200, Washington, D.C. 20036. Dr. Mann's previous professional activities include working a variety of practice, policy, and research settings that focused on addressing the developmental needs of very young at-risk children and their families. She has authored several book chapters and journal articles. She received her doctoral degree in clinical psychology with an interdisciplinary specialization in infant studies.

Melissa Manos, M.Ed., M.S.M., Executive Director, Help Me Grow of Cuyahoga County, 2412 Community College Avenue, Cleveland, Ohio, 44115. Help Me Grow is a statewide child development program that provides services to expectant parents, newborns, and infants and toddlers with or at risk for developmental delays or disabilities. Ms. Manos has worked with prevention and early intervention programs since the early 1970s.

Judith C. Meyers, Ph.D., President and Chief Executive Officer, Child Health and Development Institute of Connecticut, President and Chief Executive Officer, Children's Fund of Connecticut, 270 Farmington Avenue, Suite 367, Farmington, Connecticut 06032. Both the Child Health and Development Institute of Connecticut and the Children's Fund of Connecticut are focused on improving health outcomes for children through promoting the development of comprehensive, effective, community-based health and mental health care systems. Dr. Meyers is a clinical and community psychologist. She holds faculty appointments at the University of Connecticut School of Medicine in Pediatrics and Psychiatry and the Yale University Child Study Center.

Peggy Nikkel, Executive Director, UPLIFT (Wyoming's Federation of Families for Children's Mental Health), 145 S Durbin, Suite 201, Casper, Wyoming 82601. In addition to her work with UPLIFT, Ms. Nikkel is also the parent of a son with emotional disorders. She actively participates on a number of state and national initiatives to improve services for children.

Stephanie Powers, M.S., Editor-in-Chief, ZERO TO THREE, 2000 M Street, NW, Suite 200, Washington, D.C. 20036. Ms. Powers holds master's degrees both in child development and family studies and in infant mental health. Prior to holding her current position, she supported the healthy development of children and their families in a variety of professional roles, including child care, early intervention, child welfare, and child life programs.

Anne Gersony Provet, Ph.D., Clinical Psychologist, Westchester Medical Center, 95 Grasslands Avenue, Valhalla, New York 10595. Dr. Provet specializes in early childhood and adolescent psychology. She works as a member of the Mobile Crisis Team of Westchester Medical Center and in private practice in Mt. Kisco, New York. She is the co-author of *Mental Health Consultation in Early Childhood Settings* (Paul H. Brookes Publishing Co., 2000) with Paul J. Donahue and Beth Falk.

H. Abigail Raikes, Ph.D., Consultant, Early Childhood Development, Bill and Melinda Gates Foundation, 1706 E Galer Street, Seattle, Washington 98112. Dr. Raikes received her doctoral degree in developmental psychology from the University of Nebraska, Lincoln. She also holds a master's degree in public health from Columbia University. Her work primarily focuses on early social and emotional development, with an emphasis on children in poverty.

Jeffery D. Rosenbaum, Ph.D., Director, Early Childhood Center, Beech Brook, 3737 Landers Road, Pepper Pike, Ohio, 44124. Dr. Rosenbaum has been a child clinical psychologist since the early 1980s, working in particular with young children with behavior problems and autism spectrum disorders. He also serves as a board member of the Ohio Association of Infant Mental Health and supervises psychology graduate students from local universities in field placement experiences.

Elisa A. Rosman, Ph.D., Consultant, 874 N Greenbrier Street, Arlington, Virginia 22205. Dr. Rosman has a doctoral degree in community psychology with a focus on developmental psychology. Her research interests include children at risk and their families and the policies that affect them. She works as a consultant for nonprofit and research organizations.

Ross A. Thompson, Ph.D., Professor of Psychology, University of California, Davis, 1 Shields Avenue, Davis, California 95616. Dr. Thompson is a developmental psychologist who studies early social and emotional development, parent–child relationships, and the growth of psychological understanding. He also works on the public policy applications of developmental science, such the prevention of children malignment, divorce and custody, research ethics, and school readiness.

Michelle W. Woodbridge, Ph.D., Education Researcher, Center for Education and Human Services, SRI International, 333 Ravenswood Avenue, Menlo Park, California 94025. In her position at SRI International, Dr. Woodbridge supports and supervises the coordination of technical assistance for the statewide evaluation of First 5 California. She has worked in research and evaluation of children's systems of care services, including behavioral and mental health, education, juvenile justice, public health, and social services, since the early 1990s.

Foreword

This is an important and a timely book. It challenges policy makers and practitioners in the fields of early childhood and mental health to translate powerful research about the importance of early relationships into effective practices "on the ground."

The editors of this volume set out to achieve three core goals:

- To provide an informed perspective on why early social and emotional development is important for later school success, particularly for young children whose well-being is compromised by poverty, disability, or other threats to healthy development

- To highlight emerging prevention and early intervention strategies that help parents and other caregivers promote the emotional health of young children and the adaptive capacities of their families

- To provide ideas and guidelines for program designers and policy makers about the most effective ways to invest in young children's early social and emotional health and to prevent or reduce the costs of later serious emotional and behavioral disorders

Through the creative use of selected vignettes, case examples, and a review of the scientific literature, this book makes a strong case for the importance of supporting vulnerable young children and their families, and provides examples of feasible strategies for intervening early in the lives of those who are struggling with mental health problems. Unlike many volumes that focus exclusively on clinical issues, this book also addresses the complex challenges of delivering and paying for high quality services. Moreover, the editors have done a wonderful job of incorporating the voices of families and other caregivers, both as core partners in responsive service delivery and as primary change agents on behalf of vulnerable children.

The editors of this valuable collection have performed an important service for a struggling field. Although the book is clear in its message that all the answers are not in, it is informed by a solid developmental framework that is anchored to a rich and growing knowledge base. As such, it provides a snapshot of promising yet still fragmented approaches to the monumental task of building a system of integrated services and supports to help infants, toddlers and preschoolers who exhibit significant social and emotional vulnerability. To this end, the book identifies and addresses early warning signs and risk factors, as well as provides information on effective treatment for early childhood mental health disorders.

Finally, and of equal importance, Perry, Kaufmann, and Knitzer offer a vision and a framework for how to strengthen the policy and practice infrastructure for early childhood mental health at both the community and state levels. Collectively, the multiple contributors to this important volume make a strong case for a public health approach to emotional and social health that addresses prevention and early intervention, and not just treatment. And they embed their messages in a deep commitment to infusing innovative strategies into primary settings where young children, their families, and their caregivers are found.

In 2000, the blue ribbon committee at the Institute of Medicine and National Research Council that produced *From Neurons to Neighborhoods: The Science of Early Childhood Development* declared that "the time is long overdue for state and local decision makers to take bold actions to design and implement coordinated, functionally effective infrastructures to reduce the long-standing fragmentation of early childhood policies and programs." This book provides a valuable blueprint to guide states and communities in the pursuit of that goal. It is a rich resource and a powerful call to action from some of the finest thinking in the field. We would do well to heed its compelling messages.

Jack P. Shonkoff, M.D.
Center on the Developing Child
Harvard University

REFERENCE

Shonkoff, J.P., & Phillips, D.A. (Eds.). (2000). *From neurons to neighborhoods: The science of early childhood development.* Washington, DC: National Academies Press.

Acknowledgments

We want to begin by acknowledging the significant contributions made by our distinguished group of authors, without whom this book would not have become a reality. We also want to thank Beth Stroul and Bob Friedman, who recommended that this volume be added to the Paul H. Brookes Publishing Co. series called *Systems of Care for Children's Mental Health*— and who asked us to lead this effort. We owe a collective debt of gratitude to the many practitioners and public officials who have generously shared their lessons, triumphs, and defeats throughout the years in their quest to build comprehensive systems for young children and their families. Most of all, however, we are grateful to the families, who individually and collectively in focus groups have shared their journeys and their wisdom and their courage. We hope that their stories will inspire better integration of research, policy, and practice in communities across the country to ensure more young children grow to their full potential. Lastly, we all want to thank our own families who have been there through endless reams of electronically generated paper and evenings without dinner as this book was written and edited.

To my daughter, Grace, and my husband,
Lewis, who every day remind me of the
importance of love, laughter, and leisure
—Deborah F. Perry

To my sons, Adam and Greg, my husband, Neal,
and especially to my new granddaughters, who
bring me the magic and wonder of childhood
—Roxane K. Kaufmann

To my children, Lizbeth and Susie, who have
taught me so much about resilience, courage, and
mental health, and to my husband, Herbert
Ginsburg, who has so steadfastly supported me in
all I have done with humor, wise advice, and love
—Jane Knitzer

Social & Emotional
Health in Early Childhood

I

Understanding Early Childhood Mental Health in the Context of Child Development

1

Building Bridges

Linking Services, Strategies, and Systems for Young Children and Their Families

Deborah F. Perry, Roxane K. Kaufmann, and Jane Knitzer

> Bridge: a structure spanning and
> providing passage over a gap or barrier.
> (http://www.freedictionary.com)

In 1994, the Educate America Act set forth an ambitious national goal that "every child shall enter school ready to learn." Since then, research has emerged that paints a rich portrait of the factors that promote or inhibit early learning success. This research makes it clear that caring parental relationships and other early life experiences equip most young children with appropriate tools to support their learning and enable them to succeed in school. Thus, social-emotional development has become recognized as an essential component of optimal child development and school readiness.

The group of young children who are at risk for early school failure is sizable—somewhere between one fourth and one third of all young children. The risk factors for poor social-emotional development fall into four categories that have been repeatedly identified in research. First, poverty is the greatest risk factor for poor developmental outcomes, whether social-emotional, heath related, or academic. A second major set of risks are derived from poor quality early care and learning experiences. Unfortunately, the quality of much of the informal or formal child care and early learning experiences for young children is inadequate, especially for those from low-income families. Parental risks and behaviors pose a third set of risks. Lack of education, poor parental health, untreated parental trauma, and negative parenting all contribute to at-risk development. Parental risk factors known to have damaging effects on young children's social-emotional development, especially depression and other mental health issues, substance abuse, and domestic violence, should be the focus of increased attention. The fourth set of risk factors are seen in young children who have serious, diagnosable emotional and behavior problems. Children with chronic health problems or disabilities are also at higher risk for emotional and behavior problems. These children represent roughly one third of all children with special health care needs (Johnson & Knitzer, 2006).

Although some young children facing such risks are resilient and able to thrive despite challenges, many do not fare so well. Child care workers describe too many young children as *mad, bad, and sad*, and even the most skilled and seasoned workers tell of encounters with young children they do not know how to help. Yet, much is known about how to intervene. Just as there are deliberate strategies to promote early literacy, so there are strategies to promote healthy early social-emotional development. Such interventions need to be viewed through a family lens; that is, they must address the parents, the parent–child relationship, relationships with other important caregivers, and any possible developmental delays experienced by the child. The purpose of this book is to articulate a framework for promoting healthy social-emotional development in all young children in the context of their families and communities.

THE PURPOSE AND STRUCTURE OF THIS BOOK

This book is designed for practitioners, policy makers, and other stakeholders invested in improving social-emotional and behavioral outcomes for young children and their families. It is intended to bridge a gap in the utilization of knowledge gained from early childhood research and practice to inform the development of an intentional set of policies and effective programs targeted to this population. There is a great deal of high quality research about how young children's social-emotional development unfolds and what can lead to compromised outcomes; however, efforts to identify and address mental health problems in young children early and effectively remain limited and fragmented. Too often the research does not get translated into policies that promote cross-agency systems planning. Or, the knowledge is not used to inform an intentional approach to organizing services and supports that promote healthy social-emotional and behavioral competencies in young children (Knitzer & Lefkowitz, 2006). Therefore, this book has several goals.

- To highlight why early social-emotional development is important and its relationship to school success, particularly for young children whose development is compromised by poverty, disability, or other threats

- To provide a framework, examples, and strategies for program designers and policy makers about the most effective ways to create systems of care for young children's early social-emotional health and to prevent or reduce the costs of later serious emotional and behavior disorders

- To illustrate the ways in which mental health services and supports can be infused into early childhood environments that bridge the gaps between the different fields that serve young children and their families

This book is organized into three sections. The first section articulates the need for an approach to systems development that is anchored in developmental knowledge. It defines early childhood social-emotional development in terms of providing a foundation for school readiness (see Thompson & Raikes, Chapter 2), and explains the important role culture plays in understanding early childhood issues (see Huang & Isaacs, Chapter 3). The second section begins with a framework for building bridges between health, mental health, education, and social services and systems that are serving young children and their families. In Chapter 4, Kaufmann and Hepburn describe the critical components of an early childhood mental health system of care—the beams, trusses, struts, and bracings needed to span the gaps in our patchwork of services and supports to young children and their caregivers. The other chapters in this section describe the specific elements of this framework in more depth: work force development efforts that span different disciplines and lead to personnel who can address the mental health needs of young children in the context of their families (see Meyers, Chapter 5); outcomes assessment that needs to consider the complex interplay of services and strategies from multiple systems (see Perry, Woodbridge, & Rosman, Chapter 6); and the role of families, especially those who are raising a child with a diagnosed mental health disorder, in designing these bridges and ensuring their safe passage (see Nikkel, Chapter 7). This section concludes with two case studies that illustrate how these bridges can be constructed in a specific community or state (see Bean, Biss, & Hepburn, Chapter 8; Manos, Farwell, & Rosenbaum, Chapter 9). These examples illustrate the important role that local geography plays in designing the bridges, including the choice of materials, partner agencies, and type of approaches. The third section describes strategies to infuse early childhood mental health services and supports into typical environments in which young children are found, including primary health care environments (see Kaplan-Sanoff, Chapter 11), infant and toddler environments (see Mann, Powers, Boss, & Fraga, Chapter 12), and preschool environments (see Donohue, Falk, & Provet, Chapter 13). Fox and Dunlap (Chapter 14) summarize the evidence-based strategies for young children with and at-risk for challenging behaviors. Knitzer and Cohen (Chapter 15) conclude this book with a synthesis of lessons learned for services, strategies, and systems targeted to young children and their families at highest risk.

This book also includes five appendices for general reference. Appendix A, the Self-Assessment Guide, offers a flexible framework to support the mental health needs of young children and their families. Appendix B, the Self-Assessment Checklist for Personnel Providing Services and Supports for Children with Disabilities and Special Health Care Needs and Their Families, provides pointed questions that personnel in the human service environments can use to assess their practices. Appendix C, the Self-Assessment Checklist for Personnel Providing Services and Supports in Early Intervention and Early Childhood Environments, provides similar questions to personnel in early childhood environments. Appendix D, Spending Smarter: A Funding Guide for Policy Makers and Advocates to Promote Social-Emotional Health and School Readiness, offers a set of questions to help develop a strategic approach to social and emotional school readiness. Appendix E, the Matrix of Early Childhood Mental Health Services and Supports, provides a photocopiable workbook that arrays the continuum of services and supports with the major federal funding streams that can be used for young children and their families.

DEFINING EARLY CHILDHOOD MENTAL HEALTH

The term *early childhood mental health* has been chosen for emphasis in this book for several reasons. It underscores the inclusion of children birth to 5 years (or even through 8 years) instead of focusing only on babies and toddlers. It also helps the authors' desire to contribute to efforts to destigmatize the term *mental health*, which in many societies has come to focus exclusively on mental illness and dysfunction. The authors of this book embrace the view of the World Health Organization, which emphasizes the important role that culture plays in defining emotional and psychological well-being and underscores that mental health is defined in most cultures as broader than a lack of mental disorder (Jenkins, 2004). In much of the text, the term *social-emotional development* is used not only because many people continue to be uncomfortable with the term *mental health*, especially as it applies to young children but also because *social-emotional development* better describes a prevention and early intervention focus.

The authors have approached the task of defining early childhood mental health by drawing on two perspectives offered in the literature. The first emphasizes this term in the context of an individual child's development, whereas the second views the phenomenon in a systems context. A developmental and/or clinical definition (ZERO TO THREE, 2002) views early childhood mental health as

- The social-emotional and behavioral well-being of infants, toddlers, young children, and their families

- The developing capacity to experience, regulate, and express emotion

- The ability to form close, secure relationships

- The capacity to explore the environment and learn

A systems or service delivery perspective proposed by Knitzer (2000) defines early childhood mental health as a set of strategies to

- Promote the emotional and behavioral well-being of all young children

- Strengthen the emotional and behavioral well-being of children whose development is compromised by environmental or biological risk in order to minimize their risks and enhance the likelihood that they will enter school with appropriate skills

- Help families of young children address whatever barriers they face to ensure that their children's emotional development is not compromised

- Expand the competencies of nonfamilial caregivers and others to promote the well-being of young children and families, particularly those at risk by virtue of environmental or biological factors

- Ensure that young children experiencing clearly atypical emotional and behavioral development and their families have access to needed services and supports

In combination, these two perspectives capture the efforts to synthesize literature across a variety of fields, including early care and education and mental health, as well as apply this knowledge to building systems to support healthy social-emotional development in all young children.

These two definitions of early childhood mental health underscore the need to adopt an ecological framework in guiding the development of a new approach to systems building. Based on the pioneering work of Bronfenbrenner (1979) on ecological systems theory, the authors view early childhood mental health as intricately related to the health and well-being of the family members who care for young children in their homes. In turn, the well-being of families is influenced by the characteristics of the communities in which they reside, including such things as quality of the schools, safety of the neighborhood, and availability of services. These community level resources are affected by the broader policy and fiscal climate of the county and state in which the community is located. Finally, the national policy infrastructure sets some of the parameters within which communities and states may design systems of services and supports (Kaufmann & Perry, 2002; Kaufmann & Wischman, 1999).

WHAT TYPES OF SERVICES, STRATEGIES, AND SYSTEMS ARE NEEDED?

The authors of this book believe that to successfully bridge the chasms and, indeed, make sure there are enough bridges in the approaches to meeting the mental health needs of young children and their families, a public health framework is needed (The President's New Freedom Commission on Mental Health, 2003; Rosman, Perry, & Hepburn, 2005). Based on scientific evidence, intervention research, and real world experience, it is important to adopt a population-based approach to delivering services and supports through intentional strategies supported by enabling policies and a well-articulated infrastructure. It is the view of these authors that services are the structured interactions among children, families or caregivers, and early childhood professionals, who may be trained in early care and education, mental or physical health, and social services, that build on developmental and clinical knowledge about how to promote age-appropriate social-emotional skills as young children master relationships and regulate their own emotions. These formal services are often supplemented with informal supports that are provided by family, neighbors, or others in the child's community. They need to be directed not just to children, but to families and others who are in close contact with the children (e.g., teachers, child care providers, home visitors, pediatricians). In other words, services and supports need to be embedded within the daily routines and cultural rituals of young children and their families. To do this effectively, intentional strategies are needed to infuse these services and supports into a variety of early childhood environments, including primary health care offices, family and center-based child care programs, and early intervention programs for children with delays or disabilities. Programs that reach out to families struggling with such stressors as poverty, substance abuse, trauma, family violence, and physical and mental illness are particularly ripe for embedding within them early mental health services for the affected adults and their children. These services and strategies need to be supported by an infrastructure that ensures that professionals are trained to deliver evidence-based services, that adequate payment is available to these professionals, and that outcomes are assessed by the stakeholders who consume and finance these services.

A public health framework addresses the needs of three segments of a dynamic population of young children and their families. First, promotion strategies are those targeted to all children. Such strategies can help families and caregivers foster social skills, emotional health, and positive behaviors as a part of a school readiness agenda. These strategies include anticipatory guidance by pediatricians or others; social and emotional skill-building curricula in preschool programs; and mobilization of local community leaders, mentors, and coaches. Second, prevention and early intervention strategies target the needs of groups of young children who face special risks. Young children at risk include those whose parents are incarcerated or abuse drugs; those in foster care; those with disabilities; and those whose parents face serious mental health issues, particularly depression. These strategies focus on preventing the development of problem behaviors or poor social-emotional development in the young child. Some examples include embedding mental health consultation in child care environments and intensive home-visiting programs targeting children with family level risk factors. Finally, a third of set of strategies should ensure the availability of high quality intervention services that are sufficiently intensive to help young children who are manifesting some kind of significant mental health concern. Examples of these interventions include access to specialized mental health and other intervention services that address the behavioral health needs of young children in the context of their family and community. Ideally, they should also include access to intervention for those risks that are most likely to significantly impair effective parenting, as well as interventions targeted to the children.

A public health approach would increase the likelihood of early identification of children and families that might benefit from intentional strategies to promote healthy social-emotional development. It would allow children to receive mental health services and supports with or without a diagnosis—a barrier inherent in Medicaid and other funding sources that keeps children at risk and those with subclinical levels of problem behavior from accessing specialized services that could ultimately shift their trajectories toward positive outcomes. Finally, this framework would support efforts to destigmatize mental health services by embedding intervention within the environments and services that all children and families access as children grow and develop.

MOVING FORWARD: A NEW PARADIGM FOR EARLY CHILDHOOD MENTAL HEALTH SYSTEMS

If society is committed to the healthy social-emotional well-being of all young children in this country and to implementing this public health, bridge-building approach to delivering mental health services and supports, there are substantial implications not just for services, but also for funding and other policies. Many of the bridge-building activities can occur within communities, across child-serving agencies and providers, and even within the current policy context. Specifically, mental health professionals will need to design ways to infuse their expertise into early childhood environments, including offering mental health consultation services to child care providers, pediatricians, and home visitors and embedding behavioral health screening into existing protocols. Likewise, early care and education providers will need to share their knowledge and expertise about normal developmental milestones in young children with children's mental health professionals. In essence, bridges must be built from each side and meet in the middle; neither side owns the bridge and it requires reliance on the complementary strengths of both disciplines to ensure its structural integrity.

To be sustainable, this local bridge building will also require the development of a strong enabling policy and fiscal infrastructure at the state and federal levels that signals a long-term commitment to a more integrated approach to service delivery. At this writing, the federal responsibility for early childhood services is spread across multiple agencies that represent dozens of categorical programs, some of which share a few common principles. For example, the Maternal and Child Health Bureau (within the U.S. Department of Health and Human Services) distributes funding to states through Title V of the Social Security Act and more recently has sponsored the Early Childhood Comprehensive Systems (ECCS) initiative. At their core, these programs share a commitment to comprehensive, interagency, family centered, community-based services that is fundamental to the Infants and Toddlers Program of the Individuals with Disabilities Education Improvement Act of 2004 (PL 108-446; administered by the U.S. Department of Education) and the Comprehensive Services for Children's Mental Health initiative funded by the Substance Abuse and Mental Health Services Administration. Head Start and Early Head Start have had a long-standing commitment to comprehensive child development services that target the whole family and include mental health as well as physical health services. The Child Care Bureau has funded a number of innovative programs, including Healthy Child Care America, and states have used their Child Care Development Block Grant quality dollars to fund a number of mental health consultation activities embedded in child care environments. There is, however, no unifying federal framework that embraces a public health approach to service delivery and systems development that is paralleled in funding patterns (Johnson & Knitzer, 2005).

The authors developed this book as a way to inspire states and communities to forge ahead with their efforts to build bridges between early childhood and mental health in the absence of such a federal framework. They have brought together examples from a variety of sites, disciplines, and initiatives to nurture creative strategies for infusing a continuum of mental health services into a variety of early childhood environments. There is no single blueprint for building these bridges, but there is a common vision—if we are to prepare the next generation of young people to succeed in school, work, and life, we must embrace a population-based approach that ensures that high quality services and supports are available to all young children and their caregivers. It is the authors' hope that this volume contributes to the growing momentum across the country to extend mental health systems of care to younger children and those at risk for serious emotional disturbances, and that it supports the ongoing efforts of the early childhood community to ensure that young children enter school ready to learn. Working together, society can bridge the chasms in all efforts to provide promotion, prevention, and early intervention services to young children and their caregivers.

REFERENCES

Bronfenbrenner, U. (1979). *The ecology of human development*. Cambridge, MA: Harvard University Press.

Individuals with Disabilities Education Improvement Act of 2004, PL 108-446, 20 U.S.C.§§1400 *et seq.*

Jenkins, R. (Ed.). (2004). *World Health Organization Guide to Mental and Neurological Health in Primary Care*. London: Royal Society of Medicine Press.

Johnson, K., & Knitzer, J. (2006). *Early childhood comprehensive systems that spend smarter maximizing resources to serve vulnerable children*. New York: National Center for Children in Poverty, Columbia University, School of Public Health.

Johnson, K., & Knitzer, J. (2005). *Spending smarter: A funding guide for policymakers and advocates to promote social and emotional health and school readiness*. New York: National Center for Children in Poverty, Columbia University, School of Public Health.

Kaufmann, R., & Perry, D. (2002). Promoting social-emotional development in young children: Promising approaches at the national, state, and community levels. In The Kauffman Early Education Exchange (Ed.), *Set for success: Building a strong foundation for school readiness based on the social and emotional development of young children* (pp. 4-5). Kansas City, MO: The Ewing and Marion Kauffman Foundation.

Kaufmann, R., & Wischman, A.L. (1999) Communities supporting the mental health of young children and their families. In R.N. Roberts & P.R. Magrab (Eds.), *Where children live: Solutions for serving young children and their families*. Advances in applied developmental psychology (Vol. 17) (pp. 175-210). Stamford, CT: Ablex.

Knitzer, J. (2000). Early childhood mental health services: A policy and systems perspective. In J.P. Shonkoff & S.J. Meisels (Eds.), *Handbook of early childhood intervention* (pp. 416-438). Cambridge, England: Cambridge University Press.

Knitzer, J., & Lefkowitz, J. (2006). *Pathways to early school success: Helping the most vulnerable infants, toddlers, and their families*. New York: National Center for Children in Poverty, Columbia University, School of Public Health.

The President's New Freedom Commission on Mental Health. (2003). *Achieving the promise: Transforming mental health care in America (final report)*. (DHHS Publication No. SMA 03-3832). Washington, DC: U.S. Government Printing Office.

Rosman, E., Perry, D., & Hepburn, K. (2005). *The best beginning: Partnerships between primary health care and mental health and substance abuse services for young children and their families*. Washington, DC: National Technical Assistance Center for Children's Mental Health, Georgetown University, Center for Child and Human Development.

ZERO TO THREE Infant Mental Health Task Force. (2002, May). *Definition of infant mental health disorder*. Unpublished manuscript.

2

The Social and Emotional Foundations of School Readiness

Ross A. Thompson and H. Abigail Raikes

In the spring of 2005, two national reports were released that help to frame current thinking about the origins of school readiness. First, at the meeting of the Society for Research in Child Development, a team of developmental researchers presented a collection of papers at a session entitled *Hard Skills and Socioemotional Behavior at School Entry: What Matters Most for Subsequent Achievement?* (Dowsett & Huston, 2005; Duncan, Claessens, & Engel, 2005; Feinstein, 2005; Klebanov & Brooks-Gunn, 2005; Magnuson, 2005). Drawing on some of the most important large-scale, longitudinal studies of children's development through the early years, each researcher sought to predict scores on standardized tests of academic achievement in the early elementary grades (or later) based on kindergarten measures of cognitive competency (typically standardized achievement test scores) and socioemotional functioning (e.g., maternal or teacher ratings of social functioning or internalizing or externalizing behavior). Each of the analyses controlled for a variety of early influences, such as parent education, socioeconomic status, and family environment, to model the effects of *changes* in cognitive or socioemotional functioning late in the preschool years. Their findings were consistent: In each study, preschool measures of cognitive competence were strong predictors of early elementary academic performance, whereas measures of socioemotional functioning rarely had much predictive value. Their conclusions suggested that public resources devoted to fostering school readiness should be devoted primarily to enhancing young children's thinking, reasoning, and number skills.

The second report was a national survey of nearly 4,000 teachers in prekindergarten classrooms. Gilliam (2005) reported that roughly seven out of every 1,000 enrolled preschoolers were expelled due to behavioral concerns during the previous year. Expulsion rates were highest for older preschoolers and for African Americans. Boys were approximately 4½ times more likely than girls to be permanently prohibited from participation in preschool. Gilliam (2005) reported that expulsion rates were lowest in public school classrooms and Head Start programs, and they were highest in for-profit and faith-based child care programs. Children were much less likely to be banned from the preschool if the teacher had access to classroom-based mental health consultation when problems arose. Importantly, the preschoolers expelled from their classrooms were also likely to be those who would most benefit from the cognitive stimulation provided by a high-quality early education program.

The juxtaposition of these two reports highlights the challenges of defining the foundations of school readiness in the early years. When a national consensus emerged in the 1990s that school children in the United States were poorly prepared for the scientific and technological challenges of the future, the National Education Goals Panel (1997) urged that "all children shall enter school ready to learn" with a deadline of 2000 for accomplishing this goal. Since that time, there has been considerable attention devoted to programs that foster literacy, language, numeracy, and conceptual skills in preschoolers, with particular attention to the capabilities of children in Head Start and other programs serving disadvantaged populations.

During the same period, however, teachers of preschoolers, kindergarteners, and primary grade students voiced further concerns about the young children in their classrooms. Head Start teachers reported that their children exhibited signs of serious emotional distress, including depression, withdrawal, and problems with aggression and antisocial behavior (Yoshikawa & Knitzer, 1997). Kindergarten teachers reported that they were most concerned about the children in their classes who lacked the motivational incentives for new learning and the socioemotional capacities for getting along with others because these skills are more difficult to teach than academics (Lewit & Baker, 1995; Rimm-Kaufman, Pianta, & Cox, 2000). National studies estimate that approximately 10% of the children enrolled in typical kindergarten classrooms exhibit behaviors (e.g., fighting) that undermine school success even though they do not result in expulsion, with a much higher proportion occurring in classrooms for economically disadvantaged children (see review by Raver & Knitzer, 2002).

What are the developmental foundations necessary for young children to succeed in the primary grades? To what extent is the growth of social, emotional, and self-regulatory skills important to subsequent academic achievement? What skills are important, and how are they associated with school success? What can be done to ensure that young children, especially in circumstances of challenge or difficulty, are prepared for kindergarten?

This chapter is devoted to examining these questions. We begin with a short reflection on the nature of school readiness and then turn to research that highlights the socioemotional skills relevant to classroom success, their development during the preschool years, and their relevance to children's academic achievement. This analysis is then broadened by considering the importance of early relationships and the extrafamilial environment that prepares young children for school. In doing so, we emphasize that school readiness is not simply a matter of qualities inherent in the child; it is significantly influenced by the relationships and social contexts that shape early socioemotional and cognitive growth. In conclusion, we discuss the implications of this research for efforts to strengthen school readiness.

WHAT IS SCHOOL READINESS?

Similar to other good things, people have an intuitive sense of what *school readiness* is but often have difficulty defining it. When they do, they sometimes find that they disagree. It is not surprising that school readiness would mean somewhat different things to different people in light of divergent views of the essential contributors to early learning, the needs of the child, and the origins of individual differences in academic achievement.

Prevalent portrayals of school readiness differ, in fact, in several fundamental ways (see Carlton & Winsler, 1999; Meisels, 1999). Some views portray school readiness as primarily or exclusively the development of literacy, numeracy, language, and other cognitive skills, whereas others broaden this perspective to include young children's motivation to learn, physical health and well-being, capacities to get along with others, curiosity, and self-regulatory abilities. To some, readiness is a quality of the child, with remedial interventions focusing on deficits in cognitive, motivational, or socioemotional capabilities that are likely to impair academic success. To yet others, readiness is a quality of the child, the family, and the school and their interaction with each other to the extent that problems in readiness may arise from the underpreparation of the classroom for the child as much as of the child for the school.

Some ask whether it is suitable to apply a single standard of school readiness to all children or whether the indicators of academic preparation will vary for children from different cultures, language backgrounds, physical or emotional challenges, and other qualities. These varying portrayals of school readiness are important for many reasons, including their implications for how to assess children's preparation for school, such as by standardized assessments, observations of the child in learning situations, evaluations of work products, or other approaches that are also focused on the family, school, and community.

One way of defining school readiness is to consider the qualities that parents of young children, or kindergarten teachers, view as essential to early learning. Two national surveys of parents and kindergarten teachers conducted in the early 1990s yielded complementary conclusions (National Center for Education Statistics, 1993, 1994). For both parents and teachers, two of the three most important qualities for early learning were being "enthusiastic and curious in approaching new activities" and able to "communicate needs, wants, and thoughts verbally in child's primary language." Teachers also highly rated "physically healthy, rested, and well-nourished" and "can follow directions," whereas parents listed "takes turns and shares" and "sits still and pays attention" as essential qualities. The *lowest* rated qualities for both parents and teachers were traditional academic skills, such as "knows the letters of the alphabet," "can count to 20 or more," and "able to use pencils or paint brushes" (see Lewit & Baker, 1995).

The National Education Goals Panel (1997) outlined five dimensions of school readiness. They are 1) health and physical development, 2) emotional well-being and social competence, 3) approaches to learning, 4) communication skills, and 5) cognition and general knowledge. Recently, a consortium of representatives of 17 states sought to create a set of measurable indicators of school readiness that could be implemented in policy making and evaluation (National School Readiness Indicators Initiative, 2005). Their core readiness indicators were in the following six domains: children, families, communities, health services, early care and education, and schools. Within the child domain, there were indicators of school readiness focused on the child's physical well-being and motor development, social and emotional development, approaches to learning, language development, and cognition and general knowledge. This broad portrayal of school readiness was a means for the consortium to underscore the multiple determinants of academic readiness in young children and the diverse developmental processes that contribute to preparation for school in the early years.

Definitions of school readiness are important, therefore, for clarifying thinking about how and when young children are prepared for elementary school, and different definitions of readiness have important implications for how it is evaluated. These definitions are also important for clarifying the role of socioemotional influences on academic preparation. If young children's preparation for school is to enable them to accurately use letters and numbers in kindergarten, then early cognitive preparation is most important because of the moderately strong association between measures of cognitive competence in the preschool and kindergarten years (LaParo & Pianta, 2000).

If, however, preschool preparation is also to enable young children to cooperate successfully with classmates and the teacher, including resolving conflicts adaptively, and to exercise behavioral and emotional self-control in group learning situations, then developing socioemotional skills are likely to be more relevant to the growth of school readiness. Furthermore, if academic preparation is to foster young children's curiosity, strengthen their self-confidence as learners, and encourage their adaptability and creativity as independent problem solvers, then socioemotional influences may have even more complex relations to the other skills necessary for school readiness. Taken together, therefore, these alternative approaches to defining school readiness incorporate different portrayals of what is necessary for children to succeed in school and, in turn, how to create a foundation for the broader outcomes expected of school success in educational completion, job attainment, good citizenship, and other societal goals.

SOCIOEMOTIONAL DEVELOPMENT AND SCHOOL ACHIEVEMENT

Although these definitional issues have not been resolved, it is apparent that virtually all portrayals of school readiness incorporate children's linguistic, numerical, and conceptual preparation, and most recognize that it also requires the social, emotional, and self-regulatory capacities for learning in groups. The preschool years witness significant achievements in cognitive and socioemotional development relevant to school success, although many young children enter kindergarten behaviorally or emotionally unprepared for academic success.

Indeed, contemporary concern about school readiness is fueled by growing awareness that the academic success of many young children is undermined by early emerging emotional problems with origins in temperamental vulnerability, troubled family relationships, and traumatic early experiences, especially in disadvantaged homes (see Shonkoff & Phillips, 2000). Contrary to traditional wisdom that young children lack the capacities for the deep sadness and grief of depression, for example, recent research shows that when they are living with a depressed parent, young children are themselves at risk for affective disorders owing to the demanding, troubled emotional climate of the family as well as their inherited vulnerability (Goodman & Gotlib, 1999). Early emerging conduct disorders arise in a context of parental rejection and conflict, maternal depression, and the child's temperamental fearlessness as early as the first years of life (Rubin, Burgess, Dwyer, & Hastings, 2003; Shaw, Miles, Ingoldsby, & Nagin, 2003). Children in homes characterized by negative, coercive family interactions often reveal the emotional consequences of family life in their antagonistic peer interactions (Reid, Patterson, & Snyder, 2002).

These and related findings indicate that many children (e.g., those studied by Gilliam, 2005) arrive at kindergarten with significant social and emotional problems arising from troubled family conditions, difficult neighborhoods, and the child's own vulnerabilities. This is important because these social and emotional difficulties are also likely to impair learning in the classroom. Addressing the needs of vulnerable children such as these requires more than concerted efforts to teach them letters and numbers; it also requires services that address their emotional problems and the family difficulties that underlie them. For young children in difficult circumstances, learning and emotional well-being are connected.

Indeed, this is true for all children because learning in the classroom is affected by their socioemotional and self-regulatory capacities. In the sections that follow, we consider the importance to school success of the quality of teacher and peer relationships, conscience development, emerging capacities for cooperation and compliance, and the growth and development of self-regulation and self-understanding. How preschoolers develop competencies in each area that prepare them for school and how individual differences in children's capabilities are relevant to school success are also discussed (see also Denham & Weissberg, 2004; Raver, 2002; Thompson, 2002). Furthermore, related research issues requiring further attention are identified.

Teacher and Peer Relationships

For preschoolers, learning occurs in manageable social contexts created by focused interaction with an adult and a few playmates. Once they enter kindergarten, however, children encounter the challenges of learning in classroom activities that are directed by the teacher and may include the entire class of 10–25 children. Doing so requires that they manage their relationships with teachers and peers. The former requires skills related to focused social interaction, cooperation and compliance, and listening attentively, as well as the capacity to clearly convey needs, questions, and understanding to an adult. The latter requires equally complex capacities for social and emotional understanding, the development of skills for initiating and maintaining harmonious interaction with other children, and knowing how to handle conflict adaptively.

These are formidable challenges, but during the preschool years there are considerable advances in the development of social understanding and social behavior (see Thompson, in press, and Thompson, Goodvin, & Meyer, in press, for recent reviews). Contrary to traditional portrayals of preschoolers as egocentric, for example, young children are fascinated by how the needs, desires, beliefs, and thoughts of others compare with their own. Toddlers begin to appreciate how behavior is affected by invisible psychological motivators (e.g., desires, perceptions, feelings) and that people vary in these mental states. By ages 4–5, young children understand the influences of beliefs and thoughts on behavior and that these beliefs may be mistaken in a way that people think something is true (e.g., "Mommy is waiting outside for me") when it is not (Wellman, 2002). Throughout this period, young children also begin to understand the origins and consequences of simple emotions, the influence of psychological traits on people's behavior, and issues of fairness in social interaction, although they have considerably more to learn about the social world in the years to come.

There are important implications of these achievements for children's social experiences in the kindergarten or primary grade classroom. First, even young children respond not only to the behavior of teachers and peers but also to the emotions, intentions, desires, and motives they infer in people's actions. Given their limited psychological understanding, their inferences may be incomplete or inaccurate, which may lead to inappropriate responses. This may be especially true when children's home experiences negatively bias their expectations for others' intentions or motives. Second, their developing social awareness better enables young children to understand and cooperate with classmates, but it also permits greater deception, teasing, and manipulation as children gradually appreciate that the contents of their own minds need not always be disclosed, and the contents of others' minds can be deliberately altered or misled. Third, with increasing age young children begin to comprehend that disagreement and conflict may arise because people's goals, beliefs, and understanding are discordant. As a consequence, they become more adept at resolving conflict between themselves and others through compromise, turn-taking, persuasion, negotiation, and even humor. Their capacities for shared understanding also develop as young children become increasingly capable of balancing others' goals and viewpoints with their own.

Young children vary considerably in these capacities for social interaction and social understanding, and these differences are associated with their success in the classroom (Ladd, Birch, & Buhs, 1999). As many parents observe, children who develop warm, positive relationships with their kindergarten teachers are more excited about learning, more positive about coming to school, more self-confident, and achieve more in the classroom than do children who experience more troubled or conflicted relationships with their teachers (Birch & Ladd, 1997; NICHD Early Child Care Research Network, 2003a; Pianta & Stuhlman, 2004a). A positive teacher–child relationship may be especially important for young children who are otherwise at risk of academic difficulty because of the support it can provide for classroom involvement and self-confidence (Pianta, Steinberg, & Rollins, 1995).

The peer environment is also important. Children who experience greater peer acceptance and friendship tend to feel more positive about coming to school, participate more in classroom activities, and achieve more in kindergarten (Ladd, Kochenderfer, & Coleman, 1996, 1997). There is particular reason for concern for young children who experience early peer rejection among their kindergarten or primary school class-mates. These children are more likely to be victimized and excluded from peer activity, report feeling lonely, participate less in classroom activities, express a desire to avoid school, and do not perform as well as peers on academic achievement measures (Buhs & Ladd, 2001).

Much less is known about how particular social skills relevant to com-petence with peers and teachers contribute to children's classroom achievement. In older children, social problem-solving skills have been found to be associated with success in peer relationships, and simpler kinds of social skills may be important in younger children as well (Crick & Dodge, 1994; Lemerise & Arsenio, 2000). In one longitudinal study, how-ever, kindergarten teacher ratings of social skills and aggressiveness were each positively associated with first-grade teachers' ratings of student achievement, suggesting that assertiveness as well as cooperation may be important to peer acceptance (Dowsett & Huston, 2005). Sensitivity and appropriate response to the feelings of others is also an important con-tributor to social success with peers (Denham & Weissberg, 2004). In a recent study, Izard and his colleagues (2001) reported that measures of emotion understanding at age 5 significantly predicted academic compe-tence at age 9 after controlling for verbal ability and temperament, and suggested that this association might be mediated by the more positive classroom relationships that arise when children are more emotionally perceptive (Izard et al., 2001).

More research is needed to elucidate these relational influences and their association with early academic success. It is important to under-stand, for example, whether social relationships in the classroom affect academic achievement through children's motivation to participate in aca-demic activities, their emotions while in school, the impact of conflict with peers, or in other ways. The findings by O'Neil, Welsh, Parke, Wang, and Strand (1997), for example, that peer rejection as early as kindergarten was associated with deficits in work habits and academic achievement in the primary grades (beyond the influence of prior academic performance) sug-gest that multiple avenues of influence are likely.

Conscience and Compliance

Although social problem-solving skills and emotion understanding are likely to foster positive peer relationships in the kindergarten classroom, teachers require more from their students. A positive teacher–child rela-tionship is founded, at least in part, on the child's cooperation and compli-ance with the teacher's guidance, which includes participating in classroom activities, paying attention, staying on-task without continuous reminders, and having a positive demeanor toward learning activities. Young children must learn how to get along socially with peers, but they must also learn how to comply with adult authority.

Complying with another's behavioral expectations is challenging for young children (Kopp, 1982). They must remember what is expected, apply it to the relevant situations, alter their actions according to the remembered standard, continuously monitor their compliance, and realize when the standard no longer applies. Preschoolers are still novices in most of these skills, but they also achieve considerable progress in conscience development and their motivation to cooperate with adult authority. Contrary to traditional portrayals of preschoolers as punishment-and-obedience oriented, contemporary research reveals that young children are motivationally complex in their moral orientation (Thompson, Meyer, & McGinley, 2006). In addition to the rewards and incentives of others, preschoolers are also motivated to cooperate because of their desire to maintain warm and positive relationships with those who matter to them, such as parents and teachers, as well as by their sensitivity to others' feelings and desires (Kochanska, 1997b). An adult's angry or disapproving vocal tone after misbehavior may provoke an apology not just to avert anticipated punishment, therefore, but to restore a positive relationship on which the child is emotionally reliant. One implication is that the warmth and security of their relationships with adult authorities is an important influence on young children's attention to behavioral standards, desire to comply, and adoption of the adult's values for themselves. By contrast, when punitive coercion substitutes for relational incentives, young children are often compliant but do not as readily internalize the underlying values, and this may be especially true for children growing up in difficult family conditions.

Young children are becoming more sophisticated moralists during the preschool years in other ways. They distinguish moral violations from social-conventional rule-breaking, viewing the former as more serious and less revocable mostly because of its harm to others (Smetana, 1997). They are also beginning to see themselves as moral beings by portraying themselves as *good* boys or girls and seeking to act accordingly (Kochanska, 2002). Empathy is also an emerging resource for cooperative and moral behavior (Zahn-Waxler & Robinson, 1995). Each of these achievements is deeply influenced by the incentives and support that children experience in their family relationships.

Young children vary considerably in their cooperation with parents and teachers and for various reasons. For example, children may be incapable of complying with behavioral expectations that are developmentally inappropriate, a coercive adult–child relationship may undermine the motivation to cooperate, or a child's lack of cooperation may be a sign of other problems. In the kindergarten or primary grade classroom, individual differences in cooperation are significantly associated with academic achievement. McClelland, Morrison, and Holmes (2000) found, for example, that work-related skills (e.g., compliance with instructions, completion of work) in kindergarteners predicted children's academic achievement 3 years later, even after controlling for earlier academic achievement (see also Yen, Konold, & McDermott, 2004). Likewise, Duncan and his colleagues (2005) reported that kindergarten teacher ratings of the child's constructive learning predicted third-grade test scores, controlling for prior cognitive achievement. Alexander, Entwisle, and Dauber (1993) found that first-grade teachers' ratings of students' classroom engagement and concentration (but not compliance) predicted later achievement test scores and reading and math performance. In addition, negative and noncompliant behavior in the early years can foreshadow later difficulty. In one study, measures of the child's externalizing behavior at age 5 even predicted educational attainment at age 30 (Feinstein, 2005).

Taken together, therefore, a young child's capacity to cooperate with adult requests and participate constructively in organized activities in the classroom is associated with academic achievement. Further research is needed, however, to determine the avenues by which this association exists. Cooperation is important for several reasons. First, it establishes a more positive relationship with the teacher. Second, it enables children to benefit more from learning activities. Finally, teachers favor and give more attention to children whom they believe are compliant. These avenues from cooperation to achievement suggest significantly different ways of fostering academic achievement in young children; therefore, further exploration of the link between cooperation and academic achievement is warranted.

Self-Regulation and Self-Understanding

Young children's capacities to manage their feelings and behavior underlie the social skills and cooperative conduct that are discussed in this chapter. The growth of self-regulation, however, is broader still and encompasses developing abilities to focus and sustain attention; manage cognitive processes (e.g., thinking and reasoning); exert behavioral self-control (e.g., controlling fidgeting) in organized environments; and exhibit the emotional self-control that is entailed in sociability and cooperation. Academic achievement requires all of these features of self-regulation, and young children entering the school classroom face the significant challenge of mastering their thoughts, feelings, attention, impulses, and behavior in order to be successful students.

The preschool years witness significant advances in the growth of self-regulation, which is apparent when comparing a 3-year-old with a

6-year-old in a game of "Red Light–Green Light." One reason is the maturation of regions of the brain (primarily in the prefrontal cortex) that enable greater cognitive, emotional, and behavioral self-control (Diamond & Taylor, 1996; Gerstadt, Hong, & Diamond, 1994). Parents also foster the growth of self-regulation as they increasingly use explanations, negotiation, appeals to self-image, and other strategies to enlist children's cooperation through self-regulation rather than their coercion alone (Belsky, Woodworth, & Crnic, 1996).

Parents also coach self-regulatory strategies in their young children, such as when they suggest activities to help children remain quiet in formal environments or encourage them to use words rather than behavioral outbursts when angrily aroused (Eisenberg, Cumberland, & Spinrad, 1998; Thompson, 1994). As a consequence, young children master a broadening array of skills for self-control during the preschool years. In managing their feelings, for example, young children begin to comprehend how emotions can be regulated by seeking the assistance of another; avoiding or ignoring emotionally arousing situations; redirecting attention or activity in more emotionally satisfying ways; using reassuring self-talk; and, later, through psychological means, such as internal distraction (Thompson, 1990). Although children entering school still have far to go in learning to manage their feelings, impulses, behavior, and thoughts, they have achieved considerable progress in doing so, and many are ready for the challenges of exercising self-control in the classroom.

Preschoolers vary considerably, however, in their capacities to exert self-control. These differences are the result of several factors, including 1) temperamental individuality (a quality known as *effortful control* is associated with better emotion regulation, conscience development, and other adaptive qualities [see Kochanska, Murray, & Harlan, 2000]); 2) developmental readiness (children of any age vary considerably in their capacities for self-management); and 3) background experiences that may foster or impair the growth of self-regulation. With regard to background experiences, extensive research documents the association between self-regulatory competence in early childhood and sensitive, supportive parental care and the association between parental overcontrol, punitiveness, and negative affect and children's behavioral dysregulation (see Eisenberg, 2002; Fox & Calkins, 2003). This is one reason why children living in aversive homes where punishment is overused do not show the compliant behavior that one might expect at school or elsewhere, but instead their behavior becomes easily uncontrolled, especially during stressful or emotionally arousing circumstances.

These differences are, not surprisingly, important to academic achievement. In one study, a behavioral measure of attentional self-regulation predicted first graders' reading achievement scores independent of vocabulary and a prior measure of kindergarten reading ability (Howse, Lange, Farran, & Boyles, 2003). Other researchers have also noted the association between differences in young children's attentional skills and their reading and math achievement scores in later years (e.g., Alexander et al., 1993; Dowsett & Huston, 2005; Magnuson, 2005). In a study of more than 1,000 children, researchers with the NICHD Early Child Care Research Network (2003b) found that differences between preschoolers in behavioral measures of sustained attention and impulsivity partially mediated the association between the quality of the family environment and cognitive and social assessments of school readiness. Taken together, these findings suggest that attentional self-regulation may be especially important to early school success, perhaps because of its relevance not only to cognitive focus in learning activities but also to the social competence required of children in classrooms.

Coupled with the growth of self-regulation are advances in self-understanding that also contribute to academic achievement. During the preschool years, young children develop a more comprehensive, coherent network of self-referent beliefs concerning their behavioral competencies, personality qualities, and emotional tendencies (Thompson et al., in press). By age 3, for example, children have begun to assert their competence (e.g., by refusing assistance); describe their internal experiences (e.g., by referring to their desires, feelings, and needs); and refer to themselves in categorical terms (e.g., by gender). Moreover, 3-year-olds also take pride in their accomplishments and experience guilt when they violate standards of conduct. These and other self-referent emotions are elicited, in part, by children's sensitivity to how others evaluate them (Stipek, Recchia, & McClintic, 1992). For this reason, early self-concept is significantly influenced by children's perception of how they are regarded by the people who matter to them, which is communicated in an adult's direct references to the child, references about the child to other people (which children can overhear), and how a child's experiences are represented in conversations about everyday events (Goodvin, Meyer, Thompson, & Hayes, 2006; Miller, Potts, Fung, Hoogstra, & Mintz, 1990). These influences continue in the fourth and fifth years as young children begin to describe themselves in more explicitly characterological terms (Marsh, Ellis, & Craven, 2002; Measelle, Ablow, Cowan, & Cowan, 1998), although their use of such terms as *good* and *naughty* lacks the rich meaning inherent in how older people use these concepts. Even so, it is apparent that self-understanding in early childhood provides a foundation for the more elaborated forms of self-referential beliefs that will emerge in later years and is based partly on how children think they are viewed by caregivers.

These self-representations are important because of their influence in guiding children's choices of activities. Children who lack confidence in their cognitive skills, for example, may withdraw from participating in classroom activities. Self-representations are also important because of how a positive or negative self-concept can contribute resiliency or vulnerability when children face the challenges of academic performance. Young children who are confident in their abilities to learn, owing partly to caregiver confidence in them, are more likely to persist when faced with difficult tasks and to eagerly approach new problem-solving situations. Little, however, is known about how individual differences in young children's self-concept is related to their early academic performance, and more research on this topic is clearly needed.

THE IMPORTANCE OF RELATIONSHIPS

How do young children acquire the socioemotional skills required for school success? By contrast with academic skills that can be taught by a skilled teacher, the social skills, capacities for cooperation and compliance, and self-regulatory abilities that are described in this chapter are not so easily and explicitly instructed.

Instead, the socioemotional qualities required for school achievement develop in the context of a preschooler's experience in close relationships at home and elsewhere. In close relationships, young children become sensitive to and understand the need to respect other people's feelings, acquire skills of negotiating differences of opinion, learn how to control their impulses and desires to get along with others, and become motivated to cooperate for the social rewards it provides. Relational experience can also foster cognitive competency as children attend to cooperative learning experiences, value achievement and the praise it brings, and acquire self-confidence as problem solvers.

A number of studies have shown that the quality of the mother–child relationship in early childhood is strongly associated with how well children function in kindergarten and with subsequent school success (Burchinal, Peisner-Feinberg, Pianta, & Howes, 2002; Morrison, Rimm-Kauffman, & Pianta, 2003; NICHD Early Child Care Research Network, 2003a, 2003c, 2005; Pianta, Nimetz, & Bennett, 1997). They collectively indicate that when young children enjoy warm, supportive relationships with their mothers, they subsequently exhibit greater academic competence in kindergarten and early primary grades, are more socially competent in the classroom, show fewer conduct problems, and have better work habits. In one longitudinal study, Estrada, Arsenio, Hess, and Holloway (1987) found that a measure of the emotional quality of the mother–child relationship at age 4 was associated with the child's cognitive competence at that age and was predictive of school readiness measures at ages 5 and 6, IQ score at age 6, and school achievement at age 12. These findings are consistent with broader research literatures documenting the importance of warm, secure parent–child relationships for a variety of cognitive, socioemotional, and personality out-comes in young children (see Thompson, in press, for a review).

Other relationships are also influential. The warmth and sensitivity of the child care provider is associated with a child's classroom performance, attention skills, and social competence (Peisner-Feinberg et al., 2001; Pianta et al., 1997; see Bowman, Donovan, & Burns, 2001, and Lamb, 1998 for reviews). Kindergarten teachers' reports of their conflicted rela-tionships with children predicted poorer academic performance and greater behavior problems through eighth grade, controlling for differ-ences in cognitive ability, behavior ratings, ethnicity, and gender (Hamre & Pianta, 2001). These findings are consistent with conclusions, described earlier, concerning the importance of a positive teacher–child relationship for school adjustment and classroom engagement. There is evidence that the benefits of a positive relationship with caregivers are especially impor-tant for children who are otherwise at risk of academic or social problems in school (Peisner-Feinberg et al., 2001).

Understanding the importance of early social experiences for the so-cioemotional skills required for school success underscores that school readiness is not solely a quality within the child, but it derives from the child's relational history. Although much remains to be understood about how relational experience influences the cognitive and social competen-cies related to academic achievement, it is likely that the young child's ex-perience of warm, responsive care contributes to school readiness in mul-tiple ways. These include enhanced self-confidence, greater social skills, improved attentiveness to learning in social contexts, and greater motiva-tion to achieve because of how learning is valued by others. There are also other avenues of influence, including that warm relationships motivate parents to ensure that children attend school reliably, monitor classwork, become more involved with the school, communicate with the teacher, and foster children's school achievement in other ways. These varied av-enues by which relationships foster academic success merit further explo-ration. It is apparent, however, that young children growing up in trou-bled or stressful family circumstances or who receive care in poor quality environments experience significant relational obstacles to acquiring the socioemotional and cognitive skills needed to achieve in the classroom. Indeed, Pianta and Stuhlman (2004b) describe *relational risk* as a signifi-cant threat to school readiness for children living in poverty or other dif-ficult circumstances.

CHILD CARE AND SCHOOL READINESS

The importance of relationship history highlights that influences on school readiness arise not only from the child but also from family and extrafamilial care environments. Families vary in the constellation of supports or obstacles children experience in developing the qualities necessary for academic success, but so do child care environments. The National Institutes of Child Health and Human Development (NICHD) Study of Early Child Care has provided useful perspectives into how child care experience influences social-emotional development during the preschool years. Beginning with a sample of more than 1,000 children recruited at birth and living in nine states, the NICHD study measured diverse features of children's socioemotional functioning through school entry and beyond, as well as important family and child care predictors of development.

Several conclusions have emerged from this important study. First, both the amount and quality of child care experience in early childhood were associated with children's cognitive, behavioral, and social competence. By kindergarten, children who had spent more time in child care during their first 5 years were described by teachers and mothers as having more behavior problems, with teachers reporting more adult–child conflict, even with controls for differences in family background, child care quality, and other important influences (NICHD Early Child Care Research Network, 2003c). These associations were weaker but remained apparent by first grade (NICHD Early Child Care Research Network, 2003a). Although the influence of the amount of child care was independent of child care quality, it was apparent that the quality of care had additional influences. Children who attended higher quality care environments performed better than their peers in lower quality care environments on measures of cognitive and linguistic functioning by late preschool, although some of these advantages had disappeared by first grade (NICHD Early Child Care Research Network, 2002a, 2005). There were no consistent associations between child care quality and a preschooler's socioemotional functioning (NICHD Early Child Care Research Network, 2003d). In short, the overall amount of child care was associated with poorer social competence by school entry, but higher child care quality was associated with improved cognitive skills.

The second conclusion from this study is that the quality of the home environment and, in particular, the mother–child relationship, was consistently associated with cognitive and socioemotional functioning during the preschool years through first grade, consistent with research reviewed earlier. The benefits of a more positive family environment for young children were consistently stronger than the influences of the amount or quality of child care, and the significance of the parent–child relationship was unaffected by the amount of child care experience (NICHD Early Child Care Research Network, 2002a, 2003a, 2003c, 2003d, 2005). These conclusions underscore the preeminence of the family environment for young children's school readiness, even though child care influences are also important.

Third, although early experiences at home and child care are important, the findings of this study indicate that family and child care influences later in the preschool years were especially predictive of children's cognitive and socioemotional functioning at school entry and beyond (NICHD Early Child Care Research Network, 2003c, 2005). Although this may be due to the fact that later preschool influences are closer in time and therefore more likely to influence early school performance, these findings suggest that there remains considerable potential to redirect developmental pathways that were established early in life, especially for children in difficult circumstances.

Finally, the study found that for young children at greatest sociodemographic risk, multiple aspects of the family context were associated with the child's socioemotional functioning, including family integrity, the emotional climate of the home, as well as maternal sensitivity (NICHD Early Child Care Research Network, 2003a). Although the NICHD study did not find that high-quality child care moderated the influence of family risk factors on children's development (NICHD Early Child Care Research Network, 2002b), other studies of early child care influences have found quality to be important, especially for at-risk children, and that high-quality care moderates the effects of the amount of time children are in extrafamilial care (Love et al., 2003). Such a conclusion is consistent with the efforts of programs such as Head Start and Early Head Start, which are designed to enlist high-quality early child care in an effort to improve developmental outcomes for young children at greatest risk of difficulty after school entry. In other words, child care quality can be an important supportive influence for children who may be at greatest risk of subsequent school problems.

CONCLUSION

In the United States, considerations of school readiness inevitably evoke broader beliefs about the reasons for academic success and failure, the importance of early achievement for later success, and the value of starting early to ensure the unfolding of early developmental potential. The research on school readiness informs policy making by showing that 1) school readiness is not simply a matter of cognitive or linguistic preparation, but that it also requires the development of social skills, self-regulatory competencies, relational incentives to cooperate and comply, self-confidence, and other socioemotional qualities; 2) school readiness is not only a matter of the characteristics of the child, but it also reflects the influence of significant relationships and the social contexts of early childhood development; and 3) enhancing school readiness requires careful consideration of the multiple challenges and supports that exist within the child, family, child care, and other social environments, particularly for children at sociodemographic risk of subsequent school failure.

Developmental research on school readiness informs policy making in another way. It is easy to adopt an academic orientation toward school preparation that emphasizes the achievement of certain skills and knowledge as the prerequisite to school entry; in a sense, children who are school ready "graduate" successfully to kindergarten. School readiness, however, is not only a matter of the influences and experiences that precede school entry but also how young children are enabled to master the expectations and challenges of kindergarten and the primary grades. Viewed developmentally and relationally, early academic success is a process that continues after school entry.

What are the implications of school readiness research in fostering young children's success in the classroom? It is clear that early learning and emotional well-being are connected for young children, and that school readiness involves the preparation of children's minds as well as their emotions, social capacities, and personalities. Developmental research also suggests the following:

- Because the skills necessary for classroom success develop in the context of young children's interactions with caregivers at home and in child care, parents and child care practitioners should be assisted in understanding how they foster the development of cognitive and socioemotional skills in their everyday encounters with young children.

- Because families are central to the development of the qualities that predict school success, special efforts to provide family support when parents are stressed, depressed, or overwhelmed may be necessary to enable parents to provide the nurturant care that young children require.

- Child care practitioners are particularly important in the early identification of children with special needs that put them at risk of subsequent school failure. Because of this role, and owing to their family support function when parents encounter difficulty, child care practitioners require support in their supervisory relationships and consultation with experts in early mental health when needed.

- Because the quality of child care is associated with the development of the cognitive and socioemotional competencies related to school success, systematic efforts to improve the quality of child care in the United States are needed. This is especially true of services for children and families at risk.

- Because school success derives from children's experiences after entering school as well as before, a focus on transitional support to young children is also important to comprehensive school readiness initiatives. Such transitional support may include opportunities for parents, child care providers, and elementary school teachers to share information about the child, as well as efforts to help ensure a smooth transition to a new peer environment.

• Although many children will almost effortlessly become ready for school, other children will encounter significant obstacles because of problems in their families. Because both cognitive and socioemotional skills crucial to school success are likely to be undermined for such children, it is important that their needs are identified early and that systems of services exist to provide support to them and their families. These services are likely to be most effective if they are developmentally informed, integrated into the environments that serve children and families, culturally relevant, and accommodate children in the contexts of their social networks.

Such a system of early mental health services is, in part, what this book is all about. It is perhaps ironic to close a chapter on school readiness with a focus on early mental health services in light of the more traditional cognitivist approach to academic preparation; however, developmental research shows that the growth of minds occurs in concert with the growth of relationships, emotions, and personalities. School readiness is enhanced when the whole child is the focus.

REFERENCES

Alexander, K.L., Entwisle, D.R., & Dauber, S.L. (1993). First grade classroom behavior: Its short- and long-term consequences for school performance. *Child Development, 64*, 801–814.

Belsky, J., Woodworth, S., & Crnic, K. (1996). Through in the second year: Questions about family interaction. *Child Development, 67*, 556–578.

Birch, S., & Ladd, G. (1997). The teacher–child relationship and children's early school adjustment. *Journal of School Psychology, 35*, 61–79.

Bowman, B.T., Donovan, S., & Burns, M.S. (2001). *Eager to learn: Educating our preschoolers.* Committee on Early Childhood Pedagogy, National Research Council and Institute of Medicine. Washington, DC: National Academies Press.

Burchinal, M.R., Peisner-Feinberg, E., Pianta, R., & Howes, C. (2002). Development of academic skills from preschool through second grade: Family and classroom predictors of developmental trajectories. *Journal of School Psychology, 40*, 415–436.

Carlton, M.P., & Winsler, A. (1999). School readiness: The need for a paradigm shift. *School Psychology Review, 28*, 338–352.

Denham, S.A., & Weissberg, R.P. (2004). Social-emotional learning in early childhood: What we know and where to go from here? In E. Chesebrough, P. King, T.P. Gullotta, & M. Bloom (Eds.), *A blueprint for the promotion of prosocial behavior in early childhood* (pp. 13–50). New York: Kluwer Academic/Plenum.

Diamond, A., & Taylor, C. (1996). Development of an aspect of executive control: Development of the abilities to remember what I said and to "do as I say, not as I do." *Developmental Psychobiology, 29,* 315–334.

Dowsett, C., & Huston, A. (2005, April). The role of social-emotional behavior in school readiness. In G. Duncan (Chair), *Hard skills and socioemotional behavior at school entry: What matters most for subsequent achievement?* Symposium presented to the biennial meeting of the Society for Research in Child Development, Atlanta.

Duncan, G.J., Claessens, A., & Engel, M. (2005, April). The contributions of hard skills and socioemotional behavior to school readiness in the ECLS-K. In G. Duncan (Chair), *Hard skills and socioemotional behavior at school entry: What matters most for subsequent achievement?* Symposium presented to the biennial meeting of the Society for Research in Child Development, Atlanta.

Eisenberg, N. (2002). Emotion-related regulation and its relation to quality of social functioning. In W. Hartup & R. Weinberg (Eds.), *Minnesota Symposium on Child Psychology: Vol. 32. Child psychology in retrospect and prospect* (pp. 133–171). Mahwah, NJ: Lawrence Erlbaum Associates.

Eisenberg, N., Cumberland, A., & Spinrad, T.L. (1998). Parental socialization of emotion. *Psychological Inquiry, 9,* 241–273.

Estrada, P., Arsenio, W.F., Hess, R.D., & Holloway, S.D. (1987). Affective quality of the mother–child relationship: Longitudinal consequences for children's school-relevant cognitive functioning. *Developmental Psychology, 23,* 210–215.

Feinstein, L. (2005, April). The contributions of cognitive and behavioural development at school entry to school performance and adult outcomes. In G. Duncan (Chair), *Hard skills and socioemotional behavior at school entry: What matters most for subsequent achievement?* Symposium presented to the biennial meeting of the Society for Research in Child Development, Atlanta.

Fox, N., & Calkins, S. (2003). The development of self-control of emotion: Intrinsic and extrinsic influences. *Motivation and Emotion, 27,* 7–26.

Gerstadt, C., Hong, Y., & Diamond, A. (1994). The relationship between cognition and action: Performance of 3–7 year old children on a Stroop-like day–night test. *Cognition, 53,* 129–153.

Gilliam, W.S. (2005). *Prekindergarteners left behind: Expulsion rates in state prekindergarten systems.* Unpublished manuscript, Yale University.

Goodman, S.H., & Gotlib, I.H. (1999). Risk for psychopathology in the children of depressed mothers: A developmental model for understanding mechanisms of transmission. *Psychological Review, 106,* 458–490.

Goodvin, R., Meyer, S., Thompson, R.A., & Hayes, R. (2006). *Self-understanding in early childhood: Associations with attachment security, maternal perceptions, and the family emotional climate.* Manuscript in preparation.

Hamre, B.K., & Pianta, R.C. (2001). Early teacher–child relationships and the trajectory of children's school outcomes through eighth grade. *Child Development, 72,* 625–638.

Howse, R.B., Lange, G., Farran, D.C., & Boyles, C.D. (2003). Motivation and self-regulation as predictors of achievement in economically disadvantaged young children. *The Journal of Experimental Education, 71,* 151–174.

Izard, C., Fine, S., Schultz, D., Mostow, A., Adkerman, B., & Youngstrom, E. (2001). Emotion knowledge as a predictor of social behavior and academic competence in children at risk. *Psychological Science, 12,* 18–23.

Klebanov, P.K., & Brooks-Gunn, J. (2005, April). Assessing the contribution of preschool behavior problems and cognitive competence to elementary school achievement. In G. Duncan (Chair), *Hard skills and socioemotional behavior at school entry: What matters most for subsequent achievement?* Symposium presented to the biennial meeting of the Society for Research in Child Development, Atlanta.

Kochanska, G. (1997). Mutually responsive orientation between mothers and their young children: Implications for early socialization. *Child Development, 68,* 94–112.

Kochanska, G. (2002). Committed compliance, moral self, and internalization: A mediated model. *Developmental Psychology, 38,* 339–351.

Kochanska, G., Murray, K., & Harlan, E. (2000). Effortful control in early childhood: Continuity and change, antecedents, and implications for social development. *Developmental Psychology, 36,* 220–232.

Kopp, C. (1982). Antecedents of self-regulation: A developmental view. *Developmental Psychology, 18,* 199–214.

Ladd, G.W., Birch, S.H., & Buhs, E.S. (1999). Children's social and scholastic lives in kindergarten: Related spheres of influence? *Child Development, 70,* 1373–1400.

Lamb, M.E. (1998). Nonparental child care: Context, quality, correlates. In W. Damon (Series Ed.) & I.E. Sigel & K.A. Renninger (Vol. Eds.), *Handbook of child psychology: Vol. 4. Child psychology in practice* (5th ed.) (pp. 73–134). New York: John Wiley & Sons.

LaParo, K.M., & Pianta, R.C. (2000). Predicting children's competence in the early school years: A meta-analytic review. *Review of Educational Research, 70,* 443–484.

Lewit, E.M., & Baker, L.S. (1995). School readiness. *The Future of Children, 5,* 128–139.

Love, J., Harrison, L., Sagi-Schwartz, A., van IJzendoorn, M.H., Ross, C., Ungerer, J., et al. (2003). Child care quality matters: How conclusions may vary with context. *Child Development, 74,* 1021–1033.

Magnuson, K. (2005, April). Predicting adolescents' academic achievement: The contribution of early childhood achievement and problem behavior. In G. Duncan (Chair), *Hard skills and socioemotional behavior at school entry: What matters most for subsequent achievement?* Symposium presented to the biennial meeting of the Society for Research in Child Development, Atlanta.

Marsh, H.W., Ellis, L.A., & Craven, R.G. (2002). How do preschool children feel about themselves? Unraveling measurement and multidimensional self-concept structure. *Developmental Psychology, 38,* 376–393.

McClelland, M.M., Morrison, F.J., & Holmes, D.L. (2000). Children at risk for early academic problems: The role of learning-related social skills. *Early Childhood Research Quarterly, 15,* 307–329.

Measelle, J.R., Ablow, J.C., Cowan, P.A., & Cowan, C.P. (1998). Assessing young children's views of their academic, social, and emotional lives: An evaluation of the self-perception scales of the Berkeley Puppet Interview. *Child Development, 69,* 1556–1576.

Meisels, S.J. (1999). Assessing readiness. In R.C. Pianta & M.J. Cox (Eds.), *The transition to kindergarten* (pp. 39–66). Baltimore: Paul H. Brookes Publishing Co.

Miller, P.J., Potts, R., Fung, H., Hoogstra, L., & Mintz, J. (1990). Narrative practices and the social construction of self in childhood. *American Ethnologist, 17,* 292–311.

Morrison, E.F., Rimm-Kauffman, S., & Pianta, R.C. (2003). A longitudinal study of mother–child interactions at school entry and social and academic outcomes in middle school. *Journal of School Psychology, 41,* 185–200.

National Center for Education Statistics. (1993). *Public school kindergarten teachers' views on children's readiness for school.* (NCES 93-410). Washington, DC: U.S. Department of Education.

National Center for Education Statistics. (1994). *National Household Education Survey of 1993: School readiness data file user's manual.* (NCES 94-193). Washington, DC: U.S. Department of Education.

National Education Goals Panel. (1997). *The National Education Goals report, 1997: Building a nation of learners.* Washington, DC: U.S. Government Printing Office.

National School Readiness Indicators Initiative. (2005). *Getting ready: Findings from the National School Readiness Indicators Initiative.* Providence: Rhode Island Kids Count.

NICHD Early Child Care Research Network. (2002a). Early child care and children's development prior to school entry: Results from the NICHD Study of Early Child Care. *American Educational Research Journal, 39,* 133–164.

NICHD Early Child Care Research Network. (2002b). The interaction of child care and family risk in relation to child development at 24 and 36 months. *Applied Developmental Science, 6,* 144–156.

NICHD Early Child Care Research Network. (2003a). Social functioning in first grade: Associations with earlier home and child care predictors and with current classroom experiences. *Child Development, 74,* 1639–1662.

NICHD Early Child Care Research Network. (2003b). Do children's attention processes mediate the link between family predictors and school readiness? *Developmental Psychology, 39,* 581–593.

NICHD Early Child Care Research Network. (2003c). Does the amount of time in child care predict socioemotional adjustment during the transition to kindergarten? *Child Development, 74,* 976–1005.

NICHD Early Child Care Research Network. (2003d). Does the quality of child care affect child outcomes at 4½? *Developmental Psychology, 39,* 451–469.

NICHD Early Child Care Research Network. (2005). Predicting individual differences in attention, memory, and planning in first graders from experiences at home, child care, and school. *Developmental Psychology, 41,* 99–114.

O'Neil, R., Welsh, M., Parke, R.D., Wang, S., & Strand, C. (1997). A longitudinal assessment of the academic correlates of early peer acceptance and rejection. *Journal of Clinical Child Psychology, 26,* 290–303.

Peisner-Feinberg, E.S., Burchinal, M.R., Clifford, R.M., Culkin, M.L., Howes, C., Kagan, S.L., et al. (2001). The relation of preschool child-care quality to children's cognitive and social developmental trajectories through second grade. *Child Development, 72,* 1534–1553.

Pianta, R.C., Nimetz, S.L., & Bennett, E. (1997). Mother–child relationships, teacher–child relationships, and school outcomes in preschool and kindergarten. *Early Childhood Research Quarterly, 12,* 263–280.

Pianta, R.C., Steinberg, M.S., & Rollins, K.B. (1995). The first two years of school: Teacher–child relationships and deflections in children's classroom adjustment. *Development & Psychopathology, 7,* 295–312.

Pianta, R.C., & Stuhlman, M.W. (2004a). Teacher–child relationships and children's success in the first years of school. *School Psychology Review, 33,* 444–458.

Pianta, R.C., & Stuhlman, M.W. (2004b). Conceptualizing risk in relational terms: Associations among the quality of child–adult relationships prior to school entry and children's developmental outcomes in first grade. *Educational & Child Psychology, 21,* 32–45.

Raver, C.C. (2002). Emotions matter: Making the case for the role of young children's emotional development for early school readiness. *Social Policy Report, 16,* 1–20. Washington, DC: Society for Research in Child Development.

Raver, C.C., & Knitzer, J. (2002). *Ready to enter: What research tells policymakers about strategies to promote social and emotional school readiness among three- and four-year-old children.* New York: National Center for Children in Poverty.

Reid, J.B., Patterson, G.R., & Snyder, J. (2002). *Antisocial behavior in children and adolescents: A developmental analysis and model for intervention.* Washington, DC: American Psychological Association.

Rimm-Kaufman, S.E., Pianta, R.C., & Cox, M.J. (2000). Teachers' judgments of problems in the transition to kindergarten. *Early Childhood Research Quarterly, 15,* 147–166.

Rubin, K.H., Burgess, K.B., Dwyer, K.M., & Hastings, P.D. (2003). Predicting preschoolers' externalizing behaviors from toddler temperament, conflict, and maternal negativity. *Developmental Psychology, 39,* 164–176.

Shaw, D.S., Miles, G., Ingoldsby, E.M., & Nagin, D.S. (2003). Trajectories leading to school-age conduct problems. *Developmental Psychology, 39,* 189–200.

Shonkoff, J.P., & Phillips, D.A. (Eds.). (2000). *From neurons to neighborhoods: The science of early childhood development.* Washington, DC: National Academies Press.

Smetana, J.G. (1997). Parenting and the development of social knowledge reconceptualized: A social domain analysis. In J. Grusec & L. Kuczynski (Eds.), *Parenting and children's internalization of values* (pp. 162–192). New York: John Wiley & Sons.

Stipek, D., Recchia, S., & McClintic, S. (1992). Self-evaluation in young children. *Monographs of the Society for Research in Child Development, 57,* (Serial No. 226).

Thompson, R.A. (1990). Emotion and self-regulation. In R.A. Thompson (Ed.), *Nebraska Symposium on Motivation, Vol. 36. Socioemotional development* (pp. 383–483). Lincoln: University of Nebraska Press.

Thompson, R.A. (1994). Emotion regulation: A theme in search of definition. In N.A. Fox (Ed.), *The development of emotion regulation: Biological and behavioral considerations. Monographs of the Society for Research in Child Development* (Vol. 59., pp. 25–52).

Thompson, R.A. (2002). The roots of school readiness in social and emotional development. *The Kauffman Early Education Exchange, 1,* 8–29.

Thompson, R.A. (in press). The development of the person: Social understanding, relationships, self, conscience. In W. Damon & R.M. Lerner (Series Eds.) & N. Eisenberg (Vol. Ed.), *Handbook of child psychology: Vol. 3. Social, emotional, and personality development* (6th ed.). New York: John Wiley & Sons.

Thompson, R.A., Goodvin, R., & Meyer, S. (in press). Social development in the preschool years: Psychological understanding, self understanding, and relationships. In J. Luby (Ed.), *Preschool mental health.* New York: The Guilford Press.

Thompson, R.A., Meyer, S., & McGinley, M. (2006). Understanding values in relationship: The development of conscience. In M. Killen & J. Smetana (Eds.), *Handbook of moral development* (pp. 267–297). Mahwah, NJ: Lawrence Erlbaum Associates.

Wellman, H. (2002). Understanding the psychological world: Developing a theory of mind. In U. Goswami (Ed.), *Handbook of Childhood Cognitive Development* (pp. 167–187). Oxford: Blackwell Publishing.

Yen, C.-J., Konold, T.R., & McDermott, P.A. (2004). Does learning behavior augment cognitive ability as an indicator of academic achievement? *Journal of School Psychology, 42,* 157–169.

Yoshikawa, H., & Knitzer, J. (1997). *Lessons from the field: Head Start mental health strategies to meet changing needs.* New York: National Center for Children in Poverty.

Zahn-Waxler, C., & Robinson, J. (1995). Empathy and guilt: Early origins of feelings of responsibility. In J. Tangney & K. Fischer (Eds.), *Self-conscious emotions* (pp. 143–173). New York: The Guilford Press.

3

Early Childhood Mental Health

A Focus on Culture and Context

Larke N. Huang and Mareasa R. Isaacs

■ ■ ■

Culture and context are powerful in shaping the values, beliefs, attitudes, and behaviors that families and communities transmit to their young children. The cultural and contextual factors that influence the early socialization experiences and goals for racially and ethnically diverse children in the United States are different from those of mainstream Caucasian children (Garcia-Coll et al., 1996; Harrison, Wilson, Pine, Chan, & Buriel 1990; Ogbu, 1995). Cultural factors stemming from the ethnocultural heritage of these diverse families play a significant role in determining family child-rearing practices and expectations of appropriate or desirable behavior at different stages of the child's development (National Advisory Mental Health Council, 2001). While raising young children, families incorporate child-rearing practices that are rooted in their personal histories, family traditions, and cultural beliefs and practices. Equally significant are the contextual factors that influence parenting and socialization; such as physical, material, social, and political contexts that surround families and their children. For many ethnically and racially diverse families, their contexts are often quite distinct from Caucasian families in the United States.

The focus of this chapter is on the interaction of cultural and contextual factors that have an impact on the development of young children and are critical to understanding early childhood mental health. The key messages in this chapter are as follows:

- Changing population demographics make it imperative to grasp the significance of diversity and culture in U.S. society.

- Culture and context are key determinants in shaping family and child development and drive the need to expand existing models of child development.

- Sociocultural and contextual factors influence the mental health and the salient risk and protective factors for young children.

- Culture plays a role in how families interface with early childhood structures and caregiving systems.

- Promotion, prevention, early identification and treatment interventions, and policies need to consider the cultural context of the young child and family.

CHANGING DEMOGRAPHICS

Population growth rates among ethnically and racially diverse youth, disproportionate rates of poverty, and higher rates of immigration contribute to a rapidly changing picture of youth in the United States and an urgent demographic imperative. The population of ethnically and racially diverse youth in the United States is dramatically increasing with population growth rates significantly higher than the mainstream Caucasian population. These populations are, on average, younger than the general population and are growing rapidly due to higher birthrates and immigration. It is projected that between 1995 and 2015, African American youth will increase by 19%, Asian American youth by 74%, Latino youth by 59%, and Native American youth by 17%, which are in contrast to Caucasian youth, whose growth rate is expected to decrease by 3% (Snyder & Sickmund, 1999). These growth rates will challenge the capacity of existing service structures to meet the needs of this rapidly growing population of diverse youth.

Latinos are the fastest growing ethnic group in the United States today, and the growth rate is even greater among children under the age of 18. Currently, this group represents the largest ethnic child population in the nation (Morse, 2003). The second largest group of racially diverse youth, African Americans, are more likely to live in poor families and experience persistent poverty than children from other racial and ethnic groups. Whereas African American families represent 12.9% of the U.S. population, the poverty rate for African American children under 18 is 33% as compared to 30% for Latinos and 9% for Whites (Randolph & Koblinsky, 2000).

The changing patterns of immigration are also altering the composition of the American youth population. Recent census data show a 25% increase in the number of children living with immigrant parents; that is, 11 million children, half of whom are low-income, live in households with immigrant parents. The National Center for Children in Poverty examined national trends among children of recent immigrant parents, who are defined as parents who had immigrated within the past 10 years (Douglas-Hall & Koball, 2004). The largest percentage of children of recent immigrants (41%) lives with parents who are from Mexico; the next four largest nations of origin were India, Cuba, the Philippines, and China. Sixty-five percent of the children of recent immigrants are low income and vulnerable to the academic, physical, emotional, and social challenges associated with economic insecurity. Forty-seven percent of these children are under age 6, placing them at risk for the negative impact of low income and acculturation stresses on early development. Language barriers, the stresses of migration, acculturation, changing family role structures, and the growing federal and state restrictions on immigrants' access to safety net programs further exacerbate this situation.

What is the demographic imperative? The rapidly changing demographics among youth in the United States call for renewed attention to 1) how culturally diverse families and their children interface with existing societal structures, regulations, and policies around young children and 2) how early child-serving systems and policies take into consideration the unique needs and assets of these children and families. Understanding the cultural dynamics within these families and their ecological environment will be essential to providing appropriate, high-quality care and to developing policies that build on the cultural richness and context of their families.

THE ROLE OF CULTURE IN SOCIALIZATION

Culture, in its broadest sense, is defined as a way of life or the framework by which a group makes sense of the world. Differences related to primary and secondary cultural values influence how a family raises its children or engages with societal structures and systems. Primary culture provides the lens through which experiences are interpreted and understood. This refers to the norms, beliefs, values, languages, and socialization practices that derive from a family's ancestral homeland and continue to give direction and shape to their lives in the United States (Ogbu, 1995). For example, whereas there is much heterogeneity within any cultural group, Asian cultures have been characterized as placing a greater value on interdependence and family extendedness than Western European cultures (Gibbs & Huang, 2003). African cultures have similarly placed a greater premium on the values of collectivism and spirituality (Boykin & Toms, 1985; White & Parham, 1990). Latinos emphasize *Marianismo* as a distinctly Latino value based on the woman's role as mother and her self-sacrifice for her children and family (Ginorio, Gutierrez, Cauce, & Acosta, 1995).

Families use these cultural values to inform their parenting practices, shape their learning styles to adapt to varying societal contexts, and to organize their physical and social interactions (Emde, 1999; Phinney & Landin, 1998). For example, a study of cultural values of parents from four immigrant groups (Cambodians, Filipinos, Mexicans, and Vietnamese) contrasted with first-generation-plus Caucasian Americans and Mexican American parents (Okagaki & Divecha, 1993) found that immigrant parents placed more importance on behaviors that represented conformity to external standards. In contrast, the American-born groups placed a higher value on autonomous functioning.

These cultural values can facilitate or impede a child's negotiation of the extrafamilial world (Leung, 1990). When the culture of the family is congruent with that of its external world, clashes of values and behaviors may be minimized. For culturally and linguistically diverse families, however, a child and family's development may involve straddling disparate cultures and integrating new values and behaviors. Acculturation may also erode some primary cultural values. These clashes between primary cultural values and the external world result in secondary cultural factors that represent the adaptation of cultural values to existing sociocultural contexts. Secondary cultural values may also arise from efforts to cope with discrimination, prejudice, and the devaluation of one's cultural group. How do secondary cultural values enter into the socialization of young children?

Secondary cultural values may affect racial socialization within families as well as family decisions regarding external structures. Families may elect to proactively teach their children about racial stereotyping, potential risk factors, and strategies for handling discrimination and others forms of hurtful behaviors in schools and peer environments (Spencer, 1983; Stevenson, 1994). Secondary cultural norms may influence families' selection of child care centers and their satisfaction with those environments. For example, a Salvadoran family seeking to improve their future circumstances may select a child care center that will increase its children's exposure to the dominant language and culture. In contrast, a third generation Chicano family, concerned about the assimilation to typical American values and norms and devaluation of core cultural values, may select a child care environment that affirms Latino values and the Spanish language (Johnson et al., 2003). The family goals around cultural preservation may determine whether parents select mainstream or ethnic-specific child care environments for their children. This may also influence the choice of center-based versus family based child care with more culturally diverse groups, historically, turning to extended family members and neighbors who shared a similar culture and language.

CONTEXT AND SOCIALIZATION

Families are embedded in a sociocultural context that may have a significant impact on parenting and socialization. Contextual factors include the
physical, material, social, and political circumstances that surround a family. Whereas there are many contextual differences between racially and
ethnically diverse and mainstream Caucasian families, probably most
notable are material conditions. For example, the families of African
American, Latino, and Native American children are three times more
likely to be poor than families of white children (U.S. Bureau of the
Census, 2001). Whereas educational attainment for these groups is lower
than whites, even after education is controlled, differences in earning
power persist. Based on 1997–1999 data, the typical earning power of an
African American college graduate was $35,136 compared to $43,772 for
the average for a white worker with the same profile (U.S. Bureau of Labor
Statistics, 2002). These socioeconomic differences have direct implications
for the need for maternal employment and the use and purchase of child
care or early childhood education programs for these families. Although
less obvious than income differentials, family structure and maternal employment patterns are contextual factors that have a significant impact on
child rearing and child care arrangements.

Family structure is more fluid and variable among ethnically, racially,
and culturally diverse families. Children in these families are more likely to
be raised in single-parent, female-headed households or in extended family
households (Hunter, Pearson, Ialongo, & Kellam, 1998; Pearson, Hunter,
Ensminger, & Kellam, 1990). For these families, collective economics, provision of psychosocial and financial supports, and absorption of child care responsibilities are critical functions in extended family structures. The fluidity
of the extended family household provides important opportunities for the
care and well-being of children. Parenting is perceived as a communal family duty that enhances the development of young children. For example,
studies have shown the attachment security between African American infants and their mothers has been positively affected by the presence and involvement of their grandmothers (Chase-Lansdale, Brooks-Gunn, & Amsky
1994; Crockenberg, 1981; Egeland & Sroufe, 1981).

A critical contextual factor for ethnically diverse children is the role
of maternal employment. Women's participation in the paid labor force
has historically been much higher among African American women than
any other group of women. As percentages of working women have increased, the disparity between African American women and white women
has decreased. The greater earning contributions of African American
wives and mothers in comparison with white women have been viewed as
a critical wedge against poverty (McLoyd, 1990). Variations in these

employment patterns may have an impact on child-rearing patterns, use of child care for young children, and child outcomes (Johnson et al., 2003). Prior to 1960, child care was not widely available to African American working women (Berry, 1993). As child care was expanded for Caucasian families, African American families tended to use informal options, such as extended family members, fictive kin, or non-relatives, churches, and neighbors. Recent research shows that expanded availability of child care to African American women has increased their use of nonparental care, particularly formal child care centers. Despite stated preferences for center-based care, however, they tend to use more family based care, especially as provided by grandmothers (Smith, 2002).

As patterns of employment among women of color tend to change along with preferences and usage of out-of-home care, young children will be increasingly exposed to multiple cultures at earlier developmental stages. Young children may exhibit more behaviors associated with secondary cultural values and show more distancing from the primary cultural values of the home. For example, a qualitative study of early child care showed more assertive behaviors of a young Asian child in a day care setting. Although the staff applauded this newly assertive behavior, the parents were shocked and dismayed as they considered this behavior rude and disrespectful (Chang, 1993).

EXPANDING THE MODELS OF CHILD DEVELOPMENT TO ADDRESS CULTURAL VALIDITY

The changing demographics of the child population in the United States and emerging research on the impact of culture and context on developmental outcomes challenge the existing frameworks for understanding early childhood development. The attention to culture in theories of child development is quite variable, ranging from an *easy omission* to a *core dynamic* in the developing child and family.

Attachment Theory

Existing theories of early childhood development have generally been thought to have universal application. Cross-cultural efforts have made minor adaptations to these established theories, but usually with little change to their basic premise. Take, for example, attachment theory, which is one of the most influential theories of relatedness in child development and has dominated understanding of this concept since the late 1980s. Attachment theory has spawned one of the broadest and most creative agendas in developmental research and has provided an ideological basis for many parent intervention programs and therapeutic interventions

(Lieberman & Zeanah, 1999; Slade, 1999). Attachment theorists suggest that cultural differences are relatively minor; however, Rothbaum, Weisz, Pott, Niyake, and Morelli (2000) contend that attachment theory is infused with cultural assumptions that lead to misguided interpretation of research findings and unfortunate consequences for assessment, intervention, and intercultural understanding. They suggest that three of the core tenets in attachment theory—sensitivity, competence, and secure base—are not universal but need to be understood in a cultural context.

Sensitivity

For example, the sensitivity hypothesis claims that a primary caregiver's sensitive responsiveness to a child's signals is a major determinant of the child's attachment security (Ainsworth, Blehar, Waters, & Wall, 1978); however, much of what was considered sensitive, responsive caregiving reflected the value placed on children's autonomy. The caregiver scales used to evaluate a mother's sensitivity involved endorsing such items as mother "values the fact that the baby has a will of its own;" "finds his anger worthy of respect;" "respects that the baby has a will of its own, even when it opposes her;" "views her baby as a separate, active autonomous person;" and so forth (Rothbaum et al., 2000). This perspective on sensitive, responsive caregiving is still regarded as the standard in the field (Sroufe & Waters, 1997).

The problem in terms of generalizing to other cultures is that this value of autonomy in children may not be a shared value, and what constitutes sensitive, responsive caregiving is more likely to reflect indigenous values and goals. For example, Japanese parents prefer to anticipate their infants' needs by relying on situational cues and taking anticipatory measures to minimize stress or discomfort. In contrast, mainstream U.S. parents prefer to wait for their infants to communicate their needs before taking steps to address those needs. The different expressions of sensitivity and caretaker responsiveness suggest that Japanese caregivers focus on emotional closeness and helping infants regulate their emotional states in contrast to caregivers in the United States who facilitate helping children assert their personal desires and respect children's autonomous desires to satisfy their own needs (Keller, Voelker, & Zach, 1997; Rothbaum et al., 2000). Maternal sensitivity in Japanese mothers promotes dependence on the mother, whereas United States mothers promote exploration of the environment. Japanese maternal speech focuses on emotions rather than information as among United States mothers, and Japanese mothers prolong physical contact rather than distal eye contact. A critical difference that emerges in these cross-cultural analyses is that not only are the behaviors of these various cultural groups of mothers dissimilar, but, more importantly, the goal of sensitivity is sharply different. Japanese mothers foster dependency and emotional closeness, whereas mothers in the United States foster exploration and autonomy (Rothbaum et al., 2000).

Competence

Within attachment theory, security of attachment is linked with the social competence of the child. Competence is defined as behaviors associated with individuation, such as exploration, autonomy, independence, self-expression, affect regulation, and positive peer relationships (Weinfield, Sroufe, Egeland, & Carlson, 1999). Lack of competence is associated with relying extensively on others to meet needs. This contrasts sharply with the Japanese cultural value on dependency and reliance on others (Lebra, 1994). For example, in Japanese preschools, group-oriented achievements are more highly encouraged and valued than individual accomplishments (Peak, 1989). Dependence on others as a way of meeting one's needs and coordinating with other's needs is viewed as essential to the highly valued goal of social harmony (Kitayama, Markus, Masumoto, & Norasakkunkit, 1997). Similarly, self-expression as a developmental outcome is viewed differently in these two cultures. Among attachment theorists, emotional openness and expression is regarded as important to a child's well-being; however, among Japanese parents, emotional openness is not considered a desirable quality, and children are encouraged to contain hostile feelings within themselves or express them indirectly in order to preserve social harmony (Rothbaum et al., 2000). Japanese parents model this inhibition of expression by not scolding children openly or directly (Miyake & Yamazaki, 1995).

Secure Base

Finally, the third core concept of attachment theory focuses on the mother as the secure base. The premise is that infants and young children who are sufficiently protected and comforted by the presence of a caregiver are better able to use this caregiver as a secure base from which to explore the environment. In this framework, the secure base is linked with capacity for exploration, which is viewed as a healthy positive outcome contributing to individuation. In non-Western cultures, the link among attachment and exploration and individuation may be of less importance. In Japan, dependence serves a more valued behavioral system characterized by social accommodation (Emde, 1999). This promotes a child's empathy with others, compliance with others' wishes, and responsiveness to social cues and norms.

Baumrind's Three-Factor Classification

Other models have linked parenting style with child outcomes. Baumrind's three-factor classification of parenting into authoritative, authoritarian, and permissive has been applied to different cultural groups. The degree to which authoritative parenting is linked with positive outcomes (as documented with the mainstream Caucasian population in the United States) is variable across culturally diverse groups. In their study of African American families with young children, Querido, Warner, and Eyberg (2002) found that the authoritative parenting style proved to be most predictive of positive child outcomes. Parents who described the use of warmth, reasoning, democratic participation, responsiveness, and firm limit setting in their interactions with their young children were more likely to report fewer child behavior problems.

Different results emerged in the application of this parenting framework to Chinese and Asian Indian mothers of preschool children. Rao, McHale, and Pearson (2003) looked at socialization goals and parenting practices in these two groups of mothers. In both cultures, valuing socioemotional development was positively related to authoritative parenting practices, suggesting that the link between this type of parenting and goals related to socioemotional behaviors are consistent across mothers from different cultures (Rao et al., 2003). Mothers who reported a greater value on filial piety (a fundamental cultural value in many Asian cultures), however, were more likely to report using authoritarian practices, which suggest that the exertion of parental control is related to socialization for family responsibilities. Previous studies have shown authoritarian practices related to academic achievement among Chinese children. The goals of filial piety and socioemotional development varied between the two groups studied. These goals were directly related for Indian mothers; however, for Chinese mothers they were negatively related. For the latter, the strong emphasis on obedience and loyalty that characterizes the concept of filial piety is likely to preclude parental support for their child's assertion of individualistic sentiment. Indian mothers also value obedience; however, their cultural beliefs about socialization and childhood differ from those of Chinese mothers in that they may be more accepting of individual differences and children's emotional expression (Rao et al., 2003).

It is important to understand that the meaning and form of parental control, as associated with authoritarian parenting style, may be different in Chinese and Caucasian families. Chao (1996) suggests that the context and manner in which parental will is exercised is important. For example, when control is exerted in a loving, caring family context it may not result in the same negative outcomes as under restrictive, domineering control.

These studies suggest that application of existing early childhood models of development may need to be adapted to ensure cultural validity for diverse populations. Classic attachment theory and parenting models are rich frameworks for understanding early child–parent relationships;

however, they are each deeply value laden and must be interpreted with caution when applied to culturally different populations.

Ecological and Transitional Models of Development

From a more ecological transaction perspective, several theoretical models have taken into consideration the sociocultural context of early childhood and the caregiving environment. Whiting's (1977) work highlighted early child rearing as a reflection of the overall cultural milieu. Culture influenced the caregiving situation, determining such things as the number and identity of caregivers, feeding schedules, children's tasks, techniques of discipline, and other aspects of the child's environment (Super, 1981). Bronfenbrenner (1986) provided a detailed framework of how the ecological context influences a child's development. The child's environment consists of multiple, layered settings that vary in the amount of direct contact with the child. The sociocultural context is organized by settings and the interrelations among the settings and how their cultures influence the development of the child. The interactions of direct settings, such as the family or school or day care where the child spends time, and indirect settings, such as the parent's job, have an impact on the developing child. In another transactional model, Sameroff and Fiese (1990) introduce the concept of *cultural code* as the complex characteristics that organize a society's child rearing systems. Developmental progress is viewed as the result of the cultural, family, and individual member's codes.

Integrated Model of Development

Garcia-Coll and colleagues (1996) further expand the transactional approach in their integrated model of the development of competence in ethnically and culturally diverse children. This model considers the centrality of cultural form and meaning and broadens the role of family and kin networks beyond traditional ecological models. It recognizes that these diverse families experience different cultural expectations, family constellations, and access to economic and social resources, in addition to being subjected to prejudice, racism, classism, and segregation. The family's world view and the young child's developmental outcomes may be profoundly influenced by these life experiences. For example, racism and discrimination may directly affect children through processes such as segregation, encounters of prejudice, or parental experience of racism or oppression.

Research has documented the relationship between perceived discrimination and poor mental health functioning among adults (Brown et al., 2000; Jackson et al., 1996; Kessler, Michelson, & Williams., 1999; Krieger, 1999). Whereas all young children are exposed to similar settings, such as child care, preschool, and other early childhood environments, the impact of these settings on ethnically diverse children must be considered from the perspective of whether they inhibit, promote, or both inhibit and promote competence. Inhibiting environments are characterized by limited resources, lack of recognition of the strengths of the culturally different child, and an incompatibility between the values and goals of the family and the particular environment (i.e., the child care setting or early childhood program). A core premise of this integrative model is that ethnically diverse families develop adaptive cultures that set them apart from the dominant, mainstream culture. These adaptive cultures include a system of goals, values, behaviors, family structures, parenting strategies, and social networks that are distinct from the mainstream culture and represent a blend of their culture of origin with the immediate sociocultural context. The adaptive strategies of these families are evidenced in their child-rearing patterns and are a response to cultural and/or social stratification, the group's cultural and political history, and the demands of the immediate environment (Randolph & Koblinsky, 2000). Built around specific factors in the ecology of the child (e.g., parent's goals, values, and behaviors; parental work demands; parental mental health; family organization; social support and neighborhood context), these adaptive strategies are instrumental in the development of infants and young children.

Parents from different cultural groups may share a unique system of goals, values, and behaviors that may overlap but also differ in some ways from other cultural groups. For example, parents from different cultural groups may vary in their views about the fragility of newborns, their perceptions and responses to crying, and their view on motor development. Some researchers have speculated that the early motor maturity of African American infants is the result of their mothers' frequent handling of them during the neonatal period as well as expectations that these infants master motor tasks at earlier ages than white infants (Rosser & Randolph, 1996). Ogbu (1981) and Stevenson (1994) suggest that African American parents use child-rearing practices that foster behaviors that they feel their children need to survive in their environment. In a study of parenting in inner-city neighborhoods, Ogbu (1981) noted that African American parents expressed abundant warmth in infancy followed by an absence of warmth, inconsistent demands for obedience, and the use of physical discipline in the post-infancy period. It was felt that these strategies promoted traits that were essential for the child's survival, including self-reliance, resourcefulness, vigilance around authority, and the ability to fight back. Similarly, Chinese and Asian Indian families believe that very young children are not yet capable of *understanding* and are indulgent toward them in the early years. When the child reaches the *age of understanding*, however, strict discipline and new expectations for proper behavior are enforced (Rao et al., 2003). For Chinese children, emerging demands are placed on these children based on the cultural belief that all children, regardless of their innate ability, can achieve with effort.

The critical role of families in the development of young children has been acknowledged however, families need to be defined and examined in ways that reflect their culture and ethnicity, relationships, and economic circumstances as they influence a child's development. Dimensions such as family income, education, language, country of origin, patterns of migration, and acculturation should be considered (Randolph & Koblinsky, 2000). The family structures of diverse populations may differ from those of mainstream populations in ways that directly affect young children and determine family interactions with early childhood and mental health systems. African American families tend to be characterized by younger mothers, a higher percentage of single mothers, and large extended families. For example, low-income African American families tend to have a greater likelihood of kin residence (U.S. Bureau of the Census, 2001). The presence of multiple caregivers in kin residence may be the result of a cultural emphasis on the extended family, an economic necessity, or an adaptation to the unpredictability that many poor families encounter (Halpern, 1993). More importantly, this family organization may have both positive and negative implications for the young child. There is the potential for parenting practices that may be inconsistent among multiple caregivers and raise confusion among the children or provide opportunity for multiple social attachment. Multigenerational households may also provide for cultural richness and social and economic stability (Harrison, Wilson, Pine, Chan, & Buriel, 1990; Randolph & Koblinsky, 2000) The multigenerational family structure presents different child-rearing responsibilities and has important implications for early childhood mental health systems. Traditional approaches that assume the mother is the primary caregiver may be inappropriate for these families. The family structures of diverse cultures may require inclusion of multiple family members in parent involvement activities and educational and clinical interventions to address the young child's needs.

Social support, an aspect of family functioning that is recognized as critical to the well-being of individuals in culturally diverse families, has the potential to influence parenting and early childhood development. Relative and nonrelative (i.e., fictive) kin networks have played an essential role in providing support for poor, urban families of color. These families are more likely to receive child care assistance from and live in close proximity to extended kin than are mainstream, white families (Gibbs & Huang, 2003; Jayakody, Chatters, & Taylor, 1993; Randolph & Koblinsky, 2000). These social networks are often critical to the well-being of low-income parents in need of child care, assistance with household tasks and maintenance, and time to pursue education and employment goals (McLoyd, 1990). Conversely, social networks may introduce stress into families that results from, for example, different attitudes regarding discipline, developmental expectations for the child, and degree of adherence to cultural traditions and values (Gibbs & Huang, 2003; Randolph & Koblinsky, 2000).

The neighborhood and community characteristics help to shape the adaptive culture of the family and in turn affect parenting styles and the development of the young child. Neighborhood variables to consider include the degree of neighborhood organization or disorganization, availability of resources, neighborhood norms and expectations regarding parenting and child development, and level of safety and community violence. Randolph and Koblinsky (2000) cite studies that have found relationships between the quality of parenting and 1) the availability of resources for child rearing (Garbarino & Sherman, 1980), 2) the sense of danger in the community (Kriesberg, 1970), and 3) the proportion of older adults in the neighborhood (Cotterell, 1986). For example, due to lower socioeconomic status of many families of color or the newcomer status of immigrants, they experience neighborhoods with fewer tangible assets. These families often encounter substandard housing, seasonal migration, job displacement, residential segregation, and high levels of community violence. Some of these neighborhoods are also experiencing a breakdown of the religious, social, and economic institutions that were potential routes out of poverty (Halpern, 1993). These neighborhood trends contribute to survival-oriented patterns of parenting and relating to the outside world, which are characterized by social isolation, and restriction of young children from outdoor neighborhood play (Randolph, Koblinsky, & Roberts, 1997). In this sense, neighborhood characteristics force parents to focus on basic dimensions of caregiving, such as physical care, safety, protection at the expense of other important behaviors (e.g., play and social activities), and cognitive and language stimulation.

THE INTERFACE OF CULTURE AND EARLY CHILDHOOD SYSTEMS

The importance of early childhood programs and supports is gaining increasing attention as emerging research highlights the psychobiological malleability of young children. Emerging brain research made possible by noninvasive imaging techniques is beginning to demonstrate the effect of psychological trauma on the brain and remediation of trauma through early intervention (Rintoul, 2003). Longitudinal research is showing the long-term influence of early childhood preventive interventions and high-quality early childhood preschool education. Olds and his colleagues (1998) have found that a nurse visiting program for the first 2 years of a child's life carries positive effects on the mother and the child into the child's teen years. The High/Scope Perry Preschool study has identified both short- and long-term effects of a high-quality preschool education program for 123 young African American children living in poverty. Research on this program has found positive program effects in the domains of education, economic performance, crime prevention, family relationships, and health through age 40 (Schweinhart, 2004). Finally, increasing attention has been focused on child care environments and policy as the number of children in child care increases significantly.

With the changing ethnocultural demographics and growing national attention on the importance of the early childhood years, the systems serving these children will need to address the increasing diversity in the early childhood population. The systems of early childhood are distinct from those of other developmental stages and include, but are not limited to, early intervention programs, early child care, early education, preschools, foster care, and family courts. As the population becomes more culturally diverse, each of these interventions must be equipped to work cross-culturally. Outreach, engagement, prevention, and early intervention must be tailored to the unique cultural aspects of the young children and their families. These program efforts must recognize their strengths and limitations in working across cultures and develop effective strategies to interface with culturally diverse children and families. They must determine how well they are addressing the needs of their culturally diverse populations, how readily they are accessed and utilized by different populations, and how well they have adapted their programs to different cultural values.

Engagement with early childhood systems is variable across culturally diverse populations in the United States. For example, Latinos are now the largest ethnic minority group in the country and are growing at a faster rate than the population as a whole. The rate of population growth among Latino children is even greater as they now represent the largest minority child population in the United States (Morse, 2003). Nationally, however, they are less likely than any other racial or ethnic groups to enroll their children in early childhood education programs (Walke & Bowie, 2004), use child care centers, or receive early intervention services. In 1995, compared with 73% of white and 76% of African American first graders, only 57% of Latino first graders had participated in a center-based early childhood program prior to kindergarten (Buysse, Castro, West, & Skinner, 2004). Latino children lag behind their peers upon entry to kindergarten, and the achievement gap continues to widen as children grow older. Among 3- to 5-year-olds not yet in kindergarten, white and African American children are more likely than Latinos to recognize letters of the alphabet, count to 20, and write or draw rather than scribble (U.S. Department of Education, 2000).

Simultaneously, increasing stressors on Latino families have resulted in a dramatic increase in Latino children in foster care. For Latinos and other immigrant populations, however, the use of family child care homes as opposed to center-based care is extensive. This practice is in keeping with the higher value placed on kinship care and the increased comfort with a shared language and culture in these neighborhood homes. This preference also reflects the likelihood that family child care is more affordable than center-based care and the underlying sense of distrust of less familiar institutions.

Cultural continuity between the home and the early childhood environment is particularly important for the young child. Continuity refers to the ability of the provider to understand, respect, and build upon cultural and linguistic practices in the home to ensure smooth growth and development. Children between birth and age 2 are engaged in acquiring preferences and beliefs by incorporating the views and behaviors of adults who care for them. If the behaviors of these adults are inconsistent, there can be confusion and stress (Lally, 1994). Ensuring continuity between childrearing practices in the home and with outside caregivers is essential for the young child and family. A sense of discontinuity and cultural clashes later becomes a normal part of a child's straddling the home culture and outside environments. The older child generally possesses the adaptive skills to negotiate these conflicting cultures; however, younger children lack the cognitive and behavior skills to understand these situational determinants and may show more confusion in their behavior. For example, a parent who has been raised to believe that early mastery of skills is important may use feeding time as an opportunity to encourage an infant or toddler to build specific motor skills. A parent taught to value autonomy and independence of young children may create situations where the child self-feeds and in the process creates a mess. Conversely, for families where resources for food are scarce, the caregiver may have a greater tendency to control an infant's eating to ensure food is not wasted (Chang & Pulido, 1994).

As discussed earlier, theoretical concepts, such as attachment theory, often form the basis for early childhood programs. Consequently, independence and assertiveness are often promoted in early childhood environments. Whereas the caregivers mean well, they may inadvertently be encouraging culturally inappropriate behavior.

The sense of discontinuity is magnified for early childhood mental health systems as this is often the first time children need to negotiate a culture outside of their home environment. For parents, this may be the first encounter with challenges to their parenting strategies and values regarding child rearing. Wright and Leonhardt (1998) suggests that effective intervention with culturally and ethnically diverse young children requires that service providers deal with children's multiple developmental issues within a broader ecological context that emphasizes a cultural framework. Both developmental and cultural competence are essential in working with young, culturally diverse children and families.

CULTURE COUNTS IN DESIGNING INTERVENTION STRATEGIES AND POLICIES

The following scenarios demonstrate the issues involved with addressing the needs of culturally and ethnically diverse children. Each of these children have different backgrounds and present unique challenges.

Luis is a 3-year-old Salvadoran child whose aggressive hitting and biting behavior toward other children is threatening expulsion from his third child care center in a year. He is the only child of immigrant parents from El Salvador who were unable to use a family child care center because of Luis's behavior. His mother works in a local hotel, and his father is a day laborer. Both parents have limited English proficiency, and Luis is primarily Spanish speaking. The parents are unable to control Luis's behavior and are fearful that they will lose their jobs if Luis cannot remain in the child care center. There is some concern of the risk for domestic violence in the home.

James is a 4-year-old African American child who lives with his grandmother (his primary caretaker) and his parents. In the Head Start program, James frequently has temper outbursts, throws and breaks toys, is constantly fidgety, and is unable to sit in a chair and stay on a task. He frequently becomes enraged with his peers at little or no provocation and has occasionally hit several of the children. The parents of these other children have complained to the teachers about James's behavior. James's home life is chaotic because his parents intermittently work and frequently clash with his grandmother, who is the more stable wage-earner in the family.

Anna is a 4-year-old Vietnamese-Chinese child who lives with her parents, an 8-year-old brother, and an aunt. Anna's parents are from Vietnam. Anna barely speaks in the preschool program, plays alone, and has speech and language delays. She comes to preschool dressed in three or four layers of sweaters with a note pinned to the outer sweater asking that these not be removed. Her mother brings her to the preschool, is very reticent and nonengaging, and speaks limited English.

How do each of these settings begin to address the needs of these young children and their families? These children are among the 120,000 preschoolers in low-income neighborhoods who are increasingly needing mental health attention (Pottick & Warner, 2002). These young children, however, are different in terms of their cultural, linguistic, and socioeconomic circumstances. At this early stage of life, these three children are already at triple risk due to their minority status, their economic insecurity, and their emotional and behavioral problems. The system of care for these children must incorporate strategies for engagement and intervention that are culturally acceptable and understandable to these diverse families.

For ethnically and culturally diverse families in the United States, the stigma attached to emotional and behavioral disorders is pervasive and persistent. The sense of stigma, a general unfamiliarity with mental disorders, and a belief system that young children do not experience these disorders combine to inhibit attention to the socioemotional needs of their children. There have been numerous reports about the lack of access to mental health services for diverse ethnic and racial populations and the children within these groups (Gibbs & Huang, 2003; United States Department of Health and Human Services, 2001; Vargas & Koss-Chioino, 1992). Little attention, however, has explicitly focused on the issues for these young children with emotional and behavioral disorders.

In considering an early childhood system of care for these children, it is critical to address the cultural issues and challenges presented by these families. Cultural responsiveness and competence is manifest in the individual, person-to-person behavior as well as in the organizational policies and practices of the system. Regardless of the level of intervention, the objective is to create the conditions that will enable the child to thrive.

Five key strategies to address this objective include: 1) valuing diversity, 2) understanding the dynamics of difference, 3) conducting ongoing cultural self-assessment, 4) making cultural adaptations, and 5) institutionalizing cultural knowledge (Cross, Bazron, Dennis, & Isaacs, 1989).

The early childhood system and staff need to *value the diversity* of its children and families. The families of each of these children bring culturally determined child-rearing methods as well as expectations of the child care center, the Head Start program, or the preschool environment. The spoken languages, patterns of communication, and approach to developmental milestones may be quite different between the families and the respective centers. For example, among some Asian American families, there is simultaneously a greater indulgence in the young child and an expectation of meeting milestones, such as toilet training, earlier than most Western cultures. Staff in early childhood centers need to increase their understanding of this diversity represented in their centers and the continuity or discontinuity between the home and center cultures.

James's family composition, patterns of communication, and self-regulatory behavior would need to be understood in his family's cultural context and the tempo of his family life. Staff and programs would also need to develop strategies for responding and regrouping for inevitable clashes that occur across cultures. Anna's family deeply believes that cold air drafts and chills contribute to her developmental delays and insist that she be dressed in multiple layers, which often seem inappropriate for the tem-

perature and conditions in the center. For several weeks, Anna's family bat-
tled with the center staff who felt Anna was too encumbered by the layers
of heavy clothing until finally Anna's mother periodically removed her from
the center or pinned notes to her clothing telling the caregivers not to remove them. The staff at this center need to understand the mother's belief
system, identify the *dynamics of difference*, and *make appropriate adaptations.*

Early childhood staff need to conduct ongoing *cultural self-assessments*
and *organizational assessments.* This enables the center to inventory its cultural assets and gaps. A self-assessment enables a setting (e.g., a child care
center) to examine the capacity—the knowledge, skills, and attitudes—of
its staff for working cross-culturally, as well as the program policies and
practices that make it an inhibiting or promoting environment for culturally diverse youth and families. Regarding Luis and Anna, language issues were a barrier to connecting with the families. Identifying and prioritizing this gap may result in the acquisition of bilingual staff or
affiliation with consultants or outside agencies who could be cultural
brokers for the staff.

A cultural self-assessment and organizational assessment would also
propel the center to better understand the communities of these three
children. For example, in many racially and ethnically diverse communities there exists an invisible layer of organizations that are the backbone of
these communities. In many of these communities, particularly immigrant
communities, there are structures that preserve culture and language, provide outlets for political involvement, organize social services, and create a
sense of belonging and affiliation (Association for the Study and Development of Community, 2002). Ethnic media are sources for identifying community leaders and gathering points (e.g., churches, community centers,
grocery stores).

Cultural inventories and self-assessments, however, are useless unless
they lead to developing new behaviors and policies to improve the cultural
competence of staff, agencies, or organizations. This may take the form of
"communities of practice" that are actively engaged in building cultural
knowledge, reflecting on existing practices and programs, struggling with
the adaptations needed to better serve diverse children and families, and
collaborating with cultural entities to enhance attitudes, knowledge, and
skills (Buysse, Sparkman, & Wesley, 2003).

CONCLUSION

As the racial and ethnic diversity of the child population in the United
States continues to grow, a deep respect for culture is essential to understanding and serving these families. The recognition that culture plays a
major role in the development of young children and their families must

be translated into programs and policies that promote healthy multicultural development, identify salient risk and protective factors, and integrate cultural knowledge. Maximizing the impact of early childhood systems of care requires program developers and policy makers to expand beyond their safety zones and incorporate constructs of culture, race, cultural adaptation, disparities, and cultural discontinuities of care.

REFERENCES

Ainsworth, M., Blehar, M., Waters, E., & Wall, S. (1978). *Patterns of attachment: A psychological study of the strange situation.* Mahwah, NJ: Lawrence Erlbaum Associates.

Association for the Study and Development of Community. (2002). *Lessons learned about civic participation among immigrants.* Washington, DC: Washington Area Partnership for Immigrants.

Berry, M. (1993). *The politics of parenthood.* New York: Penguin Books.

Boykin, W., & Toms, F. (1985). Black child socialization: A conceptual framework. In H.P. McAdoo & J. McAdoo (Eds.), *Black children: Social, educational, and parental environments* (pp. 33–51). Thousand Oaks, CA: Sage Publications.

Bronfenbrenner, U. (1986). Ecology of the family as a context for human development: Research perspectives. *Developmental Psychology, 22*(6), 723–742.

Brown, T., Williams, D., Jackson, J., Neighbors, H., Torres, M., Sellers, S., et al. (2000). Being black and feeling blue: The mental health consequences of racial discrimination. *Race and Society, 2,* 117–131.

Buysse, V., Castro, D., West, T., & Skinner, M. (2004). *Addressing the needs of Latino children: A national survey of state administrators of early childhood programs.* Chapel Hill: The University of North Carolina, FPG Child Development Institute.

Buysse, V., Sparkman, K., & Wesley, P. (2003). Communities of practice: Connecting what we know with what we do. *Exceptional Children, 69*(3), 263–277.

Chang, H. (1993). *Affirming children's roots: Cultural and linguistic diversity in early care and education.* San Francisco: California Tomorrow.

Chang, H., & Pulido, D. (1994). The critical importance of cultural and linguistic continuity for infants and toddlers. *ZERO TO THREE,* 13–17. Retrieved November, 1994 from http://www.californiatomorrow.org/files/pdfs/Cultural_Linguistic_Continuity.pdf

Chao, R. (1996). Chinese and European American mothers' beliefs about the role of parenting in children's school success. *Journal of Cross-Cultural Psychology 27*(4), 402–423.

Chase-Lansdale, P., Brooks-Gunn, J., & Amsky, E. (1994). Young African American multigenerational families in poverty: Quality of mothering and grandmothering. *Child Development, 65,* 373–393.

Cotterell. J. (1986). Work and community influences on the quality of child rearing. *Child Development, 57,* 362–374.

Crockenberg, S. (1981). Infant irritability, mother responsiveness, and social support influences on the security of infant–mother attachment. *Child Development, 52,* 857–865.

Cross, T., Bazron, B., Dennis, K., & Isaacs, M. (1989). *Towards a culturally competent system of care: A monograph on effective services for minority children who are severely emotionally disabled* (Vol. 1). Washington, DC: CASSP Technical Assistance Center, Georgetown University Child Development Center.

Douglas-Hall, A., & Koball, H. (2004). *Children of recent immigrants: National and regional trends.* New York: National Center for Children in Poverty, Columbia University. Retrieved September 14, 2005, from http://www.nccp. org/pub_cli04.html

Egeland, B., & Sroufe, L.A. (1981). Attachment and early maltreatment. *Child Development, 52,* 44–52.

Emde, R. (1999). Implications for research. *NHSA Dialog: A Research-to-Practice Journal for the Early Intervention Field, 2*(2), 286–298.

Garbarino, J., & Sherman, D. (1980). High-risk neighborhoods and high-risk families: The human ecology of child maltreatment. *Child Development, 51,* 88–198.

Garcia-Coll, C., Lamberty, G., Jenkins, R., McAdoo, H ., Conic, K., Waski, B., & Vazquez Garcia, H. (1996). An integrative model for the study of developmental competencies in minority children. *Child Development, 67,* 1891–1914.

Gibbs, J., & Huang, L. (2003). *Children of color: Psychological interventions with culturally diverse youth.* San Francisco: Jossey-Bass.

Ginorio, A., Gutierrez, L., Cauce, A., & Acosta, M. (1995). The psychology of Latinas. In C. Travis (Ed.), *Feminist perspectives on the psychology of women* (pp. 89–102). Washington, DC: American Psychological Association.

Halpern, R. (1993). Poverty and infant development. In C. Zeanah, Jr. (Ed.), *Handbook of infant mental health* (pp. 73–86). New York: The Guilford Press.

Harrison, A., Wilson, M ., Pine, C., Chan, S., & Buriel, R. (1990). Family ecologies of ethnic minority children. *Child Development, 61,* 347–362.

Hunter, A., Pearson, J., Ialongo, N., & Kellam, S. (1998). Parenting alone to multiple caregivers: Child care and parenting arrangements in black and white urban families. *Family Relations, 47,* 343–353.

Jackson, J., Brown, T., Williams, D., Torres, M., Sellers, S., & Brown, K. (1996). Racism and the physical and mental health status of African Americans: A thirteen year national panel study. *Ethnicity and Disease, 6,* 132–147.

Jayakody, R., Chatters, L., & Taylor, R. (1993). Family support to single and married African American mothers: The provision of financial, emotional, and child care assistance. *Journal of Marriage and Family, 55,* 261–281.

Johnson, D., Jaeger, E., Randolph, S., Cauce, A., Ward, J., & National Institute of Child Health and Human Development Early Child Care Research Network. (2003). Studying the effects of early child care experiences on the development of children of color in the United States: Toward a more inclusive research agenda. *Child Development, 74*(5), 1227–1244.

Keller, H., Voelker, S., & Zach, U. (1997). Attachment in cultural context. *Newsletter of the International Society for the Study of Behavioral Development, (1)*31, 1–3.

Kessler, R., Michelson, K., & Williams, D. (1999). The prevalence, distribution, and mental health correlates of perceived discrimination in the United States. *Journal of Health and Social Behavior, 40,* 208–230.

Kitayama, S., Markus, H., Masumoto, H., & Norasakkunkit, V. (1997). Individual and collective processes in the construction of the self: Self-enhancement in the United States and self-criticism in Japan. *Journal of Personality and Social Psychology, 72,* 1245–1267.

Krieger, N. (1999). Embodying inequality: A review of concepts, measures, and methods for studying health consequences of discrimination. *International Journal of Health Services, 29,* 295–352.

Kriesberg, L. (1970). *Mothers in poverty: A study of fatherless families.* Chicago: Aldine.

Lally, R. (1994). Caring for infants and toddlers in groups: Necessary considerations for emotional, social and cognitive development. *ZERO TO THREE, 14*(5).

Lebra, T. (1994). Mother and child in Japanese socialization: A Japan–U.S. comparison. In P. Greenfield & R. Cocking (Eds.), *Cross-cultural roots of minority child development* (pp. 259–274). Mahwah, NJ: Lawrence Erlbaum Associates.

Leung, E.K. (1990). Early risks: Transition from culturally/linguistically diverse homes to formal schooling. *Journal of Educational Issues of Language Minority Students, 7,* 35–51.

Lieberman, A., & Zeanah, C. (1999). Contributions of attachment theory to infant–parent psychotherapy and other interventions with infants and young children. In J. Cassidy & P. Shaver (Eds.), *Handbook of attachment: Theory, research, and clinical applications* (pp. 555–574). New York: The Guilford Press.

Lynch, E.W., & Hanson, M.J. (2004). *Developing cross-cultural competence: A guide for working with children and their families (3rd ed.).* Baltimore: Paul H. Brookes Publishing Co.

McLoyd, V. (1990). The impact of economic hardship on black families and children: Psychological distress, parenting, and socioemotional development. *Child Development, 61,* 311–346.

Miyake, K., & Yamazaki, K. (1995). Self-conscious emotions, child rearing, and child psychology in Japanese culture. In J. Tangney & K. Fischer (Eds.), *Self-conscious emotions: The psychology of shame, guilt, embarrassment and pride* (pp. 488–504). New York: The Guilford Press.

Morse, A. (2003). *Language access: Helping non-English speakers navigate health and human services.* Washington, DC: National Conference of State Legislatures Children's Policy Initiative.

National Advisory Mental Health Council Workgroup on Child and Adolescent Mental Health Intervention Development and Deployment. (2001). *Blueprint for change: Research on child and adolescent mental health.* Rockville, MD: National Institutes of Mental Health.

Ogbu, J. (1981). Origins of human competence: A cultural ecological perspective. *Child Development, 52,* 413–429.

Ogbu, J. (1995). Understanding cultural diversity and learning. *Journal for the Education of the Gifted, 17,* 354–383.

Okagaki, L., & Divecha, D. (1993). Development of parental beliefs. In T. Luster & L. Okagaki (Eds.), *Parenting: An ecological perspective* (pp. 35–67). Mahwah, NJ: Lawrence Erlbaum Associates.

Olds, D., Henderson, C., Cole, R., Eckenrode, J., Kitzman, H., Luckey, D., et al. (1998). Long-term effects of nurse home visitation on children's criminal and antisocial behavior: 15-year follow-up of a randomized controlled trial. *Journal of the American Medical Association, 280,* 1238–1244.

Peak, L. (1989). Learning to become part of the group: The Japanese child's transition to preschool life. *Journal of Japanese Studies, 15,* 93–123.

Pearson, J., Hunter, A., Ensminger, M., & Kellam, S. (1990). Black grandmothers in multigenerational households: Diversity in family structure and parenting involvement in the Woodlawn community. *Child Development, 61,* 434–442.

Phinney, J., & Landin, J. (1998). Research paradigms for studying ethnic minority families within and across groups. In V. McLoyd & L. Steinberg (Eds.), *Studying minority adolescents: Conceptual, methodological, and theoretical issues* (pp. 89–109). Mahwah, NJ: Lawrence Erlbaum Associates.

Pottick, K., & Warner, L. (2002). More than 115,000 disadvantaged preschoolers receive mental health services. In Institute for Health, Health Care Policy, and Aging Research (Ed.), *Update: Latest Findings in Children's Mental Health.* Policy Report submitted to the Annie E. Casey Foundation 1(2). New Brunswick, NJ: Rutgers University.

Querido, J., Warner, T., & Eyberg, S. (2002). Parenting styles and child behavior in African American families of preschool children. *Journal of Clinical Child Psychology, 31*(2), 272–277.

Randolph, S., & Koblinsky, S. (2000). *Understanding and addressing infant mental health from a cultural perspective.* Alexandria, VA: Infant Mental Health Forum, Head Start Bureau.

Randolph, S., Koblinsky, S., & Roberts, D. (1997). Studying the role of family and school in the development of African American preschoolers in violent neighborhoods. *Journal of Negro Education, 65,* 282–294.

Rao, N., McHale, J., & Pearson, E. (2003). Links between socialization goals and child-rearing practices in Chinese and Indian mothers. *Infant and Child Development 12,* 475–492.

Rintoul, B. (October, 2003). *Early brain development: Implications for social emotional development.* Presentation at Georgetown University Center for Child and Human Development, Washington, DC.

Rosser, P., & Randolph, S. (1996). The Developmental Milestones Expectations Scale: An assessment of parents' expectations for infants' development. In R.L. Jones (Ed.), *Handbook of tests and measurements for black populations* (pp. 31–38). Berkeley, CA: Cobb & Henry.

Rothbaum, F., Weisz, J., Pott, M., Niyake, K., & Morelli, G. (2000). Attachment and culture: Security in the United States and Japan. *American Psychologist, 55*(10), 1093–1104.

Sameroff, A., & Fiese, B. (1990). Transactional regulation and early intervention. In S. Measles & J. Shonkoff (Eds.), *Handbook of early childhood intervention.* New York: Cambridge University Press.

Schweinhart, L. (2004). The High/Scope Perry preschool study through age 40. Ypsilanti, MI: High/Scope Educational Research Foundation. Retrieved September 14, 2005, from http://www.highscope.org

Shonkoff, J., & Phillips, D. (Eds.). (2000). *From neurons to neighborhoods: The science of early childhood development.* Washington, DC: National Academies Press.

Slade, A. (1999). Attachment theory and research: Implications for the theory and practice of individual psychotherapy with adults. In J. Cassidy & P. Shaver (Eds.), *Handbook of attachment: Theory, research, and clinical applications* (pp. 575–594). New York: The Guilford Press.

Smith, K. (2002). *Who's minding the kids? Child care arrangements: Spring 1997* Current Population Reports, P70-86, U.S. Census Bureau Washington, DC: U.S. Government Printing Office.

Snyder, H., & Sickmund, M. (1999). *Juvenile offenders and victims: 1999 national report.* Washington, DC: Office of Juvenile Justice and Delinquency Prevention.

Spencer, M.B. (1983). Children's cultural values and parental child rearing strategies. *Developmental Review, 3,* 351–370.

Sroufe, A., & Waters, E. (1997). Attachment in cultural context. *Newsletters of the International Society for the Study of Behavioral Development, 1*(Serial No. 31), 3–5.

Stevenson, H. (1994). Racial socialization in African American families: The art of balancing intolerance and survival. *The Family Journal: Counseling and Therapy for Couples and Families, 2,* 190–198.

Super, C.M. (1981). Cross-cultural research on infancy. In H.C. Triandis & A. Heron (Eds.), *Handbook of cross-cultural psychology: Developmental psychology (Vol. 4)* (pp. 17–53). Boston: Allyn & Bacon.

U.S. Bureau of the Census. (2001). *American's families and living arrangements: March 2000* (Current Population Reports P20-537). Washington, DC: Author.

U.S. Bureau of the Census. (2002). *Current population survey: March 2001—Annual hierographic supplement.* Washington, DC: U.S. Government Printing Office.

U.S. Bureau of Labor Statistics. (2002). *America's children: Key national indicators of well-being.* Washington, DC: U.S. Government Printing Office.

U.S. Department of Education, National Center for Educational Statistics. (2000). *Statistics in brief—March 2000: Home literacy activities and signs of children's emerging literacy, 1993–1999.* Washington, DC: U.S. Government Printing Office.

U.S. Department of Health and Human Services. (2001). *Mental health: Culture, race, and ethnicity—A supplement to mental health: A report of the surgeon general.* Rockville, MD: Author, Public Health Service, Office of the Surgeon General.

Vargas, L., & Koss-Chioino, D. (1992). *Working with culture: Psychotherapeutic interventions with ethnic minority children and adolescents.* San Francisco: Jossey-Bass.

Walke, K., & Bowie, A. (2004). *Linking the child care and health care systems: A consolation of options.* Philadelphia, PA: Private/Public ventures; retrieved October 6, 2004, from http://www.ppv.org/ppv/ppublications/assets/175pblications.pdf

Weinfield, N., Sroufe, L.A., Egeland, B., & Carlson, E. (1999). The nature of individual differences in infant–caregiver attachment. In J. Cassidy & P. Shaver (Eds.), *Handbook of attachment: Theory, research, and clinical applications* (pp. 68–88). New York: The Guilford Press.

White, J., & Parham, T. (1990). *The psychology of blacks: An African American perspective.* Upper Saddle River, NJ: Prentice Hall.

Whiting, J. (1977). A model for psychocultural research. In P. Leiderman, S. Tulkin, & A. Rosenfeld (Eds.), *Culture and infancy: Variations in the human experience.* New York: Academic Press.

Wright, H.H., & Leonhardt, T.V. (1998). Service approaches for infants, toddlers, and preschoolers: Implications for systems of care. In M. Hernandez & M.R. Isaacs (Eds.), *Promoting cultural competence in children's mental health services* (pp. 229–249). Baltimore: Paul H. Brookes Publishing Co.

II

Building Systems of Care for Young Children and Families

4

Early Childhood Mental Health Services and Supports Through a Systems Approach

Roxane K. Kaufmann and Kathy S. Hepburn

Early childhood policies and procedures are highly fragmented, with complex and confusing points of entry that are particularly problematic for underserved populations and those with special needs. This lack of an integrative early childhood infrastructure makes it difficult to advance prevention-oriented initiatives for all children and to coordinate services for those with complex problems.

Shonkoff & Phillips, 2000, p. 11

Early childhood mental health (ECMH) is everybody's business (Hanson & Martner, 2000), and every state and community can develop systems that organize services and supports for young children and families so that they are accessible, sustainable, appropriate, and of high quality. States and communities play a critical role in promoting and supporting a healthy start for young children and their families through the integration of mental health services, supports, and perspectives into existing programs and practices, and by creating or strengthening linkages among agencies, programs, families, and providers. A shared vision of early childhood mental health that crosses the boundaries and traditional perspectives of early childhood care and education, mental health, primary care, child welfare, and other service systems can reframe the traditional mental health conceptualization of a system of care to fit the developmental outcomes and programmatic resources that are right for young children and their families.

This chapter emphasizes the following points:

- The healthy social-emotional development of *all* children can be met through a continuum of services and supports informed by a public health perspective.

- The responsibility for early childhood mental health (the healthy social and/or emotional development and recovery from behavior difficulties) lies with *all* those who care about and provide services to young children and families.

- Rather than a discrete mental health service system for young children and families, most mental health services and supports can be infused into the services and environments that those children are *already* accessing in their communities.

- To make services and supports available and sustained, there must be an infrastructure that supports them (e.g., work force, financing, family advocacy).

- Opportunities to create an integrated early childhood mental health system of services and supports are afforded through different *doors* by addressing the mental health needs of young children and their families in *all* early childhood and early intervention collaborative efforts.

This chapter proposes a new approach for building systems of care for young children that addresses early childhood mental health, including a brief review of the historical context of early childhood service systems development; a framework for an early childhood mental health system of care, infrastructure building blocks, and opportunities for systems development.

A NEW APPROACH FOR BUILDING SYSTEMS TO CARE FOR YOUNG CHILDREN

Since the mid-1980s, interagency systems have been developed in states and communities in an attempt to increase access and availability of services and supports and to avoid duplication and fragmentation of services to young children and their families. Typically these efforts have focused on particular populations of children who were identified as at risk or showing evidence of developmental, physical health, or mental health difficulties (Karoly et al., 1998, Shonkoff & Phillips, 2000). Now, in a renewed focus on the needs of *all* young children and their families, states and communities are engaged in planning early childhood systems that prepare children who are ready to enter school, increase the quality of early care and education programs, and reduce risk and promote resilence in vulnerable populations. Ongoing work with states and communities reinforces the need for using *any* of the systems-building efforts that are occurring in states and communities as an opportunity to collaborate across systems and agencies to address the needs of young children and families for a continuum of mental health services, supports, and perspectives and to infuse them into early childhood environments and programs.

WHAT IS EARLY CHILDHOOD MENTAL HEALTH?

Early childhood mental health is defined in two ways. The first definition is from a developmental and/or clinical perspective, and the second is from a systems and/or service delivery view. The developmental and/or clinical definition views early childhood mental health as

- The social-emotional and behavioral well-being of infants, toddlers, young children, and their families

- The developing capacity to experience, regulate, and express emotion

- The ability to form close, secure relationships

- The capacity to explore the environment and learn (ZERO TO THREE, 2002)

A systems and/or service delivery perspective proposed by Knitzer (2000) further defines early childhood mental health as a set of strategies to

- Promote the emotional and behavioral well-being of all young children

- Strengthen the emotional and behavioral well-being of children whose development is compromised by environmental or biological risk in order to minimize their risks and enhance the likelihood that they will enter school with appropriate skills

- Help families of young children address whatever barriers they face to ensure that their children's emotional development is not compromised

- Expand the competencies of nonfamilial caregivers and others to promote well-being of young children and families, particularly those at risk by virtue of environmental or biological factors

- Ensure that young children experiencing clearly atypical emotional and behavioral development and their families have access to needed services and supports

When combined, these two perspectives help guide states, communities, providers, and families as they strive to conceptualize early childhood mental health and work to build services and supports that encourage social-emotional development in *all* young children and assist those children at risk or experiencing developmental difficulties.

EARLY CHILDHOOD MENTAL HEALTH IN THE CONTEXT OF SYSTEMS DEVELOPMENT

Four major historical efforts provide examples of how systems development has influenced the care of young children and services to address early childhood mental health concerns. They are 1) early care and education, such as Head Start and Early Head Start; 2) the federal comprehensive mental health services and mental health systems of care; 3) the early intervention system, including the Individuals with Disabilities Education Act (IDEA) of 1990 (PL 101-476) and Part C; and 4) Title V maternal and child health grant program.

Early Care and Education and Community Partnerships

Since the early 1970s, the Head Start program has promoted early childhood mental health and social competence as a core component of child development and family support services. This focus has included services delivered onsite as well as efforts to build and sustain community partnerships and services that support mental health promotion, prevention, and intervention to the country's most vulnerable children and their families. The federal effort to support consistent quality care, community partnerships, and service systems development through Head Start and Early Head Start represents an early, organized strategy for developing service linkages and systems of early care and education for young children.

Until the 1990s, much of early care and education had operated as an isolated and uncoordinated field. In response to a growing body of research on early brain development, the importance of nurturing relationships, and the effect of high-quality child care in the first 5 years of life, the early childhood community has mobilized to enhance early care and education environments. With an increased focus on outcomes for young children and school readiness, the early care and education field has successfully called attention to the need for adequate funding, policies, and practices, and it has organized through licensing, accreditation, and advocacy efforts. At the national level, policy makers have joined forces to show the important link between primary care and early childhood education and to advocate for a system that integrates services and supports that meet the health and developmental needs of young children and their families. Some states and communities now recognize the essential need to address social-emotional development and the mental health needs of young children and their families and are building new, cross-system partnerships and integrating mental health services and supports into the early care and education environment.

Mental Health Systems of Care

Since the 1980s, there have been federally funded and supported efforts to assist states and communities build what the mental health community has called *systems of care* for children and adolescents with emotional disorders and their families. As first defined by Stroul and Friedman (1986), a system of care for children with serious emotional disturbance is "a comprehensive spectrum of mental health and other necessary services which are organized into a coordinated network to meet the multiple and changing needs of children and their families" (p. 3). Starting with the Child and Adolescent Service System Program (CASSP), the National Institute of Mental Health, with funding from Congress, awarded grants to all 50 states, territories, and some local jurisdictions to plan and develop integrated systems of care for children with serious emotional disturbance. Recognizing that children with significant mental illness were often served by multiple public systems, including mental health, education, child welfare, and juvenile justice, the focus of planning and policy development was collaborative across agencies.

Using the recommendations from a diverse stakeholder work group, the Stroul and Friedman (1986) document provided a blueprint for states and communities to use in developing their service systems. At the same time, a growing movement of families began to voice their concern about their lack of meaningful involvement in the planning, design, and delivery of services for their children. Indeed, families were often blamed for their children's difficulties, having little or no say in their intervention, placement, or removal from the families. The Federation of Families for Children's Mental Health (1989) was created to build a national forum for family advocacy, empowerment, and leadership.

In 1992, Congress legislated the creation of the Comprehensive Community Mental Health Services for Children and Their Families program. This grant program now provides 6 years of funding to stimulate the development of systems of care in local communities. The intent of this program is to develop a comprehensive array of community-based services and supports that are guided by a system of care philosophy with an emphasis on individualized, strengths-based services planning, intensive care management, partnerships with families, and cultural and linguistic competence (Pires, 2002).

Although progress has been made across agencies and environments in building systems of care that support the complex and multiple needs

of children with emotional disabilities, the population served has been almost exclusively adolescents and school-age children with the most
serious disabilities. Two exceptions are Vermont (see Chapter 8) and
Colorado who have utilized their federal grants to expand the traditional
mental health perspective to a broad, public health model and provide a
full continuum of care in a range of service environments that meet the
unique needs of young children and their families. The 2003 report of The
President's New Freedom Commission on Mental Health, *Achieving the
Promise: Transforming Mental Health Care in America*, recommended a national focus on the mental health needs of young children and their families, which influenced the expanded federal grant opportunities for projects focused on this population. In 2005, the Substance Abuse and Mental
Health Services Administration (SAMHSA) funded six new sites that are
planning to serve very young children through their system of care grant.

The Early Intervention System

With the passage of the Education of the Handicapped Act Amendments
of 1986 (PL 99-457), part of which became Part C of the amendments to
IDEA, Congress intended for states to build a comprehensive system to
support infants and toddlers with and at risk for disabilities and their families. Under Part C, states and jurisdictions must provide early intervention (EI) services to any child under the age of 3 who is experiencing a developmental delay or has a diagnosed physical or mental condition that has
a high probability of resulting in delay. In addition, states may choose to
provide services for infants and toddlers who are biologically or environmentally at risk for serious developmental disabilities. In either case, states
are charged with developing a system that provides screening, assessment
and diagnosis, service coordination (case management), individualized
family service plans (IFSPs), and services provided in natural environments. As of 2006, only nine states include at-risk children in their eligibility population, which includes those children without a mental health
diagnosis but at risk of emotional and behavioral difficulties or delays. Illinois, Michigan, Florida, and New Hampshire are some of the states that
are re-examining their early intervention system; identifying opportunities
for the integration of mental health services, supports, and perspectives in
the planning and implementation of the law; and trying to better address
the mental needs of the infants, toddlers, and families they serve.

Two complementary pieces of legislation—the amended Child Abuse
Prevention and Treatment Act (CAPTA), reauthorized as Keeping Children
and Families Safe Act of 2003 (PL 108-36), and the reauthorization of IDEA
(2004)—mandate collaboration between Part C of IDEA and the child welfare system for children under 3 with a substantiated case of abuse or neglect.

Child welfare workers are required to refer these children to Part C for screening. Although screening is to be made available, children are eligible for services only if they meet the state Part C eligibility requirements. Many states are working on creative, interagency approaches to meeting this requirement. For example, Minnesota is using a common screening instrument called the *Ages & Stages Questionnaires®: Social-Emotional (ASQ:SE)* (Squires, Bricker, & Twombly, 2002) across all child-serving agencies in an effort to streamline referrals. Ohio's *Help Me Grow* is a program serving at-risk and Part C children; therefore, many of the children who might have been referred to Part C through CAPTA are already being served.

Maternal and Child Health Systems

In 1981, Maternal and Child Health (MCH) Title V programs were mandated to develop a system of comprehensive, coordinated, community-based services for children with special health care needs and their families. These systems were to be family centered and interdisciplinary and provide care coordination (case management), early screening, assessment and diagnosis, family and/or professional collaboration, and integrated care plans. State Title V programs have two primary components. They are 1) infrastructure development for screening, surveillance, and assessment; and 2) the coordination of services for children with special health care needs.

As of 2003, MCH began funding states to engage in strategic planning and systems building through the Early Childhood Comprehensive Systems grants. The grant funds states to plan, develop, and implement collaboration and partnerships at the state level that ensure families will have access to health insurance, a constantly available primary care physician (i.e., medical home), quality early care and education, social-emotional development and mental health services, parenting education, and family support. Forty-eight states, the District of Columbia, Puerto Rico, and Pilau have assessed their existing capacity and developed a strategic plan, and some are beginning to implement specific strategies, such as the following:

- Identifying a common screening instrument to use across agencies

- Developing competencies for early care and education providers that include a focus on mental health

- Focusing on early identification of maternal depression

- Providing statewide education on social-emotional development

- Expanding the skills of all early intervention providers to better address the mental health needs of young children and their families

- Coordinating, expanding, and evaluating mental health consultation

Table 4.1. Foundations supporting community and state systems-building efforts

Assuring Better Child Health and Development

State grants funded by the Commonwealth Fund to broaden the provision of child health services to low-income children ages 0–3 years to include more developmental health services, including mental health

Build Initiative

A nine-state, multi-year initiative funded by the Early Childhood Funders' Collaborative to support teams of key state stakeholders in planning and mobilization activities to build comprehensive early learning systems in their states

Starting Points Initiative

State and community grants funded by the Carnegie Corporation to build early childhood care and education systems

Success by 6

Community grants funded by the Bank of America Foundation and United Way to use the principles of collaboration and prevention; join community leaders together with parents to achieve a community vision for young children; and raise awareness, improve access to services, and advocate for public policies that improve the lives of children and families

Adapted from Floyd S., & Child and Family Policy Center Staff. (2004). *Up and running: A compendium of multi-site early childhood initiatives* (2nd ed.). Des Moines, IA: State Early Childhood Policy Technical Assistance Network, Child and Family Policy Center; adapted with permission.

Building on Existing Systems for Early Childhood Mental Health

There are many other system-building opportunities across the country that are funded by philanthropic foundations. Others are state and community driven or federally supported. All of them provide an opportunity for states and communities to meet the comprehensive mental health needs of all young children and their families, and all have contributed lessons relevant to building systems for early childhood mental health. (See Table 4.1 for a description of some of these efforts.) Some of the common themes across these initiatives reflect the *system-building elements* of shared strategic planning, interagency partnerships and collaboration, a prepared work force, coordinated services, and outcome evaluation. Other common themes across these initiatives reflect the *system quality elements.*

In a comprehensive review of the research on systems of care that promote young children's social-emotional well-being, Smith and Fox (2004) commented on the lack of an integrated early childhood mental health system of care, but described *system quality elements* thought to be most effective. They identified features, parameters, and components recommended for a system of care for young children that asserted the following

- Challenging behavior can be prevented when systems support *a comprehensive array of services* from prevention to intensive intervention.

- Services must be of *high quality* and, whenever possible, *evidence based.*

- Systems must be comprehensive and provide *individualized services and supports* related to child and family needs, including culture and language.

- In the absence of one comprehensive service delivery system, systems must be developed from *interlocking and interconnected services and programs* into a system of care.

- Systems should be *family centered.*

- The early care and education, mental health, and health and child welfare *work force must have the skills* to provide collaborative, comprehensive, individualized, evidence-based services, supports, and systems.

Although empirical evidence specific to mental health systems of care and systems research studies is limited, both the history of system development (*system building*) and the recommended components (*system qualities*) confirm and inform a framework for guiding states and communities in their current and future efforts to build systems to support early childhood mental health. The framework described in the following section reflects these lessons learned. This framework and its supporting information can serve as a blueprint to help establish a common language, further the understanding of an early childhood system of care, and promote collaborative systems building in ready states and communities.

A FRAMEWORK FOR EARLY CHILDHOOD MENTAL HEALTH SYSTEMS

The concept of a system involves more than discrete and separate services, programs, or structures located in a defined geographic area. It implies that care is organized among agencies and those people directly involved with a common understanding, shared values, enabling policies, and relational structures that are effective and deliver services that are accessible, meaningful, and result in positive outcomes for those needing supports and services (Kaufmann & Wischmann, 1999). Young children and their families need a full array of formal and informal mental health services and supports that are embedded within early childhood programs and environments and available to parents and other caregivers. A continuum of comprehensive services includes those focused on promoting positive well-being, preventing social-emotional problems, and intervening when problems arise. A system needs to be value driven and have a shared understanding and commitment by all partners across service systems (early care and education, mental health, early intervention, etc.). Families must have a voice and leadership role in guiding and designing the system and services most meaningful to them. To make this actually happen, there needs to be an infrastructure to support the delivery of these services and supports. These components are represented in Figure 4.1, and each of these will be described in more detail in the following section.

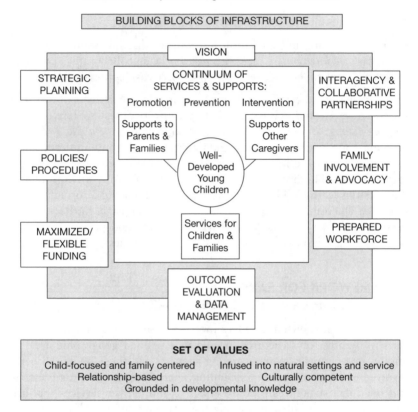

A Framework for Early Childhood Mental Health in A System of Care
Fosters the social and emotional well-being of all
infants, toddlers, preschool-age children and their families

BUILDING BLOCKS OF INFRASTRUCTURE

VISION

STRATEGIC
PLANNING

CONTINUUM OF
SERVICES & SUPPORTS:

Promotion   Prevention   Intervention

INTERAGENCY &
COLLABORATIVE
PARTNERSHIPS

Supports to
Parents &
Families

Supports to
Other
Caregivers

POLICIES/
PROCEDURES

Well-
Developed
Young
Children

FAMILY
INVOLVEMENT
& ADVOCACY

Services for
Children &
Families

MAXIMIZED/
FLEXIBLE
FUNDING

PREPARED
WORKFORCE

OUTCOME
EVALUATION
& DATA
MANAGEMENT

SET OF VALUES
Child-focused and family centered   Infused into natural settings and service
Relationship-based   Culturally competent
Grounded in developmental knowledge

Figure 4.1.   Diagram of early childhood mental health in a system of care.

Vision

An agreed-upon vision for early childhood mental health is the important
first step in galvanizing support among diverse stakeholders. A vision is often future oriented and answers the question, "What is it that our state
and/or community wants so that all children and families can be physically
and emotionally healthy and ready to learn and grow?" A vision statement
has a shared view and a shared sense of purpose, acting as a guidepost for
all activities that follow. Table 4.2 is an example of a vision statement for
the state of Florida.

Table 4.2.   An example of a vision and mission statement

Vision

One day, all children will be emotionally healthy, equipped to learn, and nurtured to develop their full potential. Our purpose is to help implement this vision by defining the need; investigating what interventions are most effective; translating these research findings into public policy; integrating infant mental health services into current programs throughout the state; building a cadre of infant mental health specialists; establishing training opportunities; securing adequate, ongoing funding; and continuing to evaluate the long-term effects on the community.

Mission statement

Our work diligently addresses the needs, develops a plan, secures the resources, and provides services necessary for strengthening the emotional development of young children. A brighter future for Florida's children can be achieved with a greater investment and collective commitment to prevention and early intervention.

Adapted from The Florida State University Center for Prevention and Early Intervention Policy for the Florida Developmental Disabilities Council. (2001). *Florida's strategic plan for infant mental health: Establishing a system of mental health services for young children and their families in Florida.* Tallahassee: Author; adapted with permission.

A Set of Values

Values represent the agreement among stakeholders on what principles should drive the development, implementation, and evaluation of the system and should be used to guide service planning and delivery. Agreed-upon values can serve to build consensus, resolve disputes, remove barriers, and address issues of territoriality among agencies. The values described in the following sections are culled from working with numerous communities and states as they have come together to build early childhood mental health systems of care. Individual community and state teams must reach their own agreement on values, mission, and guiding principles; however, these examples can serve as a starting point for these conversations.

Child and Family Centered

Partnerships between the family and service provider promote individualized services and supports that meet the needs of children and their families and move the field away from one size fits all service- or program-centered care. Family centered care acknowledges the family as the constant in a child's life and respects their skills, strengths, and expertise. In this paradigm, services and supports are available to both the child and the family, individually or together. Because families hold the key to understanding what will work in the context of their lives, they are the decision makers, the team leaders, and the evaluators of service effectiveness.

Relationship Based

By definition, early childhood mental health is reflected in the relationships that the child has with significant others and how he or she relates to the environment. Early on, every interaction between baby and parent or other caregivers has an impact on the outcome of social-emotional development in the child. Recognizing the importance of these intimate relationships, as well as those among parents, service providers, and family members, is essential in ensuring appropriate services that support child–caregiver interactions. All agencies involved in working with infants, young children, and their families must teach their providers to incorporate a relationship-based approach in service delivery. This approach has been operationalized in the field of infant mental health through a focus on the *parallel processes* that occur as relationships form between a service provider and a parent or caregiver, and how this relationship models the interactions desired between child and parent or caregiver. This perspective has influenced the growing awareness of and response to the need to support front-line workers. Programs have incorporated both team or individual reflective supervision and a safe, nonjudgmental, and relationship-based process for staff to share their successes as well as their challenges with an experienced listener.

Culturally Competent

Agencies, programs, services, and providers should be responsive to the cultural, racial, ethnic, and linguistic differences of the populations they serve. With the American population growing increasingly diverse, systems are developing policies, practices, and services that value diversity, address diverse perspectives toward mental health, and reach out to underserved populations. The work force in particular should be inclusive of natural helpers, cultural brokers, and bilingual staff.

Everything about early childhood mental health is influenced by culture. When a child is born into a family, that child enters into his or her earliest and closest relationships. The child's care and development are then influenced by the family's cultural belief systems, which become the background for all interactions and early learning within the family (Hepburn, 2004). Every family's culture, including both immigrant and native-born families, influences all factors of health and development, including sleeping patterns, the balance between encouraging autonomy versus attachment, early language and literacy, expectations of behavior and discipline, and attitudes toward mental health and illness. When the importance of a family's race, ethnicity, language, and culture is not recognized and understood, there is a risk of isolation and alienation. When the community does not offer culturally competent services and supports for diverse families and children, families may be less likely to participate in the community and access needed services and supports (Goode & Jackson, 2003; Hepburn, 2004). Building relationships with families and providing early services and supports requires a deep understanding of the cultural and linguistic preferences of each family and a willingness by staff to adapt interventions to make them more culturally relevant (see Chapter 3).

Infused into Natural Environments and Services

Young children and families are best served in a holistic way at home; through child care or preschool programs; during primary care visits; in Women, Infants, and Children (WIC) offices; in homeless shelters; through adult-serving programs; and in their neighborhoods. Mental health consultation to child care, Head Start, home visitation programs, and in primary care environments allows easy access to supports and services. Co-location of services, such as primary care and behavioral health care, makes for one-stop shopping and greatly increases access to and utilization of care (Rosman, Perry, & Hepburn, 2005). The use of evidence-based interventions and programs in child care and preschools, Head Start, Early Head Start, child welfare, and home visitation helps promote mental health and ensures earlier intervention and compliance with intervention.

Services infused into natural environments allow multiple points of entry into the system to ensure early access to supports and services. Services, however, must be coordinated to avoid having families who fall through the cracks or receive fragmented services. In a system of services, coordinating care can be supported through a variety of strategies, such as centralized resource and referral services, interagency agreements, integrated service plans, service coordination, and collaborative councils or committees. Children and families with more complex problems may need service coordination, case management, or wrap-around processes to assist them in accessing, organizing, and using multiple services and supports.

Grounded in Developmental Knowledge

When does a temper tantrum raise red flags? When is maternal depression a worrisome factor in a child's development? What practices in child care promote optimal social-emotional wellness? Understanding typical child development is essential to those working with infants, young children, and their families. Early care and education providers are often unaware of how important consistent, nurturing care is to the overall growth and development of young children in their program or to early signs of mental health problems in young children. In addition, mental health providers, who understand pathology, are not often versed in typical child development or group care. In a system, work force development includes cross agency and provider education; competency-based learning opportunities; and ongoing teaching, technical assistance, and supervision to providers to build a cadre of professionals who understand both early childhood development and infant mental health. For families, access to reading materials and emerging information about the importance of early relationships, brain development, typical developmental milestones, and warning signs can help them promote and make informed decisions about their child's mental health.

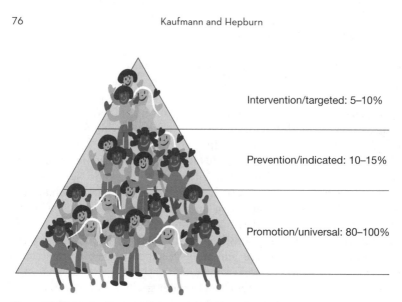

Intervention/targeted: 5–10%

Prevention/indicated: 10–15%

Promotion/universal: 80–100%

Figure 4.2. Public health approach to mental health services and supports.

A CONTINUUM OF SERVICES AND SUPPORTS

States and communities can develop a system that offers a continuum of mental health services by adopting a public health perspective toward intervention. By starting with the provision of universal interventions— mental health promotion for all children and families—planners have the advantage of promoting positive interactions, supporting health and wellness, and preventing the developmental and economic costs of children with behavioral health difficulties. As the pathway continues from promotion to prevention and intervention, the community as a whole benefits from the services and supports provided. Edwall (2005) further explains this process.

> Early childhood mental health care provides a continuum of services and supports from prevention through intervention. It includes children who will never have a mental health diagnosis, those who may develop a problem at some point, and those who have evident problems early on. It relies on a wide range of both professional helpers and "natural" helpers—those grandparents, child care workers, neighbors, church members or others who understand and are willing to support young children and their families. It embraces families as the most important people in their children's mental health development, but it also acknowledges the importance of the quality of relationships that children begin to establish outside the family during their early years.

Children who are at risk for mental disorders, those with health or developmental disabilities, and those exhibiting emotional and behavioral disorders need a range of multiple, diverse, formal, and informal services and supports that recognize child and family strengths and address individual needs (Kaufmann & Wischmann, 1999).

Conceptually, the public health approach to mental health services and supports easily lends itself to the population of young children and their families as illustrated in Figure 4.2. The majority of children and families require only universal interventions and/or promotion services and supports. A smaller subgroup of children and families with identified risk factors, 10%–15% of the population, will also need indicated interventions. Only 5%–10% will need additional targeted mental health services.

Promotion and Universal Services and Supports

Promotion activities target all young children and their families and include approaches aimed at improving parenting knowledge and skills, child development, and social-emotional health. These activities often take place in homes, early care and education programs, primary care, family support, and other community environments, such as recreation centers, libraries, and play groups. Communities that provide home visits to all newborns, parent education focusing on social-emotional development, high-quality child care and universal preschool, and social-emotional screening as part of well-child check-ups are examples of social-emotional health promotion activities. The following are several examples of such services in Michigan, North Carolina, and Oklahoma.

- Michigan provides a Baby Stages Wheel, which is a family-friendly, hands-on wheel that provides social and emotional development milestones in the first 3 years of life. It is widely distributed to parents as well as early care and education providers.

- North Carolina provides an Office Resource Guide to pediatric practices to support easy use of the standard screening instrument—the *Ages & Stages Questionnaires® (ASQ)* (Bricker & Squires, 1999). The state also updated their Medicaid regulations to allow easy billing for screening.

- Oklahoma offers the Tulsa Public School's Parents as Teachers home visiting program, which is designed to provide information on child development and engage interested parents in age-appropriate activities with their child, identify any concerns, make referrals for care, and link families to community services as needed.

Prevention and Indicated Services and Supports

Preventive measures are targeted to specific populations considered to be at risk because of biological or environmental factors. Preventive services are available before there are diagnosable symptoms. These interventions can be integrated into environments that serve children and families at risk, such as Head Start, homeless shelters, family resource centers, adult literacy programs, and adult mental health or substance abuse treatment centers. Examples include intensive home visitation programs for parents involved with child protective services, experienced parent mentors for teen mothers, and mental health consultation to Head Start and child care programs in an effort to retain children whose behaviors put them at risk of being expelled (Cohen & Kaufmann, 2000; Donohue et al., 2000; Gilliam, 2005). The following are some examples of prevention and indicated services and supports in the states of Colorado, Kentucky, Indiana, and New Jersey.

- Colorado offers Invest in Kids, which is a private, nonprofit organization that is helping communities across the state improve the health and well-being of young children by supporting the implementation of *The Incredible Years* curriculum to promote social-emotional development, prevent social-emotional problems in young children, and provide an education to parents to promote positive social skills in their children and prevent or reduce behavior difficulties.

- Kentucky offers Kentucky Kids Now, which provides mental health consultation to child care programs across the state in an effort to decrease behavior problems that might lead to expulsion and later school failure. The initiative is partly funded through the state tobacco settlement dollars.

- Indiana offers Healthy Families Indiana as a statewide system of nationally credentialed home-visiting programs that offer the Partnership in Parenting Education (PIPE) program to promote healthy family relationships by strengthening attachment, emotional availability, and relationship skills between the parent and child.

- New Jersey offers a volunteer mentoring program for teenage mothers that pairs them with experienced moms for as long as it takes to promote positive relationships between mother and baby and to help the mother finish high school and go on to college or work.

Intervention and Targeted Services and Supports

Intervention services and supports for children who have a significant delay or disability in psychosocial development are essential to help them achieve their full potential and improve the quality of their relationships. Intervention services are often provided by mental health clinicians and can be delivered in homes, early intervention programs, early care and education environments, therapeutic nurseries, adult treatment centers, and therapeutic foster care homes. By using appropriate diagnostic tools (e.g., *Diagnostic Classification of Mental Health and Developmental Disorders of In-*

fancy and Early Childhood:0–3R [DC:0–3R] [ZERO TO THREE, 2005]), keen observation, clinical judgment, and attention to the concerns of families, early intervention for autism, failure to thrive, and attachment disorders, among others, can lead to positive outcomes (Tableman, 2005). When preschool children with such disorders as posttraumatic stress disorder, depression, early conduct disorder, and attentional difficulties are provided with evidence-based interventions, the likelihood of improvement is greatly enhanced (Center for Evidence Based Practice: Young Children with Challenging Behavior, 2004; Dunlop et al., 2003; Raver, 2002). The number of promising, effective, and evidence-based interventions for young children and families is growing, which is allowing states and communities to select and implement those that best match their needs for intervention services. The following are some examples of intervention and targeted services and supports in Kansas, Tennessee, Ohio, Washington, and Massachusetts.

- The Southeast Kansas Community Action Program has invested in program-wide Positive Behavior Supports in Head Start centers to enhance the skills of teachers and administrators and educational consultants to work with children who have challenging behaviors.

- Tennessee; Cleveland, Ohio; and Yakima, Washington offer the Regional Intervention Program (RIP), Intervention Center of the Positive Education Program, and Valley Intervention Program, respectively, that provide a parent-driven intervention approach that includes behavioral intervention for children, individualized learning and support for parents, and group support for parents and children. Parents learn from parent and professional coaches, practice skills, and test these skills in real-life situations.

- Massachusetts has residential substance abuse agencies, treatment shelters, and community housing programs that offer The Nurturing Program for Families in Substance Abuse Treatment and Recovery, which is an intervention that supports and assists parents in developing self-awareness and nurturing skills, understanding the impact of substance abuse and pursuing recovery, and understanding child development.

SCREENING, ASSESSMENT, AND EVALUATION

Screening, assessment, and *evaluation* are terms often used interchangeably with definitions that vary across disciplines, programs, and systems. *Screening* has the most consistent meaning across environments. It is typically seen as a brief procedure that is often done universally at regular intervals and is not dependent on signs of delay or disorder. Because a screening tool is never sufficient for confirming a developmental delay or disorder, children whose screening results indicate a possible delay should undergo a comprehensive assessment and/or evaluation. Whereas there is generally consensus on the meaning of *screening*, the term *assessment* often has different meanings for different disciplines and programs. In IDEA, for example, assessment is described as the process of gathering an array of information about a child's strengths and needs. It is used to develop individualized plans and determine changes in individual children. The *process* of assessing a child is dynamic as it synthesizes information from diverse sources, including families, health care and other related professionals, and child care providers. *Assessment* often includes naturalistic observation. Sometimes in primary care, mental health, and other disciplines, the term *assessment* is used synonymously with evaluation and is used to make a diagnosis. *Evaluation* is usually the term used to describe the process for determining atypical development, making a diagnosis, and determining eligibility (Nuttall, 1992; Sosna & Mastergeorge, 2005).

In a system of care, screening and assessment activities occur across multiple environments, often governed by diverse mandates and administered by an array of multidisciplinary providers; therefore, it is essential that the terms *screening, assessment,* and *evaluation* be clarified and, if possible, used commonly across environments. If, because of conflicting regulations, common definitions are not possible, families and providers should clearly understand the different meanings for each environment in which they are involved. Fortunately, since 2000, many new screening and assessment tools have been developed that examine social-emotional and behavioral development in children birth to 5. Increasingly, these tools are being used in pediatricians' offices; child care environments; Part C and preschool special education environments; child welfare offices; and in homes where they are administered by home visitors, nurses, and mental health consultants. Several communities are using a common screening tool across these environments, teaching a wide group of providers to administer the tool, developing a central referral process, and attempting to make access to services and supports more effective.

DELIVERING SERVICES AND SUPPORTS

Every community has a unique combination of assets, priorities, and needs that influence the types of services and supports that are delivered, the manner in which they are delivered, and the individuals providing the services. Services, or formal intervention strategies, tend to be provided by licensed personnel, be more clinical in focus, have an evidence base, and be evaluated for efficacy. Supports can be less formal; may be provided by families, volunteers, paraprofessionals, or unlicensed personnel; and may be more informational, educational, or supportive in nature with particular sensitivity to the cultural and linguistic preferences of the families served. An early childhood mental health system recognizes the need for both formal services and informal supports by developing a cross-agency, interdisciplinary process that is accessible, family driven, and individualized.

Services and supports that meet the needs of young children and families defy simple categorization. Whereas the public health approach described in this chapter illustrates the continuum of services and supports, it does not illustrate the true range of services provided to children and families with varying needs. Some services are specifically designed and delivered to fit each of these categories or levels of intervention, but in practice they can cross these boundaries to meet the unique needs of children and families in combinations of services. They can change in mix, intensity, and frequency and should ebb and flow with a child's development, the needs of the family, and specifically identified mental health concerns or difficulties. An *individualized care plan* can include a variety of levels and types of services at any one point in time for an individual child and their family.

For young children, services to benefit the child always involve working with the people who care for and about them, such as parents and other caregivers. Services that build the capacity of parents, teachers, and other caregivers to support a child's healthy development and mental health are as valuable as those interventions designed and individualized for a specific child and family in response to behavioral health concerns or a mental health disorder.

Services must also bridge the perspectives of early care and education, early intervention, mental health, and other service systems so that there is mutual respect for and understanding of the contribution of diverse types and levels of services to promote, prevent, and intervene in early childhood mental health. All parties involved in a system of care must understand this shared perspective and their unique roles and responsibilities in early childhood mental health services when crossing system boundaries.

An Individualized Care Plan and a Continuum of Services and Supports Across Agencies and/or Systems

Sandra, a teenage, single mother with two children under 5, is living in Bridgeport, Connecticut. Her children receive primary care at the Bridgeport Hospital Clinic and are enrolled in Head Start. Through a partnership with a community mental health center, the hospital, and child protective services, Sandra has a case manager who is coordinating multiple family services, helping her find a job, and encouraging her to attend Alcoholics Anonymous (AA) meetings weekly. John, Sandra's 3-year-old son receives speech and language therapy in Head Start provided by the early intervention program. He was almost expelled from child care, but the services of a state-provided mental health consultant helped the staff and Sandra cope with John's challenging behavior. Sandra has just enrolled in Head Start's family literacy program and hopes that she and her sister (with whom she and her children live) will be part of a pilot training project using *The Incredible Years* (see the section on Prevention and Indicated Services and Supports in this chapter for a description of *The Incredible Years*) with staff and families.

■ ■ ■

WHERE TO BEGIN: BUILDING BLOCKS AND INFRASTRUCTURE

The *infrastructure* for a system of care, or the foundation for organizing a system or having a system function, is the outcome of joining together *processes* and *structures* to achieve system-level integration and comprehensive services and supports (Pires, 2002). Similar to the trajectory of growth and development for a young child, building *infrastructure* for a system of care to address early childhood mental health has developmental milestones (or core elements) that are not always addressed or met in a linear process. There are also influences of both nature and nurture. By *nature*, each community or state approaches early childhood mental health system of care development with certain given features. These include existing organization and agency structures; policies and procedures; service delivery strategies; and, often, diverse understanding, philosophy, and perspectives on early childhood mental health services to young children and their families. By *nurture*, every community or state has champions or those who take on leadership roles, are open to change, and see opportunities to encourage the growth and development of new and more responsive ways of doing business.

Building systems is a multifaceted, multilevel process. It involves making changes at the state, local, and neighborhood levels. It entails changes at policy and service delivery levels, and it involves joining together *processes* (e.g., roles, responsibilities, and interactions of key partners) and *structures* (e.g., how services are organized, delivered, and funded; how staff is prepared for work; how outcomes are measured) to achieve system-level integration and comprehensive services and supports (Pires, 2002). For lasting change, a community or state's approach to early childhood mental health and comprehensive services and supports must be supported by a defined *infrastructure*, which is the outcome of strategic planning, interagency collaboration, and establishing policies and procedures for maximized and flexible funding, family advocacy, a prepared work force, and outcome evaluation and data management. Too often, model demonstration projects, community-based service programs, family support organizations, respite services, and other needed supports and services are not sustained, regardless of popularity, need, efficacy, or will. An organized, cross-system effort informed through partnerships with families and based on shared vision and values helps stabilize the revolving door of programs ands services that hamper early treatment and intervention.

STRATEGIC PLANNING

Strategic planning is key to defining and implementing the vision and values of an early childhood system of care with a strong mental health component. A strategic plan presents a unified vision based on agreed-on values and principles with articulated goals, objectives, and desired outcomes (Pires, 2002). This plan guides decisions and activities and requires ongoing, regular review to determine achievement of desired outcomes and/or need for revisions to increase success. Operationally, strategic planning is a process that involves critical elements—gathering key partners (including family members), openness to new ways of thinking and doing business, facilitated discussion and decision making, and timing and opportunity.

There are many ways to move through the strategic planning process at both the state and community levels, such as one planning body with multiple subcommittees or work groups or a state-level collaborative with local planning bodies. To encourage openness to new ways of thinking and doing business, some states and communities increase the capacity of all stakeholders by providing information and increasing common knowledge related to early childhood mental health, school readiness, and promising practices in other communities. Some states and communities engage informed, neutral parties as facilitators to help move key partners through the discovery, discussion, planning, and decision-making process. Moving from planning to decision making and action requires that any planning group address their governance function, that is, clarity of roles and responsibilities and capacity to act and/or sanction authority by an appropriate state or community body (e.g., the governor's office, state-level department, established early childhood council).

One final factor in strategic planning relates to timing and opportunity. It is sometimes described as being strategic or having a strategic mind-set. Effective system builders are continually scanning the environment and looking for opportunities to generate interest, build constituencies, create buy-in, reengineer financing streams, utilize existing structures, and capitalize on other initiatives (Pires, 2002), as well as be aware of the basic time cycle for critical legislative and budget decisions, new initiatives, and funding opportunities. By building on diverse opportunities, such as grants, statewide legislation, pilot projects, advocacy efforts, and even court orders, states and communities can organize and plan services and supports through a variety of mechanisms that are supported by numerous stakeholders. Strategic planning and being strategic, when combined, are a powerful force toward building early childhood mental health systems. (See Chapter 8 and Chapter 9 for more information on systems of care in Vermont and in Cuyahoga County, Ohio.)

A Strategic Planning Process for Building an Early Childhood Mental Health System of Care in Maryland

Maryland has a statewide early childhood mental health steering committee led by two key agencies—Mental Health and Mental Hygiene and the Department of Education—and includes integral people from advocacy groups, other child and family serving agencies, family members, and providers. Guided by a clearly stated vision and four long-term goals, the steering committee contracted with Georgetown University to facilitate the planning process. Before planning statewide services and supports, the committee wanted an accurate picture of what was already available to children and families in each county and what services were missing or inadequate. As a first step, the steering committee engaged in a county-by-county capacity assessment process. In recognition of strong county autonomy in Maryland, regional forums were convened across the state to develop community buy-in, gather information about county priorities, and provide the latest research findings on early childhood mental health. These meetings and the mapping process helped cement a partnership between communities and the state, thereby ensuring local buy-in from the beginning of the planning process. Data from county self-assessments combined with outcome data from several state-funded pilot sites led to the legislature appropriating funding for mental health consultation statewide (Perry, 2003, 2005).

INTERAGENCY AND COLLABORATIVE PARTNERSHIPS

Collaboration is at the heart of system building. A truly effective early childhood mental health system encourages broad-based collaboration of services, supports, and system-level integration (Kaufmann & Wischmann, 1999). For young children and their families, a system of mental health services and supports must include partnerships and linkages across those programs, services, and supports already accessed by this population. For young children at the system level, this generally includes early care and education, primary care, mental health, child welfare, early intervention, and special education It should, although it does not always, include substance abuse and domestic violence, as well as court-linked agencies. States and communities that have success at building collaborations take specific steps to generate public interest and support, engage service system and agency leadership, partner with family and community advocacy groups, and build on or expand existing partnerships. In addition to agency, business, and advocacy organizations, families themselves should be collaborative partners in identifying what is needed to create a comprehensive and integrated system that works for them.

Rallying around early childhood mental health requires partners to build trust, agree on core values and concepts, develop common language and terminology, and identify common goals. As conflicts, challenges, and barriers arise, previously agreed-on decision-making processes, such as reaching consensus, voting, and using nominal group process, help resolve issues in a less impassioned way. Strong alliances with family advocates and community organizations, always an important part of collaboration, become critical to sustaining and building a system of services and supports, especially in times of fiscal constraints. Although it takes time and energy to build these strong alliances, they, along with effective communication and decision making, are key to building lasting partnerships and moving from simply meeting together to action planning and developing and delivering new services and supports, especially in times of fiscal constraints.

A Unique Collaboration Across Service Systems in Florida

The Miami-Dade County, Florida Juvenile Court, Early Head Start, Part C of IDEA, and Mental Health joined as partners for a pilot project (2004) that addresses the well-being of infants, toddlers, and their families who are at risk of foster care placement. Screening and assessment are provided to all infants with referral to services as needed. An Early Head Start Program is directly connected to the court. An evaluation of the pilot showed that 100% of the infants were reunited with their families.

POLICIES AND PROCEDURES

Many states and communities across the country are engaged in strategic planning, interagency collaboration, and building system infrastructure. Policies and procedures concretize the hard work that occurs in committees and task forces. Whereas the development of a plan provides a blueprint for action, policies and procedures help implement and sustain systems and the resulting services and supports. Policies guide decisions, actions, and practices. They might explain which type of providers can deliver services, establish billing codes for reimbursement, and establish eligibility criteria, typically statewide. Procedures are less formalized, describe how business is accomplished, and may vary by community. One component of policy development is governance or formalizing a decision-making body and process. Governance structures ensure authority, accountability, and legitimacy. Governing bodies occur at all levels—state, community, and neighborhood. Some are created by legislation and others by executive order, memoranda of agreement, or community will (Pires, 2002). State interagency collaborating committees legislated by Part C of IDEA are one such body. State Early Childhood Cabinets convened by governors are another, and the Early Childhood Comprehensive Systems grants provide another governing entity. Governance and well-developed policies help states and communities deal with unforeseen events, such as changes in leadership, funding cuts, and shifts in priorities that can impede the progress of system development. States and communities can avoid losing ground during these contextual changes through formalizing their work. The development of memoranda of understanding, interagency agreements, and legislation help to address clarity, credibility, and shared liability aspects of governance and can maintain efforts over time.

The following are some examples of policies and procedures that support an ECMH system of care in Colorado, Illinois, and Ohio.

- Colorado's Project BLOOM (SAMHSA-funded system of care grant) is part of a state leadership commission created by the governor to coordinate early childhood initiatives across agencies to ensure that children are ready to succeed at school and in life.

- The Illinois Legislature's Children's Mental Health Act of 2003 addresses mental health for children birth to 18 and brings mental health and education together to create social-emotional learning standards and policies for school districts and school buildings.

- The Ohio General Assembly directed the Department of Mental Health to ensure that mental health clinicians, early childhood educators, and parents receive information and education on how to support the social-emotional development of all children birth through age 6.

FAMILY INVOLVEMENT AND ADVOCACY

A system of care is greatly enhanced through authentic involvement of consumers in all phases of needs assessment, planning, implementation, and evaluation (Pires, 2002). Effective systems actively support and engage families by

- Providing tangible supports, such as respite or child care assistance, transportation, translation, or interpretation services

- Recognizing and using the knowledge, skills, and experiences of families

- Building capacity that provides families with information, skills, and confidence to partner in system-building efforts, such as training, committee work, mentoring, and educating the community about early childhood mental health

- Partnering with families to design and deliver services

Parent Involvement in an Early Childhood Mental Health System of Care in New York

Building on a strong partnership between a family organization known as Family Ties and the county children's mental health system, Westchester County, New York, is expanding a focus from older children with a variety of mental health needs to include young children and their families. One new service provided is a Family Strengthening Team that provides home-based crisis intervention to families struggling to keep their young children from being hospitalized or placed in foster care. The partnership is currently expanding its three levels of services and supports to reach out to young children and their families across the county. Level one brings *circles of support* teams together to develop and monitor individual plans to improve child and family outcomes. Level two links community organizations that are charged to provide diverse child and family services to address issues that act as barriers to accessing services. Level three addresses policy, infrastructure, and program issues at the county level.

Family advocacy organizations continue to play a critical role in supporting families, promoting best practices, providing educational opportunities for families and providers, promoting legislation, and keeping systems relevant. One goal of family involvement is to have family members *drive* the service system for their own children and for the well-being of all children. In the previous example in New York, a family organization advocated for earlier intervention services, became partners in the planning of those services, and were included in the *circles of support* teams. Family involvement and advocacy must be structured, well-funded, and valued by states and communities as an essential cornerstone of service systems. Historically, the mission of family organizations and advocacy groups was often founded on serving older children or those with more intense intervention needs. The end result of that perspective is that many families of young children have been overlooked as potential resources for strengthening advocacy, education, support, and services. An understanding of the early childhood mental health perspective and a shift in focus to include promotion and prevention can provide advocacy organizations the opportunity to educate the public about promoting mental health and the importance of early identification, expanding their family voice, and bolstering their mission to reduce the stigma associated with mental health and mental illness.

Unfortunately, at the time of this writing, no national advocacy organization adequately addresses early childhood mental health. Strategies that are being implemented to ensure that mental health issues have an impact on young children and their families include

- Advocacy organizations that support children with serious emotional disorders reaching out to families of young children.

- Advocacy organizations that address disabilities and special health care needs that are including a stronger focus on early childhood mental health issues.

- Consortia being formed among diverse family organizations at the state and community levels.

Regardless of the strategy chosen, the importance of reaching out to families of very young children is an important component of an early childhood system of care. Head Start and Early Head Start policy councils and parent organizations, parent education and information centers funded through IDEA, the Federation of Families for Children's Mental Health, United Advocates of Children of California (UACC), National Alliance for the Mentally Ill Child and Adolescent Network (NAMICAN), and other advocacy organizations are recognizing the importance of early outreach and intervention and promoting a focus on early childhood mental health. Family advocacy organizations do play a critical role in supporting families, promoting best practices, providing educational opportunities for families and providers, promoting legislation, and keeping systems responsive to the needs of children and families.

Reaching Out to Families in California

In an effort to reach out to diverse families, the Los Angeles All About Children (ABC) project, a newly funded SAMHSA system of care grantee, has established relationships with multiple, ethnic-specific, community-based family support agencies. Many of these programs have not addressed the mental health needs of children and families in the past but are willing to do so with support and training from ABC.

MAXIMIZED AND FLEXIBLE FUNDING

Interagency public and private collaboration is essential to developing and financing a system of care that provides a continuum of early childhood mental health services (Johnson, Knitzer, & Kaufmann, 2002). Yet, even the most successful collaboration can be challenged by restrictive funding and limited resources. The following are some of the major challenges to funding early childhood mental health services and supports.

- Serving children without a diagnosis through Medicaid

- Paying for dyadic interventions between infant or young child and caregiver

- Focusing on at-risk children and their families

- Paying for promotion and program-level interventions

Building a systemic approach to financing early childhood mental health services and supports is a complex process that includes the identification, understanding, and full utilization of all existing funding resources. Because early childhood mental health addresses relationships among infants, toddlers, and preschool-age children and their adult caregivers, both adult and child funding streams must be accessed (Wishmann, Kates, & Kaufmann, 2001). Each state or community must determine how it will pay for each component of its comprehensive system of services, including screening, direct services, flexible dollars for informal supports (e.g., money for a double stroller, a baby sitter, a child's birthday party), and infrastructure (see the Appendix E, Matrix of Early Childhood Mental Health Services and Supports).

Many states and communities have identified ways to maximize funding from different federal, state, and local resources. For example, Medicaid cannot be used for infrastructure development, but Title V funds through the Maternal and Child Health Bureau can be used. Paying for intentional early childhood mental health services, however, particularly those targeted to young children experiencing significant risk factors (known to be related to later serious mental health issues), remains difficult. To be successful, states and communities have to be creative in funding program-level interventions, such as mental health consultation; reflective supervision; and multigenerational efforts, such as mentoring and grandparent support groups. Therefore, having a strategic process for fiscal planning that maximizes the impact of multiple funding sources from existing funding streams, redirected budget line items, and billable sources (e.g., Medicaid and state general revenues) is key (Hayes, 2002; Johnson & Knitzer, 2005; Johnson, Knitzer, & Kaufmann, 2002). Foundations have been instrumental in providing a vision and funding for a variety of early childhood mental health initiatives. Foundation leadership (e.g., the Commonwealth Fund's Assuring Better Child Health and Development projects) has been very helpful in providing technical assistance to states for needed mapping of current resources and identifying and building support for necessary modifications.

States and communities can use multiple strategies for financing their system. Cheryl Hayes of the Finance Project in Washington, DC (Hayes, 2002), described five key strategies for financing programs and services for children and families:

1. Make better use of existing resources through redeployment, efficiency, and reinvestment.

2. Maximize federal and state resources through leveraging, refinancing, and use of administrative claims.

3. Create more flexibility in existing categories through pooling, better coordinating, and de-categorization of eligibility for services.

4. Build public–private partnerships.

5. Create new dedicated revenue streams through levies, special taxes, trust funds, and so forth.

The following are examples of efforts to maximize funding opportunities in Ohio, Vermont, and Illinois:

• After successful pilot efforts in Ohio, state general funds pay for mental health consultation across the state. Many counties are adding to state funds using local dollars and billing Medicaid.

• In Vermont, Medicaid match funds, increased by using state and local dollars spent by child care, are used to provide services to families not eligible for Medicaid and to pay for mental health consultation.

• A modified Medicaid reimbursement policy in Illinois allows for perinatal depression screening and consultation service and clarifies billing policies related to children's developmental screening.

PREPARED WORK FORCE

A fully designed and developed early childhood mental health service system provides services and supports to young children, their parents, and other caregivers and addresses all three levels of care: 1) promotion, 2) prevention, and 3) intervention. The three levels of care include an array of services and supports, such as parent education, consultation, care coordination, crisis intervention, screening, assessment, and therapeutic intervention. A prepared work force must be available to support all services within a state or community's system. Those who provide or oversee the provision of services and supports to prevent problems and restore emotional health to young children and their families need a range of skills. These include developmental knowledge, clinical sensitivity and expertise, understanding of family dynamics, and skill in working with individuals and families from diverse cultures (Cohen & Kaufmann, 2000; Knitzer, 2001).

Unfortunately, far too few mental health providers are taught to work specifically with infants, toddlers, and preschool-age children. Even fewer have those skills and the experience consulting early care and education providers. Typically, early childhood educators are not taught to work with children displaying atypical behaviors. They lack the needed skills to intervene effectively and receive little support to change their teaching methods. Often early childhood higher education programs include no coursework in family systems and early intervention.

There are efforts underway to address issues of personnel shortages (see Chapter 5). Specialized education and masters' or certificate programs in early childhood and family mental health are in development or in place in only a few states. More commonly, states and communities build work force capacity by establishing provider competencies; implementing self-assessments; providing in-service training; and offering consultation, reflective supervision, and support.

The following are examples of work force development efforts in building an ECMH system of care in Colorado, Florida, Michigan, and California:

- In Colorado, the Early Childhood Comprehensive System interagency group is broadening a focus on professional development for child care providers to one that includes all service providers of young children and families. Core competencies for different levels of personnel will be developed to ensure that social-emotional mental health modules are infused into the professional development of early care and education providers, mental health clinicians, physicians, nurses, and social workers.

- After developing infant and toddler standards, Florida created Learning in Everyday Moments, an education program for child care providers that helps them enhance their skills to implement the new standards, thereby having an impact on the quality of care.

- The Michigan Association for Infant Mental Health has developed an endorsement for professionals from many disciplines at the following levels: Infant Family Associate, Infant Family Specialist, Infant Mental Health Specialist, and Infant Mental Health Mentor. Each level recognizes knowledge, education, and best practice standards.

- California has developed certification and accompanying education in four areas: 1) Infant–Family (for individuals from disciplines other than mental health), 2) Preschool–Family (for individuals from disciplines other than mental health), 3) Infant–Family Mental Health Professional (only for individuals with mental health degrees), and 4) Preschool–Family Mental Health Professional (only for individuals with mental health degrees).

OUTCOME EVALUATION AND DATA MANAGEMENT

Outcome evaluation is an essential part of a strategic plan for building an early childhood system of care. Early on, data (census data, survey data, extent data from research, or evaluation data from other efforts) help to inform the strategic planning process. Data, along with unique state and community information, allow stakeholders to refine their theory of change (i.e., expectations for children and families, goals and objectives, and how to effectively achieve these goals) (Hernandez & Hodges, 2003) using outcomes, indicators (both qualitative and quantitative), and data management procedures that are relevant and useful to all involved. Evaluation at all system levels—state, community, and provider—is part of building an infrastructure to deliver services (see Chapter 6).

The following are examples of outcome evaluation and data management in Connecticut and Vermont:

- Connecticut's Early Childhood Consultation Partnership developed a statewide data system to collect information and measure outcomes for the more than 4,000 people served through mental health consultation. Results showed a 94% increase in the quality of child care, and 98% of children at risk for expulsion remained in care.

- The Vermont Children's UPstream Services (CUPS) system of care used quantitative and qualitative methods to look at outcomes. The qualitative study consisted of focus groups with parents and providers across the state and found that services and supports reduced incidents of child abuse, helped families stay together, and increased adult use of services. The quantitative results showed lower rates of behavior problems and reduced family stress (see Chapter 8 for more information).

Data management and information sharing has its own challenges. The nature of creating a system of care is to cross-service system boundaries and find ways for inclusive or systemwide, as well as local and provider level, evaluation. Decisions about data management and information sharing must include thoughtful analysis and address issues of confidentiality, standardization, and collection and reporting mechanisms that can be implemented systemwide. Effective states and communities use valid data collection measures and instruments that are consistent with system values, gather data at multiple levels of the system structure, and provide a system of reporting back to stakeholders. In turn, all of the data collected inform multiple sustainability strategies.

MAKING THE MOST OF OPPORTUNITIES FOR SYSTEMS DEVELOPMENT

It is the right time to build systems of services, supports, and care for early childhood mental health. Although a relatively new field, early childhood mental health is receiving the recognition it has long deserved backed by research and a growing evidence base. Across the country, there is increased political will, public and private interest, a commitment to invest in early childhood, a growing culture of collaboration among service systems and agencies, and a strong voice of testimony by families and caregivers. For example, in Kaufmann and Hepburn's 2003 survey of state children's mental health directors, the 22 states that responded indicated that they were actively involved in developing services, programs, or systems to meet the mental health needs of young children birth-to-5. Most are using the service system-building processes identified in this chapter, including strategic planning and capacity mapping, expansion of mental health services and early intervention, and education and work force development, all of which are the building blocks for system of care development. They are taking on common challenges, including restrictive eligibility criteria that limits access to services, lack of funding for promotion and prevention services, the difficulty in using DC:0–3R for billing Medicaid, the stigma associated with mental health, and the lack of qualified early childhood mental health professionals. Furthermore, they are exploring solutions to these challenges.

The time is right to understand early childhood mental health services and supports through a systems approach framework, to learn from states and communities that have forged ahead, and to make the most of current and upcoming opportunities for building an early childhood mental health system of care.

REFERENCES

Bricker, D., & Squires, J. (1999). *Ages & Stages Questionnaires® (ASQ): A parent-completed, child-monitoring system* (2nd ed.). Baltimore: Paul H. Brookes Publishing Co.

Center for Evidence-Based Practice: Young Children with Challenging Behavior. (2004, November). *Facts about young children with challenging behavior.* Available: http://www.challengingbehavior.org

Cohen, E., & Kaufmann, R. (2000). *Early childhood education Consultation.* Washington, DC: Center for Mental Health Services, U.S. Department of Health and Human Services.

Donahue, P.J., Falk, B., & Gersony Provet, A. (2000). *Mental health consultation in early childhood.* Baltimore: Paul H. Brookes Publishing Co.

Dunlop, G., Conroy, M., Kern, L., DuPaul, G., VanBrakle, J., Strain, P., et al. (2003). *Research synthesis on effective intervention procedures: Executive summary.* Tampa: University of South Florida, Center for Evidence-Based Practice: Young Children with Challenging Behavior.

Education of the Handicapped Act Amendments of 1986, PL 99-457, 20 U.S.C. §§ 1400 *et seq.*

Edwall, G. (2005). *Early childhood mental health: The continuum.* St. Paul: Minnesota Association for Children's Mental Health.

Florida State University Center for Prevention and Early Intervention Policy for the Florida Developmental Disabilities Council. (2001). *Florida's strategic plan for infant mental health: Establishing a system of mental health services for young children and their families in Florida.* Tallahassee: Author.

Floyd, S., & Child and Family Policy Center Staff. (2004). *Up and running: A compendium of multi-site early childhood initiatives* (2nd ed.). Des Moines, IA: State Early Childhood Policy Technical Assistance Network, Child and Family Policy Center.

Gilliam, W.S. (2005). *Pre-kindergarteners left behind: Expulsion rates in state pre-kindergarten systems.* New Haven, CT: Yale University Child Study Center.

Goode, T., & Jackson, V. (2003). *Getting started and moving on: Planning, implementing and evaluating cultural competency for comprehensive community mental health services for children and families.* Washington, DC: Georgetown University, National Center for Cultural Competence.

Hanson, K., & Martner, J. (2000). *Mental health in Head Start: It's everybody's business* (video tape). Washington, DC: Head Start Information and Publication Center, Administration for Children and Families.

Hayes, C. (2002). *Thinking broadly: Financing strategies for comprehensive child and family initiatives.* Washington, DC: The Finance Project.

Hepburn, K. (2004). *Building culturally and linguistically competent services to support young children, their families, and school readiness.* Baltimore: Annie E. Casey Foundation.

Hernandez, M., & Hodges, S. (2003). *Making children's mental health services successful: Crafting logic models for systems of care: Ideas into action.* Tampa: University of South Florida, Department of Child and Family Studies, Louis de la Parte, Florida Mental Health Institute.

Individuals with Disabilities Education Act (IDEA) of 1990, PL 101-476, 20 U.S.C. §§ 1400 *et seq.*

Individuals with Disabilities Education Improvement Act (IDEA) of 2004, PL 108-446, 20 U.S.C. §§ 1400 *et seq.*

Johnson, K., & Knitzer, J. (2005). *Spending smarter: A funding guide for policymakers and advocates to promote social and emotional health and school readiness.* New York: Columbia University, National Center for Children in Poverty, Mailman School of Public Health.

Johnson, K., Knitzer, J., & Kaufmann, R. (2002). *Making dollars follow sense: Financing early childhood mental health services to promote healthy social and emotional development in young children.* Promoting the Emotional Well-Being of Children and Families, Policy Paper No. 4. New York: Columbia University, National Center for Children in Poverty, Mailman School of Public Health.

Karoly, L., Greenwood, P., Everingham, S., Hoube, J., Kilburn, M.R., Rydell, C.P., et al. (1998). *Investing in our children: What we know and don't know about the costs and benefits of early childhood interventions.* Santa Monica, CA: Rand Corporation

Kaufmann, R. (2005). Early childhood mental health in a system of care. Retrieved January 20, 2006, from http://gucchd.georgetown.edu/programs/ta_center/topics/earlychildhood.html

Kaufmann, R., & Hepburn, K. (2003). *Early childhood mental health initiatives survey.* Compiled for the State Commissioners of Mental Health. Washington, DC: Georgetown University.

Kaufmann, R., & Wischmann, A.L. (1999). Communities supporting the mental health of young children and their families. In R.N. Roberts & P.R. Magrab (Eds.), *Where children live: Solutions for serving young children and their families.* Stamford, CT: Ablex Publishing Corporations.

Keeping Children and Families Safe Act of 2003, PL 108-36, 42 U.S.C. §§ 5101 *et seq.*

Knitzer, J. (2000). Early childhood mental health services: A policy and systems perspective. In J.P. Shonkoff & S.J. Meisels (Eds.), *Handbook of early childhood intervention.* New York: Cambridge University Press.

Knitzer, J. (2001). *Building services and systems to support the healthy emotional development of young children: An action guide for policymakers.* New York: Columbia University, National Center for Children in Poverty, Mailman School of Public Health.

Nuttal, E. (1992). Introduction. In E. Nuttal, I. Romero, & J. Kalesnik (Eds.), *Assessing and screening preschoolers psychological and educational dimensions.* Boston: Allyn and Bacon.

Perry, D. (2003). *Report on the early childhood mental health capacity assessment.* Presented to Maryland Legislature in March 2004. Washington, DC: Georgetown University, Center for Child and Human Development.

Perry, D. (2005). *Evaluation results for the early childhood mental health consultation pilot sites.* Washington, DC: Georgetown University, Center for Child and Human Development.

Pires, S.A. (2002). *Building systems of care: A primer.* Washington, DC: Georgetown University, Center for Child and Human Development.

The President's New Freedom Commission on Mental Health. (2003). *Achieving the promise: Transforming mental health care in America. Final report* (DHHS Publication No. SMA 03-3832). Rockville, MD: U.S. Government Printing Office.

Raver, C. (2002). Emotions matter: Making the case for the role of young children's emotional development for early school readiness. *Social Policy Report of the Society for Research in Child Development, 16*(1), 3–23.

Rosman, E., Perry, D., & Hepburn, K. (2005). *The best beginning: Partnerships between primary health care and mental health and substance abuse services for young children and their families.* Washington, DC: Georgetown University, Center for Child and Human Development.

Shonkoff, J.P., & Phillips, D.A. (Eds.). (2000). *From neurons to neighborhoods: The science of early childhood development.* Washington, DC: National Academies Press.

Smith, B., & Fox, L. (2004). *Systems of service delivery: A synthesis of evidence relevant to young children at risk of or who have challenging behavior.* Washington, DC: , U.S. Department of Education, Office of Special Education Programs.

Sosna, T., & Mastergeorge, A. (2005). *The infant, preschool, family, mental health initiative compendium of screening tools for early childhood social-emotional development.* Sacramento: California Institute for Mental Health

Squires, J., Bricker, D., & Twombly, E. (2002). *Ages & Stages Questionnaire®: Social-Emotional (ASQ:SE): A parent-completed, child-monitoring system for social-emotional behaviors.* Baltimore: Paul H. Brookes Publishing Co.

Stroul, B., & Friedman, R. (1986). *A system of care for children and youth with severe emotional disturbances* (rev. ed.). Washington, DC: Georgetown University, Child Development Center.

Tableman, B. (2005, September). Paper presented at the Infant and Early Childhood Mental Health Summit, Washington, DC.

Wishmann, A., Kates, D., & Kaufmann, K. (2001). *Funding early childhood mental health services and supports.* Washington, DC: Georgetown University, Child Development Center.

ZERO TO THREE. (2002). *Definition of infant mental health disorder.* Unpublished manuscript.

ZERO TO THREE. (2005). *Diagnostic classification of mental health and developmental disorders of infancy and early childhood* (rev. ed.). Washington, DC: ZERO TO THREE.

5

Developing the Work Force for an Infant and Early Childhood Mental Health System of Care

Judith C. Meyers

■ ■ ■

In 2003, The President's New Freedom Commission on Mental Health released a report that provided a blueprint for transforming the mental health service delivery system. Changes in the values, skills, and attitudes of the work force were seen as a key to the success of this transformation. A subsequent article, based on the work of the Commission's Subcommittee on Children and Families (Huang, MacBeth, Dodge, & Jacobstein, 2004), addressed the work force issues as they pertain to children. The authors noted "Children with mental health needs and their families present challenges very different from the adult population. Therefore, the strategies must be different for transforming pre-service education and in-service training in order to ensure a qualified workforce" (p. 184). They went on to say that professionals working with children need to be educated in child development, family contexts, and the multiple service systems where children are seen, including primary care, education, child welfare, and juvenile justice.

It was not all that many years ago that the mental health profession came to appreciate the need to understand and treat children as different from adults (Meyers & Davis, 1997). The field of early childhood mental health (ECMH) is now at a new frontier as its advocates increasingly appreciate that not all children are alike and that a system of services and supports that meets the needs of our nation's youngest children—infants, toddlers, and preschoolers—has to take into account some unique considerations to successfully promote their social-emotional development and identify and provide intervention for their mental health concerns. The President's New Freedom Commission on Mental Health report (2003) directly addresses the need for a coordinated, national approach to meeting the mental health needs of young children and their families. As an understanding of children's mental health becomes more refined, it is clear that further distinctions are needed to build a work force prepared to address the mental health needs of children in their earliest years, from birth to 5, that are rooted in the knowledge and skills specific to that developmental period.

This chapter examines what is known about the need for educated professionals in infant and early childhood mental health, who comprise the early childhood work force, and what competencies they ought to possess. Descriptions of some promising approaches to educating the work force are highlighted and followed by a set of recommendations.

CRITICAL ISSUES IN THE EARLY CHILDHOOD MENTAL HEALTH WORK FORCE

In the forums where work force issues in early childhood mental health are addressed, two main concerns are expressed: 1) a shortage of professionals with the necessary knowledge, skills, and work experiences; and 2) the need for quality education at colleges and universities and in community in-service programs.

As cited in the groundbreaking work *From Neurons to Neighborhoods* (Shonkoff & Phillips, 2000), there is a critical need to expand the number of individuals available to work in environments with young children to successfully promote healthy social-emotional development and provide early detection and intervention through effective screening, referral, and intervention of serious early childhood mental health problems. This need occurs within the context of an already existing shortage of providers in the overall children's mental health system who are prepared to work in the context of a home- and community-based, family centered, culturally competent, strengths-based systems of care approach (Meyers, Kaufman, & Goldman, 1999; Pires, 1996).

The concern about a sufficient cadre of professionals to work in early childhood mental health is coupled with the need for high-quality training for such a work force. There are a few training opportunities for professionals in the field of infant and early childhood mental health but there is a significant absence of such an emphasis in most graduate clinical education programs in psychology, psychiatry, social work, education, and related fields. Because early childhood mental health is still a nascent field, there is little agreement about what knowledge, skills, and work experiences are needed and the best way to ensure that professionals who provide the care possess them. There are, however, individuals and states working together to reach consensus on the competencies that provide the foundation in infant and early childhood mental health.

Michael Hoge, with the Annapolis Task Force on Behavioral Health Workforce Education, writes about a training gap between the theories and practices being taught and the theories and practices considered cutting edge in mental health.

> It is the gap between the settings in which we train and the settings in which we expect providers to practice. (Hoge, 2002, p. 311)

This training gap clearly exists when it comes to preparation of professionals to work in early childhood mental health where both early childhood professionals with mental health expertise as well as mental health providers with early childhood expertise are needed. That crossover, however, rarely occurs.

The shortage of individuals with expertise in the social-emotional development of young children is clearly being experienced across the nation. As more and more states begin to develop statewide plans for services and supports to address the mental health of young children, there is repeated attention to the challenge of an inadequate work force and the struggle to identify professionals with the appropriate training, experience, or knowledge.

At an Early Childhood Mental Health Summit hosted by the Ounce of Prevention Fund in Chicago in 2000, 100 leaders from six midwestern states met to discuss comprehensive strategies for states to meet the social-emotional needs of young children. In a report of the proceedings, they noted the lack of adequately trained and qualified staff as one of the key challenges, including both of the following:

> (1) The lack of training for early childhood providers regarding the promotion of social and emotional development and the early identification of mental health issues and (2) the shortage of mental health therapists who are trained to work with the birth to five population. (Ounce of Prevention Fund, 2000, p. 6)

The report rightly concluded

> Without an infrastructure to meet these training and workforce challenges, states will fall short of being able to provide comprehensive statewide services. (p. 6)

In a policy paper by the National Center for Children in Poverty, Knitzer put it most succinctly. She said, "There are simply not enough people with these skills to address the need" (2001, p. 20). She went on to note that there is nearly universal consensus from programs across the country that recruiting and hiring early childhood mental health specialists is a major challenge.

Examples of state or local plans developed in three states—Florida, Vermont, and California—echo the concerns about work force capacity or programs to address it. Florida's Infant Mental Health Plan cites the lack of any professional education program, degree, and certification or continuing education program in their state for infant mental health professionals (The Florida State University Center for Prevention and Early Intervention Policy, 2001). A report by the Vermont Children's UPstream Services (CUPS) Core Competencies Task Force (2001) states

> First, there are few people in the state who have the skills in both early childhood development and mental health to fill positions as early childhood mental health clinicians. Second, many people who already work with families and young children . . . could benefit from learning more about the evolving field of early childhood mental health. (p. 1)

In Alameda County, California, an early childhood mental health systems development work group specifically notes a dearth of trained early childhood mental health providers, especially those who are bicultural and bilingual (Alameda County, 2003).

WHO COMPRISES THE EARLY CHILDHOOD MENTAL HEALTH WORK FORCE?

An array of providers touch the lives of young children. Many of these professionals are in a position to promote social-emotional needs and identify and provide intervention for mental health problems. Early care and education providers and primary health care providers often are the frontlines for the majority of children who will interact with one or more such providers during their early years. Therefore, the providers in education and health care are particularly important players in promoting healthy emotional development and identifying early signs of problems. In addition, for a subset of children and families who are at risk or have an identified problem, there are a host of other professionals.

The Florida Infant Mental Health Plan describes three levels of care that provide a starting point to frame three groups of caregivers, all of whom can play a role in a comprehensive early childhood system of care:

Level 1 includes those people in a position to strengthen the social-emotional development of all children, including parents and early care and education providers who need to be able to provide a supportive climate for emotional development.

Level 2 consists of professionals who are not specialists in mental health but who are in a position to promote the social-emotional development of young children and identify early warning signs for difficulties or delays. These include primary health care providers (e.g., pediatricians, family physicians, pediatric nurse practitioners); child welfare staff who work with children and families where abuse or neglect has occurred; home visitors; parent educators; early interventionists who work with children in the Individuals with Disabilities Education Improvement Act (IDEA) Part B and C system; occupational and physical therapists; and speech pathologists.

Level 3 is made up of clinically trained professionals who focus on children diagnosed with emotional or mental health problems, including child psychiatrists and psychologists, clinical social workers, marriage and family therapists, and psychiatric nurse practitioners.

Although there is a clear perception that there is not a sufficient number of professionals to meet the ever increasing need in early childhood mental health, to date there is no way to quantify the gap and know how many among those in any of the three categories have had specific training in early childhood social-emotional development and/or mental health. Because there is only the beginnings of specific certification or specialization in this arena, there is no way to track either the number of professionals from early care and education providers to child psychiatrists available or the number of training programs that address this topic.

WHAT COMPETENCIES ARE NEEDED?

The field of mental health is beginning to develop an appreciation for, and a more sophisticated understanding of, a competency-based approach to intervention. As defined in a monograph prepared by Meyers, Kaufman, and Goldman (1999) that examined promising practices for intervention related to children's mental health in a system of care approach, competency is defined simply as a set of values, knowledge, and skills that result in a person being able to do the right thing for the right reason at the right time.

The Annapolis Coalition on Behavioral Health Workforce Education, meeting since 2001, has recently focused on identification of an agreed-on set of competencies for a behavioral health work force that includes providers within the formal mental health system and those in the broader health and human services system, as well as people with disorders and their families. Going beyond what they term *armchair competency development model* (Annapolis Coalition on Behavioral Workforce Education, 2004, p. 3) by which a list of required knowledge and skills is developed by various experts, they call for a more rigorous and systematic state-of-the-art approach to defining competencies. This includes a systematic method of data collection to identify and define competencies using multiple sources of data (e.g., focus groups, structured interviews, surveys, observations). They recommend a framework that differentiates core competencies needed for all individuals from competencies common to all individuals performing the same job or function (job family competencies) and tiered level competencies for those at different levels, ranging from direct care to supervisor to program manager.

This cutting edge work provides a template for beginning to address competencies within the infant and early childhood mental health arena. For the most part, the field of early childhood mental health is still at the stage of armchair competency development, although several efforts to define competencies in infant and early childhood mental health were developed in Michigan and Vermont in the early 2000s. Both are described in more detail later in this chapter. Other efforts are under way in California and Colorado.

Core Competences in Early Childhood Mental Health

In examining a range of sources recommending a set of competencies, there is sufficient commonality to offer a starting point for developing a common set of core competencies for any professional working with infants, young children, and their families (Cohen & Kaufmann, 2000; Florida State University Center for Prevention and Early Intervention Policy, 2001; Hepburn, Kaufmann, Dodge, & Hansen, 2004; Jellinek, Patel, & Froehle, 2002; Vermont CUPS Core Competencies Task Force, 2001; Weatherston, 2002; Yoshikawa & Knitzer, 1997). A concerted nationwide effort to reach agreement across disciplines around a core set of competencies, as is happening in the broader health and behavioral health field, is, however, recommended (Expert Panel on Behavioral Health Workforce Development, 2004; Institute of Medicine, 2003). This section presents a core set of values, knowledge, and skills as the starting point.

Values and/or Beliefs

Those in a position to influence the social-emotional development of infants and young children and/or provide intervention to address mental health problems are expected to reflect certain values in their work. The starting point is no different than the core set of values for the broader children's mental health systems of care, with an emphasis on viewing children in the context of their families and communities, understanding the role of parents as central, and practicing cultural competence (Meyers et al., 1999). The following eight tenets are specifically appropriate for any caregiver who works with young children:

1. Children are best understood within the context of family, caregiving, and community relationships.

2. What happens in the early years affects the course of development across the life span.

3. Nurturing relationships with parents and other people in their lives from birth onward are the most important contribution to children's positive social-emotional development and well-being.

4. Children deserve to be in safe, stable, caring, and nurturing environments that promote their health and development, protect them from harm, and are supportive of appropriate social-emotional well-being.

5. Families play the leading role in children's social-emotional development, and they are to be full participants in all aspects of the design, implementation, and evaluation of programs and services for their young children.

6. Families and caregivers need to be respected and supported in their roles by building on their skills and knowledge and supporting their mental health.

7. Individuality, as well as social, economic, and cultural diversity, must be understood, honored, appreciated, and reflected in practice.

8. Caregivers' work is collaborative and interdisciplinary and comprises health, mental health, early care and education, and human services.

Knowledge

When it comes to knowledge and understanding, apart from what anyone working with children of all ages should know (e.g., cultural competence, working with families, working in cross-disciplinary teams), there are areas of knowledge specific to infants, toddlers, and preschoolers. The ten areas most often noted are the following:

1. Early childhood development: typical and atypical early childhood development, including developmental milestones and a basis for identifying atypical behavior in infants and young children; mental health and mental health promotion in a developmental context

2. The importance of relationships: attachment and separation in early social-emotional development; how early experience with disrupted attachment through hospitalization, foster care, adoption, parental death, or divorce is manifested in later life; the role of temperament in relationships

3. Gender differences: how girls and boys differ in early childhood social-emotional development

4. Cultural competence: the role of culture in early childhood mental health

5. Other systems: familiarity with child care, health care, family support, and early intervention systems needed for good mental health

6. Risk and protective factors: familiarity with risk factors (e.g., prenatal and neonatal risks, teen parents, parental depression, parental substance abuse, exposure to domestic and community violence) and protective factors (e.g., child characteristics of good-natured temperament, compliance, social relatedness; family characteristics relating to maternal education, steady and supportive relationship with at least one caring adult, warm caring family, structured environment with reasonable expectations of child's development); and early interventions to diminish risk and enhance protective factors

7. Mental illness: psychopathology in infants and young children, including internalizing (e.g., anxiety, depression); externalizing (e.g., aggression, impulsivity); and dysregulation (e.g., eating and sleeping disturbances) domains

8. Early warning signs: recognition of early signs of emotional, social, and behavioral concerns and specific disorders of infancy and early childhood

9. Assessment: assessing the mental health needs of infants, young children, and their families, including the quality of young child–parent relationships; familiarity with the *Diagnostic Classification of Mental Health and Developmental Disorders of Infancy and Early Childhood (DC:0–3R)* (2005).

10. Intervention: evidence-based preventive and specialized mental health interventions for infants, young children, and their families

Skills

As important as what ECMH professionals believe and know is what they can do. The expectations for what professionals ought to know how to do will differ depending on the level of care they are providing. Early childhood mental health professionals clearly need to know the most about identifying, assessing, and providing intervention for mental illness in young children. For all professionals interacting with young children, some level of exposure or experience with the following 11 competencies is useful.

1. Informal and formal observation; listening; interviewing and assessment skills with infants, young children, and their families

2. Ability to identify early signs of emotional and behavioral concerns or developmental delays and detect when infants, young children, and their families need more specialized assistance

3. Developmental screening for infants and young children

4. Assessing relationships between a parent and infant or toddler

5. Recognizing signs of distress or trauma in infants and young children

6. Managing challenging behaviors in a way that teaches young children to develop self-awareness, problem-solving, and reciprocal interactions; supporting and strengthening attachment relationships

7. Teaching other caregivers about the importance of attachment in the development of nurturing relationships

8. Use of psychotropic medications in early childhood

9. Determining diagnostic categories and approaches

10. Knowing where to turn to make appropriate referrals for mental health assessments and intervention or to keep an infant or young child safe from harm

11. Caring for infants and young children with challenging behaviors or problematic emotional development

Reflective Capacities

An underlying principle and practice central to infant and early childhood mental health is that of *reflective practice*. Defined as the art of "stepping back" to examine what one is observing or doing (Emde, Bertacchi, & Mann, 2001, p. 67), the infant and early childhood mental health professional needs to develop the capacity to reflect on the complexity of work with very young children and their families. Coupled with this is the need for reflective supervision, guidance, and support to reflect on one's personal beliefs, values, and responses as they are awakened by their professional work with infants and young children.

This list of values, knowledge, skills, and reflective capacities serves only as a starting point to be further developed. Ideally, this development will occur at the national level as part of the broader efforts of a national coalition on work force development for behavioral health or efforts beginning to take shape through the national organization, ZERO TO THREE. Two states, Michigan and Vermont, appear to be the most advanced in developing a competency-based approach to infant and early childhood mental health. Michigan's work focuses on infant mental health (birth to 3), but has implications for birth to 5, as well. Vermont's focus is broader than that of Michigan.

Michigan

The Michigan Association for Infant Mental Health (MI-AIMH) has demonstrated the most advanced work in developing competencies for those working with infants, toddlers, and families in the infant and family field. MI-AIMH has developed a set of competencies that lead to endorsement at one of four professional levels. The MI-AIMH endorsement was designed to recognize competency, specifically to verify that someone

> has attained a level of education as specified, participated in specialized in-service trainings, worked with guidance from mentors or supervisors, and acquired knowledge to promote the delivery of high quality, culturally sensitive, relationship-based services to infants, toddlers, parents, other caregivers and families. (Michigan Association For Infant Mental Health, 2002, p.1)

Each level has guidelines describing areas of expertise, responsibilities, and behaviors that demonstrate competency. The following is a description of the four levels:

Level 1: Infant Family Associate—This level requires an associate's degree, Child Development Associate Credential, or 2 years paid work experience relevant to infancy and early childhood; 30 hours of relationship-based training pertaining to the social-emotional development of infants, young children, and their families; professional reference ratings; and professional membership in MI-AIMH.

Level 2: Infant Family Specialist—This level requires a bachelor's degree in education, science, social work, nursing, or related fields; 30 hours of relevant relationship-based education; 2 years early childhood professional work experience; 1 year (24 hours minimum) reflective supervision or consultation; professional reference ratings; and professional membership in MI-AIMH.

Level 3: Infant Mental Health Specialist—This level requires a master's or doctoral degree in social work, psychology, nursing, education, or a related field; coursework with a focus in infant mental health in accordance with the MI-AIMH competencies; 30 hours of relationship-based education specific to infant mental health; 2 years of supervised work experience in infant mental health; 50 hours minimum of reflective supervision or consultation; professional reference ratings; successful completion of the endorsement exam; and membership in an infant mental health association.

Table 5.1. Required areas of knowledge for the Michigan Association for Infant Mental Health endorsement across professional levels

Theoretical foundations
   Pregnancy and early parenthood
   Infant and young child development and behavior
   Infant and/or young child and family centered practice
   Relationship-based therapeutic practice
   Family relationships and dynamics
   Attachment, separation, and loss
   Disorders of infancy and/or early childhood
   Cultural competence
Law, regulations, and agency policy
   Ethical practice
   Government and/or law and regulation
   Agency policy
Systems expertise
   Service delivery systems
   Community resources

Level 4: Infant Mental Health Mentor—This level has the same requirements as level 3 with the addition of a 3-year postgraduate work experience requirement as a policy leader, supervisor, faculty member, researcher, trainer, program administrator, or related assignment.

Each level requires the preparation of a portfolio, references, and evidence of having met the competency-based requirements for work experience and education. Those applying for endorsement at levels 3 and 4 must successfully complete a 3-hour written exam as additional documentation of competency specific to infant mental health practice. The exam has been designed and field tested by university faculty, senior infant mental health professionals, and members of MI-AIMH. The areas of knowledge and skills, as well as requirement for reflective practice, become increasingly more complex at each level. Required areas of knowledge across all four levels are shown in Table 5.1.

At levels 3 and 4, one is expected to have knowledge of psychotherapeutic and behavioral theories of change and mental and behavioral disorders in adults. In addition, for endorsement at level 4, one is expected to have knowledge of research. The following skills are also expected for all four levels:

- Observing and listening

- Screening and assessment

- Responding with empathy

- Advocating for services needed by children and families

- Promoting life skills

- Being aware of risks to health and safety

- Working with others (building and maintaining relationships, supporting others, collaborating, resolving conflict, empathy, and compassion)

- Communicating (listening, speaking, writing)

- Thinking (analyzing information, solving problems, exercising sound judgment, maintaining perspective, planning, and organizing)

- Reflecting (contemplation, self-awareness, curiosity, professional and/ or personal development, emotional response)

In addition, at levels 3 and 4, one is expected to have competency in intervention planning, developmental guidance, supportive counseling, and parent–infant or parent–toddler psychotherapy. For endorsement at level 4, one should also be able to demonstrate skills in consulting, group process, developing talent, and advocacy at the systems level and in administration and research and evaluation.

The first applications for competency-based endorsement were received in 2003. As of 2006, 90 candidates have successfully met requirements for endorsement. Most of the candidates have earned endorsement at levels 3 and 4, including the infant mental health specialist and the infant mental health mentor. As evidence of the importance of competency-based professional endorsement, it is worth noting that employers within the community mental health system have begun to list the MI-AIMH endorsement as a qualification for hiring within the early childhood mental health community in Michigan.

Vermont

The state of Vermont, through its CUPS, has developed a set of competencies that include a range of knowledge and practices that cover the four domains of the infant and young child: child, family, community, and interpersonal relationships and teamwork (Vermont CUPS Core Competencies Task Force, 2001). Examples of a competency in each domain are described here.

Child Domain

The domain of the infant and young child addresses the knowledge and skills needed to understand the young child's social-emotional development. There are 18 competencies within this domain with an additional seven competencies specific to early childhood care and educational group environments.

An example of a competency in the child domain is knowledge about how nurturing relationships develop between an infant and parent or caregiver and related skills, such as how to observe and inquire about these relationships or how to use informal resources to strengthen nurturing relationships and make referrals for formal services when needed.

Family Domain

The family domain explores the characteristics of family life, the dynamics and tasks within a family system, and how to support families in nurturing the emotional development of their young children. There are 10 competencies within this domain.

An example of a competency in the family domain is knowledge about the role of a parent's mental health and relationships with regard to infant and childhood growth and development and knowing how to recognize mental health problems in parents or caregivers that adversely affect infant and child development.

Community Domain

The community domain pertains to relationships between a family and its community. It focuses on how to connect families to supports and resources and how to provide positive community building experiences for children and families. There are eight competencies within this domain.

An example of a competency in the community domain is knowledge about how differences in culture, race, ethnicity, and class influence a family's development and sense of connection to their community, and how a mental health professional can work in a nonbiased, inclusive, and accepting way with families from different backgrounds.

Interpersonal Relationships and Teamwork Domain

This domain has 11 competencies and focuses on personal and professional beliefs, values, and life experiences; building effective relationships with families; and working as part of a team.

An example of a competency in interpersonal relationships and teamwork is knowledge of the value of working in partnership with families and others on the child's team, and how to communicate honestly, sensitively, and empathically with families and other team members using nontechnical language.

EXAMPLES OF APPROACHES TO DEVELOPING A TRAINED WORK FORCE

Several states and communities are implementing innovative approaches to building the capacity of their early childhood mental health work force.

Those at the forefront, including Vermont, Florida, Maryland, and Illinois, have developed comprehensive approaches to an early childhood system of care. Other states, such as Connecticut, are developing promising approaches for various components of a system without necessarily having yet connected them to a statewide plan. The following descriptions of work in Florida, Vermont, and Connecticut highlight promising efforts.

Florida

As part of a state Infant Mental Health Plan, Florida issued a comprehensive set of strategies and implementation recommendations for building a training infrastructure that serves as a model for other states. They addressed personnel at all three levels of their system with specific recommendations about how to infuse knowledge on the emotional, behavioral, and social development of children birth-to-5 years and introduce relationship-based practices into all relevant existing preservice and inservice training programs.

One of eight goals of the plan—Goal 5—focuses specifically on training (The Florida State University Center for Prevention and Early Intervention Policy, 2001, p. 15), quoted as follows

> Goal Five builds a training infrastructure for infant mental health for three levels. At Level 1, training would be provided for frontline caregivers including early care and education providers and home visitors, schools, faith-based organizations, law enforcement and the judicial systems. At Level 2, families and professionals caring for children in IDEA Part B & Part C system, and the child protection system would be trained including social workers, therapists, pediatricians, nurses, psychologists, and other healthcare providers to incorporate relationship based principles into care provided for families with children age birth to age five. Level 3 creates new university graduate programs to train professionals with clinical skills in infant mental health psychotherapy, as well as continuing education opportunities for specialized, advanced training for currently practicing mental health professionals.

The plan includes the five related strategies with examples of specific implementation as shown in Table 5.2. An example of one recommendation for implementation from among several included in the plan for each strategy is provided.

Vermont

As part of CUPS, the state organized a Learning Team to bring together a range of people to address the kinds of training and technical assistance needed to support the development of their early childhood system of care (Simpson, Jivanjee, Koroloff, Doerfler, & García, 2001). The team met monthly and brought together state-level staff from mental health and

Table 5.2. Training strategies and examples of implementation recommendations for Level 1 frontline caregivers from the Florida Infant Mental Health Plan

1. For level 1 from the caregivers, infuse training on the emotional, behavioral, and social development of children birth to 5 years and relationship-based practices into all programs serving children birth to 5 years, including but not limited to Healthy Start, Healthy Families, Early Head Start and Head Start, teen parent programs, home visiting programs, health care providers, subsidized and other early care and education providers, and prekindergarten early intervention and other school programs.
   Modify current mandated trainings, Child Development Associate coursework, and college curricula to incorporate infant mental health concepts and best practices.

2. Provide inservice training on infant mental health issues to people involved in law enforcement and the judicial systems.
   Present information on infant mental health principles and services at law enforcement conferences, meetings, and web sites.

3. Train level 2 staff, including IDEA Part B and Part C therapists, interventionists, and other professionals, such as pediatricians, nurses, therapists, and other health care providers to incorporate relationship-based principles into care provided for families with children birth-to-5 years.
   Contact the professional associations (e.g., physical, occupational, speech therapy, nursing, medical associations) to arrange workshops with continuing education units on incorporating infant mental health principles into therapies and health care.

4. Provide training for staff and foster parents on emotional, behavioral, and social development and mental health services for children birth to 5 years in the child protection system.
   Meet with staff from the Department of Children and Families responsible for the professional training of child protection workers to develop specific training components on infant mental health and the risks associated with abuse and neglect.

5. Provide adequate and appropriate education and training to build a cadre of level 3 infant mental health therapists.
   Partner with universities in the state to create an interdisciplinary graduate program in infant mental health (IMH) to prepare professionals in the fields of education, nursing, social work, psychiatry, and psychology for specialized intervention and clinical practice in IMH. The program should include academic coursework, clinical practicum, and continuing education.

Source: The Florida State University Center for Prevention and Early Intervention Policy, 2001.

early childhood, representatives of higher education institutions, family members, and representatives of family organizations. They assessed the training needs of each region in the state and developed a series of workshops and coordinated training activities across the state to avoid duplication and better target identified needs. The Learning Team developed the Core Competencies described earlier in this chapter.

Connecticut

Connecticut is an example of a state that is in the process of building a comprehensive plan for early childhood with the assistance of the federal Maternal and Child Health Early Childhood Comprehensive Systems grants. Social-emotional development is one of five core areas required in the plan. The other four areas are 1) medical homes for all children, 2) quality early care and education, 3) family support, and 4) parent education. In addressing the need to build the infrastructure to support program development in each of these areas, work force development is central.

Although still in its developmental stages, the state is building on several exemplary programs and initiatives, including the Early Childhood Consultation Partnership (ECCP), training for health care practitioners through Educating Practices in the Community (EPIC), and training for early care and education providers through Connecticut Charts-A-Course.

ECCP is a statewide mental health consultation program in Connecticut designed to meet the social-emotional needs of children birth-to-5 years by offering support, education, and consultation to early childhood educators and providers, thereby enhancing their skills and competencies. Funded by the Department of Children and Families and several philanthropic foundations, the program is managed by Advanced Behavioral Health, which subcontracts with community-based organizations to hire mental health consultants. The program has 11 master's degree–level consultants positioned throughout the state. Minimum hiring requirements include a master's degree in human services and knowledge of and experience with early childhood development and mental health. ECCP began operations in January 2003 and offers a continuum of services from brief phone consultation to child-specific, classroom, and center-based consultation services. Because there is no certification or organized training program for mental health consultants, the consultants receive intensive training and ongoing supervision arranged by Advanced Behavioral Health. The training curriculum includes the following topics: early childhood social-emotional development; early identification, intervention, and referral; attachment and bonding; abuse and/or neglect issues, including mandated reporting; helping young children cope with trauma; staff stress management and team building; managing behavior challenges in the classroom; cultural competence; healthy classroom environment and routine; and the use of screening tools, such as the *Devereux Early Childhood Assessment* (DECA) (LeBuffe & Naglieri, 1999), the *Brief Infant–Toddler Social Emotional Assessment* (BITSEA) (Briggs-Gowan & Carter, 2002), and the *Ages & Stages Questionnaires®* (ASQ) (Bricker & Squires, 1999).

Connecticut also has developed an integrated training model for training both health and mental health consultants to child care and is considering adding education consultants to the mix. Such an approach ensures that the various specialists who work with child care providers have the knowledge and skills to recognize and respond to the needs of children and early care providers across the spectrum, expanding the numbers of people who can be responsive to the mental health needs of the children in these environments. During these joint trainings, the consultants learn about health promotion, child mental health, abuse and neglect, the field of child care, children with special needs, models of consultation, assessing quality care, team building, state and community resources, and partnering with other systems. Child Care Health Consultants also receive additional training using a version of the National Training Institute for Child Care Health Consultants Curriculum (NTI) (developed by NTI at the University of North Carolina, Chapel Hill School of Public Health) adapted for Connecticut. This 30-hour training conducted during a 5-month period includes a section on mental health.

Through a statewide training system for early care and education professionals called Connecticut-Charts-A-Course, a 3-hour course for entry level child care providers on early childhood mental health is offered. The course provides information on the following:

- Identifying and coping with children with mental health issues

- Addressing challenging behaviors with intervention

- Enhancing classroom experiences for professionals and children

- Identifying stressors at different developmental stages

- Identifying behaviors of children in distress

- Recognizing signs of depression, anxiety, disruptive behaviors, and stress reactions

- Knowing when to refer

In addition to being offered through community colleges and community-based organizations, the ECCP mental health consultants offer this course on site in child care centers.

Reaching Health Care Practitioners

As noted earlier in this chapter, pediatricians and other primary care health providers are becoming increasingly important participants in the mental health delivery system; yet, there is concern about their preparation and training to take on this role. The American Academy of Pediatrics has taken an active role by developing practice guidelines, including a two volume set on mental health that addresses prevention and early identification of childhood psychological problems; promotes mental health as an essential component of overall health and well-being; includes developmental guidelines for infancy and early childhood; and provides tools for health professionals and families for use in screening, care management, and health education (Jellinek, Patel, & Froehle, 2002). These materials provide a framework that can be used in other environments, including child care and parent education programs.

Connecticut has developed a system for training health care practitioners called Educating Practices in their Communities (EPIC). Based on a model developed in Pennsylvania, EPIC is a statewide community-based provider education program using an academic detailing approach, which has been found to be a more effective way to modify the practice of individual health care providers than the passive approach of lectures, conferences, and printed materials (Trowbrige & Weingarten, 2001). In this system, experts visit individual primary health care practices bringing lunch and the opportunity to receive continuing education credits. During a 1–1½ hour session, they deliver information to both health care and office staff on specific topics. Trainings have been developed and delivered on the topics of suspected child abuse and neglect, early detection and developmental surveillance for children birth to 5 years at risk for developmental delays, and oral health in a pediatric practice. Plans are in place to develop a series on behavioral health for primary care providers. One component will include early childhood mental health. In addition, a work group has been formed to address the inclusion of information on mental health and health consultation and early childhood mental health in training programs for nurse practitioners and medical school and pediatric and family practice residency training programs at professional schools in Connecticut.

SPECIALIZED CLINICAL TRAINING FOR INFANT AND EARLY CHILDHOOD MENTAL HEALTH PRACTITIONERS

The examples in the previous section provide illustrations of statewide approaches to building competence within the range of professions working with young children. In addition, there is the need for more trained mental health professionals skilled in working with young children. The Irving Harris Foundation has been a major force behind building such a work force. Since the mid-1990s, the foundation has funded 15 programs around the nation and two in Israel to create a network of clinicians skilled in working with infants, toddlers, and preschoolers.

The Harris Infancy and Early Childhood Professional Development Network

The programs in the Harris Infancy and Early Childhood Professional Development Network are funded to address the severe shortage of professionals qualified to work with the range of mental health problems babies and young children through age 5 can experience. Eight programs were

Table 5.3. Harris Infancy and Early Childhood Professional Development Network
Training Programs in the United States in 2004

1. Boston, MA: Boston Institute for Early Child Development, Boston Medical Center,
    Boston University School of Medicine
2. Chicago, IL: Irving B. Harris Infant Studies Program, Erikson Institute
3. Chicago, IL: Harris Infant Mental Health Program, The University of Chicago
4. Denver, CO: Irving Harris Program in Child Development and Infant Mental Health,
    Department of Psychiatry, University of Colorado Health Sciences Center
5. Minneapolis, MN: Irving B. Harris Training Center for Infant and Toddler Develop-
    ment, College of Education and Human Development, Institute of Child Develop-
    ment, University of Minnesota
6. New Haven, CT: Harris Program in Early Childhood, Yale University Child Study Center
7. New Orleans, LA: Harris Center for Infant Mental Health, Department of Psychia-
    try, Louisiana State University Health Sciences Center
8. New Orleans, LA: Harris Training Programs in Infant Mental Health, Institute of In-
    fant and Early Childhood Mental Health, Tulane University Health Sciences Center
9. New York, NY: Institute for Infants, Children, and Families, Jewish Board of Family
    and Children's Services
10. Oakland, CA: Early Childhood Mental Health Training Program, Children's Hospital
    and Research Center
11. Phoenix, AZ: Harris Infant and Early Childhood Mental Health Training Institute,
    Southwest Human Development and Department of Family and Human Develop-
    ment, Arizona State University
12. San Francisco, CA: Infant–Parent Program, University of California
13. San Francisco, CA: Child Trauma Research Project, University of California
14. Seattle, WA: Graduate Certification Program in Infant Mental Health, University of
    Washington
15. Tallahassee, FL: Harris Institute for Infant Mental Health Training, Center for Pre-
    vention and Early Intervention Policy, Florida State University

Source: Harris Network at ZERO TO THREE, 2004.

initially funded during a 3-year period (1994–1997), and more have been
added since then. The most recent addition opened at Florida State University in June 2004. Together the programs now reach more than 4,000
persons each year from the full range of disciplines related to infant mental
health. (See Table 5.3 for a list of the programs participating in the network.)

Although each is somewhat unique, the range of activities include
training for professionals from a variety of disciplines (e.g., psychology,
child and adolescent psychiatry, social work, special education, nursing,
early childhood education) in evaluation; assessment; intervention with infants, toddlers, and families; training in child development for pediatric residents and practicing physicians; training and mentoring for other frontline
caregivers in infant and toddler development in their region; development
of competencies for the states in which they are located; and a range of consultation and education programs for their communities. As an example,
the Irving B. Harris Institute for Infant Mental Health at Florida State
University will help implement Florida's Strategic Plan for Infant Mental

Health described earlier in this chapter, addressing the needs of the three levels of the work force. The Institute plans to address the following four goals (Florida Association for Infant Mental Health, 2003):

1. To establish competencies for Infant Mental Health Specialists in Florida tied to Medicaid reimbursement in collaboration with the Florida Department of Children and Families Bureau of Children's Mental Health, Agency for Health Care Administration, and Florida Mental Health Association;

2. To build a cadre of well-trained infant mental health specialists at Florida State University through the School of Social Work;

3. To train medical students and physicians in infant mental health;

4. To build infant mental health capacity statewide through expansion of in-service trainings. (p. 1)

Wayne State University/ Merrill Palmer Institute

The Graduate Certificate Program in Infant Mental Health at the Merrill Palmer Institute of Wayne State University in Detroit, Michigan is one example of a specialized program. It was developed in 1988 by faculty and community professionals. Faculty on staff at Wayne State University contributed to the design of the MI-AIMH competencies and the endorsement. The graduate certificate program reflects these competencies and is aligned with the endorsement described earlier in this chapter. The program is interdisciplinary in design, drawing on graduate students and professionals in the Colleges of Science, Education, Liberal Arts, Nursing, and the School of Social Work. As of August 2005, hundreds of students have taken coursework in the infant mental health program and 85 professionals have earned the full 22-credit graduate certificate. All graduates are working within the infant and early childhood mental health field. These specialists are defined

> not as a member of a particular discipline, but rather as someone with a distinct set of core beliefs, skills, training experiences, and clinical strategies who incorporates a comprehensive, intensive and relationship-based approach to working with young children and families. (Weatherston, 2002, p. 5)

Infant mental health (IMH) specialists learn clinical strategies to address the emotional health and development of both parent and child. They are trained to work in prevention, early identification of risks, and intensive assessment and intervention of serious emotional disturbances or jeopardized relationships. IMH specialists may be trained at the master's, post-master's, doctoral, or post-doctoral levels. The field is broad and interdisciplinary, including professionals from social work, child welfare, education, speech and language, occupational and physical therapy, child and family development, psychology, nursing, pediatrics, and psychiatry. Each specialist develops knowledge and skills specific to their own discipline, as well as competencies described as follows:

> quite specific to the optimal development of infants and toddlers within the context of nurturing relationships—for example, knowledge of attachment and early development, infant and family observation for the purpose of early assessment and care, the identification of disorders in infancy, and strategies for intervention with parent and child. It is the overlay of specialized studies, opportunities for skill-building and supervised service experiences with children birth to three and their families that contribute to the optimal development of an Infant Mental Health professional. (Weatherston, 2002, p. 10)

CHALLENGES AND RECOMMENDATIONS

The major work force and training challenges facing the early childhood mental health field stem from its interdisciplinary nature. Given the range of providers who comprise the relevant work force, agreements about curricula and credentialing have to be agreed on by a diverse array of stakeholders. This could be done state by state, institution by institution, or a national model could be developed. Given the work underway by the Annapolis Coalition on Behavioral Health Workforce Education and ZERO TO THREE, this author recommends a national collaborative effort to develop a core set of competencies for infant and early childhood mental health with the participation of key national representatives across disciplines and from educational institutions, professional organizations, and family members. The goal of such an effort would be to reach agreement about the knowledge, skills, and experiences required to effectively meet the social-emotional needs of infants and young children across the continuum of promotion, prevention, and intervention. These core competencies would be useful at the national level and guide the development of curricula and training programs for infancy and early childhood mental health. Building on the work of the MI-AIMH, as several states are already doing, could provide a national training model for translating these agreed-on competencies into practice and addressing how to ensure that those working with infants and young children have the necessary knowledge and skills. Once this work is done, the question of a national endorsement or certification program can be considered.

Such a national approach would advance the work in each state. States could then work through government and academic partnerships to create systems to teach the skills and knowledge needed and develop their own endorsement or certification programs.

In the meantime, states can build on the examples provided in this chapter to accomplish the following:

- Partner with higher education institutions to integrate relevant knowledge and skill development into existing training programs across a range of disciplines.

- Develop interdisciplinary graduate programs to prepare professionals in education, nursing, social work, psychiatry, and psychology for specialized intervention and clinical practice.

- Increase the understanding of state and local child serving agencies about the importance of providing mental health services to young children and embed training on early childhood mental health into existing training programs for all those who come into contact with young children.

- Create opportunities for continuing education through institutions of higher education, professional associations, and state agencies for ongoing local and statewide seminars and intensive training series for students, paraprofessionals, faculty, and community professionals.

CONCLUSION

An effective system of care for young children is dependent on a well-qualified and well-trained work force that consists of individuals well prepared for this most important work. Mental health professionals are increasingly advancing their understanding of the special competencies needed by the range of professionals who work with young children in health, early care and education, and mental health programs. Whereas the majority of professionals in those environments have not yet had the opportunity to avail themselves of specialized training, through the work of such states as Michigan and Florida, the Harris Professional Development Network, and the national efforts of ZERO TO THREE and the Annapolis Coalition, they are seeing the foundational work that will help establish the competencies needed across a range of providers and the examples of what quality education and training entails.

REFERENCES

Annapolis Coalition on Behavioral Health Workforce Education. (2004). *Report of core recommendations: Conference on behavioral health workforce competencies.* Available from Michael A. Hoge, Ph.D., at michael.hoge@yale.edu

Bricker, D., & Squires, J. (1999). *Ages & Stages Questionnaires® (ASQ): A parent-completed, child-monitoring system* (2nd ed.). Baltimore: Paul H. Brookes Publishing Co.

Briggs-Gowan, M., & Carter, A. (2002). *Brief Infant-Toddler Social and Emotional Assessment (BITSEA).* San Antonio, TX: Harcourt Assessment.

Cohen. E., & Kaufmann, R. (2000). *Early childhood mental health consultation.* Washington, DC: Georgetown University, National Technical Assistance Center for Children's Mental Health, Center for Child and Human Development.

Early Childhood Mental Health Systems Development Workgroup, Alameda County. (October 15, 2003). (Meeting minutes). Retrieved November 21, 2004, from http://www.co.alameda.ca.us/childcare/ecmh_mn_101503.pdf

Emde, R., Bertacchi, J., & Mann, T. (2001). Organizational environments that support mental health. *ZERO TO THREE, 22*(1), 67–69.

Expert Panel on Behavioral Health Workforce Development. (2004). *Recommendations to the Institute of Medicine committee on crossing the quality chasm.* Available from Michael A. Hoge, Ph.D., at michael.hoge@yale.edu

Florida Association for Infant Mental Health. (2003). *Irving B. Harris Institute for Infant Mental Health is established at Florida State University.* Retrieved December 24, 2004, from http://www.fsu.edu/~cpeip/FAIMHSummer03.pdf

Florida State University Center for Prevention and Early Intervention Policy. (2001). *Florida's strategic plan for infant mental health: Establishing a system of mental health services for young children and their families in Florida.* Tallahassee: Author.

Harris Network at ZERO TO THREE. (2006) *Early childhood and infant mental health training programs.* Retrieved December 24, 2004, from http://harrisnetwork.org/programs.html

Hepburn, K., Kaufmann, R., Dodge, J., & Hansen, K. (2004). *Early childhood MH consultation: A training guide for the early childhood services community.* Washington, DC: Georgetown University, National Technical Assistance Center for Children's Mental Health, Center for Child and Human Development.

Hoge, M. (2002). The training gap: An acute crisis in behavioral health education. *Administration and Policy in Mental Health, 29*(4/5), 305–317.

Huang, L., MacBeth, G., Dodge, J., & Jacobstein, D. (2004). Transforming the workforce in children's mental health. *Administration and Policy in Mental Health, 32*(2), 167–187.

Individuals with Disabilities Education Improvement Act of 2004, PL 108-446, 20 U.S.C. §§ 1400 et seq.

Institute of Medicine. (2001). *Crossing the quality chasm: A new health system for the 21st century.* Washington, DC: National Academies Press.

Institute of Medicine. (2003). *Health professions education: A bridge to quality.* Washington, DC: National Academies Press.

Jellinek, M., Patel, B.P., & Froehle, M.C. (Eds.). (2002). *Bright futures in practice: Mental health: Volume I: Practice guide.* Arlington, VA: National Center for Education in Maternal and Child Health.

Knitzer, J. (2001). *Building services and systems to support the healthy emotional development of young children: An action guide for policymakers.* New York: National Center for Children in Poverty.

LeBuffe, P., & Naglieri, J.A. (1999). *Devereux Early Childhood Assessment* (DECA). Rutland, MA: Devereux Foundation.

Meyers, J., & Davis, K. (1997). State and foundation partnerships to promote mental health systems reform for children and families. In C. Nixon & D. Northrup (Eds.), *Evaluating mental health services: How do programs for children "work" in the real world* (pp. 95–116). Thousand Oaks, CA: Sage Publications.

Meyers, J., Kaufman, M., & Goldman, S. (1999). *Promising practices: Training strategies for serving children with serious emotional disturbance and their families in a system of care.* Systems of care: Promising practices in children's mental health (Vol. V, 1998 Series). Washington, DC: American Institutes for Research, Center for Effective Collaboration and Practice.

Michigan Association for Infant Mental Health. (2002). *MI-AIMH endorsement for culturally sensitive, relationship-focused practice promoting infant mental health competency guidelines.* Southgate, MI: Author.

Ounce of Prevention Fund. (2000). *First steps: Early childhood mental health regional summit 2000.* Chicago: Author.

Pires. S. (1996). Human resource development. In B. Stroule (Ed.), *Children's mental health: Creating systems of care in a changing society* (pp. 281–207). Baltimore: Paul H. Brookes Publishing Co.

The President's New Freedom Commission on Mental Health. (2003). *Achieving the promise: Transforming mental health care in America. Final report.* (DHHS Publication No. SMA 03-3832). Rockville, MD: US Government Printing Office.

Shonkoff, J., & Phillips, D. (Eds.). (2000). *From neurons to neighborhoods: The science of early childhood development.* Washington, DC: National Academies Press.

Simpson, J., Jivanjee, P., Koroloff, N., Doerfler, A., & García, M. (2001). *Promising practices in early childhood mental health.* Systems of care: Promising practices in children's mental health (Vol. III). Washington, DC: American Institutes for Research, Center for Effective Collaboration and Practice.

Trowbridge, R., & Weingarten, S. (2001). *Educational techniques used in changing provider behavior.* In K. Shojania, B. Duncan, K. McDonald, & R. Wachter (Eds.), *Making health care safer: A critical analysis of patient safety practices* (pp. 595–600). AltRQ Publication No, 01-E058, Rockville, MD: Agency for Healthcare Research and Quality.

Vermont CUPS Core Competencies Task Force. (2001). *Knowledge and practice to promote the emotional and social development of young children.* Waterbury, VT: Author. [Prepared with support from the Federal Center for Mental Health Services Initiative Grant #HSM52151.]

Weatherston, D. (2000). The infant mental health specialist. *ZERO TO THREE* (Vol. 21, No. 3), 3–10.

Yoshikawa, H., & Knitzer, J. (1997). *Lessons from the field: Head Start mental health strategies to meet changing needs.* New York: National Center for Children in Poverty.

ZERO TO THREE. (2005). *Diagnostic classification of mental health and developmental disorders of infancy and early childhood* (DC:0–3R) (rev. ed.). Washington, DC: ZERO TO THREE.

6

Evaluating Outcomes in Systems Delivering Early Childhood Mental Health Services

Deborah F. Perry, Michelle W. Woodbridge, and Elisa A. Rosman

Since the 1980s, there have been a series of parallel efforts to build more comprehensive, coordinated "systems" to deliver services for young children and their families. These efforts have been fueled by a confluence of scientific and anecdotal evidence. Data from the scientific community (Shonkoff & Phillips, 2000) demonstrate the importance of the first years of life for brain development. These early years not only establish the hardware for the brain's later functioning, but also set the stage for achieving critical social-emotional developmental milestones. In particular, the formation of positive attachments to caregivers lays the foundation for future relationships with peers, teachers, and loved ones and a sense of competence that predicts later self-esteem and approaches to learning (see Chapter 2). At the same time, greater numbers of families are raising children who are exposed to a variety of risk factors that may compromise their emotional well-being, including poverty, parental depression and/or substance abuse, domestic violence, and developmental delays or disabilities (see Chapter 15). Finally, focus groups conducted with families of children who have a serious emotional disturbance have revealed a consistent truth—the vast majority of these parents knew something was different about their children early in their children's lives, often in their first year (see Chapter 7).

Taken together, these insights document the continuing need to develop service systems that can simultaneously promote positive social-emotional well-being and school readiness in all young children; target preventive services and supports for children in families at highest risk for developing mental health problems; and provide individualized, family centered interventions for those children who may be manifesting problematic behavior in the first 5 years of life. To accomplish these ambitious goals requires a new vision for how services and supports for young children and their caregivers should be delivered. Rather than build a stand-alone mental health system to deliver services to young children and their families, these services and supports must be woven into the fabric of the existing service systems that families with young children are accessing.

A framework for infusing mental health promotion, prevention, and intervention services has been described in Chapter 4 of this volume. This framework is being operationalized in many different ways in communities and states across the country, depending on the unique needs of the target population the stakeholders have defined. Successful states and communities have strategically built on the variety of systems reforms that are underway in the early care and education, maternal and child health, early intervention and/or special education, and mental health arenas. One of the common challenges faced by consumers, policy makers, program managers, and service providers is how to evaluate the effectiveness of their systems. Specifically

- Is there a system of services and supports, or is there a set of coordinated programs?

- What are the meaningful outcomes of a system at the child–family level, provider–program level, and system level? How are these outcomes measured?

- How can data from outcome evaluations be used to improve service delivery, system development, and outcomes for children and families?

This chapter provides an overview of critical issues in evaluating systems for delivering early childhood mental health services and supports. First, the critical challenges that stakeholders face as they evaluate complex systems change are discussed, as well as some tools and strategies that have been useful to others. Next, the chapter describes the framework for the national evaluation of the Substance Abuse and Mental Health Services Administration (SAMHSA) grants to foster the development of children's mental health systems of care. The chapter then explores the efforts to evaluate early childhood systems of care, highlighting one state's experience with a large-scale effort. The chapter concludes with a discussion of the challenges and opportunities for systems evaluation and outcomes measurement for young children's mental health.

THE CURRENT CONTEXT

Increasingly, policy makers are recognizing that the best way to provide comprehensive services to young children and their families, including those that promote mental health, is not through individual programs but through well-integrated systems of services. Unfortunately, the current array of services for children under the age of 5 years is a patchwork of public and private programs, with varying eligibility criteria and categorical funding streams. Furthermore, the lack of any one lead agency for providing early childhood services leads to a service delivery system for early childhood services that is highly fragmented.

Comprehensive approaches to integrating services must be accompanied by evaluation designs capable of providing data on the effectiveness of the services and systems reforms. Rigorous evaluations are necessary to understand whether or not an individual program, or a larger system of programs and services, is working, and if it is having the desired effect. They are also necessary for identifying what gaps in services still exist, as well as how the system can be improved. In their progress report on the status of evaluation of comprehensive community initiatives, Kubisch, Fulbright-Anderson, and Connell (1998) highlight three important components of a successful evaluation: 1) a political component, 2) a practical component, and 3) a teaching/learning component. Politically, it is important that funders, stakeholders, and key players know what sort of progress their initiative is making and whether or not it is paying off. Practically, good evaluation data are vital to feedback into the system to improve implementation. From a teaching/learning perspective, evaluation is vital for researchers and practitioners to discover what works and for that knowledge to be available for improving services and systems for young children and their families.

There are inherent difficulties in evaluating systems of services. Kubisch and colleagues (1998) identified six primary challenges that manifest at the community level:

1. Horizontal complexity—systems are operating across multiple sectors of the community.

2. Vertical complexity—systems attempt to have an impact on multiple levels of a community (e.g., individuals, families, communities).

3. Community building—desired outcomes, such as neighborhood empowerment, may be difficult to measure.

4. Contextual issues—external political and economic conditions may be outside the control of the initiative.

5. Community responsiveness and flexibility—systems have to be continuously evolving in response to community needs.

6. Community saturation—there are inherent limitations in conducting program evaluations in real-world environments.

This set of challenges underscores the inherent tension between conducting a rigorous community-based evaluation and the realities of complex systems change implementation. Rarely is there an opportunity to conduct a randomized controlled trial, except in the cases of implementing a particular evidence-based practice in a program or environment. Often, no true control group can be identified, nor does funding exist to collect similar data on a comparison community or population. Without a control or comparison group, attributing changes in positive outcomes to the intervention (in this example, a systems-reform initiative) becomes significantly more difficult.

These complexities are magnified when the level of analysis is a state. States are increasingly under pressure to be accountable for results, by requirements placed on them by the federal government as well as by taxpayers. The Government Performance and Results Act (1993) mandated that each federal agency develop performance measures for the programs they administer. As a condition of receipt of federal funds, states must provide data on a common set of indicators defined by the federal agency. These data are then aggregated by the federal program managers and used to determine if the programs are having the desired effect. Ideally, these indicators should be defined through a collaborative process that builds on the expertise and experience of state and local stakeholders, researchers, and families or consumers.

TOOLS AND TERMINOLOGY IN SYSTEMS EVALUATION

In response to these dilemmas, program evaluators, researchers, and other stakeholders have proposed a range of approaches to determining whether or not systems are achieving their desired effects. There are two major types of program evaluations that are conducted: 1) process (summative) evaluations and 2) outcome (formative) evaluations. Process evaluations collect data in a systematic way to document the activities that were implemented and the quality of those activities (Chinman, Imm, & Wandersman, 2004). A good process evaluation provides essential data on the extent to which the target population was served, what services they accessed, and which barriers were encountered while accessing needed services. A specific example of important process evaluation data is measuring the extent to which an evidence-based program has been implemented with fidelity when it is brought to a community. Without knowing if the interventions or systems-reform efforts were actually implemented, no assessment of the impact or outcomes can be made. Formative evaluations document the extent to which these interventions or actions may need to be modified and whether they resulted in measurable changes for the target population. When these efforts are successful, they allow stakeholders to assess the extent to which systems are in place, as well as what effect those systems are having on child and family level outcomes. Defining these outcomes requires a participatory process among families, program developers, evaluators, and sometimes the funders.

Consistent with the values of an early childhood mental health system articulated by Kaufmann and Hepburn (see Chapter 4), high-quality evaluations are those that adopt a participatory action approach. A participatory action approach is a collaborative process between researchers and stakeholders (those who potentially benefit from or have an interest in or commitment to the evaluation results) throughout the entire research process (Whyte, 1991). When implemented well, evaluators and community stakeholders work together in all phases of the evaluation; that is, from the specification of questions, the research design (including selecting measures), data collection, data analysis, and dissemination and utilization of the evaluation information. This type of model often results in increased relevance and utilization of the evaluation findings, as well as educating and empowering all participants. Substantive involvement of families, consumers, and other stakeholder groups as members of the evaluation team lead to better use of the data, especially for program change, advocacy, and sustainability.

High-quality program evaluations are built on a well thought-out set of assumptions about how and why a particular set of strategies is likely to lead to a specific set of measurable outcomes. This is often referred to as a *theory of change* (Granger, 1998; Hernandez & Hodges, 2001; Weiss, 1995). By engaging in a substantive conversation with a diverse group of stakeholders, including families, program managers, and front-line practitioners, a skilled evaluator can help articulate the connections between the activities that a community has selected to implement and the goals (outcomes) that they are seeking to address. This leads to the creation of a comprehensive evaluation plan. The role of the evaluator is to help bring to light the underlying theory—the assumptions about the pathways through which behavior or systems change will result—to determine what will need to be measured and how. This is possible because the theory explicitly links program activities and processes with specific short- and long-term outcomes (Hernandez & Hodges, 2001).

A logic model is one tool that evaluators often use to graphically depict the connections between the problem or need and a set of actions to be undertaken by a state or community (Chinman et al., 2004). The use of logic models is being promoted across many disciplines (Gabriel, 2000; National Association for the Education of Young Children and the National Associations of Early Childhood Specialists in State Departments of Education, 2003). Many federal agencies now require that grants include a logic model. In its ideal form, a logic model is driven by a theory of change that comes from previous research on the type of intervention being conducted, prior studies with the population in question, and discussions with stakeholders and practitioners in the community (Gabriel, 2000). Logic models are typically read from left to right; that is, beginning with current conditions, linking these to a set of activities designed to address those conditions, and then connecting to short-term and long-term outcomes. Other components of a logic model are a description of the target population and an articulation of the values underlying the system. There should also be a *goal* that states the desired impact or outcome of the program or initiative. Impact, which is also used interchangeably with long-term outcomes, is generally measured in terms of *indicators*.

Using a logic model can be instrumental to a community in defining their short- and long-term outcomes (*outcomes* is often used interchangeably with the term *results*). These outcomes need to be operationalized in such a way that they can be measured over time with accuracy and using indicators. Outcome indicators are specific data that will be used to determine if the initiative has had the desired effect. In addition, when moving from outcomes to indicators, it is vital that the indicator itself be meaningful to the community, passing what Friedman refers to as the *public square test* (Friedman, 2004, p. 16). That is, if someone were standing in the middle of the community's public square explaining the results of an evaluation as measured by specific indicators, would anyone stay to listen? Friedman provides extensive examples of potentially meaningful indicators, ranging from rate of preterm deliveries in a community, to percent of children fully immunized at ages 2 and 5, to rate of entry into foster care for children birth through age 5. Whereas these examples of potential indicators provide a useful pool from which to draw, it is vital that, for any specific project, the indicators (and outcomes) chosen be specifically tied to the initial logic model (or theory of change model) proposed (Taylor-Powell, Rossing, & Geran, 1998). The case study presented at the end of this chapter from First 5 California includes two tables of indicators drawing from data already collected by a variety of stakeholders in the state (see the section Lessons Learned from First 5 California in this chapter for more information).

One important outcome of using a theory of change approach and developing a detailed logic model is that these strategies can help stakeholders identify (and measure) critical *mediating* variables; that is, those factors that are the mechanisms through which a program or intervention may be having its effect or the barriers that interfere with achieving this outcome. For example, states and communities have implemented mental health consultation programs as a strategy to reduce the number of children who are being expelled from preschool (Brennan, Bradley, Allen, Perry, & Tsega, 2005; Gilliam, 2005). There are a number of ways in which mental health consultation could lead to reductions in preschool expulsions. For example, the consultant could work directly with the child and the teacher to extinguish a specific challenging behavior (e.g., biting other children). In another example, the mental health consultant might guide changes in the child care environment (i.e., modify how long circle time is and how transitions are managed). If the model of consultation is child-focused, and a theoretical link is made between reductions in levels of problem behaviors, then child-level outcomes should be included in the evaluation. If a program-focused model is being implemented, changes in the child care environment (including specific teacher behaviors) should be measured. The failure to specify and measure these key mediating variables means that if reductions in expulsion rates are not seen, stakeholders cannot distinguish among a number of plausible explanations. For example, did the consultation have no effect on children's behaviors? Did the consultation have no effect on teacher behaviors or the child care environment? If there were changes in these mediators, but children were still expelled, there may be other variables that should be examined in the next evaluation.

Although logic models can help demonstrate positive results, they do not necessarily capture the system component of the services being provided; that is, what is the value added from having a collaborative or system of services rather than individual services functioning independently (Taylor-Powell et al., 1998). Provan and Milward (2001) present a model for explicitly evaluating functioning as a network (as well as functioning on the community level and the organization and/or participant level). They recommend the following criteria for measuring network effectiveness: growth of membership in the network, the range of services provided, efficiency of services provided, lack of service duplication, multiplexity (strength of relationships among members of the network), presence of a network administrative organization (NAO), coordination of services, cost of maintaining the network, and member commitment to network goals.

Measuring Early Childhood Systems

The Federal Maternal and Child Health Bureau initiated the Early Childhood Comprehensive Systems (ECCS) program in 2003 to provide a mechanism for state maternal and child health agencies to collaborate with other stakeholders to create comprehensive early childhood systems. Overall goals are clearly stated, and all participating early childhood systems must develop access for families to 1) health insurance and ongoing pediatric services through a medical home, 2) quality early care and education, 3) social-emotional development and mental health services, 4) parenting education, and 5) family support. Although different individual systems may chose different goals, Friedman (2004) argues that, regardless of particular priorities, the focus is on creating a "comprehensive, collaborative, integrated, consumer oriented and easily accessible system of services and supports for young children and their families" (p. 22-23).

Through the work of an interagency team of policy makers and program managers, an evaluation tool was developed to assist the ECCS grantees in system-building efforts. This tool (Ruderman & Grason, 2004) examines outcomes at multiple levels—system, program, and child and family across the five topical areas that ECCS focuses on, listed earlier. The tool is made up of four main sections: 1) shared goals, 2) system partnerships, 3) generic strategies, and 4) examples of specific public health and/or Title V activities. The tool is designed to assist with articulating goals, identifying measurable outcomes, providing a baseline for monitoring and improving system-building efforts, building a framework for common concerns, providing both internal and external education, and offering a justification for infrastructure needs.

■ ■ ■

One example of where many of these strategies have been used to measure changes in the development of systems for delivering mental health services has been the grant program operated since 1994 by SAMHSA's Comprehensive Community Mental Health Services for Children and their Families program. This large-scale effort has been informed by the work of a large group of advocates, researchers, and state and federal policy makers, including the publication of *Unclaimed Children* (Knitzer, 1982) and *A System of Care for Seriously Emotionally Disturbed Children and Youth* (Stroul & Friedman, 1986). In response to a lack of coordinated, comprehensive, community-based, culturally competent services for children with serious emotional disturbance, communities received up to 6 years of federal funding to build systems of care across multiple child-serving agencies. Typically, these involved child welfare, juvenile justice, special education, Medicaid, and mental health working together to address the needs of adolescents with a mental health diagnoses; however, in recent years, communities have sought to extend this framework to younger children.

NATIONAL EVALUATION OF THE MENTAL HEALTH SYSTEM OF CARE SITES

The Center for Mental Health Services, a division of the Substance Abuse and Mental Health Services Administration of the U.S. Department of Health and Human Services, makes a significant commitment to implementing of the systems of care through the multiyear Comprehensive Community Mental Health Services for Children and Their Families Program. A multisite, rigorous national evaluation is required by the program's authorizing legislation. Since 1993, 121 federal grants have been awarded to communities, tribal nations, and states for the development and implementation of systems of care (Substance Abuse and Mental Health Services Administration, 2004). Although there is a preponderance of research and evaluation to support policy and fiscal reforms promoted in systems of care (e.g., Brannan, Baughman, Reed, & Katz Leavy, 2002; Manteuffel, Stephens, & Santiago, 2002; Rosenblatt, 1998; Stroul, Pires, Armstrong, & Zaro, 2002), there still are insufficient empirical data to demonstrate their differential effectiveness on children's behavioral and functional outcomes over traditional practices (e.g., Bickman, 1996a; Bickman, 1996b; Bickman, Noser, & Summerfelt, 1999). Data collected through the national evaluation, however, are productive additional empirical support for systems of care approaches, though these are not publicly available at the time this book went to press. In addition, there is widespread acceptance and implementation of many critical facets of the model and lessons that can be applied to the evaluation of efforts to meet the mental health needs of young children and their families.

What is clear from decades of studies on systems of care is that a multi-level structure is essential to adequately capture and assess the effectiveness of the systemic, programmatic, and practice-level interventions on which systems of care are based (Rosenblatt & Woodbridge, 2003). These levels are described in more detail in the following sections.

System Level

System level reforms seek to alter the organizational, structural, and financial dimensions of the service system. The system of care model proposes multiple systems-level modifications, including the development of interagency policies and services across child-serving agencies (e.g., mental health, juvenile justice, child welfare, education); the use of a continuum of community-based care in lieu of restrictive placements; and the restructuring of service financing (i.e., blended or pooled funding).

Evaluation designs to measure and assess the implementation, maintenance, and progress regarding system level changes have included both qualitative and quantitative methodology with a strong emphasis on descriptive data. Comprehensive approaches that triangulate data from various sources and through various methods are particularly popular, including surveys of administrators and front-line staff, audits of service plans and fiscal planning information, interviews of providers and consumers, and observation protocols of management and service team planning meetings. Most methods function to document and gauge the behavior and perceptions of system staff and consumers in promoting service access, cultural appropriateness, service linkage, continuous quality improvement, and cost effectiveness.

The national evaluation has developed a process to assess fidelity to the system of care values and principles in grant-funded communities. The tool relies on data collected from multiple informants, including primary caregivers, direct-service providers, and informal helpers as well as record reviews. Findings have implications at both the practice and systems level. To date, this System of Care Assessment has gathered data in communities funded since 1997, and gains have been seen over time and across domains. Stronger gains have been seen in domains related to service delivery as compared to infrastructure. For example, communities showed progress in developing and implementing individualized family service plans (IFSPs) and individualized education programs (IEPs); however, efforts to engage interagency partners in program management and operations activities were more difficult (SAMHSA, 2006).

Program Level

Program-level interventions seek to offer a more comprehensive continuum of *wrap-around* services that can include both traditional clinical services (e.g., outpatient and inpatient care) as well as more state-of-the-art innovations (e.g., respite, therapeutic foster care, case management). Systems of care have been shown to promote programmatic innovations that expand the service array, the availability of providers (including nontraditional), and the cultural appropriateness of options.

Evaluation designs to measure and assess the program-level changes in systems of care have also included both qualitative and quantitative methodology, again with a strong emphasis on descriptive data. Most methods function to document and gauge the spectrum of services available within a system through interviews and surveys with children and families, staff, and administrators.

Although the national outcomes demonstrate a wider variety of service options generally available in systems of care, a critical lesson learned is the need to assess not only these options but the degree to which the programs are implemented with adequate fidelity. The state of the field in measuring fidelity is still in its infancy, with research demonstrating the challenges and inconsistency in assessing adherence, quality, and dosage of services with rigor.

Practice and Individual Level

Practice level reforms seek to enhance the way care providers interact directly with consumers—children, their families, and their support sytems— and achieve client level outcomes using various approaches from traditional, office-based psychotherapies to newer models, such as wrap-around and multisystemic therapy. Evaluation designs to measure and assess the practice level and individual level changes in systems of care have also included both qualitative and quantitative methodology, with the stronger emphasis on outcome data. Most methods function to assess behavioral and functional gains through standardized interview or survey methods with children, families, and providers.

EARLY CHILDHOOD DEVELOPMENTS IN MENTAL HEALTH SYSTEMS OF CARE

Although many of the grant-funded system of care sites have included children under the age of 5 in their system of care initiatives, only one of the system of care sites funded from 1992 to 2004 focused exclusively on building a system of care for young children and their families. The state of Vermont received their federal grant in 1997 and completed their transition to a sustainable statewide system of care in 2004. It was the first state to complete this ambitious accomplishment. Their 6 years of quantitative and qualitative evaluation data provide a snapshot of how systems of care can reduce parenting stress, improve child-level outcomes, and create systems reforms that have a lasting effect on generations to come.

After Vermont received its grant in 1997, Children's UPstream Services (CUPS) was founded in 1998. It was formed by issuing invitations to each of the 12 human services regions in Vermont to work together to provide direct behavioral health services to families with young children, as well as to receive behavioral health training and consultation for an early childhood system of care. CUPS now consists of 12 regional teams, which include 26 full-time employees who provide both direct services to children and families and training and consultation for child care and other service providers; a learning team that is made up of approximately 12 experts in early childhood who provide training and technical assistance for the regional teams; a state outreach team made up of state agency and department directors, as well as parent representatives; a family consortium that provides advice on family participation; and an evaluation team. Aside from offering ongoing consultation to help children remain in their natural environments, CUPS provides training events across the state. (For a review, see Chapter 8 and Burchard, Tighe, & Pandina, 2003).

Between April 1999 and June 2003, nearly 2,400 families were served by CUPS. These families all had children ages birth through 6 years who were either experiencing or at risk for severe emotional disturbance, or the families had a parent with a severe emotional disorder who was under age 22. The evaluation team conducted an evaluation with 134 of the 2,400 families. Families who participated in the evaluation were interviewed at

Table 6.1.   Examples of tools used by Vermont for the Children's UPstream Services
evaluation

Domain and/or construct problem behaviors	Instrument	Source
Internalizing and externalizing	Achenbach System of Empirically-Based Assessment, Child Behavior Checklist (Achenbach & Rescorla, 2000)	National evaluation protocol
Child temperament and parenting stress	Parenting Stress Index (Abidin, 1993)	Local evaluation protocol
Caregiver strain	The Caregiver Strain Questionnaire (Brannan, Heflinger, & Bickman, 1998)	National evaluation protocol
Satisfaction with services and cultural competence	Family Satisfaction Questionnaire (ORC Macro, nd)	National evaluation protocol
Adequacy of shelter, income, nutrition, and child care	Family Resources Questionnaire (ORC Macro, nd)	National evaluation protocol
Factors critical to positive outcomes	Open-ended interviews with caregivers	Local evaluation protocol

6-month intervals during the course of 3 years. Researchers found that 6 months after intake, parents reported a significant reduction in their stress related to both their children's temperament and to more general parenting stress. Parents also reported significantly lower levels of severe behavior problems 6 months after intake. In smaller, more in-depth focus groups, families spoke of the following ways that CUPS helps and supports families. According to them, CUPS is successful because it teaches parenting skills, prevents child abuse, prevents future costs to society, prevents the loss of children as our country's most valuable resource, and supports communities (Pandina et al., 2004). Table 6.1 provides examples of the tools used by Vermont for the CUPS evaluations.

In the most recent round of grants funded by SAMHSA in 2005, six communities have focused their systems of care development on young children and their families beginning at birth. These communities join Colorado's Project BLOOM and the Vermont CUPS project as a cadre of communities seeking to extend the lessons learned from mental systems of care to young children and their families. These sites will benefit from the rigorous national evaluation funded by SAMHSA, as well as their local evaluations that will measure some of the unique outcomes that will result from early childhood systems reforms.

Another large-scale example of the combination of ambitious systems reform and rigorous evaluation can be seen in the First 5 initiative in

California. Focused on the whole population of young children and their families and implemented county by county, this comprehensive approach provides additional lessons learned for stakeholders seeking to implement and evaluate early childhood mental health systems reforms.

Lessons Learned from First 5 California

In 1998, the voters of California passed Proposition 10, The California Children and Families First Act, a statewide initiative that levied a 50-cent per pack tax on cigarettes to support services and programs targeting children birth to 5 years and their families. Collectively called First 5 California, the program's mission is for "all young children in the State of California [to] reach age five physically and emotionally healthy, learning and ready to achieve their greatest potential in school" (Center for Education and Human Services, 2005, pp. 1–2). Eighty percent of the total tax revenues, which have generated approximately $600 million annually, are allocated to County Commissions to disburse to early childhood programs according to local needs and priorities. The ultimate goal of First 5 California is to improve the lives of California's children and families through innovative strategies that are informed by outcome-based evaluations. The remaining 20% of funds are allocated to the California Children and Families Commissions (CCFC) to fund special statewide initiatives, media campaigns, development of educational materials for parents and caregivers, training activities for child care providers, and research and evaluation activities.

To support more effective funding decisions, program planning, and policies, the CCFC, overseers of First 5 California, called for an outcome-based accountability system to track progress in four priority areas: 1) improved child health, 2) improved child development, 3) improved family functioning, and 4) improved systems of care. In 2002, the CCFC contracted with SRI International, a private nonprofit research organization, to carry out a comprehensive statewide evaluation of the First 5 California initiative according to these guidelines. SRI, in collaboration with partner firms, the CCFC, and County Commissions, developed and implemented evaluation activities to support results-based accountability and continuous improvement efforts at both the state and local levels.

SRI launched the First 5 California statewide evaluation framework with the production and dissemination of the *First 5 California: Child, Family, and Community Indicators Book* (Child Trends & SRI International, 2002), which defined more clearly potential statewide outcomes, performance measures, and indicators for review and consideration by the CCFC and County Commissions. The indicators included in the publication were selected by drawing on documentation of the outcomes and indicators being used in evaluations conducted locally by County

Commissions and familiarity with national and statewide efforts to define outcomes and indicators for children and families (e.g., Healthy People 2010, the Health Plan Employer Data Information Set, the National Committee for Quality Assurance, and county level score cards in use in California and other states). The following criteria were also taken into consideration (Child Trends & SRI International, 2002):

Importance: How important is the indicator as a component or determinant of child and family well-being?

Validity and reliability: Does the indicator measure what it is supposed to measure? Is the indicator reproducible over repeated measurements and observers?

Sensitivity to change: Is the indicator sensitive enough to capture and respond to the impact of interventions that may reasonably be expected to influence the indicators? Is the indicator sensitive enough to reflect meaningful changes in the phenomenon of interest?

Data availability and quality: Are data readily and consistently available over time to track changes in the indicator?

Meaningfulness: Can the public and policy-makers easily understand what the indicator means and its implications for child and family well-being?

The indicators that County Commissions rated as being most important for tracking the success of First 5 California statewide were recommended for measurement in its statewide evaluation. The CCFC then added several additional indicators to track the impact of the initiative on tobacco cessation and school success in subsequent years of the child's life. Some examples of agreed-on indicators appear in Table 6.2, which delineates the First 5 child and family level outcomes and indicators. Table 6.3 delineates examples of the agreed-upon system level outcomes and indicators.

Development of Data Collection Training and Reporting Tools

The First 5 California statewide evaluators created a repertoire of instruments and training resources to assist County Commissions and their staff in the collection, entry, analysis, and dissemination of statewide evaluation data. This includes a large investment in the development of a web-based data entry and reporting system called Proposition 10 Evaluation Data System (PEDS), which is offered at no cost to County Commissions and their contracted programs that choose to use it. Statewide evaluators continually monitor PEDS for quality and user satisfaction, adding advanced functions and reports to PEDS and disseminating continuous quality improvement reports to PEDS users. Evaluation technical assistance coaches, assigned to each of the 58 County Commissions, also provide

Table 6.2.   First 5 child and family outcomes and indicators

1.   Children receive early screening and intervention for developmental delays and other special needs.

Number and percentage of children under age 3 who receive a developmental screening from their primary care provider

Number and percentage of children identified as having special needs by the time of kindergarten entry

Number and percentage of children identified with disabilities who receive developmental services by the time of kindergarten entry

Number and percentage of early childhood care and education providers who receive training and/or technical support for caring for children with special needs

2.   Children enter kindergarten ready for school

Number and percentage of children entering kindergarten ready for school as determined by assessments completed by teachers and parents that indicate the child is ready in the areas of cognitive, social-emotional, language, approaches to learning, and health and physical development

Number and percentage of children who participate in school-linked transitional practices

Number and percentage of students retained a second year in kindergarten

State standardized test scores for reading and math in second grade

3.   Parents provide nurturing and positive emotional support to their children

Number and percentage of mothers screened for depression

Table 6.3.   First 5 systems change outcomes and indicators

1.   Increased accessibility of services and/or activities

Increased number of service locations

Provision of co-located services (i.e., multiple agencies providing services at a shared location)

Provision of services in conveniently located places (e.g., schools)

Provision of home-based services

Provision of transportation to services

Expansion of service hours or provision of flexible scheduling

Increased outreach and public awareness of services

Provision of services for special needs population(s)

Provision of services for underserved population(s)

2.   Improved service delivery

Provision of training and technical assistance to program staff to improve the quality of services

Increased family focus of services (i.e., addressing the needs of multiple family members)

Increased attention to preventive services and/or activities

3.   Increased cultural competence

Cultural diversity training for providers

The provision of training and technical assistance to improve knowledge, attitudes, and skills of service providers to increase their capacity to work with children with disabilities and other special needs

Service providers who are culturally and linguistically reflective of the community

The provision of print, audiovisual, and electronic materials that are culturally and linguistically appropriate for communities being served and written at appropriate literacy levels

(continued)

Table 6.3. *(continued)*

The availability of adapted and specialized services and supports for children with special needs and their families

Data collected and reported by ethnicity, language, age, gender, geographic areas, special needs populations, or other significant subgroups

4. Increased service integration

Providing comprehensive services (a combination of health, educational or social-emotional support services)

Undertaking joint planning and decision-making among multiple agencies

Seeking joint funding and/or pooling resources with other agencies

Using a centralized registry or database across agencies to share information on program participants

Advocating for policy change in collaboration with other agencies

5. Increased accountability for results

Using a shared accountability system across agencies (e.g., using common measures to assess results, examining findings jointly)

Using data to inform program refinement and future program funding

6. Increased civic engagement of program participants

Increasing public input (e.g., surveys, community hearings, advisory boards)

7. Increased sustainability of First 5 California funded programs

Percentage of programs with a fund-raising plan for the current year and for at least 1 year into the future

Percentage of First 5 funds versus funds from other sources and supporting services

Percentage of programs that leverage First 5 funds

Percentage of programs able to reduce duplication and save money through collaboration

8. Improvements in school readiness service system

The number and percentage of elementary schools with formal linkages to preschools, Head Start and Early Head Start programs, child care centers, home-visiting programs, and community resources

The number and percentage of preschools with formal linkages to public and private elementary schools, child care centers, home-visiting programs, and community resources

customized training on data collection, the PEDS application, and data findings to help build local capacity to collect and use information, coordinate local and state evaluation efforts, and minimize local data collection burden. All evaluation tools and resources are available electronically on the statewide evaluation website (http://www.first5eval.org) and in multiple languages (e.g., English, Spanish, Hmong, Vietnamese, Cantonese, and Mandarin). Table 6.4 shows some examples of tools used to measure Early Childhood Mental Health outcomes.

Results from the First 5 California Annual Report (2004–2005)

In the 2004–2005 year alone, First 5 services and programs touched the lives of almost 20 million young children and their families, particularly children most at risk of not having access to the services and supports

Table 6.4.   Examples of tools to measure early childhood mental health outcomes

Level	Domain	Examples of tools
Child level outcomes	Children's problem behaviors	*Ages & Stages Questionnaire®: Social-Emotional (ASQ:SE)* (Squires, Bricker, & Twombly, 2002)
		Brief Infant Toddler Social Emotional Assessment (BITSEA) (Briggs-Gowan & Carter, 2002)
	Children's social skills	*Devereux Early Childhood Assessment (DECA)* (LeBuffe & Naglieri, 1999)
		Preschool Kindergarten Behavior Scales (Merrell, 2002)
Family and/or caregiver outcomes	Family strengths and/or needs	*Family Needs Scale* (Dunst, Cooper, Weeldreyer, Snyder, & Chase, 1988)
		Family Resource Scale (Dunst & Leet, 1988)
		Family Support Scale (Dunst, Trivette, & Jenkins)
	Caregiver depression	*Beck Depression Inventory* (Beck, Ward, Mock, & Erbaugh, 1961)
		Center for Epidemiological Studies Depression (CES-D) Scale (Radloff, 1977)
Program level outcomes	Child care provider behavior	*Arnett Global Rating Scale of Caregiver Behavior* (Arnett, 1989)
	Teachers' attitudes	*Teacher Opinion Survey* (Geller & Lynch, 1999)
System level outcomes	Cultural and linguistic competence	*Promoting Cultural and Linguistic Competency* (Goode, 2004, 2005)
	Integrated funding plan	*Spending Smarter* checklist (Johnson & Knitzer, 2005)
		Early Childhood Mental Health Services Funding Matrix (Wischman, Kates, & Kaufmann, 2001)
	System of care implementation	*Early childhood mental health systems of care: a self-assessment guide for states and communities* (Kaufmann, 2006)

they need for their optimal early development and school readiness. First 5 successfully reached out to culturally and linguistically diverse populations and to families with children with disabilities and other special needs. Approximately 3.5 million people received intensive direct services from First 5 funded programs, including activities such as early education classes, developmental screenings and assessments, parenting education, health insurance enrollment, and preventive health care services (including dental care). Of the children and families intensively served, 79% were Latino, 13% were children with disabilities or special needs, 67% spoke a language other than English, and 68% were living under the federal poverty level.

In addition, more than 16 million people were provided with information about child health, education, and development through community outreach events such as health fairs, media campaigns, and information dissemination. Programs also served more than 400,000 service providers (including more than 250,000 early care and education providers) by conducting provider capacity trainings and professional development activities to improve skills and resources. More than 1,000 First 5 programs were funded to implement systems change activities, including efforts to fill service gaps, make services more accessible and family friendly, reach out more effectively to diverse and often underserved communities, and improve the quality and effectiveness of services.

Preliminary outcome data show positive effects on children's health, development, early education, and family well-being after 6–12 months of intensive First 5 services. For example

- More children had health insurance.

- More children had an ongoing source of primary health care.

- More children had routine medical and dental care.

- More children regularly attended preschool.

- More families regularly read and told stories to their children.

- More doctors provided developmental assessments of young children, resulting in more children being identified as having disabilities or special needs.

- More mothers acquired their high school diploma or general education degree.

- Fewer children were exposed to secondhand smoke in their homes.

These beneficial effects on the health and early growth experiences of children are the very factors known from research to lead to children's greater success in school and in life. In addition, results from various stakeholder surveys measuring system change factors indicate that First 5 services are increasingly more accessible, comprehensive, high quality, integrated, family focused, and outcomes based.

Key Challenges and Lessons Learned
from the Statewide Evaluation of First 5 California

The First 5 statewide evaluation team made significant accomplishments that have given the CCFC and County Commissions information essential to meeting their strategic funding priorities, accountability requirements, and program improvement needs; however, they have also faced numerous challenges. Lessons are shared here for the purpose of providing insight for other possible renditions to support and evaluate early childhood systems of care.

The CCFC's contract with the First 5 statewide evaluation team specified collection of a range of data to answer multiple evaluation questions (including questions addressing the population, system, program, and participant levels); however, the legislation supporting First 5 California made participation in the statewide evaluation voluntary. County Commissions perceived the amount and variety of data required in the statewide evaluation as burdensome; therefore, their willingness to cooperate has dictated the pace, quantity, and quality of the submitted data. Future approaches should consider mandating participation in a comprehensive systemwide evaluation to ensure commitment to systemwide implementation.

Furthermore, fluid political environments at both the state and county levels have frequently resulted in the need to rethink information needs and adapt evaluation processes accordingly. This fluidity has resulted in the loss of some data quality and consistency, and it has increased County Commissions' reluctance to participate in the statewide evaluation given that changes to the data collection structure and procedures have an impact on human and fiscal resources.

These challenges have not overshadowed the statewide evaluator's belief in the importance of measuring systemwide indicators to assess the impact of such an immense statewide initiative. The First 5 evaluators actively worked to address challenges by conducting the project through a collaborative and inclusive process with the state and County Commissions. They attended regional meetings, routinely communicated data collection plans and findings, visited program sites to learn about services and local evaluation, and often sought County Commission input through surveys and group discussions. Identification of the four priority result areas (i.e., improved child health, improved child development, improved family functioning, and improved systems of care) was an especially useful framework to encourage First 5 administrators and stakeholders in building more comprehensive support systems for children and families. Consensus to evaluate these result areas was achieved among County Commissions because stakeholders understood and rallied behind First 5's mission to improve key systemwide outcomes through a diverse set of programs. Furthermore, to support continued local level learning and program improvement, the statewide evaluation incorporates qualitative data collection and dissemination of findings. The annual report includes individual County Commission profiles, local stories, and case study reports that describe promising practices being used by high-quality preschools and early literacy programs.

CHALLENGES AND OPPORTUNITIES

The case studies and examples presented in this chapter underscore the array of challenges that stakeholders face as they seek to evaluate comprehensive early childhood mental health systems reforms. Some of these challenges are shared by others trying to conduct rigorous evaluations of any complex systems change efforts. For example, there is a lack of consensus on what the most important system level outcomes are and how to reliably measure them. There are ongoing concerns about how to measure the implementation of evidence-based practices; that is, balancing concerns about fidelity with the need to adapt these interventions for the unique program and population features present in individual communities. In addition, there is a continued need to systematically build capacity at the local level to collect, analyze, and utilize evaluation data for continuous program improvement. Other challenges are unique to those attempting to measure the impact of infusing mental health into the existing, diverse array of early childhood, beginning with how to measure the degree to which *infusion* has occurred and how to assess the quality of those services and supports in the context of early childhood programs and environments that are of variable quality.

Lessons Learned from Starting Early, Starting Smart

One of the few large scale efforts to infuse mental health into early childhood environments was launched in 12 communities across the United States as part of the Starting Early, Starting Smart (SESS) initiative. Funded through a public-private partnership between the Substance Abuse and Mental Health Services Administration and the Casey Family Foundation, behavioral health services (including mental health and substance abuse) were embedded within either primary care sites or early care and education environments. The integration of behavioral health services into accessible, nonthreatening environments where families naturally take their children was motivated by concerns about stigma and a desire to increase utilization of these services by high-risk families. SESS also included a rigorous cross-site external evaluation as part of its implementation. This 12-site study was guided by two research questions. First, will integrating behavioral health services into primary and early childhood care environments lead to higher rates of entry into prevention or early intervention services? Second, will integrating these services lead to sustained improvements in the outcomes of participating children and families? Service use and outcomes were compared for those families at intervention sites and control sites. Using a rigorous set of tools to measure child and parent level outcomes, data were collected on roughly 1,500 children served in SESS sites and a comparison group of children in similar environments of about the same size. Outcomes were measured a minimum of three times, and service use data were collected even more often. Impact was measured primarily at the child and family level, and the findings were positive, such as reduced drug use in problem users, lower levels of verbal aggression and parenting stress, and more positive parent-child interactions in families that participated in the SESS sites. Classroom teachers reported reductions in problem behaviors, both for internalizing and externalizing (Springer, 2003). Limited data on system and program level outcomes were noted in the final report.

■ ■ ■

The framework for infusing mental health services and supports is based on an articulated set of values, which must also be reflected in how services are delivered and outcomes are measured. Early childhood mental health is defined within the context of the child's relationships with parents and other caregivers; therefore, it is important to measure family level variables in addition to child level changes in social-emotional behaviors. Reductions in levels of caregiver depression, for example, are likely to be a critical link in reducing the level of risk for young children's mental health. Changes in levels of family support, access to resources, and other family level risk and protective factors will have an impact on family's stress, which also has direct effects on young children's social-emotional well-being. Finally, a comprehensive evaluation should include measures of system level variables, such as the extent to which the services and supports are culturally relevant and delivered to families in a manner that respects their cultural and/or linguistic background; the degree to which varied funding sources have been mobilized to support services and infrastructure; and an overall assessment of the extent to which there is a *system* at all, that is one that is consistent with the state or community's vision.

To evaluate the impact of embedding mental health services into early childhood environments, new tools and models are needed. For example, one strategy to infuse mental health into early care and education environments is to embed a mental health consultant in a child care program.

Evaluating the impact of this type of service requires a multiple level protocol, including tools to assess the overall quality of the child care environment, the effectiveness of the consultation (likely mediated by the quality of the consultant's relationship with the early childhood provider), the impact of the consultation on the overall emotional climate of the environment, and the impact on a target child if identified. Currently, there are well-validated tools to measure the overall quality of a range of child care environments and a growing number of instruments to measure young children's social skills and problem behaviors (see Sosna & Mastergeorge, 2005). Tools to measure the quality of child care environments (e.g., the Early Childhood Environmental Rating Scales), however, have not proven to be sensitive enough to detect the micro-level changes in teacher behaviors and interactions that are likely to mediate the effects of mental health consultation (Brennan, Bradley, Allen, Perry, & Tsega, 2005). Furthermore, there are a very limited number of standardized measures of the effectiveness of consultation on teacher behaviors and attitudes and even fewer tools to quantify the quality of the consultant–teacher relationship. Green and Everhart (2006) found that the effectiveness of mental health consultation in Head Start environments was related to the perceived quality of the relationship between the consultant and the teacher; this was measured by a few questions on a self-reported survey. This finding suggests that new tools are needed to assess the quality of these relationships so that additional data can be collected in other environments.

This points to another component of the framework for early childhood mental health systems that represents both an opportunity and an ongoing challenge—engaging a diverse group of families in all levels of the system. When this is accomplished, families will not only determine the array of services and supports they access (and have choices about who provides these services), but families will also be engaged in the design and implementation of system evaluations and assist with data analysis and interpretation. As mentioned earlier, this type of participatory action framework is critical to the success of evaluation efforts. Only through the meaningful involvement of a diverse array of stakeholders, including families, will relevant early childhood mental health outcomes be defined and appropriate tools developed.

Engaging a variety of stakeholders across systems represents an opportunity to be more strategic about how and where to infuse mental health into services and environments, and how to team with and learn from other efforts to evaluate the impact of early childhood systems reforms. The Child and Family Policy Center has documented an array of early childhood systems-building efforts that are currently underway (State Early Childhood Policy Technical Assistance Network, 2004). Some are taking place in a targeted number of states (e.g., the Build Initiative funded by a consortium of philanthropic organizations), whereas others are funded through ongoing federal programs, such as Part C of the Individuals with Disabilities Education Act or the Early Childhood Comprehensive Systems program. These efforts represent vehicles to leverage systems level implementation and evaluation of commonly shared outcomes.

Ultimately, the mental health needs of young children and their families will only be met through the adoption of a public health approach that infuses services and supports into a variety of environments. As more family focused mental health services are embedded within these early childhood programs and environments, including early care and education, primary health care, and home visiting, evaluation strategies will have to adapt to this complex climate of implementation. Adopting multi-level models, articulating the theories of change, and developing tools that are consistent with the values of the systems and their stakeholders will yield data that will drive improvements in the delivery of effective services and supports, inform ongoing efforts to reform early childhood systems, and lead to healthy social-emotional development for all young children and their families.

REFERENCES

Abidin, R. (1983). *Parenting stress index* (3rd ed.). Odessa, FL: Psychological Assessment Resources.

Achenbach, T.M. (1991). *Integrative guide to the 1991 CBCL/4-18, YSR, and TRF profiles.* Burlington: University of Vermont, Department of Psychology.

Achenbach, T., & Rescorla, L. (2000). *Achenbach system of empirically-based assessment, child behavior checklist: Manual for the ASEBA preschool forms and profiles.* Burlington: University of Vermont, Department of Psychiatry.

Arnett, J. (1989). Caregivers in day-care centers: Does training matter? *Journal of Applied Developmental Psychology, 10,* 541–552.

Beck, A.T., Ward, C.H., Mock, J., & Erbaugh, J. (1961). An inventory for measuring depression. *Archives of General Psychiatry, 4,* 561–571.

Bickman, L. (1996a). The evaluation of a children's mental health managed care demonstration. *The Journal of Mental Health Administration, 23,* 7–15.

Bickman, L. (1996b). Reinterpreting the Fort Bragg evaluation findings: The message does not change. *The Journal of Mental Health Administration, 23,* 137–145.

Bickman, L., Noser, K., & Summerfelt, W.T. (1999). Long-term effects of a system of care on children and adolescents. *The Journal of Behavioral Health Services & Research, 26,* 185–202.

Brannan, A.M., Baughman, L.N., Reed, E.D., & Katz Leavy, J. (2002). System-of-care assessment: Cross-site comparison of findings. *Children's Services: Social Policy, Research, and Practice, 5*(1), 37–56.

Brannan, A., Heflinger, C., & Bickman, L. (1998). The caregiver strain questionnaire: Measuring the impact on the family of living with a child with serious emotional disturbances. *Journal of Emotional and Behavioral Disorders, 5,* 212–222.

Brennan, E., Bradley, J., Allen, M.D., Perry, D., & Tsega, A. (2005, March). *The evidence base for mental health consultation in early childhood settings: Research synthesis and review.* Paper presented at an invitational meeting sponsored by the Georgetown University National Technical Assistance Center for Children's Mental Health, Tampa, FL.

Briggs-Gowan, M.J., & Carter A.S. (2002). *Brief-Infant-Toddler Social and Emotional Assessment (BITSEA): Manual* (Version 2.0). New Haven, CT: Yale University.

Burchard, J.D., Tighe, T.A., & Pandina, N.G. (2003). *Children's UPstream Services outcome report.* Waterbury: Child Adolescent and Family Unit, Vermont Department of Developmental and Mental Health Services.

Carter, A., & Briggs-Gowan, M., Jones, S., Little, T. (2003). The Infant–Toddler Social and Emotional Assessment (ITSEA): Factor structure, reliability, and validity. *Journal of Abnormal Child Psychology, 31*(5), 495–514.

Center for Education and Human Services. (2005). *Annual report fiscal year 2005–2005: California Children & Families Commission—First 5 California.* Retrieved on October 1, 2006, from http://www.ccfc.ca.gov/pdf/research/f5ar_fy2004-05.pdf

Child Trends & SRI International. (August 2002). *First 5 California: Child, family, and community indicators book.* Menlo Park, CA: SRI International.

Chinman, M., Imm, P., & Wandersman, A. (2004). *Getting to outcomes 2004: Promoting accountability through methods and tools for planning, implementation and evaluation.* Santa Monica, CA: Rand Corporation.

Dunst, C., Cooper, C., Weeldreyer, J., Snyder, K., & Chase, J. (1988). *Family needs scale.* Cambridge, MA: Brookline Books.

Dunst, C., & Leet, H. (1988). *Family resource scale.* Cambridge, MA: Brookline Books.

Dunst, C., Trivette, C., & Jenkins, V. (1988). *Family support scale.* Cambridge, MA: Brookline Books.

Friedman, M. (2004). Results accountability for state early childhood comprehensive systems: A planning guide for improving the well-being of young children and their families. In N. Halfon, T. Rice, & M. Inkelas (Eds.), *Building state early childhood comprehensive systems* (Series No. 4). Los Angeles: National Center for Infant and Early Childhood Health Policy.

Gabriel, R.M. (2000). Methodological challenges in evaluating community partnerships & coalitions: Still crazy after all these years. *Journal of Community Psychology, 28,* 339–352.

Geller, S., & Lynch, K. (1999). *Teacher opinion survey.* Richmond, VA: Commonwealth University Intellectual Property Foundation and Wingspan, LLC.

Gilliam, W.S. (2005). *Pre-kindergarteners left behind: Expulsion rates in state pre-kindergarten systems.* New Haven, CT: Yale University Child Study Center.

Goode, T. (2004). *Promoting cultural diversity and linguistic competency: Self-assessment checklist for personnel providing services and supports to children with disabilities and special health care needs and their families.* Washington DC: Georgetown University, Center for Child and Human Development.

Goode, T. (2005). *Promoting cultural diversity and linguistic competency: Self-assessment checklist for personnel providing services and supports in early intervention and early childhood settings.* Washington, DC: Georgetown University, Center for Child and Human Development.

Granger, R. (1998). Establishing causality in evaluations of comprehensive community initiatives. In K. Fulbright-Anderson, A.C. Kubisch, & J.P. Connell (Eds.), *New approaches to evaluating community initiatives: Volume 2, Theory, measurement, and analysis* (pp. 221–246). Queenstown, MD: The Aspen Institute.

Green, B., & Everhart, M. (2006). *Multi-level determinants of effective mental health consultation in early childhood settings: Results from a national survey.* Paper presented at the 19th Annual Research Conference on Children's Mental Health, Tampa, FL.

Hernandez, M., & Hodges, S. (2001). Theory-based accountability. In M. Hernandez & S. Hodges (Eds.), *Developing outcome strategies in children's mental health* (pp. 21–40). Baltimore: Paul H. Brookes Publishing Co.

Johnson, K., & Knitzer, J. (2005). *Spending smarter: A funding guide for policymakers and advocates to promote social and emotional health and school readiness.* New York: National Center for Children in Poverty.

Kaufmann, R. (2006). *Early childhood mental health systems of care: A self assessment guide for states and communities.* Washington, DC: Georgetown University, Center for Child and Human Development.

Knitzer, J. (1982). *Unclaimed children: The failure of public responsibility to children and adolescents in need of mental health services.* Washington, DC: Children's Defense Fund.

Kubisch, A.C., Fulbright-Anderson, K., & Connell, J.P. (1998). Evaluating community initiatives: A progress report. In K. Fulbright-Anderson, A.C. Kubisch, & J.P. Connell (Eds.), *New approaches to evaluating community initiatives: Volume 2, Theory, measurement, and analysis* (pp. 1–13). Queenstown, MD: The Aspen Institute.

LeBuffe, P., & Naglieri, J. (1999). The Devereux Early Childhood Assessment (DECA): A measure of within-child protective factors in preschool children. *NHSA Dialog: A Research-to-Practice Journal for the Early Intervention Field,* Vol. 3(1), 75–80.

Manteuffel, B., Stephens, R.L., & Santiago, R. (2002). Overview of the national evaluation of the Comprehensive Community Mental Health Services for Children and Their Families Program and summary of current findings. *Children's Services: Social Policy, Research, and Practice,* 5(1), 3–20.

Merrell, K. (2002). *Preschool and kindergarten behavior scales* (2nd ed.). Austin, TX: PRO-ED.

National Association for the Education of Young Children and the National Associations of Early Childhood Specialists in State Departments of Education. (2003). *Early childhood curriculum, assessment, and program evaluation: Building an effective, accountable system in programs for children birth through age 8.* Washington, DC: Author.

ORC Macro. (nd). *Children's mental health initiative.* Retrieved September 10, 2006, from http://www.orcmacro.com/projects/cmhi/default.aspx

Pandina, N.G., Burchard, J.D., Tighe, T.A., Wise, M., Ursu, K., & Morse, M. (2004). *Children's Upstream Services: Qualitative evaluation report.* Waterbury: Child Adolescent and Family Unit, Vermont Department of Developmental and Mental Health Services.

Provan, K.G., & Milward, H.B. (2001). Do networks really work? A framework for evaluating public-sector organizational networks. *Public Administration Review,* 61, 414–423.

Radloff, L. (1977). The CES-D scale: A self report depression scale for research in the general population. *Applied Psychological Measurement,* 1, 385–401.

Rosenblatt, A. (1998). Assessing the child and family outcomes of systems of care for youth with severe emotional disturbance. In M.H. Epstein, K. Kutash, & A. Duchnowski (Eds.), *Outcomes for children and youth with emotional and behavioral disorders and their families: Programs and evaluation best practices* (pp. 329–362). Austin, TX: PRO-ED.

Rosenblatt, A. (2005). Assessing the child and family outcomes of systems of care for youth with severe emotional disturbance. In M.H. Epstein, K. Kutash, & A. Duchnowski (Eds.), *Outcomes for children and youth with emotional and behavioral disorders and their families: Programs and evaluation best practices* (2nd ed.) (pp. 143–173). Austin, TX: PRO-ED.

Rosenblatt, A., & Woodbridge, M. W. (2003). Deconstructing research on systems of care for youth with EBD: Frameworks for policy research. *Journal of Emotional and Behavioral Disorders, 11*(1), 27–37.

Ruderman, M., & Grason, H. (2004). *Early childhood system building tool*. Baltimore: Johns Hopkins Bloomberg School of Public Health, and Los Angeles: UCLA Center for Healthier Children, Families and Communities.

Shonkoff, J.P., & Phillips, D.A. (Eds.) (2000). *From neurons to neighborhoods: The science of early childhood development*. Washington, DC: National Academies Press.

Sosna, T., & Mastergeorge, A. (2005). *Compendium of screening tools for early childhood social-emotional development*. Sacramento: California Institute of Mental Health.

Springer, J. (2003). *Starting Early Starting Smart final report*. Rockville, MD: Substance Abuse and Mental Health Services Administration.

Squires, J., Bricker, D., & Twombly, E. (2002). *Ages & Stages Questionnaires®: Social-Emotional (ASQ:SE): A parent-completed, child-monitoring system for social-emotional behaviors*. Baltimore: Paul H. Brookes Publishing Co.

State Early Childhood Policy Technical Assistance Network. (2004). *Up and running: A compendium of multi-site early childhood initiatives*. Iowa: Child and Family Policy Center.

Stroul, B.A. (2002). *Systems of care issue brief: A framework for system reform in children's mental health*. Washington, DC: Georgetown University, Child Development Center, National Technical Assistance Center for Children's Mental Health.

Stroul, B.A., & Friedman, R. M. (1986). *A system of care for seriously emotionally disturbed children and youth*. Washington, DC: Georgetown University Child Development Center.

Stroul, B.A., Pires, S.A., Armstrong, M.I., & Zaro, S. (2002). The impact of managed care on systems of care that serve children with serious emotional disturbances and their families. *Children's Services: Social Policy, Research, and Practice, 5*(1), 21–36.

Substance Abuse and Mental Health Services Administration (SAMHSA). (2004). *Comprehensive community mental health services program for children and their families*. Retrieved February 9, 2006, from http://www.mentalhealth.samhsa.gov/publications/allpubs/CA-0013/default.asp

Substance Abuse and Mental Health Services Administration. (2006). *Services evaluation committee, briefing materials: National evaluation of the comprehensive community mental health services program for children and their families*. Rockville, MD: Author.

Taylor-Powell, E., Rossing, B., & Geran, J. (1998). *Evaluating collaboratives: Reaching the potential*. Madison: University of Wisconsin, Program Development and Evaluation, Cooperative Extension.

Weiss, C.H. (1995). Nothing as practical as good theory: Exploring theory-based evaluation for comprehensive community initiatives for children and families. In J.P. Connell, A.C. Kubisch, L.B. Schorr, & C.H. Weiss (Eds.), *New approaches to evaluating community initiatives* (pp. 65–92). Washington, DC: The Aspen Institute.

Wischman, A., Katzes, D., & Kaufmann, R. (2001). *Funding early childhood mental heath services and supports*. Washington, DC: Georgetown University Center for Child and Human Development.

Whyte, W. (1991) *Participatory action research*. Thousand Oaks, CA: Sage Publications.

7

Building Partnerships with Families

Peggy Nikkel

2:00 A.M. The young mom rocks and sings to her 6-month-old son. He continues to cry as he arches his back and pushes away from her. In exhaustion, a single tear slides down her cheek. Another night with little sleep and no relief in sight.

12:30 A.M. The shouting and yelling, combined with intermittent crying has been coming from the bedroom at the end of the hall for more than 45 minutes. The sound of toys and other objects hitting the wall is distinguishable. Dad sits in the living room staring at the blank television screen. This is the fourth night this week. How can a 3-year-old child be so out of control?

10:25 A.M. Pleased that their preschoolers were playing so well together, two young mothers were enjoying engaging conversation and their second cup of coffee when a scream jolted them out of their chairs. They ran to the backyard to find the 4-year-old boy repeatedly beating the 2-year-old girl with a plastic baseball bat. The attack was apparently unprovoked. It will be some time before the little girl and her mom return for a visit.

Sadly, these scenes and countless others are played out daily in the homes of many young children across our country regardless of socioeconomic status, ethnicity, culture, or education. This chapter describes the realities faced by many families of children with serious emotional and behavioral challenges as they seek an early and accurate diagnosis, evidence-based intervention services, family supports in their homes and communities, and a meaningful role in reforming the systems that are providing mental health services to children. In reality, options for early childhood mental health services and supports for families whose children are manifesting problematic behaviors are often very limited. Although many family members voice concerns about their young children prior to their second birthday, they also frequently report the quick dismissal of their concerns by clinicians. Parental blame for a child's problem is pervasive among clinicians and educators. The frustration that families often feel can lead them to become hostile or resistant when working with professionals or to simply withdraw and cease their efforts to find help for their child.

Families also experience frustration while seeking help due to the lack of a coordinated system that includes a full continuum of support and care opportunities for families of young children. In their efforts to access services, families find themselves filling out reams of paper, repeatedly sharing their very personal story, and exhausting their physical strength and financial reserves, but often to no avail. In some states families are required to relinquish custody of their child to access needed services that are otherwise cost prohibitive. Failure to access effective early intervention services can set a family on a course toward increased frustration, stress, isolation, and hopelessness.

This chapter follows the story of my family and our struggle to understand our son's mental illness and navigate the many challenges of finding appropriate care and services for him. I will also share how my family's journey with our son, Jeremy, led me into advocacy work for children's mental health. I share my family's story in an effort to prompt system change and to give hope to other families who are facing similar struggles.

| **Family Voices** |
| Every time we had to go to a new clinician, his or her starting point in helping our son was to find out what was wrong with us as parents. This happened repeatedly, regardless of the fact that we adopted our son as an infant and his biological mom had used alcohol and cocaine during her pregnancy. It would have been easy for us to just give up in our search for appropriate intervention for our son and help for our family. It would have been easy for us to build a wall of defense and withdraw from all those offering help. But, thankfully, we persisted until we found the help we needed. |

Family Voices sections were taken from responses at focus groups about early childhood mental health convened by Peggy Nikkel, Roxane K. Kaufmann, and Deborah F. Perry at the Georgetown Training Institutes in San Francisco in 2004.

One Family's Journey: Jeremy's Early Years

When my husband and I first married in 1977, we wanted a big family. Our first child was cute, intelligent, and very compliant. Of course, we attributed our son's success to our parenting skills. We did not have a clue what was in store for us down the road. Subsequent efforts to have more children were unsuccessful, so we adopted. We picked up our second son, Jeremy, from the hospital when he was just 3 days old. The only information we were given was that his biological mother was 16 years old and had received no prenatal care. Years later we received information that indicated she had actually used alcohol and cocaine during her pregnancy.

As an infant, Jeremy was hard to comfort. At times he would even arch his back and try to push away from me. He struggled with bonding and had horrible sleeping patterns. At 13 months of age he suffered a grand mal seizure that was triggered by a high fever. It lasted 1½ hours, and he was in a coma for 24 hours. At the time, doctors treated it as simply a febrile seizure and did not medicate him. (He had several other episodes of seizure activity between the ages of 3 and 4 years, even though he was medicated for seizures at that time. He stayed on those medications until he was 6 years old and was determined to be seizure free.)

His motor and verbal developments were fairly normal, but we knew things were not right socially and emotionally. As a toddler, Jeremy quickly learned how to climb out of his crib, so we put an accordion gate across his bedroom door. He soon learned how to climb over the gate, and at night, when the rest of the family was trying to sleep, Jeremy would be up screaming and yelling or wandering around the house. At times he would hit his brother to awaken him. One night he climbed over his gate and tried to start a fire in the fireplace like his daddy had done the day before. He unsuccessfully tried to strike a whole box of matches and then fell asleep on the floor in front of the hearth. After this event, we disassembled his crib and contrived a cage of sorts using a bunk bed and the sides from his crib.

> **Family Voices**
>
> We began to seek help for our son's behavior problems before he was a year old, but his behavior was dismissed as "normal." A pediatrician finally agreed to help us when our son was 3 years old. After years of different medications, therapy, hospitalization, and residential care he finally received an accurate diagnosis and effective, lasting treatment when he was 17 years old.

> **Family Voices**
>
> As an infant our son didn't sleep well. He was hard to comfort and even became rigid or pushed away when we tried to comfort him.

This allowed us to keep him and the rest of us safe at night. It did not stop the screaming and yelling, however.

Before Jeremy was 2 years old, we tried to get our pediatrician to consider additional evaluations, but we were told that Jeremy was a normal toddler. I am sure the doctor would have reconsidered his professional opinion if he had to live with Jeremy! When Jeremy was 3 years old, a new pediatrician sent him for his first neurological and mental health evaluation, which consisted of a 2-week stay at an inpatient children's psychiatric hospital. It was extremely difficult to leave him there as the doors locked behind us. We were able to have brief visits, and we also took part in the evaluations and consultations with the doctors. During Jeremy's first few days at the hospital, staff members were questioning why he was there, but then the honeymoon ended. They were amazed to see the level of defiance and violence he displayed at such a young age and began to see what we lived with every day.

■ ■ ■

THE NEED FOR SYSTEMS REFORM

In *Achieving the Promise: Transforming Mental Health Care in America*, the report from The President's New Freedom Commission on Mental Health (2003), evidence of a fragmented mental health delivery system and lack of coordinated individualized care plans (e.g., individualized education program, individualized family service plan, standard treatment plan) are cited as contributing factors in a family's sense of hopelessness. The fragmented service system is extremely complex for families because there are so many different plans. In a fragmented system, families are forced to work with separate caseworkers from multiple agencies and often when their family is in crisis. Few states offer a coordinated care plan or support services that assist families in identifying and receiving necessary services. Many times, clinicians lack the knowledge and skills to work with young children and their caregivers. Finally, there are far fewer evidence-based interventions for this age group.

Several recent findings seem to indicate that the families themselves may hold the key to positive outcomes for these children. When families are given the opportunity to choose their providers and have more control over funds spent on care and supports for their family, they have an increased sense of personal responsibility. Increased choice for families is shown to protect individuals and encourage quality care (The President's New Freedom Commission on Mental Health, 2003). Family members are capable of identifying and meeting their own needs when given appropriate and sufficient information and support. Families also view help as being more beneficial when they are allowed to meet their needs and goals (Dunst, 1993). Conversely, clinicians often do not know what help to offer families of young children. Parents should be recognized as special educators—the true experts on their children. Other professionals should learn to be consultants to the parents (Hobbs, 1982).

Common Values in Early Childhood Mental Health Systems

Consensus is building around a core set of values that should drive reform in the mental health system. These values have also been embraced by other child-serving systems, such as maternal and child health, early intervention, and child welfare. Families need to be actively engaged in planning the array of services that their children need. Intervention planning needs to be conducted from a strengths-based framework that avoids blaming families for their children's mental health problems. A continuum of services and supports must be available so that families have choices about the "who, what, and where." In addition, families should be active participants in designing and evaluating services, policies, and systems. To accomplish this, program managers and policy makers need to implement (and fund) family centered practices that allow family members to enter these discussions as a full partner. All of this requires a commitment to engaging in meaningful parent–professional partnerships with a diverse array of family members.

Families Engaged in Intervention Planning

Early mental health services are most effective when family members are viewed as an important part of the intervention team and given appropriate and adequate supports to care for their children in their home and other early childhood environments within their community. Families of young children need adequate support to strengthen their competencies to promote healthy emotional development in their children. Mental health services to young children and families should be delivered in natural environments that are sensitive to the cultural and ethnic values of each individual family (Kaufmann & Wischmann, 1998).

When services are provided from a strengths-based perspective, families are more inclined to invest their best efforts to cooperate and participate in achievement of intervention goals. Outcomes from the Starting Early Starting Smart (SESS) initiative clearly show that if early childhood mental health services are to achieve maximum success, families must be viewed as full partners. If families are to benefit from services, they need to be actively involved in the planning, implementation, and monitoring of the services being offered. When early childhood service providers value and support family members, they model strategies for parents to value and support their children (Hanson, Deere, Lee, Lewin, & Seval, 2001).

Families will be more responsive to services that are strengths based and uniquely tailored to the needs of their family instead of those that are designed with the one-size-fits-all mentality. Early childhood mental health services have the potential for being as unique and varied as the diverse families raising young children in today's communities.

The *family centered care* approach presents a challenge to clinicians and service providers because it shifts its focus from the deficits of children and families to their strengths. This can be a significant challenge for practitioners who have been trained in the deficit approach of working with families. Meaningful family partnership and participation can change the practitioner's service delivery approach. The family centered care model promotes collaboration and partnership with families as it fosters family decision making and independence. Key supports that communities can provide to support parents and families of young children include expansion of quality child care options, parent education, adequate physical and mental health care, and strong community networks (Carnegie Task Force on Meeting the Needs of Young Children, 1994).

Securing meaningful family involvement in planning, implementation, and evaluation of services will foster important ongoing relationships among agencies, clinicians, and families. Family driven services can only be built when respect among participants is evident at all levels. Building a relationship of respect and trust between clinicians and families takes time to develop, but the investment of time is imperative to achieve positive outcomes for young children and their families. When families are collaborators in all stages of intervention programs, their level of investment and engagement will increase (Hanson, Deere, Lee, Lewin, & Seval, 2001).

Lessons Learned About Family Engagement from Starting Early, Starting Smart

The Starting Early, Starting Smart (SESS) initiative was a collaborative between the Substance Abuse and Mental Health Services Administration and Casey Family Programs to study integrated behavioral health services for young children and their families. Behavioral health services are defined as substance abuse prevention, substance abuse treatment, mental health services, and family services. Bringing these areas together in a service integration approach is the provision of family support, advocacy, and care coordination that addresses medical, educational, and basic needs, as well as coordinating behavioral health and other services for families (Hanson, Deere, Lee, Lewin, & Seval, 2001).

As an integral part of the SESS project, a Family Strengths Institute was conducted to empower families to be effective advocates and remain actively involved in their family's intervention (Casey Family Programs and the U.S. Department of Health and Human Services, 2001). Seven representative families from the project sites were identified to participate with trained parent mentors and the staff of the Federation of Families for Children's Mental Health to form the Family Advisory Council. This council planned the Family Strengths Institute. Through these planning sessions, the following key guide points were identified for effective family involvement that could be used or modified to ensure meaningful family involvement throughout the planning and implementation of early childhood mental health services:

- It is important to incorporate the expertise of family member mentors when engaging family members who do not have the experience of participating in planning processes.
- Family members need to receive child care, transportation, and food allotments before they leave home. In addition, stipends should be offered as a token of appreciation for their time.
- A family member should be assigned the task of preparing and engaging other family members to participate in the planning process.
- Family members need to meet, greet, and relax in an informal environment before the actual meeting begins.
- Take as much time as needed to allow family members to tell their stories in an unrushed manner during introductions.
- Family members respond well to brainstorming sessions. It is the responsibility of the facilitator, however, to synthesize the information and present the result to the family members before continuing with the planning process.
- Family members need to receive information from the institute that will help them with their unique situations.
- Family members need scheduled breaks every 1½ hours to keep them engaged for the entire day's planning process.
- Family members expressed their belief that cultural competence needs to be stressed to give all institute participants, especially professionals, a better understanding of how to value, support, and engage families in all aspects of the SESS program.
- Family members need to be a part of the presentations during the institute. The opportunity to speak and not just be spoken to is very empowering and allows them to express their abilities to all institute participants.
- The committee structure for planning the institute gives family members an opportunity for continued participation without overburdening them with too many tasks.
- A facilitated process that is staffed and scheduled by a contractor is needed to support the ongoing planning process that requires conference calls, mailings, and e-mails.

The Need for A Continuum of Services and Supports

To meet the mental health needs of young children and their caregivers, there must be a range of services and supports available in communities across the country. This continuum needs to include both formal services— those provided by professionals—as well as informal supports, such as parent–parent networks. In *Promising Practices in Early Childhood Mental Health, Systems of Care* (Simpson, Jivanjee, Koroloff, Doerfler, & Garcia, 2001), the combination of family centered supports and services with a high level of family participation in decision making is cited as a key component of an effective early childhood mental health continuum. Site visits to successful early childhood mental health programs in Vermont, Illinois, Kansas, Maine, and Ohio provided specific examples of an array of services that span promotion, prevention, and intervention. Promotion services, such as information on child development, behavior management, and community supports, help with parenting skills. Play groups are available to all families, including those who may have a mental health concern. Prevention services are focused on children in families that may be at greater risk for developing a social-emotional or behavioral disorder, such as those parents with depression or substance abuse. These services might include care coordination, periodic screening and monitoring, or home visits. In addition, effective intervention services that are culturally competent, strengths based, and family centered would also be available to families whose child may be manifesting problematic behavior (e.g., family therapy, play therapy).

Parent–parent support should be available to all families, including those families who have a child with mental health needs. Data from rigorous research are beginning to document what families have known for a long time, which is that this is a highly effective and very valuable service. One-on-one parent support has been shown to have positive outcomes for parents of children with a chronic illness, as well as those with serious mental health issues (Ireys, Chernoff, Stein, DeVet, & Silver, 2001; Silver, Ireys, & Bauman, 1997). Mothers who received emotional and informational support in natural environments from trained parents who had also raised a child with special needs experienced a reduction in anxiety and were better equipped to handle life stressors. Support services included weekly phone calls and occasional social outings.

Parents of children with special emotional and behavioral needs are also finding this type of mutual support from community-based groups across the country. The Federation of Families for Children's Mental Health and members of the Center for Mental Health Services Statewide Family Network Grant communities focus their information, referral, support, and advocacy efforts on families of children with emotional and behavioral needs. Addressing the ongoing mental health needs of young children is often demanding, time consuming, and very stressful for families. The knowledge that they are not facing these challenges alone can bring hope and strength to face another day. Additional studies on the effectiveness of these nonclinical approaches to family support could greatly enhance the acceptance and expansion of these services.

A few programs are beginning to recognize the lack of services focused on siblings within a family of a child with emotional and behavioral challenges. The Simplifying Mental Illness + Life Enhancement Skills (SMILES) program is for children who have a parent or sibling with a mental disorder. SMILES is a 3-day age-appropriate educational program that focuses on increasing the child's knowledge of mental illness and skill development to better function within their family. Skill development is targeted at coping mechanisms, building resilience, problem solving, enhancing self-esteem and self-expression, and decreasing the child's feelings of isolation (Pitman & Matthey, 2004).

> **Family Voices**
>
> When I was growing up I saw how much stress my brother brought to my parents and how he made them unsure of their parenting skills. I didn't know at the time how to talk about it, but I knew that without saying any words and just by being a good kid I could show them they were doing things right and that it wasn't their fault. It got to the point, though, that I couldn't take the pressure of having to be good all the time.

One Family's Journey: The Struggle to Find an Accurate Diagnosis and Community-Based Services

As a result of evaluations conducted when Jeremy was admitted to the children's psychiatric hospital at the age of 3, as well as subsequent evaluations throughout grade school, he was diagnosed with a number of disorders, including reactive attachment disorder, attention-deficit/hyperactivity disorder (ADHD), mild cerebral palsy, central auditory processing disorder, bipolar disorder, oppositional defiant disorder, and cognitive delays leading to learning disabilities. He has experienced numerous medication therapies, as well as behavior management strategies. We have had every kind of star chart and reward system imaginable on our refrigerator. I even kept a daily journal documenting his behaviors as we kept looking for some pattern or a trigger to his behaviors.

When Jeremy was a preschooler, therapists encouraged us to find a preschool or child care environment for him to participate in several days a week to build his social skills. Because we lived in a small community, our options were limited. None of the preschools in town would accept him with his special needs, but we were able to find one private child care facility willing to allow him to enroll for 2–3 half days each week. This child care provider worked with us to implement behavior management techniques consistent with what we were doing at home. Jeremy had great difficulty with any type of social interaction. His tendency was to either withdraw or to become very aggressive; consequently many children were afraid of him or chose to exclude him from activities.

With multiple challenges and an IQ of 86, Jeremy was placed in special education classes beginning in kindergarten. Even though an individualized education program (IEP) was developed and maintained throughout his school experience, teachers struggled to find successful strategies for working with Jeremy.

From age 3 to 9 years, Jeremy experienced about half a dozen inpatient hospital stays lasting from 2 weeks to 3 months. With each of these hospital admissions, my husband and I encountered clinicians who were determined that we had somehow caused Jeremy's problems. Repeatedly facing those accusations was hard on our family and certainly not helpful towards achieving successful outcomes. When Jeremy was 9 years old,

> **Family Voices**
>
> I had both my kids at age 18. They were just 11 months apart. I knew right off that my daughter was not like other children. She regressed, especially after the birth of her brother. She rages and goes after her brother. I chose to have my children, and I love my children. My daughter will not let me love her. She does not make eye contact. She is territorial. It is hard on her brother. I feel bad because I cannot give him the attention he needs. As a teen mom, I get the "look" everywhere I go—the "You are just another statistic" look.

his violence was a daily occurrence, and our family was rapidly disintegrating. We struggled for weeks with the hardest decision of our lives, which was to place Jeremy in residential care. The only facility in our state (Oklahoma) that was willing to take him was located 90 miles away. As difficult as it was, it was a very helpful intervention for all of us. When Jeremy had been out of our home for about 2 weeks, I told his older brother that there was not as much yelling in the house now. He responded, "Mom, Jeremy wasn't the only one yelling." He was so right. We were a very strong, loving family with good parenting skills and strong support from extended family, but we quickly became dysfunctional when faced with Jeremy's daily assaults and our lack of specialized skills to parent him. We had so much more than many families do today, and yet we still could not handle him on our own. Throughout the ordeal our faith in God, supportive extended family

and faith community were all that kept us together and sane.

Jeremy stayed at the residential facility
for 18 months. During that time we traveled
at least twice a week to work with him, his
house parents, and his therapist who specialized in working with adopted children. Jeremy was also able to attend a school that
had a classroom specifically designed for
children with serious emotional disturbances. His teacher was not only trained in
special education, but was also a psychologist. The teacher worked with only six students and an instructional aid. This environ-

> **Family Voices**
>
> When our son needed
> intensive care, there
> was only one residen-
> tial facility in the state
> that would take him.
> He was only 9 years
> old and so violent and
> out of control that he
> was destroying our
> whole family.

ment was ideal for Jeremy. After making significant progress in education,
social, and home living goals, Jeremy returned home with us. That was in
1994 when Jeremy was 11 years old, and it was his last out-of-home placement. Even though Jeremy's behaviors continued to be extremely challenging at times, we had all learned better coping and behavior management
skills as a result of that experience.

Just two months after Jeremy returned to our home, my husband accepted a new job and our family moved to Wyoming. In an effort to help
Jeremy have a positive experience in his new school, we provided the
school with all of Jeremy's records. They, however, wanted to do a new evaluation and develop a new IEP. We felt it was important for his new school
to be aware of his medical, educational, and behavioral history so they
could be prepared, and we also wanted them to continue to support the
positive gains Jeremy had made while in residential care. While recognizing
our son's learning disabilities, the new school determined that my husband
and I had exaggerated Jeremy's emotional and behavioral disorders. Consequently, Jeremy's new IEP included supports for his learning disabilities,
but the school refused to plan adequate supports for his emotional disabilities. It took three years of struggling through failed educational strategies,
multiple suspensions and disciplinary referrals before the school district
would acknowledge that Jeremy's primary disability was an emotional
disability.

Accessing appropriate mental health care in Wyoming was also a challenge. We began work with a child psychologist shortly after our move to
Wyoming, but he was located 150 miles away in Colorado. We determined it
was worth the drive several times each month because the psychologist had
been referred by the successful clinicians who worked with Jeremy in
Oklahoma. After about a year of traveling to Colorado for mental health

care, we were able to transfer to a clinician in Wyoming who lived just 70 miles away. Through the years, Jeremy's mental health care was provided in a clinic, but home and community supports were never offered. From the ages of 11–16 we continued to struggle with different medication therapies and behavior management techniques, but we were able to maintain Jeremy at home. Numerous times his suicidal threats or violence would escalate to the point that we developed an emergency plan with his therapist and increased supervision at home, but we always managed to keep him at home.

When Jeremy was 17 years old, I had the opportunity to attend a training conference in Wyoming that focused on brain development and behavior in children and adolescents. The speakers talked about contributing factors that led to violence. After speaking with one of the conference presenters, I discovered that Jeremy was just the type of child with whom their neurological treatment center worked. Consequently, we planned our family vacation that summer around Jeremy's outpatient evaluation in Austin, Texas, where the facility was located. After 2 days of testing, which included a brain electrical activity mapping (BEAM) scan, neuropsychological testing, and family interviews, Jeremy was diagnosed not only with ADHD, bipolar disorder, and cognitive deficits, but he also had fetal alcohol effects (FAE) and fetal cocaine effects (FCE) accompanied by complex partial seizure disorder of limbic origin. Evidence from the BEAM scan indicated that Jeremy had been having seizures in the limbic region of the brain that can manifest themselves as living on an emotional rollercoaster, with a specific tendency toward violence. The neurologist changed Jeremy's medications and put him on an anticonvulsant. Remarkably, that change allowed Jeremy's emotions to remain stable enough to allow us to really get to know our son. We were able to have discussions without him yelling and throwing things. He was finally able to spontaneously hug us and tell us that he loved us. We were able to begin to heal.

■ ■ ■

Challenges

One of the greatest challenges facing parents of young children with emotional and behavioral disorders is an inescapable societal stigma. Many people in society have a difficult time believing that preschool children could really have disorders that have a severe effect on their behavior. The natural assumption is that the parents must be doing something terribly wrong. Consequently, these families are often dismissed by professionals and excluded and isolated from family gatherings and social events. Shame and blame quickly become the mantle these families wear most often.

Extended family members often fail to understand the true nature of the challenges being faced by their family members who are desperately trying to raise a young child with emotional concerns. They may be quick to judge the parents as lacking adequate skills to discipline the child. Everyone from a grandfather to a cousin has just the right technique or solution for their inadequate parenting skills. In many cases, extended family members begin to distance themselves from the struggling child, compounding the isolation felt by the child's family. Clinicians and other professionals frequently dismiss the parents' concerns as being exaggerated and unrealistic. Many parents would gladly allow these professionals extended time with their children in a more natural environment to better determine the children's needs. Sadly, this type of evaluation and observation seldom occurs. Families are left to their own resources to find help.

The disparity of service provision and insurance coverage for children with emotional and mental health disorders compared with those for other childhood disorders adds tremendously to the stigma and frustration that fami-lies face. A broad array of services is available for children with developmental or physical disorders, but the same is not true for children with emotional and behavioral disorders.

Limited resources are available for early childhood mental health programs and family supports. This resource shortage includes both funding and human resources. This presents numerous challenges when trying to effectively address prevention and early intervention that will truly make a difference for young children and their families.

In most communities, early childhood mental health services are very fragmented or nonexistent. Typically, families are required to seek help from multiple service agencies and professionals. At each separate location, the family is required to complete an extensive medical and family history. Professionals fail to comprehend the emotional drain this causes for parents. Retelling their story is painful no matter how many times it is told. It is very disheartening for parents to make such a personal investment in detailing their family's difficulties only to be dismissed or blamed by professionals.

Many communities around the country are beginning the work to develop integrated systems of care for children's mental health services, but the focus is on older children already diagnosed with serious emotional disturbances (SED). Even family advocacy and support organizations tend to focus their efforts on families of older children and are ill-equipped to support families of young children. Very few states are targeting their system development efforts on early childhood mental health, even though research strongly indicates the effectiveness of prevention and early intervention when treating mental health disorders in children. Vermont,

Colorado, Maryland, Ohio, Florida, Illinois, Kansas, Maine, and Wyoming are some of the states currently addressing early childhood mental health services through a coordinated system of care planning effort. System planning models encourage strong participation and input from family members; however, most families are not able to actively participate in these efforts due to the demands of caring for their children with special needs in addition to other family members. Adequate compensation and support must be provided if families are expected to be active members of system planning efforts.

One Family's Journey: Relating Family Experience to State Systems Reform

My personal experience of raising my son, Jeremy, with multiple emotional, behavioral, and learning disorders led me to become involved in advocacy efforts to reform a state mental health service system with a focus on early childhood. I am convinced that early screening and evaluation accompanied by appropriate services and supports could have drastically diminished the level and duration of crises for our son and our family. When I was in the midst of the crisis with my son, I did not have the time or energy to focus on anyone or anything except the conflict and needs in my own family.

As my son began to stabilize somewhat in his early teens, I had the opportunity to begin work as the executive director of a family advocacy organization called UPLIFT. (UPLIFT is not an acronym; however, the capital letters symbolize the lift they hope to give to families.) UPLIFT is also Wyoming's Federation of Families for Children's Mental Health. I saw my employment with UPLIFT as an opportunity to help make a difference for other families. Having lived in Wyoming for only 3 years when I accepted this position, I began to explore the scope and type of children's mental health services and supports that were available to families in the state. From personal experience with Jeremy, I knew that some of Wyoming's elementary and middle schools were ill equipped to serve the educational and social needs of children with emotional disorders. I also knew that there were very few mental health services and providers who worked with children under the age of 12. Knowing the inadequacy of early childhood mental health services that had been available to Jeremy when we lived in Oklahoma, I began to suspect the same was true for Wyoming.

A review of early childhood services and data in Wyoming in 1997 indicated that no children birth to 5 years had been identified as having an emotional disorder. Although Wyoming had exemplary child find programs and child development centers across the state, the focus was on developmental and physical special needs. Existing child development screeners only included two or three questions relating to the child's social-emotional development in the preschool years. Although there were state-funded programs for children with special health care needs, a child was dropped from the program if the needs were identified as social or emotional. Respite care was not available for families if their child had an emotional or mental health disorder. There was definitely a gap in services!

In my search for strategies to plug this gap in children's mental health services, I discovered a copy of *Lessons from the Field: Head Start Mental Health Strategies to Meet Changing Needs* (Yoshikawa, & Knitzer, 1997). I was excited to read of early childhood programs across the country that were having success in implementing early mental health screening and intervention in community-based programs. Several Head Start programs cited were using the *Early Screening Project (ESP): A Proven Child Find Process.* (Walker, Severson, Feil, 1995). The ESP had some key characteristics that would lend to successful implementation in a state such as Wyoming—low cost and user friendly. (With a total population of just over 500,000 people, Wyoming's population density is just 5 people per square mile. This results in Wyoming's designation as a frontier state which implies unique challenges in the provision of all types of medical services, and especially mental health services.) Dr. Ed Feil from the Oregon Research Institute was listed as one of the developers of the ESP, so I called him and asked about his screening instrument and how he might be able to help us in Wyoming. Dr. Feil was eager to work with us to implement this evidence-based approach in Wyoming.

A search for funding opportunities to enhance community awareness of the need for early childhood mental health screening and intervention led me to submit a grant application from UPLIFT to the Center for Mental Health Services Community Action Grant program. In 1998, our family advocacy organization was awarded a 2-year grant to build community consensus around the need for early screening. Our project included community readiness assessments, community consensus building meetings, ongoing consultation with Dr. Feil, and an evaluation component by the University of Wyoming. During the 2 years of the grant, consensus building meetings were conducted in five regions of the state in addition to training on early screening and intervention for early childhood providers.

Successful implementation of the activities of the Mental Health Services Community Action Grant led to further program development and expansion. Through my work with UPLIFT we were persistent in maintaining family member participation on numerous state councils and committees addressing early childhood development. UPLIFT's message was always the same—do not forget early childhood social and emotional development, and screen and intervene early.

This work led to the development of UPLIFT's Wyoming Early Start Program. Qualified staff members continue to offer screening and intervention training to early childhood care providers. Over the past few years, UPLIFT has been an active partner in a number of new state projects addressing early childhood mental health needs including the At-Risk Preschool Program, Kindergarten Readiness, and the Mental Health Pilot Project.

Other Challenges

A heightened awareness of the need for children's mental health services has uncovered a significant work force shortage, especially in rural and frontier areas (Bird, Dempsey, & Hartley, 2001; Peterson, West, Tanielian, & Pincus, 1998). The need is even greater for providers of early childhood mental health services. This work force shortage contributes to an inability to access early, appropriate services for children whose need is so great.

Another challenge facing families is the struggle over appropriately identifying or labeling their children's mental health needs. Most families interviewed voiced the desire to have access to appropriate, quality services regardless of the label that is given to their children. The struggle over labeling often is generated within the service provider community as an increased measure of liability and cost once an emotional disorder label or diagnosis is given to a young child. Strong opinions are held regarding the adequacy of existing assessments and diagnostic instruments for use with young children.

In addition to the numerous challenges, there is one that many families are unprepared to work through—the death of a dream. Families of young children with emotional and mental health challenges often find themselves facing a sense of grief over unrealized dreams for their child. Most parents anxiously anticipate the birth or adoption of their child, often planning what their future will hold in store. With emotional disabilities comes the realization that many aspects of life will never be "normal" or what the parent had anticipated. Regardless of these challenges, families can begin to envision a hopeful future with the help of understanding and compassionate professionals and family support groups.

KEY PRACTICE RECOMMENDATIONS

In an effort to equip families to better care for their children with mental health disorders, service providers should accept and support the family as a unit. Cornwell and Korteland (1997) recommend a family–professional partnership model to facilitate effective approaches to supporting families in early intervention that includes the following key elements:

- Partnerships should be based on mutual acceptance, respect, and caring.

- Partners should be able to trust each other.

- Partnerships are reciprocal relationships.

- Partnership relationships take time to develop.

- Partners should be open to sharing some of themselves in their relationships.

- Families maintain the final decision-making authority in partnerships.

- Partners should share responsibility for their work together to achieve their goals.

- Partners offer help to families in response to their identified needs and concerns.

- Open and effective communication is needed in partnerships.

- Disagreement and negotiation are allowed in partnerships.

Simeonsson and Bailey (1990) reported that greater parental involvement is believed to have positive consequences for a child. They recommend three approaches to families in early intervention. They are 1) educating parents on how to teach their child; 2) providing information and support to parents to reduce parental stress and depression and increase coping skills; and 3) offering individualized interventions to help parents gain the skills to help the family and the child with disabilities adapt and develop, such as the family empowerment model. The following list highlights the lessons learned about family–professional partnerships from Starting Early Starting Smart's Family Strengths Institute.

The Family Strengths Institute, mentioned earlier in this chapter, was conducted in October 2000 for family participants from the 12 Starting Early Starting Smart grant sites across the country. The purpose of the institute was to learn from the families how to keep families empowered and involved in their child's care. Family participants also learned important advocacy skills to assist them in accessing the most appropriate services for their children:

- A comfort level needs to be established at the onset, that is during the registration process, so that family members and professionals understand that both are necessary for a positive outcome from the institute.

- It is important for family members, especially for those new to these types of meetings, to relax with other family members and gain additional encouragement and information from meeting facilitators before the meeting convenes.

- Professionals need to understand that their presence at the initial family activity would inhibit the empowering and networking processes that are critical to preparing family members for institute participation.

- Family members many times do not have credit cards, so access to hotel phone service and even check-in is difficult. Therefore, prepaid telephone cards and setting up master billing for hotel check-in avoids inconvenience and embarrassment.

- The support of substance abuse meetings during the institute helps family members continue their regimens of sobriety.

- Beginning the day with a demonstration of spirituality prepares institute participants emotionally and mentally for the activities of the day. This also affords an opportunity to demonstrate cultural competence because this demonstration can be expressed through various cultural frameworks.

- Given the opportunity to present on issues and topics other than their personal stories helps to break down the stereotype of family members as just *consumers*.

- Presenters should use a strengths-based approach regardless of topic.

- The response panel format allows family members an opportunity to tell their stories and experiences within a topical framework.

- Presenters should make every effort to convey information in language that everyone can understand and to use visual aids.

- Presenters with a reputation for delivering information in a creative and entertaining way should be sought to participate in the institute.

- Families are supported and served best by professionals who work in a culturally competent way.

- Subjectivity in research is lessened if there is input from and feedback to the persons being researched.

- Working together as a site team jump starts the process of demystifying professionals for family members and helps professionals see family members as more than just consumers. In addition, planning to continue interaction after returning home helps to build the family–professional relationship that ultimately affords better outcomes for the family members and their children.

- Playing and socializing together helps to build relationships other than professional and consumer.

Building effective partnerships with families will only occur when the needs of families are recognized. Regardless of the environment and location of various focus groups and systems planning groups, several themes quickly surface regarding family needs. The most commonly heard is that of respite care. Daily activities can present unique challenges for these families; the simplest of tasks can become a major battle. When the family schedule fluctuates depending on the behavior of a preschooler, family stress and conflict are heightened. Quality child care or respite care providers are seldom available for these families, and this only adds to the pressure and stress. Respite care can defuse a volatile situation in the home and give parents and siblings a much-needed opportunity to be refreshed and renew their strength for the days ahead.

Families also voice a strong desire for practical strategies to assist them in daily care and activities. When families receive adequate support and intervention, they are better equipped to care for their child in their own home without costly out-of-home interventions. Most families interviewed indicated that they were well aware of their child's difficulties before they were able to persuade clinicians to take their concerns seriously and do a full evaluation. Parents are frequently told that their child is too young or just acting like a typical toddler. Practitioners must begin to really listen to the concerns of parents as the first important step in providing more timely diagnosis and intervention.

Universal early screening in a variety of primary care and child care environments will greatly enhance the ability to intervene early and effectively. Screening children for their risk of emotional disorders should be included in other mandatory developmental and physical screenings that occur in early childhood environments.

Even though there is an emergence of evidence-based practices when intervening with families of children struggling with mental health challenges, there are no evidence-based practices for parent support or engaging families in meaningful partnerships for systems planning. Researchers should be encouraged to document the effectiveness of parent–parent support and advocacy being provided by community-based family organizations. There are very limited funding opportunities to support this work and yet families recognize the importance and effectiveness of these activities.

If communities truly desire to build partnerships with families, they must begin to respect family members as equal partners and recognize the wealth of knowledge they can bring to the discussion regarding their child's needs or the needs of a community's system of care. Communities must listen to family members to learn what supports they need so they can be actively involved in their child's care or systems planning efforts. An environment of trust and acceptance must be established to remove the paralyzing stigma of mental health. Then and only then will family members be able to remove the mantle of shame and blame worn for so long, and take up the mantle of hope.

One Family's Journey: Jeremy's Transition to Adulthood

In 2001, Jeremy graduated from high school after 12 years of special education classes. We were so proud of him as he walked across the stage with his graduating classmates. He had achieved what many children struggling with mental health challenges never achieve. After graduation Jeremy enrolled in a technical program at our community college to become a diesel mechanic. Upon successfully completion of the program, he has been able to work as a diesel mechanic for several different companies in the area. Consistent employment is always a challenge for adults with mental illness. Jeremy has been dismissed from almost every job he has had with most jobs lasting only 6–8 months. We have tried to stay as involved in his life as he will let us, but it is also important for him to be independent. As a young adult who is now 23 years old, Jeremy maintains his own housing and is paying for most of his own living expenses. Keeping up with his counseling appointments and medication therapy seems to be an ongoing challenge, however, we have every hope that he will learn to find balance and consistency in this area of his adult life.

Our family experience has taught us how important appropriate, early, and consistent childhood mental health services are for children and their families. We have also learned how vital nontraditional supports and respite care are for these families. There is hope for children struggling with mental illness, but successful outcomes will only be achieved by a group effort as policy makers, clinicians, communities, and families rally around a child to support his or her journey.

REFERENCES

Bird, D.C., Dempsey, P., & Hartley, D. (2001). *Addressing mental health workforce needs in underserved rural areas: Accomplishments and challenges.* Portland: Maine Rural Health Research Center, University of Southern Maine.

Carnegie Task Force on Meeting the Needs of Young Children. (1994, April). *Starting points: Meeting the needs of our youngest children.* New York: Carnegie Corporation.

Casey Family Programs and the U.S. Department of Health and Human Services. (2001). *The Starting Early Starting Smart Family Strengths Institute: A journal of the convening.* Washington, DC: Casey Family Programs and the U.S. Department of Health and Human Services, Substance Abuse and Mental Health Services Administration.

Cornwell, J.R., & Korteland, C. (1997). The family as a system and a context for early intervention. In S.K. Thurman, J.R. Cornwell, & S.R. Gottwald (Eds.), *Contexts of early intervention: Systems and settings* (pp. 93–109). Baltimore: Paul H. Brookes Publishing Co.

Dunst, C.J. (1993). Implications of risk and opportunity factors for assessment and intervention practices. *Topics in Early Childhood Special Education.* 13(2), (pp. 145-146).

Hanson, L., Deere, D., Lee, C., Lewin, A., & Seval, C. (2001). *Key principles in providing integrated behavioral health services for young children and their families: The Starting Early Starting Smart experience.* Washington, DC: Casey Family Programs and the U.S. Department of Health and Human Services, Substance Abuse and Mental Health Services Administration.

Hobbs, N. (1982). *The troubled and troubling child: Reeducation in mental health, education, and human services programs for children and youth.* San Francisco: Jossey-Bass.

Ireys, H.T., Chernoff, R., Stein, R., DeVet, K.A., & Silver, E.J. (2001). Outcomes of community based family-to-family support: Lessons learned from a decade of randomized trials. *Children's Services: Social Policy, Research and Practice, 4*(4), 203–216.

Kaufmann, R., & Wischmann, A. (1998). Communities supporting the mental health of young children and their families. In R. N. Roberts & P.R. Magrab (Eds.), *Where children live: Solutions for serving children and their families: Vol. 17; Advances in applied developmental psychology* (pp. 175-210). Stamford, CT: Ablex.

Peterson, B., West, J., Tanielian, T., & Pincus, H. (1998). Mental health practitioners and trainees. In R. Anderschied & M. Henderson (Eds.), *Mental Health United States 1998* (pp. 214–246). Rockville, MD: Substance Abuse and Mental Health Services Administration.

Pitman, E., & Matthey, S. (2004). The SMILES program: A group program for children with mentally ill parents or siblings. *American Journal of Orthopsychiatry, 74*(3), 383–388.

The President's New Freedom Commission on Mental Health. (2003). *Achieving the promise: Transforming mental health care in America (final report).* (DHHS Publication No. SMA 03-3832). Washington, DC: U.S. Government Printing Office.

Silver, E.J., Ireys, H.T., & Bauman, L.J. (1997). Psychological outcomes of a support intervention in mothers of children with ongoing health conditions: The parent-to-parent network. *Journal of Community Psychology, 25*(3), 249–264.

Simeonsson, J., & Bailey, D.B. (1990). Family dimensions in early intervention. In J. Shonkoff & S. Meisels (Eds.), *Handbook of early childhood intervention* (pp. 428–444). New York: Cambridge University Press.

Simpson, J.S., Jivanjee, P., Koroloff, N., Doerfler, A., & Garcia, M. (2001). *Promising practices in early childhood mental health, systems of care: Promising practices in children's mental health, Volume III.* Washington, DC: Center for Effective Collaboration and Practice, American Institutes for Research.

Walker, H.M., Severson, H.H., Feil, E.G. (1995). *The early screening project: A proven child-find process.* Longmont, CO: Sopris West.

Yoshikawa, H., & Knitzer, J. (1997). *Lessons from the field: Head start mental health strategies to meet changing needs.* New York: National Center for Children in Poverty.

8

Vermont's Children's UPstream Project

Statewide Early Childhood Mental Health Services and Supports

Brenda J. Bean, Charles A. Biss, and Kathy S. Hepburn

One Child's Story

Ray entered the Children's UPstream Services (CUPS) program when he was 3 years old and in one of the best preschools in the state. The preschool had never expelled anyone for behavior incidents, but Ray was on the verge of being the first. He was punching and hitting children and staff, and he had broken a staff member's nose. The preschool director called the CUPS worker, who met with Ray, his mother, the director, and the classroom teacher. They developed a plan that included consultation with the mother and teacher, coordination with the pediatrician, a behavioral assessment, a one-on-one classroom aid, and in-classroom and at-home strategies to support Ray.

One classroom strategy was a *feeling board* that allowed Ray to identify a face that expressed his emotion at the time and place it in an agreed-on place in the room. This "game" became so popular in the class that all the children wanted a feeling board, which resulted in the activity becoming part of the preschool curriculum.

Ray, his mother, teacher, and pediatrician met regularly with the CUPS worker to discuss Ray's progress. Each team member was supportive of the other and of Ray, and his behavior began to improve.

When the time came to enroll Ray in kindergarten, his team met with the elementary school and presented a detailed plan of care. The school said that it was unable to implement such a detailed and expensive plan.

The team then decided to keep Ray in the preschool for another year so that he could maintain and solidify his improved behavior. When he entered public school in first grade Ray had an Individualized Education Plan (IEP) to help teachers address his special needs within the classroom and with his family. He progressed so well that he no longer needed an IEP, only a special accommodations plan for second grade. By the end of second grade, Ray was continuing to improve his behavior and was reading on grade level, excellent predictors of future success.

As a result of collaboration among his preschool and mental health team, the trajectory of Ray's life changed dramatically. Ray will probably need little if any special education services, will most likely graduate from high school, and will become a successful taxpaying citizen. Without this early intervention, Ray's personal outcomes would most likely have been poor and the cost to society of these poor outcomes potentially extensive. This true story speaks volumes about the impact that early childhood mental health services can have on individual children and their families and the value of building and implementing a system of care.

The State of Vermont has been at the forefront of establishing ongoing, statewide services and supports to promote and intervene with early childhood mental health. It is the only state that has successfully built a statewide system of mental health services and supports that is integrated into the early childhood system, through a program known as CUPS. Interest, timing, and opportunity contributed to the initiation of this effort, and statewide strategic planning and the development of infrastructure contributed to its establishment and continued success. This chapter describes the development of CUPS. It begins with the context and then describes the details of building an infrastructure to support and sustain this system of care, which was initially largely funded through a grant from the federal Substance Abuse and Mental Health Services Administration (SAMHSA). Findings from a rigorous outcome evaluation are presented, and one region's experience at the local level is discussed.

THE START OF CUPS

The interest in planning for early childhood mental health services and support in Vermont grew from two major observations. One was from Vermont parents of 20- to 23-year-old children who were involved in mental health services for their children and families and who were engaged in the state's chapter of The Federation of Families for Children's

Mental Health (the Federation), a family advocacy group. During a broad discussion about children's mental health services, a question was asked about when the parents first knew something was wrong with their son or daughter. The parents replied with such answers as in utero, the first day, as a toddler, or when he or she entered preschool. They expressed frustration that their children and families only received significant help once their children were 12 or 13 years old; had performed poorly in school or been suspended; and the families had suffered stress, lost work due to absenteeism, and experienced financial ruin. Out of this discussion grew interest in exploring the mental health issues and concerns for very young children.

The Vermont Agency of Human Services (AHS) initiated its first statewide survey of kindergarten teachers, which led to the second observation. This survey showed that at least 26% of the state's young children at the time of kindergarten entry lacked the social-emotional and other skills to succeed in school. At the same time, anecdotal reports of children exhibiting increasingly disturbing behaviors were emerging from the early childhood community.

The convergence of these two key observations and the timing of increased national focus on the importance of early childhood social-emotional development and school readiness spurred the state's interest in early childhood mental health. Vermont's subsequent needs assessment positioned the state well for any grant opportunity that would allow development of mental health services and supports for young children and their families.

A suitable grant opportunity presented itself in the form of available funding from the federal Children's Mental Health Services (CMHS) division of SAMHSA. Vermont used the data it had already gathered to apply for a *Services Initiative* grant, available from CMHS/SAMHSA, with the purpose of creating a system of care for children who are experiencing severe emotional disturbance and their families. Vermont's application was the first to link the system of care for children's mental health with the early childhood field to address early childhood mental health.

Vermont's grant, $5.7 million for 5 years (later extended to 7 years—from September 1997 to August 2004), was awarded to the former Vermont State Department of Developmental and Mental Health Services (now the Division of Mental Health in the Department of Health). The grant-funded program was called Children's UPstream Services (CUPS) to reflect the intent for early intervention. The name is derived from an old story about people rescuing children one by one from a river until someone wisely goes upstream to investigate why the children are in the river and to prevent them from falling or being thrown into it in the first place. Before CUPS, most of Vermont's children's mental health services were devoted to keeping children who were *in the river* from being washed over a *waterfall of crises.*

With this new grant, Vermont could begin to work *upstream* and focus efforts on early intervention with young children ages birth-to-6 years and their families. Every year since its inception in 1997, CUPS enrolls and serves 500–600 new families with young children. As a result of its success, CUPS received continuation funding from the Vermont legislature beginning in state fiscal year 2005. It is now administered by the Child Development Division of the Department for Children and Families in the newly reorganized AHS.

THE BUILDING BLOCKS OF INFRASTRUCTURE

Although the concept, values, and principles of systems of care for children and adolescents with serious emotional disturbances and their families came forward as early as 1986 (Stroul & Friedman, 1996), the application of systems of care ideas to early childhood mental health is a more recent development. In her work to address the unique features of systems of care for young children and their families, Roxane Kaufmann has identified the *building blocks* of infrastructure needed to create and maintain early childhood mental health services and supports (Kaufmann, 2003, 2005; Kaufmann & Wischmann, 1999). The rest of the story of CUPS and its development addresses each of the following building blocks, which are discussed individually in this chapter:

- Strategic planning
- Interagency partnerships
- Maximized and flexible funding
- Prepared work force
- Outcome evaluation

Strategic Planning

Strategic planning for CUPS began at the state level, clarifying the vision for early childhood mental health services and supports, and then shifted to the regional level for identifying local needs, resources, and strategies for creating the capacity to fund, administer, and deliver services and supports. The process for strategic planning involved the following three key structures or entities: 1) a Task Force on Mental Health Needs of Young Children and Their Families, 2) the State Outreach Team, and 3) each region's Community Partnership.

Before submitting the grant application for CUPS in 1997, Vermont had already formed a Task Force on Mental Health Needs of Young Children and Their Families as a passionate continuation of the initial discussions among mental health, family, and early childhood community representatives. The Task Force was chaired by the director of the Child, Adolescent and Family Unit of Vermont's Division of Mental Health and by the executive director of the Vermont Federation of Families for Children's Mental Health.

The Task Force conducted a survey of early childhood providers to learn what they considered the top mental health issues and needs of the children and families they served. This survey helped the Task Force to better understand and develop an agenda related to the social-emotional development of young children and early childhood mental health. The results of this survey indicated that the predominant mental health issues that early childhood providers encountered among young children were physical, sexual, and/or emotional abuse; neglect; depression; aggression; unspecified behavior, emotional, and learning problems; attention-deficit/hyperactivity disorder (ADHD); attachment disorders; and developmental disabilities, including autism. The predominant mental health issues that early childhood providers encountered among the parents of young children were depression, substance abuse, domestic violence, posttraumatic stress disorder or other effects of prior abuse, lack of parenting skills or understanding, stress (especially from poverty), anxiety, and grief from loss. These widespread concerns contributed to the position statement of the Task Force on the Mental Health Needs of Young Children and Their Families (Santarcangelo & Mikkelsen, 1997). They informed the Task Force's vision, agenda, and action plan for a full continuum of integrated early childhood services, including those supporting social-emotional development, physical health, mental health, and strong family functioning throughout Vermont.

The Task Force's action plan became the basis for the CUPS grant application. The CUPS project application to CMHS/SAMHSA proposed to support and preserve families of young children experiencing or at risk for experiencing severe emotional disturbance by ensuring access to behavioral health and other community-based services designed to meet their individual needs and build on their strengths. The Vermont Department of Developmental and Mental Health Services planned to provide behavioral health intervention and consultation for the early childhood system of care and for families with young children ages birth-to-6 years. The grant would support and strengthen local interagency partnerships, services, and care coordination. Using grant funding, Vermont would expand key services aimed at strengthening the behavioral health of young families and decreasing the incidence of children entering kindergarten without the emotional and social skills necessary for being active learners in school. Key statewide services would include crisis outreach, intensive home-based services, respite care, intensive case management, and individualized or wrap-around services and related training. The local expansion of services for these families and young children would include parenting education and support, family literacy, home–preschool coordination, and mental health consultation services to both families and early care and education providers (Cohen & Kaufmann, 2000; Hepburn & Kaufmann, 2006).

Immediately after the grant was awarded, the director of the Child, Adolescent and Family Unit of Vermont's Division of Mental Health repeatedly invited key stakeholders to come together to implement the grant, determine how to carry out the action plan, and develop strategies for sustaining services beyond the grant-funded period. The key stakeholders included representatives from family organizations and state departments, such as Mental Health, the Head Start State Collaboration Office, the Child Care Division, Part C, Special Supplemental Nutrition Program for Women, Infants, and Children (WIC), child welfare, Temporary Aid to Needy Families (TANF) and the Department of Education (especially Part B), that had interests in young children and families as well as funding that could support this new focus. This group ultimately became the State Outreach Team that worked to garner broad support and moved to implement the proposed plan.

Convening this team helped to build *state-level*, cross-system partnerships and bring together those service systems that could be affected or that could bring resources to CUPS. The strategic planning work of the State Outreach Team concluded that strong *local* partnerships and a collaborative plan for local implementation could best address early childhood mental health services. They believed that local communities would be inspired to engage in planning, forge strong partnerships, and design and support local services if grant funds could be made readily available. Therefore, the State Outreach Team, with an accompanying letter of support from the deputy secretary of AHS, issued an *Invitation to Communities* (Mitchell, 1998) to undertake a planning process in each of the 12 human services districts in Vermont.

The *Invitation to Communities* recommended that the local planning process be steered by a Community Partnership that would identify important local outcomes, priority needs and services, and a regional management team; recommend a budget and fiscal agent; and address participation in outcome evaluation. The Community Partnership was to appoint a steering committee to be composed of family members, early care and education community representatives, mental health services providers, primary (health) care providers, special education providers, domestic safety representatives, and substance abuse prevention and treatment service providers, as well as others invested in young children and their families. Each plan was to address the desired outcomes of supporting and preserving families with young children; strengthening the behavioral health of families with young children; and increasing the incidence of children entering kindergarten with the emotional and social skills necessary to be active learners in school. Other than the regional planning process and the grant's evaluation requirements to be implemented at the state level (see "Outcome Evaluation" later in this chapter), few additional parameters were imposed on the Community Partnerships or the eventual local service providers to carry out their local plan for CUPS. The resulting plans from the 12 regional teams became the basis for CUPS services and supports in each region. Regional CUPS services plans generally included outreach, information, and referral; interagency training and technical assistance; early childhood mental health consultation; and direct intervention services, such as the following:

- Crisis outreach

- Observations, assessments, and referrals

- Case management, service coordination, and collaborative intervention planning

- Intensive home-based services

- Respite care

- Intensive child care services

Interagency Partnerships

Interagency partnerships, at both state and local levels, are key to building a system of care and were essential to building widespread support for CUPS before and after the grant award. In Vermont, the forging of these interagency partnerships involved cross-organizational and thus cross-cultural conversations, facilitation by experts, collaborative strategic planning, and shared training experiences. As described in the preceding Strategic Planning section, two important structures for facilitating and forging these partnerships were the State Outreach Team and the regional steering committees (often based in emerging Early Childhood Councils of the 12 Community Partnerships).

To ensure widespread support for CUPS and set the stage for interagency partnerships, the Division of Mental Health invited national experts Jane Knitzer (National Center for Children in Poverty, Columbia University) and Roxane K. Kaufmann (National Technical Assistance Center for Children's Mental Health, Georgetown University) to meet with key stakeholders from mental health, health, and early care and education immediately after the announcement of the grant award. These stakeholders, from both the state and local levels across Vermont, were unaccustomed to working together and were unfamiliar with each other's fields of knowledge and terminology. The national experts counseled that CUPS could not be successful if it was imposed by mental health on the early care and education field; it could be successful only if mental health expertise comes to be valued and sought by early care and education providers. Likewise, they stressed that this would most likely occur if all parties maintained awareness that early childhood mental health is inherently cross-disciplinary and therefore a *cross-cultural* phenomenon requiring sensitivity about varying realms of knowledge and education, expectations, use of language, work environments, rates of pay, and so forth. This initial meeting set the stage for all future CUPS planning and implementation activities, reinforced the importance of cross-system and interagency partnerships, and led the Division of Mental Health to contract with a Continuous Learning Consultant (described further in the Prepared Work Force section of this chapter) to attend to bringing together the different cultures of mental health and early care and education to facilitate the cultural exchange process.

The State Outreach Team modeled the interagency and interdisciplinary partnerships intended for the regional planning efforts and functioned to provide oversight and on-site technical assistance to the CUPS regional teams for the remainder of the federal grant. The Early Childhood Councils, or regionally organized groups of early care and education providers and early childhood services agencies, were simultaneously being supported and formalized through the combined efforts of Success by Six coordinators (who were engaged in different school readiness initiatives) and the State Team for Children and Families (with its Early Childhood Steering Committee's focus on unifying early care and education systems). Both the State Outreach Team and the Early Childhood Councils had many opportunities to model, build, and refine the local interagency partnerships that could support and sustain responsive and effective early childhood mental health (and other) services.

The State Outreach Team's contribution to and use of the *Invitation to Communities* to kick-off a regional planning process for CUPS sanctioned and reinforced the local partnerships required for a collaborative response to the Invitation with a regional proposal for funding. In support of these partnerships, CUPS planning funds were made available for consultation and facilitation so that the regional groups would have assistance in forging their partnerships and achieving consensus around their plans. The State Outreach Team also modeled new ways of partnering and doing business. In addition to their more formal strategies, they took their "show" on the road and traveled together across the state to meet with each regional steering committee to respond to policy and funding questions concerning early childhood mental health. By traveling together and co-training together, the State Outreach Team members formed their own new relationships and problem-solving strategies related to state issues. Also, by reporting regularly to the State Team for Children and Families and to its Early Childhood Steering Committee, they extended their reach to many family representatives and middle managers with state and/or regional governance responsibilities. This investment in building partnerships and achieving local consensus has held up over the years as these interdisciplinary, interagency groups developed strong and lasting partnerships to become the core of Vermont's strong network of Early Childhood Councils and Community Partnerships.

The Early Childhood Councils learned from existing relationships and partnerships among early childhood serving agencies the importance of early childhood mental health concerns. The councils used the support of the State Outreach Team and the grant opportunity for expanded services to address social-emotional and behavioral health for young children, to build new partnerships, and to further their efforts to integrate all early childhood services.

In combination, the State Outreach Team and the Early Childhood Councils linked two functioning systems and promoted partnerships that designed and delivered accessible and effective mental health services to young children and families. These new partnerships, their shared experiences, and the widening circles of people with knowledge about CUPS and its positive outcomes helped to ensure the shared interest and popular support needed to ultimately obtain new funding to continue the services beyond the end of the federal grant.

Maximized and Flexible Funding

Maximized and flexible funding enables communities and agencies to collaborate more fully and creatively. To support the creative planning in the 12 regions, the State Outreach Team encouraged communities to stretch the federal CMHS/SAMHSA grant funds and to rethink, restructure, and refinance existing services. In particular, the State Outreach Team encouraged the regions to maximize Medicaid by understanding different program and service requirements and utilizing this funding stream through a variety of agencies. These three strategies (federal funding, redirecting existing funding, and maximizing Medicaid) made up the fiscal infrastructure or building block for CUPS in Vermont.

The director of the Child, Adolescent and Family Unit of the Division of Mental Health and the regional children's mental health directors knew that the CUPS services had to be designed and delivered in a way that could be funded by Medicaid to ensure sustainability after the end of the grant. At the beginning of the regional planning process for CUPS, the director of the Child, Adolescent and Family Unit challenged each region to "think big" and develop a plan that could make use of the federal grant funds plus an equal amount of Medicaid. The challenge was heightened by the fact that the state could not offer the necessary match for Medicaid, so each region had to identify its own match through interagency sharing of State General Fund dollars already allocated to the region.

Within each region, some community agencies were accustomed to using and maximizing Medicaid and others were not. For mental health services providers, Medicaid was a familiar source of funding as virtually all the mental health services in Vermont are funded by Medicaid (children in households up to 300% of the federal poverty level are eligible for Medicaid in Vermont, as are other individuals based on income and/or disability). The early care and education providers, however, had limited knowledge of Medicaid and were reluctant to participate in the diagnostic and paperwork requirements associated with this funding source. As the relationships and trust grew stronger over time, both at the state and regional levels, funding strategies and agreements grew.

The mental health and early care and education providers formed early childhood mental health agreements that maximized both the use of Medicaid and the use of state general funds that had not previously been matched. In these types of agreements, the State General Funds came mostly from school and parent–child center budgets. The organizations (with agreement from the respective state departments that were actually the source of the match) entered into contracts with their regional mental health center to deliver services to children enrolled in Medicaid, as well as to serve other children. The regions with Medicaid agreements were able to charge their direct intervention costs for CUPS to fee-for-service Medicaid rather than to the grant, which freed up the grant funds to pay for more preventive activities, such as training and mental health consultation.

Those who chose to add Medicaid to the grant funds to further grow their services had to follow Medicaid rules. The process of forming and implementing these agreements between community mental health agencies and early care and education providers (and their respective state partners) helped the providers become more informed about and comfortable with Medicaid and its many federal and state rules. Another major development was the adoption of a policy by the Division of Mental Health to pay for services for children through age 6 whose diagnosis is given as a parent–child relationship disorder (a V code in the *Diagnostic and Statistical Manual of Mental Disorders [DSM]*). Although the Division of Mental Health had refused in the past to pay for mental health intervention for people whose primary diagnosis was a V code, the division's new policy made the use of Medicaid more palatable to early care and education providers.

Greater sharing of State General Funds for matching Medicaid contributed to the expansion of direct and indirect services to meet the needs of young children experiencing or at risk for serious emotional disturbance. This expansion included more mental health services on-site at child care centers (e.g., consultation, one-on-one social support from community integrationists); in pediatric practices (e.g., targeted case management, therapies from clinicians, psychiatric consultation); and in the community (e.g., more in-home and community crisis services). Table 8.1 provides numerous examples of the expanded services.

Prepared Work Force

As the 12 regional CUPS teams organized and began to develop plans for new and enhanced services for young children and their families, two work force issues became clear. First, there were few people who had the skills in both early childhood development and mental health to fill positions as early childhood mental health clinicians. Second, many people who already worked with families and young children (e.g., child care providers, early childhood educators, health care providers, child protection workers) could benefit from learning more about the evolving field of early childhood mental health. Similar to most states across the country, Vermont's mental health work force was limited in its capacity to address early childhood mental health. Unlike most states, Vermont had a new grant and could make work force development a priority to address these specific concerns.

Two major steps for putting infrastructure in place included 1) creating two key roles and positions—the CUPS Continuous Learning Consultant and the CUPS Training and Technical Assistance Coordinator; and 2) hosting a 2-day retreat to develop Vermont's Plan for CUPS Learning Opportunities.

By establishing the Consultant and Coordinator positions, CUPS provided leadership for work force development. Both positions were very influential in facilitating, designing, and implementing Vermont's plan for CUPS Learning Opportunities and building each region's capacity to deliver CUPS services. The success of their work was based on the incumbents' capacity to champion for and coach others in early childhood mental health, their knowledge and experience from the fields of mental health and early care and education, their keen sense of organizational development, and their skills and experience in training and technical assistance. Both positions supported the involvement of diverse audiences (parents, mental health and child care providers, advocates, and so forth)

Table 8.1. Examples of expanded services

Mental health consultation services

Available to nearly 20% of the child care centers across the state (T. Tighe, personal communication, February 2005)

Includes regular on-site and available on-call outreach services to support child care workers in both center-based and home-based environments through observations, individual child and programmatic recommendations, and reflective supervision

Includes consultation about individual concerns to parents or other primary caregivers of children who are not enrolled in a mental health treatment. Consultants gather information, discuss ways to support the child at home, and make any necessary referrals for direct intervention services

Consultation may also be about the mental health concerns of child care centers beyond application to only one child

Provided by qualified (although not necessarily licensed) mental health staff contractors

Reimbursed through administrative Medicaid

Pediatric primary care collaboration services

Currently in place in five pediatric practices across the state

Includes outreach services to children and families, including screening, assessment, case coordination, some therapies, referral services, and psychiatric consultation to primary care practitioners regarding social-emotional development, intervention, and best practice

Provided by full-time, licensed mental health clinicians housed in the primary care office, who are employed by the mental health agency, which contracts with the primary care practice, and reimbursed for services by fee-for-service and Early Periodic Screening, Diagnosis, and Treatment (EPSDT) outreach funds

Board-certified child psychiatrist available for on-site consultation for the practice (minimum of 1 hour per week), who are contracted by the primary care practice and reimbursed by the department of health using Medicaid EPSDT outreach funds

Crisis and/or respite services

Available in all 12 regions across Vermont on a daily 24-hour basis for children and families who need immediate response for crisis stabilization

Individualized and flexible home and community supports to stabilize the crisis, including crisis counseling; respite services (e.g., through home aides, immediate child care, overnight care in specialized foster homes); a crisis plan developed and coordinated with and by the family that includes specific contacts and strategies (e.g., notification of kin, use of other community resources, supports in place to help avert or address future crises)

Provided by a well-trained team of qualified mental health professionals, paraprofessionals, and a child psychiatrist able to clinically assess a complex situation for safety and stabilization and address the need for ongoing services and supports

Funded generally with Medicaid fee-for-service and EPSDT outreach funds with State General Fund dollars from the Division of Mental Health and the Department for Children and Families

in work force development, with participants learning from national and in-state experts about early childhood mental health for young children and families.

The 2-day retreat in the fall of 1998 that resulted in Vermont's Plan for CUPS Learning Opportunities was convened under the leadership of both the CUPS Continuous Learning Consultant and the CUPS Training and Technical Assistance Coordinator. Fifty family members and providers from early care and education, health, mental health, and other fields across the state identified and explored specific learning needs related to early childhood mental health and systems change. All agreed there was a need to describe the knowledge and skills that individuals involved with the social-emotional development of infants, young children, and their families should possess and practice and the essential value of interdisciplinary perspectives and expertise.

In addition to the Learning Opportunities Plan, the retreat process led to the creation of two key resources: 1) the Learning Team, and 2) the Family Consortium. The Learning Team (a group of university or agency-affiliated trainers and educators) and the Family Consortium (a group of advocacy or family organization affiliated parents or other family members) provided ongoing training and work force development for CUPS. These groups worked together, with administrative support from the University of Vermont, which was contracted to carry out the work related to training and work force development.

The Learning Team guided the training and technical assistance work outlined in the CUPS Learning Opportunities Plan and addressed such areas as the identification of competencies for promoting and intervening with early childhood mental health. Once identified, the competencies were available for guiding individual and group professional development. Other Learning Team activities include sponsoring reflective supervision (with peer consultation and mentoring) opportunities and inservice events to meet specific needs of regions and statewide priorities. To carry out this work, the Division of Mental Health awarded a grant to the University of Vermont for the position of the Training and Technical Assistance Coordinator and for the CUPS Learning Team, including the Continuous Learning Consultant as chair of the Learning Team. The Learning Team included members from higher education, early childhood, and family mental health fields, which ensured interdisciplinary perspectives and expertise.

The Family Consortium, an association of representatives from statewide family organizations (Vermont Federation of Families for Children's Mental Health, Vermont Parent Information Center, Parent to Parent of Vermont, and others), advised the learning team to ensure the inclusion of activities that build capacity for support, advocacy, and involvement for families. Thus, family advocates were included in group reflective systems and sessions with CUPS workers. The Family Consortium also had control over some of the Learning Team budget and used these funds, in combination with other grant funds, to award mini grants to strengthen the capacity of regions for family support, involvement (including in governance), and advocacy.

In tandem, the Learning Team and the Family Consortium guided the work force development plan and efforts. Each member of the Learning Team and the Family Consortium assumed responsibility for or par-

Table 8.2. Sample work force development products and activities

Key publications

Knowledge and Practices to Promote the Emotional and Social Development of Young Children (Moroz, 2001), a self-assessment tool for individuals and teams

Finding Help for Young Children with Social-Emotional-Behavioral Challenges and Their Families: The Vermont Children's Upstream Services (CUPS) Handbook (Lezak, 2004), a service access guide

Training events

To increase the awareness and skills about early childhood mental health of families, direct services workers, and administrators for a variety of organizations and fields

To focus on foundational issues, such as the importance of parent–child and parent–provider relationships

To explore how to intervene with difficult situations, such as domestic violence, substance abuse, and parental depression

Staff development services

Reflective supervision for frontline workers, including parent advocates

Scholarships for individuals to attend out-of-state conferences

Subgrants for regions to hold training events of local importance

---

ticipated in one or more of the team's products and activities completed throughout the duration of the grant. Table 8.2 provides samples of work force development products and activities.

The CUPS Plan for Learning Opportunities and the activities and products of the Learning Team and Family Consortium benefited CUPS workers and early childhood mental health services as documented in the report *CUPS Documentation Project: Experiences of Providers and Consumers of Early Childhood Mental Health Services in Vermont* (Sullivan, Moroz, Baker, & Bean, 2005). In this report, CUPS workers (services providers) and child care providers and family members (consumers) describe their experience delivering and receiving CUPS services. Themes identified by this small study are the principles and best practices that CUPS workers demonstrated, delivering both direct and indirect early childhood mental health services. Some of the practices are shown in Table 8.3.

Continuous training and technical assistance efforts can help bridge gaps created by staff turnover in the mental health and early care and education work force, keep the existing work force current with the knowledge and evidence base, and offer support to avoid burnout. Although the training and technical assistance activities ended when the federal grant funds ended, the need for work force development remains. Based on CUPS, and with help from additional small grants from the IDEA Partnership, Vermont continues to promote the use of core competencies and reflective supervision to prepare and support providers to deliver early childhood and family mental health intervention. Vermont's Child Development Division has redesigned its professional development activities to include early childhood mental health consultants and other early interventionists.

Table 8.3. Sample best practices demonstrated by Children's UPstream project workers

Knowledge of child development

Knowledge of child development to understand child behavior

Skills to observe the child and family to understand the child's behavior and family interaction

Service coordination

Linking families with needed services

Facilitating the coordination of services

Working with families

Offering access, comfort, and crisis support in a trusted relationship

Utilizing a family-centered approach involving respect for diversity, careful listening, being responsive to family concerns, and partnering with families in problem solving

Integrating families into their communities

Meeting in the everyday environment of the family and child

Weaving a network of support for families through parent groups

Using parent groups to help families become involved in community activities

Working with child care providers

Offering support and technical assistance to child care providers

Adopting a consumer-centered approach in their work with child care providers, similar to work with families, such as listening, valuing, and collaborating

Facilitating communication between child care providers and families

Adapted from Sullivan, M., Moroz, K., Baker, P., & Bean, B. (2005). *CUPS documentation project: Experiences of providers and consumers of early childhood mental health services in Vermont.* Waterbury: Vermont State Department of Health, Division of Mental Health; adapted with permission.

Outcome Evaluation

Evaluation data is useful for assessing program or intervention effectiveness as well as for addressing issues related to sustainability, such as advocating for a program, justifying program continuation, and seeking ongoing funding. Effective outcome evaluation requires specific structures and processes to identify data points, gather data, complete data analysis, and generate reports. Vermont CUPS participated in the national evaluation associated with the CMHS/SAMHSA federal grant and in-state and locally defined evaluation activities.

The federal CMHS requires all Services Initiative grantees to participate in a standard evaluation about the process and outcomes of each grant. Thus, CUPS had specific evaluation requirements as part of the grant award. Macro International, contracted by CMHS/SAMHSA, gathered child and family data from grantees and conducted annual on-site interviews about system issues. At the state level, evaluation activities included operationally defining and deciding how to measure progress toward the desired outcomes and indicators for CUPS that were not specific to individual children and families, gathering the data, and analyzing the data from each region and statewide. At the regional level, each region collected any data they wanted that was separate from the federal or state requirements for the evaluation.

To carry out the state evaluation, the Child, Adolescent and Family unit of Vermont's Division of Mental Health contracted with the University of Vermont psychology department to conduct the CUPS evaluation using a CUPS Evaluation Team. The professors and their students on the CUPS Evaluation Team helped the 12 regions to enroll families in the evaluation and to obtain the necessary interviews with a sample of the parents served by CUPS. Extensive 1-year follow-up data was reported for more than 130 families statewide (Burchard, Tighe, & Pandina, 2003). Regional reports were delivered to regions with more than 20 people in the follow-up. Also, the CUPS Evaluation Team produced a qualitative report exploring differences between matched families that had improved versus those that had not improved after receiving 6 months of CUPS services (Pandina et al., 2004). Some of these families were later interviewed and videotaped in a production of *Parents Speak Up! Help for Young Children's Social and Emotional Challenges* about early childhood mental health, which was aired over cable television stations in Vermont (Pandina, 2003). The evaluation data and the testimony of parents indicated that CUPS services were helpful for nearly all children and families; those with more complex difficulties sometimes needed serves for more than 6 months before experiencing improvement. The following are examples of recipients of CUPS services (Sullivan et al., 2005):

Families who are struggling with their children's behavior problems or with depression and isolation

Children with significant mental health needs

Families that have special needs not met by other agencies

Families and providers that need help recognizing and responding to the mental health needs of young children

A decrease in children's emotional problems

A reduction of parental stress

An increase in parents' satisfaction with their children's progress

Both the Evaluation Team Data and the Documentation Report of the Learning Team confirm that CUPS provides essential services and supports. Table 8.4 highlights findings from the report.

Unfortunately, the evaluation activities ended when the federal grant funds ended. The data, however, still exists, and Vermont would like to use it as the basis for longitudinal research about the effects of early childhood mental health services on children's readiness for school. Meanwhile, the MACRO evaluation helped to establish that families who receive direct in-

Table 8.4. Additional findings from the *CUPS Documentation Project*

Evidence of positive changes in children

Children were happier and more involved with parents.

Children were less aggressive.

Evidence of positive changes for families

Parents gained an understanding of how to parent their child.

Parents felt better about themselves and their family's future.

Some parents wanted to reach out to other families with similar struggles.

Increased support and strength in marital partnerships.

Evidence of positive change in the larger system

Reduction in child and family involvement as consumers of mandated services.

Agencies serving young children and their families understand the mental health needs of young children and their families.

Key: CUPS = Children's UPstream project. (Adapted from Sullivan, M., Moroz, K., Baker, P., & Bean, B. [2005]. *CUPS documentation project: Experiences of providers and consumers of early childhood mental health services in Vermont.* Waterbury: Vermont State Department of Health, Division of Mental Health; adapted with permission.)

tervention through national CMHS Services Initiative grants do experience positive outcomes. Also, the data and powerful testimony from local communities documented the value and effectiveness of CUPS consultation, training, and direct services, which resulted in continuation funding from the Vermont legislature.

One Region's Story: Washington County, Vermont

The early childhood mental health system of care in Washington County, Vermont has grown out of an active, ongoing strategic planning process and community vision to better serve vulnerable children and families. In the mid-1990s, the regional Family Services Collaborating Council, which is a group of school superintendents, and the directors of the local social welfare, child protection, public health, mental health, parent–child center, youth advocacy agency, and community action council came together to plan for a system of prevention and early intervention for young children and their families. As a result of that planning effort, the group obtained a legislative appropriation to develop Success By Six services in the county. The mental health services in the plan became known as the *Success by Six Therapeutic Outreach Project.* This project joined together the local parent–child center (The Family Center of Washington County) with the community mental health center (Washington County Mental Health Services) to better serve families with children ages birth to 6 years at-risk for social-emotional disturbance through a home visiting therapeutic outreach model. The project was one of two in Vermont that pre-existed and inspired the statewide development of CUPS.

Then, in response to the 1998 state of Vermont, AHS Invitation to Communities to apply for federal grant monies through CUPS, Washington County initiated local strategic planning by gathering input from a broad spectrum of community members through a broadly distributed community needs survey and an evening community forum. The results prompted a proposed plan for direct, in-home therapeutic and consultation services to children ages birth-to-6 years who are experiencing behavior and emotional challenges and/or to parents with mental health challenges. In addition, CUPS would provide service planning and coordination for families with young children; training opportunities for parents and child care providers; and behavioral consultation in child care, school, and, eventually, health environments.

Washington County continued to build a continuum of services for its system of care through committed, stable, and knowledgeable leadership in key regional and state early childhood and mental health agencies and through its creative approach to maximizing opportunities to design and deliver early childhood mental health services. These efforts included integrating, merging, and creating new services as described here:

- Forming a partnership among CUPS staff, the Central Vermont Medical Center, and the Vermont department of health to provide therapeutic services to postpartum women identified in the hospital or at WIC clinics.
- Collaborating with the Central Vermont Community Response team, a multidisciplinary empanelled team in Washington County to provide outreach and community-based intervention, services planning, coordination, and support for pregnant women and mothers with co-occurring substance abuse and mental health disorders and their children.
- Forming the Child Care Outreach Project (CCOP) by merging the CUPS consultation services of Washington County Mental Health Services with the Family Center of Washington County's Resource and Referral program to increase capacity for consultation services and reduce the number of children dismissed from child care due to challenging behaviors. CCOP offers consultation, mentoring, and wrap-around services to the family–provider team and short-term direct support to maintain the child's placement.
- Developing the New Leaf Family Child Care Center, an integrated full-day, full-year child care program offering therapeutic and psycho-educational services to children birth to 5 years of age (and their families) who are at risk of developing mental illness due to actual or potential dismissals from child care or placements in protective services. The project, funded by the state of Vermont Child Care Services Division and the Division of Mental Health, collaborates with a number of community staff from the State Department for Children and Families (child welfare and child protection), Central Vermont Home Health and Hospice, Head Start, Associates in Pediatrics, and Early Essential Education (Part B) programs to ensure that children and families facing the greatest risks are receiving high-quality child care and family support.

- Concurrently developing the Central Vermont Collaborative for Children with Autism Spectrum Disorders, established by Washington County Mental Health Services in conjunction with each of the school districts in Washington County, to provide empirically based intensive direct services in public schools, child care centers (including New Leaf), and family homes, as well as staff and/or parent training for young children with autism spectrum disorders.

(D'Haene & Curtis, personal communication, February, 2005)

CONCLUSION

This story of Vermont's CUPS and the building blocks of its infrastructure conveys the developmental history of the state's system of care, a now well-organized, modestly funded system of early childhood mental health services for young children in each of the 12 regions across the state. A close look at individual features and evidence of change and maturation in one region, Washington County, illustrates how CUPS supplemented several already successful services and led to the availability of expanded mental health services for young children and their families.

The developmental story of Vermont's CUPS and statewide system of care also leads to the most powerful lessons learned by them. Serving children where they are and where they already receive other services (e.g., child care, health care, in home, community) increases access to care and support for families and providers. Services must include direct therapeutic intervention but must also be complemented by mental health consultation and family and provider education to effectively meet the needs of young children and families. By using the SAMHSA/CMHS grant as seed money, strengthening the building blocks for systems of care infrastructure, and expanding mental health services in these ways, Vermont has been able to continue the CUPS program fully supported by a combination of state general funds, fee-for-service income, and administrative Medicaid dollars to do the right thing for young children and families in Vermont.

REFERENCES

Burchard, J., Tighe, T., & Pandina, N. (December, 2003). *Children's UPstream Services outcome report.* Waterbury: Vermont State Department of Developmental and Mental Health Services and University of Vermont.

Cohen, E., & Kaufmann, R. (April, 2000). *Early childhood mental health consultation.* Rockville, MD: Center for Mental Health Services, Substance Abuse and Mental Health Services Administration.

Hepburn, K., & Kaufmann, R. (2006). *Early childhood mental health consultation: A training guide for the early childhood services community.* Rockville, MD: Center for Mental Health Services in the Federal Substance Abuse and Mental Health Services Administration.

Kaufmann, R. (2003). *Early childhood mental health in a system of care.* Paper presented at The Georgetown Early Childhood Mental Health Academy, Baltimore, MD.

Kaufmann, R. (2005). *Early childhood mental health in a system of care.* Retrieved January 20, 2006, from http://gucchd.georgetown.edu/programs/ta_center/topics/early_childhood.html

Kaufmann, R., & Wischmann, A.L. (1999). Communities supporting the mental health of young children and their families. In R.N. Roberts & P.R. Magrab (Eds.), *Where children live: Solutions for serving young children and their families. Advances in Applied Developmental Psychology, 17.* Stamford, CT: Ablex Publishing.

Lezak, A. (Ed.). (March, 2004). *Finding help for young children with social-emotional-behavioral challenges and their families: The Vermont Children's Upstream Services (CUPS) handbook.* Waterbury: Vermont State Department of Developmental and Mental Health Services.

Mitchell, C. (January, 1998). *An invitation to promote Children's UPstream Services (CUPS).* Waterbury: Vermont State Department of Developmental and Mental Health Services.

Moroz, K. (January, 2001). *Knowledge and practices to promote the emotional and social development of young children.* Waterbury: Vermont State Department of Developmental and Mental Health Services.

Pandina, N. (December, 2003). *Parents speak up! Help for young children's social and emotional challenges* [video]. Waterbury: Vermont State Department of Developmental and Mental Health Services.

Pandina, N., Burchard, J., Tighe, T., Wise, M., Ursu, K., & Morse, M. (March 2004). *Children's Upstream Services qualitative evaluation report.* Waterbury: Vermont State Department of Developmental and Mental Health Services.

Pires, S.A. (2002). *Building systems of care: A primer.* Washington, DC: Georgetown University Center for Child and Human Development.

Santarcangelo, S., & Mikkelsen, K. (September, 1997). *Prevention and early intervention: Vermont's necessary next steps.* Position statement of the Task Force on the Mental Health Needs of Young Children and Their Families. Montpelier: Vermont State Department of Education.

Stroul, B., & Friedman, R. (1996). *A system of care for children and youth with severe emotional disturbances (rev. ed.).* Washington, DC: Georgetown University Child Development Center, National Technical Assistance Center for Children's Mental Health.

Sullivan, M., Moroz, K., Baker, P., & Bean, B. (March, 2005). *CUPS documentation project: Experiences of providers and consumers of early childhood mental health services in Vermont.* Waterbury: Vermont State Department of Health, Division of Mental Health.

9

Early Childhood Mental Health in Cuyahoga County, Ohio

Melissa Manos, Sally Farwell, and Jeffrey D. Rosenbaum

■ ■ ■

For nothing is fixed, forever and forever and forever, it is not
fixed; the earth is always shifting, the light is always changing, the sea does not cease to grind down rock. Generations
do not cease to be born, and we are responsible to them because we are the only witnesses they have. The sea rises, the
light fails, lovers cling to each other, and children cling to
us. The moment we cease to hold each other, the sea
engulfs us and the light goes out.
(J. Baldwin, 1998, p. 706)

YOUNG CHILDREN IN CUYAHOGA COUNTY

Cleveland, the largest city in Cuyahoga County, Ohio, is one of the poorest
large cities in America. It was officially considered as such in 2004, but child-
serving agencies in Cuyahoga County had suspected the truth long before
that. For years, young children in this community have been increasingly
subject to the most intractable problems associated with child poverty—
abuse, neglect, and witnesses to violence. Cuyahoga County has also experienced locally what a recent study at Yale University's Edward Zigler Center
for Child Development and Social Policy has documented nationally—an
increase in the number of very young children being suspended or removed
from child care and Head Start programs (Gilliam, 2005).

Cuyahoga County's family serving agencies, neighborhood centers,
and governmental supports have had some success in combating the effects

of endemic poverty among its youngest children. A strong history of public–private partnerships, a county government open to supportive family services and prevention strategies, and a philanthropic commitment to the community have put the county in the forefront for new initiatives. Since 1999, a communitywide, public–private partnership to mobilize resources and energy to ensure the well-being of the county's youngest children has been under way. The vision of this initiative was to provide a seamless system of services to parents and caregivers and to build awareness and advocacy for young children's issues. This chapter documents the development of a coordinated system of services and supports focused on the needs of young children and their families that have evolved since the late 1990s.

BUILDING AN EARLY CHILDHOOD SYSTEM: HISTORY OF CUYAHOGA COUNTY'S INVEST IN CHILDREN INITIATIVE

In 1999, inspired by research showing the importance of brain development during the first 5 years of life, 23 private foundations and corporations joined with county government to begin the work of developing a network of family focused services that would address the needs of children from birth through age 5. Table 9.1 lists the foundations and corporations that formed this partnership committee. These community leaders and providers, working together, launched a countywide program, known as Early Childhood Initiative (ECI), and strategic plan for early childhood that is centered on three goals: 1) effective parenting, 2) healthy children, and 3) quality child care.

This was the beginning of a comprehensive and integrated network of services for young children in Cuyahoga County—bringing to the table for the first time representatives of health, family serving, and child care providers with private and public funding. ECI reached out to families at birth and offered home visits, enrollment in health insurance, home-based child care options, and information about the importance of the early years of life. Families who received services from one part of this network were easily linked to other relevant services. The philosophy of *no wrong door* for families seeking services took on real meaning. More than 80 public and private provider agencies in the community were now connected in a more unified, comprehensive manner.

In the initiative's first 3 years, 83,000 children were reached by the services under its umbrella. An evaluation of the first 3 years of implementation found that more children in the county received services at younger ages and with greater continuity of care than before the initiative was implemented. Powerful baseline data collected demonstrated increases in a number of key measures, including the number of newborn home visits (from 0 in 1998 to 5,916 in 2005); the number of children served in ongoing home visiting

Table 9.1. Cuyahoga County Early Childhood Initiative Partners: The Partnership Committee, Cuyahoga County, Ohio

The Abington Foundation	Florence Crittendon Services Fund	The Billie Howland Steffee Family Fund
The Eva L. and Joseph M. Bruening Foundation	Hershey Foundation	The Treu-Mart Fund
Charitable Foundation	Initiatives in Urban Education Foundation	The TRW Foundation
The Cleveland Clearing House Association	Mount Sinai Health Care Foundation	Verizon Foundation
The Cleveland Foundation	The Reinburger Foundation	The Raymond John Wean Foundation
The George W. Codrington Charitable Foundation	Saint Ann Foundation	The Thomas H. White Foundation
Deaconess Community Foundation	Saint Luke's Foundation	The Woodruff Foundation
Eaton Corporation	The Sherwick Fund	United Way Services

Adapted from Cuyahoga County Early Childhood Initiative. (2002). Retrieved April 3, 2006, from http://www.researchforum.org/project_printable_302.html; adapted with permission.

services (from 1,118 in 1998 to 6,209 in 2005); and the number of children served in special needs child care (from 0 in 1998 to 847 in 2005). Since 1999, almost 70% of the children born in Cuyahoga County have received one or more of the services that are part of the initiative. The number of children who are at risk or have special needs that were identified during their first 6 months of life doubled, and more than 4,000 children with developmental delays and disabilities were linked to early intervention services. Fully 98% of children under the age of 6 years were enrolled in health insurance.

Similar to any new initiative, the effort has changed and evolved. In October 2003, the board of county commissioners, the philanthropic community, parents, and hundreds of representatives of the community's public and private sectors planned for the second phase of the initiative. Now called Invest In Children, a new strategic 5-year plan recommended the continuation of the network of services while proposing to increase its comprehensiveness. The goals of Invest In Children were amended to include effective parents and families, safe and healthy children, children prepared for school, and a community committed to children.

From the beginning of this countywide early childhood strategic planning,

> We began to look at interceding in children's lives in a way that this community hadn't done before. In fact, there were people who didn't believe that infants could have emotional problems.
>
> *(G. Avis, personal communication)*

there was growing concern about the gap in early childhood mental health (ECMH) services in Cuyahoga County. Leaders working in child care and early intervention shared their concern about the prevalence of social-emotional problems among very young children, which for some manifested themselves in expulsion from child care and preschool. Community leaders also had a broader concern. With more than 42% of the county's young children living in families under 200% of the federal poverty level, many children in the county are particularly vulnerable to the social-emotional difficulties associated with poverty. Leaders estimated that almost 9,000 children ages birth-to-5 years are in need of mental health services, which is approximately 10% of the population of children this age. These concerns propelled the desire to explore strategies to ensure young children would have access to quality mental health services (Safford, Mahoney, & Espe-Sherwindt, 2003).

CUYAHOGA COUNTY'S EARLY CHILDHOOD MENTAL HEALTH MOVEMENT

Cuyahoga County's ECMH movement preceded and then merged with ECI, now called Invest In Children. Simi-lar to many states and communities, building a system of care often involves parallel beginnings in similar or related service systems. In Cuyahoga County, the early childhood mental health movement and the pilot projects represented collaboration between early intervention and mental health; both were related and complementary to the work of ECI (Safford, 2001) and later became embedded in Invest In Children's strategic plan. Table 9.2 provides a timeline of ECMH activities and ECI development.

First Steps (1997–2001)

To begin to address the emerging concern and awareness of the need for early childhood mental health services, members of the community involved in the local early intervention collaborating group, along with child care providers, explored three strategies focused on determining best practices for the delivery of early childhood mental health services. These early strategies included Day Care Plus, the Individualized Family Service Plan (IFSP) Pilot, and the establishment of an ECMH committee. These strategies raised community awareness, harnessed the concerns of the community, and offered valuable early insight into the issues of early childhood mental health. Eventually they evolved into a more comprehensive approach to mental health services and became an integral part of the 2003 Invest In Children's strategic plan.

The first strategy that helped to address the delivery of mental health services was Day Care Plus. In January 1997, the Cuyahoga County

Table 9.2. Cuyahoga County Timeline for Early Childhood Mental Health (ECMH) activities and Early Childhood Initiative (ECI) development

January 1997	Day Care Plus (Cuyahoga County Mental Health Board, Starting Point, and Positive Education Program)
June 1997	Individualized Family Service Plan Pilot (Ohio Department of Health, Ohio Department of Mental Health, Cuyahoga County Community Mental Health Board, Help Me Grow)
January 1998	Initial planning for the ECI (Cuyahoga County Commissioners, Cuyahoga County Family and Children First Council)
March 1998	Early Childhood Advisory Committee formed
December 1998	Help Me Grow Collaborative's ECMH committee established
May 1999	Funding for ECI finalized
June 1999	ECI launched with more than 50 agencies and 3-year project with more than $40 million
July 1999	ECI in full scale operation serving children born in 2000
January 2001	ECMH pilot in three agencies (United Way's Success by Six, Cuyahoga County Mental Health Board)
January 2003	ECI strategic planning focus on ECMH Project Tapestry; federal grant received
May 2004	ECMH pilot expansion to six agencies (ECI and Ohio Department of Mental Health); Voices for Children Advocacy effort
Late 2004	ECI renamed Invest In Children

Community Mental Health Board, Starting Point for Child Care and Early Education (a child care resource and referral organization), and Positive Education Program (a large nonprofit service provider agency) came together as partners to improve the social, behavioral, and emotional functioning of at-risk children in child care. Through Day Care Plus, early childhood mental health consultation services and staff training are offered to child care providers who are experiencing concerns about a child's behavior. In addition, intervention programs for parents are available. Day Care Plus ultimately inspired a statewide pilot program based on this consultative model, and it continues to be a significant service offered by Positive Education Program. Now funded through the Cuyahoga County Community Mental Health Board and Invest In Children, Day Care Plus paved the way for additional ECMH service providers in the county.

The IFSP Pilot, which began 6 months after Day Care Plus, focused on incorporating mental health requirements into the IFSP. Through Part C of the Individuals with Disabilities Education Improvement Act (2004), a family whose child is eligible for early intervention services has an IFSP that outlines outcomes and services for the family. Yet, if a child is receiving intervention from a mental health provider, the child must also have an intervention plan for those mental health services. Having several plans for an individual child and his or her family who is involved with several systems can be confusing and challenging.

Through collaboration with the Ohio Department of Health, the Ohio Department of Mental Health, the Cuyahoga County Community Mental Health Board, and the local early intervention collaborative group (now known as Help Me Grow Cuyahoga County), community stakeholders sought to use the IFSP as the sole intervention plan for children birth to 3 years, incorporating mental health services. Evaluation of the IFSP Pilot proved this strategy was a turning point; that is, it illustrated that different state agency regulations governing Medicaid services for mental health and early intervention services were often in conflict with one another and presented barriers to providing care at the local level. It also revealed that families do not want all of their providers to know the details of the mental health services that they are receiving. As a result of the pilot and at the request of the families, mental health agencies did not use the IFSP to document specific mental health services due to the stigma of including them on the IFSP. In addition to this valuable lesson learned, the IFSP Pilot increased awareness of the need to include social-emotional delays in determining eligibility for Part C early intervention services.

At the end of 1998, county stakeholders convened a planning committee focused on building an early childhood mental health system. This planning committee, known as The Early Childhood Mental Health Committee, could share best practices, identify service gaps, and serve as a forum for current research and new knowledge. In addition, the committee could help to identify funding sources. The logical coordinating body for the ECMH committee was the local early intervention collaborating group, now known as the Help Me Grow Collaborative of Cuyahoga County. Help Me Grow is a statewide program for parents, newborns, and toddlers that provides developmental services, family support, and education that includes newborn home visits, ongoing in-home parent education, and early intervention services. The Help Me Grow Collaborative, which comprises early childhood providers, families, and advocates, is the county planning body committed to ensuring a comprehensive, family centered system for children prenatal to 3 years old.

Once established, the ECMH committee began its work by developing a position paper on early childhood mental health, offering training for child-serving and mental health professionals and providing outreach to community officials, physicians, and early childhood professionals on the importance of early childhood mental health services. In addition, the ECMH committee began to address long-range needs for early childhood mental health services, including establishing guiding principles, identifying service delivery components, and gathering best practices from other communities and states. The guiding principles that were established are as follows (Center on Urban Poverty and Social Change, 2005):

- Interventions that begin earlier in a child's life are more likely to produce positive results.

- Prevention is more effective and less costly than intervention.

- Program models should be research based, drawing on evidence and best practices.

This work led to an opportunity to train clinicians in the *Diagnostic Classification of Mental Health and Developmental Disorders of Infancy and Early Childhood* (DC:0–3). Other early projects of the ECMH committee included a survey to assess early childhood mental health needs and a forum convening Cuyahoga County leaders to examine promising early childhood mental health practices in other states to inform the continued work of the committee. One of the most influential efforts of the committee was the process of regularly convening leaders and clinicians from across the community to meet and discuss the need for early childhood mental health services. This provided energy and passion for the issue. With the evolving early childhood initiative, children could now be identified for services at many different access points. The ECMH committee provided the foundation that ensured early childhood mental health services expanded across the county.

These early strategies (Day Care Plus, IFSP Pilot, Early Childhood Mental Health Committee) provided the momentum to encourage local leaders and county officials to take further initiative to expand early childhood mental health services. In 2001, with encouragement from the ECMH committee, United Way of Greater Cleveland designated young children's social-emotional needs as a major funding priority. The United Way partnered with The Cleveland Foundation and the Ohio Department of Mental Health's Early Childhood Mental Health Initiative (through the Cuyahoga County Mental Health Board) to begin a new countywide pilot focused on expanding services for early childhood mental health. The ECMH Pilot would

- Continue to evaluate the types of mental health services the community's young children needed

- Establish an infrastructure of early childhood mental health service providers

- Develop public and private funding streams to support the services

- Advocate for local and state policy that would support early childhood mental health.

Initially, three private, nonprofit agencies were awarded funding to provide direct mental health services to children and their families. In May 2004, additional private and public funding through Invest In Children and the Ohio Department of Mental Health expanded these services to three more private, nonprofit agencies. All six providers address early childhood mental health issues in a transactional, family systems context, with particular attention to the relationship between the very young child and his or her primary caregiver. Five of the programs are home based and one is center based. The approaches and intervention options of each provider agency's early childhood mental health program vary, providing choices for families as they seek support. The majority of the personnel delivering these services are independently licensed mental health clinicians.

Early Childhood Mental Health Services Agencies in Cuyahoga County

Beech Brook

Beech Brook's model of therapy is a short-term, home-based, 90-day intervention designed to help the child and caregiver get back on track. The therapy involves intensive home-based visits and continuous telephone contact that helps parents and caregivers learn and implement parenting practices that foster healthier attachment and improved learning in preschool by reducing various behavioral issues.

Applewood Centers

Applewood Centers' home-based model of therapy typically lasts 6 months and emphasizes psychotherapy and emotional support for the caregiver, play therapy with the child, and coaching for the parent to provide developmental guidance to the child. Many of the children referred to Applewood Centers are experiencing traumatic stress syndrome because they have witnessed violence, often against their mothers.

Positive Education Program

The Positive Education Program (PEP) model of intervention is primarily center based, incorporating peer activities for both children and parents or caregivers. It emphasizes the participation of trained parents and professional staff in the intervention program. The program seeks to improve the ability of the child to participate in family functions, typical group environments, and ultimately in school.

The Achievement Centers for Children

The Achievement Centers for Children provide relationship based counseling to families with young children who are experiencing difficulties in their social-emotional development, as well as to children who are cared for by a family member who is experiencing emotional difficulties that affect parenting. The Achievement Centers for Children specialize in providing comprehensive, coordinated services to children experiencing delays in multiple domains of development.

Bellfaire Jewish Children's Bureau

Bellfaire Jewish Children's Bureau provides services to families with an infant or toddler who is experiencing a problem with social-emotional development, especially due to trauma, separation, loss, medical concerns, developmental, and sensory or neurological conditions. The program provides a comprehensive assessment and in-home intervention services for 3–4 hours per week for 3–6 months.

Berea Children's Home and Family Services

Berea Children's Home and Family Services model of prevention typically lasts 6 months. The model focuses on the parent as the *agent of change* while it works to improve or create a home environment suitable for addressing attachment and emotional regulation issues. This model strives to improve the young child's ability to regulate emotions and to support the parents in developing and improving a nurturing relationship with their infant or toddler.

CHILDREN AND FAMILIES IN EARLY CHILDHOOD MENTAL HEALTH INTERVENTION

Although the six agency programs offer a range of intervention options, clinicians in every program see children presenting with similar behaviors. Even though acting out or externalizing behaviors are sometimes considered to be the most common indicator of a need for early childhood mental health treatment, some children manifest internalizing behaviors, including social withdrawal, depressive features, self-defeating or self-harming behaviors, detachment, and loss of previously attained developmental milestones. The early childhood mental health services have reached a variety of children with social-emotional concerns, as well as a substantial number of children who have been victims of physical abuse, sexual abuse, and emotional abuse and neglect. The following is a list of common concerns presenting for ECMH intervention:

- Children with difficult behavior in foster care and child care

- Parents with mental health needs affecting the parent–child relationship

- Children exhibiting aggressive behaviors, excessive tantrums, night-mares, and anxiety

Who are the children and families seeking intervention? These fol-lowing three stories provide an illustration of the children and families who are receiving services in the early childhood mental health programs in Cuyahoga County. The anecdotes describe the child and family inter-vention as well as a snapshot of successful early childhood mental health services.

An Overwhelmed Mother

Feeling overwhelmed was a not a new experience for Mary—money was al-ways tight and she had separated from John, her children's father. In spite of all of this, Mary felt that she was a good mother. Things, however, were not going well with the baby, John, Jr. He was born by emergency cesarean section, and they were apart for 5 days before she finally was able to take him home. He was not as chubby or as easy to feed as his big sister, and soon he was losing weight and diagnosed with failure to thrive by his doc-tor. John, Jr. was hospitalized, and the Department of Child and Family Ser-vices (DCFS) (the county child welfare system) became involved. In learn-ing to care for John, Jr. at home, Mary had to learn to manage a feeding tube and a stream of people coming to her home to help. She began to doubt her abilities to help her son and became depressed and resentful. She was sure that the DCFS would take the baby from her, and she saw no way to stop it.

A referral was made by the hospital social worker to the Help Me Grow central intake and referral site. At the site, Mary met Joyce, a mental health social worker at the Achievement Centers for Children. Joyce understood the resentment and fear Mary was experiencing and became a partner to not only Mary, but also to baby John's father. Joyce provided supportive counseling in both of their homes, at the hospital, and with the rehabilitation therapist involved with baby John's care. Joyce also maintained communica-tion about the parents' progress with the DCFS caseworker. In her work with each of the parents, Joyce provided a safe emotional environment for Mary to explore and repair the disconnection that occurred during the early months with John, Jr., while also inviting the father to develop a more sus-taining role in his son's life.

The family, with Joyce's support, allowed themselves to make changes they had not let themselves consider before, such as deciding to have baby John move to his father's home where his complicated feeding schedule could be better managed. Mary, relieved of the pressure of the baby's feed-ing regimen, now focused on other aspects of nurturing her son in her work with Joyce. John, Jr. is now a thriving toddler with regular visits between his two homes where both parents have developed respect for the unique role each parent is contributing to their son's life.

A Family's Success Story

David was referred to Beech Brook when he was 2 years old and having difficulty in his foster home where he was showing developmental delays and aggressive behavior. During that time, he was having weekly visits with his biological family as part of the DCFS family service plan and goal to reunify him with his family.

After the initial assessment, the Beech Brook therapist established intervention goals of decreasing David's aggression and assisting his foster parents with managing his anger and destructive behaviors. Intervention sessions took place at three locations—the family visit center; the foster home; and, eventually, at the home of his biological parents.

David was sad and angry that he had been taken out of his parents' home, and he expressed it in the only way that he could—through aggressive behavior. The therapist assisted the foster family in dealing with his feelings and making him feel safe and secure. The therapist also offered to help David's biological parents to learn how to relate to him as a 2-year-old child (e.g., playing on the floor with him) and giving him firm limits and boundaries. This also included helping David's biological mother learn to better manage David's anger. As David started to have longer visits with his biological parents, his aggressive behaviors began to diminish.

Throughout intervention, the foster family, the biological family, and David did well. David and his mother developed a stronger bond, which was very helpful as reunification occurred. The therapist was able to see David in various environments and was able to observe how his behaviors and moods changed over time and as living arrangements changed. At the end of intervention, the therapist determined that David did not have any lasting developmental delays and that his anger and sadness at being removed from his biological family had temporarily interfered with his achieving normal developmental milestones.

Literally Climbing the Walls

Susan had always wanted to be a mother, but she and her husband were unable to conceive a child and decided to adopt. Their first adopted son adapted beautifully to his new home and eventually to preschool. Their second son, Sam, however, presented a new set of parenting challenges. Susan recalls that even as a toddler, he was "literally climbing the walls." Their family life became stressful and difficult, especially after the joyful surprise of the birth of their daughter. Their attentions were now stretched among an infant, a typically developing son, and a son with special needs.

> In child care across the country, issues surfaced over the past few years around children with challenging behaviors. Many of them are expelled from child care programs because providers feel that they cannot manage the child's behavior or that the child becomes a threat to himself or herself or to the other children in the center.
>
> *(B. Osborne-Fears, personal communication)*

After Sam was asked to leave several preschools, Susan was referred to the Positive Education Program's Day Care Plus Program. Sam was evaluated and diagnosed with learning and behavior disorders. Therapists were able to work with him in both therapeutic and child care environments, as well as providing the family with information, intervention, and strategies to help stabilize their relationships and family life. As a result of the intervention, Sam is an elementary school student performing at grade level in a mainstream public school and has overcome his behavior challenges that once threatened to disrupt his life with his family and at school.

■ ■ ■

EARLY CHILDHOOD MENTAL HEALTH PILOT EVALUATION

As Cuyahoga County implemented the early childhood mental health pilot initiative, there was a need for a comprehensive independent evaluation. The purpose of the evaluation was to provide

> evidence of the efficacy of mental health services in the context of early intervention, and of the comparative efficacy of the alternative service delivery models, provided to young children with diverse social-emotional developmental needs. (Safford et al. 2003, p. 39)

Children who received services would be less stressed, cope better, have fewer problems, have better relationships with their parents, and catch up emotionally if necessary. Expected family outcomes could include (Safford et al., 2003, p. 40) the following:

- Stabilizing children's home environments by alleviating stressors where possible and enhancing the coping abilities of children and their caregivers

- Enhancing parenting skills and the ability of parents and caregivers to use personal resources and external, as well as internal, supports effectively

- Fostering positive and satisfying caregiver–child relationships and constructive caregiver–child interactions

- Relieving children's presenting symptoms that interfere with positive social-emotional development

- Helping children get back on track with respect to social-emotional developmental progress

Evaluation efforts gathered a combination of qualitative (interview, document analysis, and participant observation) and quantitative data. The evaluation data gathered from three sources (parent or caregiver, service providers, and standardized assessment protocol) suggested that the early childhood mental health services provided through the agencies were effective in having a positive impact on family relationships "in order to promote children's positive social-emotional development" (Safford et al., 2003, p. 53).

An analysis of 42 parent or caregiver interviews conducted by the evaluators revealed the following statistics (Safford et al., 2003):

- 79% of the parents or caregivers stated that either the intervention had enabled them to understand their child better or to interact with their child more effectively or both.

- 83% indicated their parenting skills had improved.

- 86% perceived that, in a variety of ways, the services had significantly helped to stabilize their domestic circumstances.

- 90% of those interviewed indicated that their child's inappropriate or problematic behavior had decreased.

- 81% saw a corresponding increase in positive coping or prosocial behavior.

A survey of therapeutic providers supported the findings reported by families. Staff believed 74% of the children they served made either substantial or moderate improvement. Safford and colleagues (2003) asserted that improvement rates that are greater than 70% are generally accepted as indicating valid psychotherapeutic procedures.

The positive impact of the early childhood mental health services was also demonstrated by analysis of standardized assessments. The therapists completed the Parent–Infant Relationship Global Assessment Scale (PIR-GAS). The PIR-GAS delineates different child–caregiver relational challenges and was completed at the onset of the mental health intervention through the diagnostic process. The PIR-GAS was later completed following intervention for 43 children. The post-intervention scores were significantly higher for these children when compared to their pre-intervention scores, which indicates improvement.

The results of this comprehensive evaluation indicated positive effects of the early childhood mental health interventions. Although, at this writing, the children served are too young to assess their success in school, these services are part of an intentional strategy to foster stable home environments, teach appropriate behavior and self-control, and teach effective parenting skills to increase the likelihood that these children will begin school ready to learn. Future evaluations will attempt to follow the children who participated in intervention and provide longitudinal data on their success in school.

> The message is simple. Babies can't wait. The first 3 years are an enormous opportunity for growth and development for infants, toddlers, and their families. It also brings tremendous opportunity for vulnerability and harm; and if we are going to be serious about getting our children ready for school and success later in life, we've got to take advantage of those early years.
> *(C. Oser, personal communication, 2003)*

THE BROADER CONTEXT: SYSTEMS OF CARE FOR YOUNG CHILDREN'S MENTAL HEALTH IN OHIO

Ohio's system of care for children with social-emotional and behavioral concerns is constantly evolving and changing. There are several initiatives across the state that are addressing important related issues such as financing the ECMH system as well as advocating for effective policy changes that support a statewide comprehensive system of care.

Funding, Access, and Policy Challenges

The success that Cuyahoga County has experienced in improving local services and supports to young children and their families can only go to scale and be sustained through partnerships with state agencies. Publicly funded mental health services for young children in Ohio are limited.

Restrictive program eligibility (set by state agencies) and the limited array of available services (administered and implemented differently by each county) contribute to this shortfall. Ohio has 88 counties and abides by *local rule*, making the establishment of a statewide comprehensive system of care for young children's mental health politically and administratively challenging.

For example, Ohio's eligibility for Individuals with Disabilities Education Improvement Act (IDEA) of 2004 (PL 108-446) Part C services requires either a delay in one developmental domain or a diagnosed condition that has a high probability of leading to a delay. Part C funds have covered only service coordination, global evaluations, IFSP development, transition services, family support, and procedural safeguards. Young children's clinical mental health therapies and specialized services have not been covered by Part C funds, and in Cuyahoga County, the pool of additional funds are insufficient to address the needs for clinical services. As a result, Cuyahoga County has an increasingly large number of Part C eligible children who have identified mental health needs but few financial avenues to pay for needed services. Across Ohio there is a disparity between the mental health services available and those funded for young children and their families. The Ohio Department of Job and Family Services administers the Medicaid program, which also functions through county-based rules in each of the 88 counties. Ohio's Medicaid program for children (called Healthy Start) was expanded with State Child Health Insurance Program (SCHIP) funds in 1997. Children from birth through 18 years in families with incomes up to 200% of the federal poverty guidelines are eligible for SCHIP, and enrollment in Cuyahoga County is the highest in the state. Advocates for early childhood mental health services, however, have not been successful at changing Medicaid regulations to accept the DC:0–3 diagnostic tool as an indicator of medical necessity. Therefore, many young children with social-emotional concerns that present in the context of the family are not eligible for Medicaid coverage, which continues to be driven by the *identified patient's* diagnosis.

One notable exception to these state-level funding challenges is the Ohio Department of Mental Health's (ODMH) initiative that provides grant funds for early childhood mental health services. In several areas of the state, ODMH funds for early childhood intervention have been used primarily to fund programs that provide mental health consultation to child care and preschool environments. Consultants provide resources and assistance to teachers and families of children experiencing social-emotional difficulties.

This labyrinth of state programs, services, county rule, and funding inconsistencies has been the greatest barrier to instituting a statewide, comprehensive, and coordinated system of care for young children's mental health. Many public agencies provide important services to young children with mental health needs, and the public system's multiple points of intervention and service provision have provided the impetus for a range of clinical and advocacy initiatives; however, linking and funding these services as a continuum of care equitably across the state remains a challenge.

Advocating for a Public Policy for Early Childhood Mental Health

Given the complex web of state services for young children, the early childhood mental health community in Cuyahoga County recognized that local and state advocacy has a vital role in successfully establishing a comprehensive system of care. Early advocacy efforts involved consultants who worked on public policy and advocacy measures as well as grant seeking and coalition building with local philanthropic foundations.

In 2004, Voices for Greater Cleveland's Children, a local children's advocacy group focused their efforts on advocating for early childhood mental health issues. This advocacy effort involved countless meetings with local officials and opinion leaders. One of the most critical steps was a community leadership breakfast and public forum in November 2003 that featured Dr. Wil Blechman, a lead participant in Florida's early childhood mental health planning team, and Cindy Oser, Director of State Policy Initiatives for ZERO TO THREE in Washington, DC.

These national speakers participated in strategic meetings with public officials and focused on strategies for enhancing public–private partnerships for early childhood mental health and next steps in building the ECMH system of services. Their expert guidance and facilitation helped advance the cause of early childhood mental health funding with the Cuyahoga County Commissioners most invested in the Early Childhood Initiative. The speakers also spoke at a public forum on the importance of early relationships and social-emotional development. Their message highlighted early childhood mental health as a school readiness strategy. These timely presentations and public forums helped the commissioners bring issues related to early childhood mental health to the forefront as they discussed funding priorities to address broad community needs, including school readiness. Several months after the public forum, which was the culmination of many advocacy efforts, the commissioners announced that they had allotted $700,000 in funding for early childhood mental health services. This county funding, as well as funding secured from five local foundations, ensured the survival and expansion of the early childhood mental health services. Invest In Children's strategic 5-year plan also clearly supports the increased capacity to provide mental health services to children and their families.

THE FUTURE: INFRASTRUCTURE
FOR A COMMUNITY SYSTEM OF CARE

Building a system of care for early childhood development in Cuyahoga County is an ongoing process that requires a significant amount of planning and development. Fully integrating existing services, expanding them to meet the needs of children, and implementing new programs will not only necessitate new financial resources but also require additional administrative and management capabilities throughout the system.

During its first 5 years, Cuyahoga County's Invest In Children established a strong foundation for services for young children prenatal to 6 years and their families. Greater numbers of children are receiving more of the services they need at younger ages than ever before, and those services are beginning to produce real benefits for the children and their families. It is tempting to sit back and acknowledge a job well done, but the recent countywide strategic planning process for the next 5 years of Invest In Children revealed that there is much more work to accomplish. A more firmly defined organizational structure that identifies lead agencies and defines how services and systems will be aligned helps to build an infrastructure that can keep a focus on early childhood mental health services.

Figure 9.1 provides a chart of the organizational structure of the Cuyahoga County Early Childhood Initiative and Invest In Children programs. This organizational structure provides a way to ensure that services and supports provided by an array of community partners can be linked together. As part of the Help Me Grow program, Welcome Home and Early Start both offer home visits. Welcome Home provides a newborn home visit by a registered nurse to all first time and teen mothers shortly after the baby leaves the hospital. Early Start focuses on families who have a child at risk for developmental delays and disabilities. Starting Point is the child care resource and referral agency. Working with the Cuyahoga County Health and Human Services agency and their contractors, Help Me Grow and Starting Point are able to provide an array of services that meets the needs of children, families, and the early childhood community.

Additional strategies will help to strengthen the ties among community service providers, bolster quality, strengthen connections to families, and summon the community to action. Stronger cross-system partnerships and linkages must be developed and can be supported as opportunities arise. For example, in 2002, Cuyahoga County's Department of Justice Affairs was awarded a federal Strengthening Communities' Youth (SCY) grant by the Substance Abuse and Mental Health Services Administration (SAMSHA). Through the SCY project, evidence-based and promising practice for alcohol and drug treatment approaches are being piloted for youth. Then, in 2003, the Cuyahoga County Community Mental Health

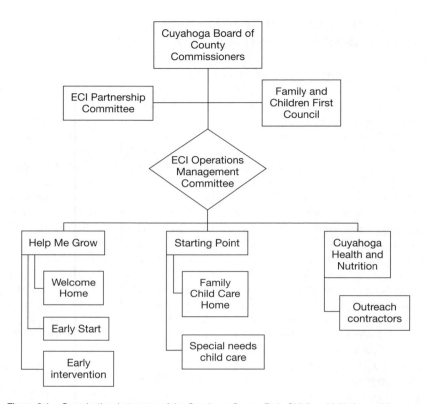

Figure 9.1. Organizational structure of the Cuyahoga County Early Childhood Initiative and Invest In Children. (*Key:* ECI = Early Childhood Initiative.) (Adapted from Center on Urban Poverty and Social Change. [2005]. *Cuyahoga County Early Childhood Initiative evaluation: Phase II final report.* Cleveland, OH: Case Western Reserve University, Mandel School of Applied Social Sciences; adapted with permission.)

Board was also awarded a SAMHSA grant that focused on the mental health needs of children with severe emotional disturbance (SED). Locally, this pilot is called the Tapestry Project. As a result of an overlap in these two populations, funding from both SAMHSA projects is allowing an integrated intervention program for youth with co-occurring disorders that is provided through intensive home-based services. Both of these SAMHSA grants have emphasized the need to create a system of care for youth and families with multiple needs—in other words, a team approach to serving and supporting families in their communities and neighborhoods.

Ohio's Early Childhood Mental Health State Plan and Access to Better Care Initiative

At the state level, the Ohio Department of Mental Health (ODMH) has established its early childhood project, funded for approximately $2.6 million in the 2004–2005 biennial budget, to be focused primarily on mental health consultation throughout the state. ODMH also set a goal of developing an Early Childhood Mental Health State Plan to "secure long-term, stable funding which supports a continuum of high quality mental health services for children birth to age six and their families" (ECMH Advisory Council, June 29, 2004).

Through regional meetings and other ODMH-sponsored discussions, early childhood mental health providers from other counties identified the following goals for the state plan:.

- All children ages birth to 6 years and their families will have access to a full continuum of high-quality mental health services and supports.

- Those who serve and/or care for children birth to 6 years will demonstrate knowledge of social-emotional development of children.

- Secure, long-term, stable funding will support a continuum of high quality mental health services for children birth to 6 years and their families. (This includes the full use of EPSDT funding.)

- Public awareness efforts will promote the mental health needs of children ages birth to 6 years and their families and the benefits of positive intervention and consequences of poor social-emotional development.

- Evaluation will measure desired outcomes for the goals and strategies within the state ECMH plan and promote research and program evaluation on early childhood mental health.

Based on past experience and interest in future efforts, advocates from Cuyahoga County's Invest In Children and Voices for Greater Cleveland's Children have been working closely with another advocacy group—the Public Children's Services Association of Ohio—a proactive coalition of agencies that promotes the development of sound public policy and program excellence for safe children, stable families, and supportive communities to secure inclusion of early childhood mental health services for children ages birth to 5 years in Ohio's Access to Better Care (ABC) initiative (2006) (The Public Services Association of Ohio Two-Year Strategic Plan 2006 & 2007, 2005).

ABC is a major children's initiative enacted in 2006 as part of the state of Ohio's fiscal year 2006–2007 biennial budget. The initiative was developed to respond to the growing realization that failing to appropriately serve youth with alcohol, drug, and/or mental health services needs results in increased costs in other parts of the system. Specifically, lack of access to care can lead to school failure, suicide, criminal behavior, unwanted pregnancy, and other expensive problems that present a growing challenge for Ohio's foster care and juvenile justice systems. With the involvement and input of parents, advocates, and state and local leaders, the ABC initiative was developed with an emphasis on three strategies: 1) promotion, 2) prevention, and 3) intervention. The initiative creates an opportunity to build on the crucial role of the behavioral health system to provide a supportive leadership role for Family and Children First councils (FCF) and their member agencies to better address the needs of children with behavioral health issues (mental health and substance abuse) across the developmental spectrum and across the many environments where these children need or receive care. The ABC initiative honors FCF's commitment to children and families by strengthening the role of parents as empowered advocates for their children via a more parent- and child-focused definition of service coordination and by reinforcing the spirit of local collaboration, which is already strong in Cuyahoga County (Access to Better Care, 2006).

Both the Ohio Early Childhood Mental Health state plan and the Access to Better Care initiative offer opportunities for increased attention to the mental health needs of young children and systems-building activities. These statewide efforts emphasize the need to create a system of care, and they are opportunities to continue to build this effort in Cuyahoga County.

CUYAHOGA'S COUNTY'S COMMITMENT TO THE FUTURE

Cuyahoga County has made significant efforts to make Cleveland a more positive and supportive community for young children and families. The following letter from the Cuyahoga County commissioners eloquently restates the county's commitment to early childhood. The champions articulate the county's continued commitment to promote child and family development; enhance, access, and have an impact on service systems; and improve child and family outcomes.

> Our youngest children are our community's highest priority. They do not have years to wait for change. In our community, our ultimate goal is to see every child succeed. For this to happen, we must propel our efforts to the next level, making investment in early childhood a priority for the entire community. The investment we make as a community in early childhood programming is an investment in Greater Cleveland's future. Together we can make a difference in the lives of our children. They deserve no less. (County Commissioners, J. Dimora, T. Hagan, and P. Lawson-Jones, personal communication, July 1, 1999–June 30, 2000)

REFERENCES

Access to Better Care. (2006). Retrieved April 4, 2006, from http://www.ohiofcf.org/features.asp?learn=abc

Baldwin, J. (1998). *Collected essays* (T. Morrison, Ed.). New York: Library of America.

Center on Urban Poverty and Social Change. (2005). *Cuyahoga County Early Childhood Initiative evaluation: Phase II final report.* Cleveland, OH: Case Western Reserve University, Mandel School of Applied Social Sciences.

Cuyahoga County Early Childhood Initiative. (2002). Retrieved April 3, 2006, from http://www.researchforum.org/project_printable_302.html

Gilliam, W. (2005). *Prekindergarteners left behind: Expulsion rates in state prekindergarten systems.* New Haven, CT: Yale University Child Study Center.

Individuals with Disabilities Education Improvement Act of 2004, PL 108-446, 20 U.S.C. §§ 1400 *et seq.*

Safford, P.L. (2001). Early childhood mental health pilot. Retrieved April 3, 2006, from http://www.case.edu/artsci/schubert/newsletter01.pdf

Safford, P.L., Mahoney, G.J., & Espe-Sherwindt, M. (2003). *The Cuyahoga County early childhood mental health pilot: Final evaluation report.* Cleveland, OH: Case Western Reserve University.

The Public Services Association of Ohio Two-Year Strategic Plan 2006 & 2007. (2005). Retrieved April 4, 2006, from http://www.pcsao.org

10

Strategic Financing of Early Childhood Mental Health Services

Deborah F. Perry

As state and local policy makers seek to develop a continuum of early childhood mental health services—promotion, prevention, and intervention—they are faced with a daunting task of how to pay for many of these services and supports. At one end of the continuum are mental health promotion activities, which are sometimes embedded in home visiting or parent education programs. At the other end of the continuum are intervention services, which can be paid for by Medicaid and private insurance for those children with a mental health diagnosis. It is services for those children who are at high risk for developing social-emotional problems, if early intervention and prevention are not provided to them and their caregivers, that are the most difficult to pay for with the current array of federal and state programs.

The purpose of this chapter is to describe a strategic approach to developing a comprehensive, interagency financing plan that supports a broad continuum of early childhood mental health services and supports. The chapter begins with a process that has been effective for states and communities in building interagency financing systems for young children. Then, some of the most common strategies states and communities have used to spend existing resources *smarter* are described (Johnson & Knitzer, 2005). The chapter concludes with a discussion of how the federal policy and fiscal framework must change to be more aligned with emerging knowledge about the importance of intentional strategies to support families and other caregivers and effective interventions that allow young children to develop the kinds of relationships and regulatory skills they will need to succeed in school and in life.

This chapter was written with help from Jane Knitzer and Roxane K. Kaufmann.

THE CURRENT POLICY AND FISCAL CONTEXT

There is growing recognition about the effectiveness of a range of preventive interventions delivered during the early childhood period as the best way to shift the developmental trajectories of children at risk for poor outcomes (Aber, Pedersen, Brown, Jones & Gershoff, 2003; Conduct Problems Prevention Research Group, 1992; Dunlap et al., 2003; Knitzer, 2002; Shonkoff & Phillips, 2000). Rhetoric about the importance of early intervention for children who experience risk factors is widespread; yet, finding funds to pay for these preventive and early intervention services remains particularly challenging. These children essentially fall between the cracks of two major types of programs requiring state and federal funding—programs to support the broad-based needs of children and categorical programs to address the needs of a specific subgroup of children and families.

Many federal programs that focus on services for children are smaller, categorical funding streams. Although categorical programs are an important way that the federal government targets assistance to particular subgroups of needy children and families, they create obstacles to state and community efforts to adopt a systems-based approach to meeting the mental health needs of all young children and their caregivers. Flynn and Hayes (2003) identify three specific barriers that states and communities encounter with categorical programs: 1) eligibility, 2) program regulations, and 3) flow of funds or administrative barriers. Narrowly defined or disparate categorical criteria that restrict who can be served by the program combined with specific requirements about how or where services can be provided are two examples of these barriers. For instance, many programs focus exclusively on low-income families, whereas others require that the child meet certain diagnostic criteria to receive services, regardless of a family's income (e.g., Part C of the Individuals with Disabilities Education Improvement Act [IDEA] of 2004 [PL 108-446]). In addition, many federal funds flow to the state, whereas others (e.g., Head Start) are granted directly to communities. All of this incongruity serves to complicate state and local efforts to build a continuum of services and supports to young children and their families.

This problem is confounded by the chasm that exists between early care and education programs and the public mental health system in this country. The largest federal programs that finance services for young children often do not include provisions that specifically promote positive social-emotional outcomes. (Table 10.1 provides a chart of federal funding streams that can support a continuum of early childhood mental health services.) Because these funds are limited, there is rarely enough left over for intentional interventions embedded into early childhood en-

Catalog of Federal Domestic Assistance program numbers	Funding source	Fiscal year 2007 appropriation (in thousands)	Federal Administrative Agency	Type of grant and/or flow of funds	Focus on birth to 5 only
93.778	Medical Assistance Program (Medicaid, Title XIX)	$199,445,145	Centers for Medicare and Medicaid Services (CMS);Department of Health and Human Services (DHHS)	Entitlement grants to states	
93.558	Temporary Assistance to Needy Families (TANF)	$16,488,667	Administration for Children and Families (ACF); DHHS	Formula grants to states	
84.010	Title I Grants to local educational agencies (Title I basic, concentration, targeted, and education finance incentive grants)	$12,713,125	Office of Elementary and Secondary Education, Department of Education	Formula grants to local education agencies through state departments of education	
93.600	Head Start	$6,722,410	ACF; DHHS	Project grants to local organizations	X
93.767	State Children's Health Insurance Program (CHIP); (SCHIP)	$5,040,000	CMS; DHHS	Formula grants to states	
10.557	Special Supplemental Nutrition Program for Women, Infants, and Children (WIC Program)	$3,877,495	Food and Nutrition Service, Department of Agriculture	Formula grants to local agencies through the state department of health	X
93.755	Child Care and Development Block Grant [Child Care and Development Fund [CCDF])	$2,062,081	ACF; DHHS	Formula grants to states	
93.944	Maternal and Child Health Services Block Grant to the states (MCH Block Grants)	$573,957	Human Resources and Services Administration (HRSA); DHHS	Formula grants to states	
84.181	Special education—grants for infants and families with disabilities	$436,400	Office of Special Educational Rehabilitative Services (OSERS); Department of Education	Formula grants to states	X
84.173	Special education—preschool grants	$380,751	OSERS; Department of Education	Formula grants to states	X
93.104	Comprehensive Community Mental Health Services for Children with Serious Emotional Disturbances (SED) (CMHS Child Mental Health Service Initiative)	$56,538	Substance Abuse and Mental Health Services Administration (SAMHSA); DHHS	Project grants to local communities or states	

vironments of the kind described in this book. Similarly, young children at risk for developing more serious problems are ignored in public mental health funding streams. The vast majority of public mental health funding in this country focuses on chronically mentally ill adults. The only federal funding that is targeted to children's mental health is a grant program administered by SAMHSA known as the Comprehensive Community Mental Health Services for Children and their Families Program. These grants are funded directly to communities who are engaged in efforts to create systems of care for children with serious emotional disturbances. Although there has been greater interest in including younger children in these systems-building grants, there is still a legislative mandate to target these dollars to children with significant mental health challenges, which has often been interpreted by communities to mean the children must have a diagnosable condition. In the most recent cohort of funded communities, six sites have opted to focus their systems of care on young children, providing a natural laboratory to explore creative strategies for addressing the needs of young children who may be at risk for developing a serious emotional disturbance.

Similarly, the federal early intervention program for infants and toddlers—often referred to as Part C of IDEA—should be an important source of funding because it permits states to serve very young children at risk of developmental delays (including social-emotional and attachment delays). Very few children whose primary need is a mental health issue, however, are served by Part C programs. After 2 decades of implementation, the majority of the services provided under Part C remain occupational and physical and speech therapy (Office of Special Education Programs, 2002). One barrier to children who present primarily with a social-emotional delay is that this program has traditionally focused on children with cognitive and/or physical developmental delays. Many of the multidisciplinary assessment teams do not include personnel who understand infant mental health disabilities, nor are they using tools that specifically assess delays in social-emotional development. In addition, there has been no increase in federal funding to encourage more states to include children at risk for developing delays in their definitions of who is eligible. At this writing, only nine states include children at risk. This small number reflects states' concerns about the fiscal implications of taking on such a large population of needy families under a program framework that *entitles* all eligible families to any services identified on the individualized family service plan (IFSP). Absent a coherent set of new fiscal and programmatic policies and a more proactive federal response, states and communities must essentially *ad hoc* craft a strategy of piecing together a rational fiscal policy. The good news is that, increasingly, states and communities are doing this successfully.

A STRATEGIC PROCESS FOR INTERAGENCY FINANCING

States and communities face the daunting challenge of quilting together pieces from a variety of federal, state, public, and private financing sources to build a financing system to support a comprehensive continuum of early childhood mental health services and supports. This task can be facilitated by a strategic process model (outlined in Figure 10.1) adapted from work done with states as they sought to implement the Part C of IDEA (Striffler, Perry, & Kates, 1997). The steps in this process are rarely accomplished in a linear fashion; rather, as the financing plan is developed, shifts in the political and fiscal climate invariably occur, forcing reconsideration of earlier agreed to decisions or priorities.

The first step in this process actually occurs early and often—any major effort to coordinate a variety of funding streams to support new mental health services for young children begins with an assessment of the

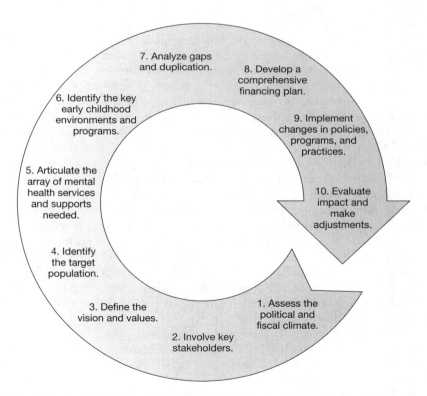

Figure 10.1.   Ten-step strategic planning process for building an early childhood mental health financing system.

current political and fiscal climate. States and communities have different ongoing priorities and initiatives, and many of these relate to school readiness—a natural fit with efforts to support young children's healthy social-emotional development. Being strategic in selecting which of these initiatives "has legs" can be a critical part of a successful interagency financing plan.

One outcome of this scan of the current fiscal and political climate is the identification of the key stakeholders who need to be involved in the strategic fiscal process. Who are the key decision makers in terms of allocating existing resources? Where are new moneys likely to come from (e.g., philanthropic organizations, the state legislature)? How might families of young children be involved in deciding which services and supports would meet their needs? Is there an existing interagency group that is working on similar issues that could add this to their scope of work? A number of states, for example, have developed cross-agency early childhood mental health task forces as part of their efforts to build comprehensive early childhood systems through the Maternal and Child Health Bureau Early Childhood Comprehensive Services grants.

Once key stakeholders have been engaged, consensus on the vision and values needs to be forged. Is there a common vision for what the goal of an early childhood mental health system might produce? What values would drive the development of such a system? Kaufmann and Hepburn (see Chapter 4) describe some of these characteristics. Each state or community needs to discuss these as they relate to the culture of their own locale and how they address local demographic trends.

The vision for an early childhood mental health system of care described by Kaufmann and Hepburn embraces a public health approach, which includes services and supports that promote healthy social-emotional development in all young children and their caregivers. As the planning group refines their approach to financing early childhood mental health services, a major decision will be how to define the target population for this work. Will the focus be on young children who are currently manifesting social-emotional or behavior problems? Will children at risk for developing such problems be the focus, and, if so, how will they be identified? Decisions about the target population have direct implications for which funding streams can be considered, as well as the array of services and supports that will be needed.

Depending on the breadth and inclusiveness of the definition of the target population, discussions about the continuum of services and supports that would reflect the vision and values will drive the next step of the process. What mental health intervention services will be covered? Will these include family-focused intervention? For example, will they help parents receive help with depression, but also address parent–child relationships? How will support to other caregivers (who are not necessarily parents) be provided and paid for? Will it support classroom interventions that address not just individual children, but the staff and program directors through case and program consultation?

The vision for early childhood mental health systems advocated throughout this book is one that infuses mental health promotion, prevention, and intervention into an array of early childhood environments. To accomplish this, the strategic fiscal team will need to know the inventory of programs that serve young children and their caregivers. These will include major public programs, such as Head Start or prekindergarten, as well as private and nonprofit programs run by organizations, such as United Way, and the patchwork of public and private providers of child care. Home visiting programs offer an entry into families' homes, reaching those families who are not yet accessing center-based, out-of-home services. Pediatricians and other health care providers regularly see young children and their families in the first several years of life. This inventory will identify some of the major sources of funding that are supporting the current infrastructure of early childhood services across a variety of environments and providers.

Once the array of mental health services is defined and the early childhood environments are identified, the difficult work of analyzing the gaps and duplication in the services and supports begins. Often, there are several sources of funding for support services, such as case management, but few available resources for mental health consultation services. Likewise, funding is available for evaluation and assessment services, for example under Part C of IDEA, but there are insufficient resources for dyadic therapy or play therapy for children birth-to-age 5 (see the Capacity Assessment Process in Maryland case study, this chapter).

The results of the analysis of gaps and areas of duplication form the basis for the development of a comprehensive financing plan. There are more than 50 different federal funding streams that can be used for young children's services (Fisher, Cohen, & Flynn, 2000), and they fall into four different types of programs: 1) entitlement programs (e.g., Medicaid); 2) formula grants (e.g., Title V Maternal and Child Health Block Grant); 3) discretionary grants (e.g., Head Start); and 4) direct payments (e.g., Supplemental Security Income [SSI]). Some funding streams have more flexibility than others. For example, there are some funding sources (e.g., the Mental Health Block Grant) that could be used to support services to young children, but historically have been targeted to older children. Others could be used to support prevention activities, but have been focused on *deep-end* services (see the Federal Funding for Early Childhood Services and Supports case study, this chapter). There are several documents that describe the array of funding sources that could be used to support young children and their families (see Fisher, Cohen, & Flynn, 2000; Flynn & Hayes, 2003; Johnson & Knitzer, 2005; Johnson & Knitzer, 2006; Wischman, Kates, & Kaufmann, 2001), and these can assist in the search for the right match of fiscal resources and strategies. There are two tools in the appendix to this book that can be helpful in undertaking these activities. Appendix D, Spending Smarter: A Funding Guide for Policy Makers and Advocates to Promote Social-Emotional Health and School Readiness, is a checklist that outlines key questions for the fiscal planning team to guide the development of the plan. Appendix E, the Matrix of Early Childhood Mental Health Services and Supports, is a matrix that arrays the continuum of services and supports with the major federal funding streams that can be used for young children and their families.

Implementing the financing plan often requires changes to existing procedures, policies, and personnel development. Changes to the state Medicaid plan may be needed to allow for reimbursement of different types of services (see the Small Changes Yield Big Impacts in Florida and Vermont case study, this chapter). Some of these changes can be done through agency level administrative changes, whereas others may require public comment or legislative changes (e.g., if new revenues are raised to support services for young children).

Finally, the impact of these changes should be monitored, both in terms of process level indicators (i.e., number of children and families served and services provided), as well as the extent to which families with young children are benefiting from these services and supports (see Chapter 6). Feedback on the impact should inform ongoing and future efforts to finance services and supports for young children and their caregivers (see the Capacity Assessment Process in Maryland case study, this chapter).

Capacity Assessment Process in Maryland

Following a search conference convened with more than 100 stakeholders in 1999, the state of Maryland formed an Early Childhood Mental Health Steering Committee. This group agreed to a common vision for a system of mental health services and supports that would be infused into the early childhood environments where children and families lived, worked, and played. One of their initial five goals was to conduct an inventory of the services and supports that currently exist in each of Maryland's 24 counties. This *capacity assessment* process was a collaboration between members of the steering committee, faculty at Georgetown University, and interagency teams led by the local management boards. A continuum of mental health services (including promotion, prevention, and intervention services) was identified, and a list of the major early childhood programs and environments was provided to each local team. Each team completed the inventory tool, and the data were aggregated into a statewide picture. Many services and supports were available in the majority of the counties, including evaluation and assessment and case management; other services were not available in most of the jurisdictions (e.g., therapeutic nursery programs, play therapy). Interestingly, mental health consultation services were reported as being available in most counties; however, through follow-up calls, the definition of this service varied tremendously. Some counties had a *warm line* that parents could call to ask about specific behavior problems (e.g., biting, temper tantrums); others had master's level specialists who provided on-site, intensive consultation to child care providers (Perry, 2003).

Federal Funding for Early Childhood Services and Supports

The Finance Project conducted a comprehensive analysis of the availability of federal funding for early childhood services and supports in 2000 (Fisher, Cohen, & Flynn, 2000). At that time, there were 59 federal programs totaling more than $230 billion; however, only 11 of these programs focused exclusively on young children. This first category of child-focused programs was discretionary grants, and they accounted for roughly $6 billion, with Head Start accounting for the vast majority of these allocations. The second category of federal expenditures for young children comes from programs that focus on a broader population, such as Medicaid, Temporary Assistance for Needy Families (TANF), and food stamps. In 2000, there were eight such programs accounting for roughly $30 billion of expenditures targeted to young children under age 6. The last category of federal commitments to young children and families accounted for the remaining 40 programs and approximately $72 billion in 2000. It was not possible to estimate the amount of funds that were spent on services and supports for young children; these programs include a combination of entitlements (e.g., SSI, Title IV-E); formula grants (e.g., SCHIP, Title V); discretionary grants (e.g., Healthy Schools, Healthy Communities; Safe Schools, Healthy Students); and direct payments (e.g., Section 8 Rental Certificate Vouchers).

Small Changes Yield Big Impacts in Florida and Vermont

In Florida, one result of their comprehensive Infant Mental Health state planning was accomplished through a minor change to the state's Medicaid plan. By substituting the term *family* for the term *child or parent* in front of the word *therapy*, mental health professionals are now able to be reimbursed for dyadic infant mental health work. The collaborative relationship with Medicaid also led to the ability to use a crosswalk between the diagnostic codes from DC:0-3R (ZERO TO THREE, 2005) and DSM-IV for billing for young children's mental health services.

In Vermont, the Department for Children and Families is working with their colleges in the Medicaid agency (the Agency for Human Services) to expand the availably of mental health consultation for young children with mental health problems. This special grant program defines mental health consultation that is financed through their administrations claiming that, "Consultation and Education with family and community-based groups to improve circumstances and environments for young children (0-6) and their families. The consultation and education (e.g., training) should aim to assist parents and community groups to use health care resources effectively and efficiently as t hey gain knowledge, attitudes, and skill to enhance early identification, intervention, screening, and referral for mental health Medicaid services." The consultation must be provided by "qualified staff or contractors [with] clinical education, training, and experience" including licensed mental health professionals and those with a master's degree in human services (State of Vermont, 2002).

■ ■ ■

BUILDING A COMPREHENSIVE FINANCING SYSTEM

Building a comprehensive financing system to support young children's social-emotional development is part creativity, part tenacity, and part serendipity. It requires the right people working together with a clear vision of what they are trying to fund. It involves risk taking combined with attention to details of the specific requirements of federal funding streams. In addition, it often relies on taking advantage of those strategic opportunities that present at the state or local policy scene. This section describes some of the strategies that states and communities have used to integrate funding across agencies and sectors.

Much of what is considered an early childhood mental health system involves services directed to young children, their caregivers, or both young children and their caregivers; however, there must also be funding available to pay for the infrastructure to support this system (see Chapter 4 for more information). In addition to the provision of high-quality therapeutic and early intervention services for children and their families, funding for such things as personnel development; surveillance (i.e., screening and monitoring in multiple environments); and outcome evaluations are needed. Some funding sources can only pay for direct child and/or family services, whereas others are better suited to supporting the infrastructure. Other funding resources may be needed to pay for informal supports to families and caregivers, such as faith-based or nongovernmental organizations. A comprehensive financing system will blend funding from public and private sources to create and sustain both the infrastructure and service delivery activities.

Funding Mechanisms and Strategies

Because the majority of federal funding available for services for young children and their families are categorical programs, states and communities must implement creative strategies to knit together these funding streams into their systems. In their work with The Finance Project, Flynn and Hayes (2003) describe three types of approaches to *blending* categorical funding streams: 1) coordination, which is also referred to as *braiding*; 2) pooling; and 3) decategorizing. In general terms, coordination strategies maintain the categorical funding structure but allow communities or programs the flexibility to use these separate funding streams in a more unified way. Pooling, a strategy most often used at the state or county level, generates a single pot of funding that can be used flexibly. Similarly, by decategorizing funding streams—essentially removing the restrictions or criteria imposed by the federal legislative or regulatory requirements— funds from more than one program can be used together. The latter two strategies cannot be accomplished at the community or program level in the absence of state or federal action (e.g., waivers).

Coordination is the main strategy that communities and programs can use to *braid* together different categorical funding streams. For example, one funding source might provide support for low-income children; whereas another might be tapped for children with a specific diagnosis being served in the same program. This approach avoids reliance on a single funding source; however, it requires a sophisticated record-keeping system and vigilance, which means many smaller organizations find this too onerous. To address this concern in many communities, multiple agencies are coming together and identifying one partner who can serve as the fiscal agent for the other partners (Flynn & Hayes, 2003). On a statewide scale, Indiana created a Central Reimbursement Office (CRO) to manage the wide variety of categorical funding streams that can pay for early intervention services through their Part C system (Johnson, Knitzer, & Kaufmann, 2002). (See the Indiana's Central Reimbursement Office case study, this chapter.)

Pooling typically occurs at the state level, and these funds are then made available to communities and programs. Most often, funding from federal block grants, which carry fewer specific regulations, and state dollars are pooled to support broader systems reforms (Johnson & Knitzer, 2005). In many jurisdictions, pooled funds are available to be mobilized to support program planning and coordination efforts at the local level, which encourages decision making based on local needs and resources. Another advantage of this type of approach is that these pooled funds can be used to support the infrastructure of local systems, which can supplement categorical dollars that are focused on direct services (Flynn & Hayes, 2003).

Decategorizing funds is a strategy that often requires changes in state-level legislation or administrative procedures (often codified in regulations). Contrary to popular belief, many federal categorical programs actually provide a framework within which states have a good deal of latitude in how they target these funds. Often decisions about whether to focus federal dollars on a particular subgroup has been made at the state level, and federal regulations do not prohibit their being used for a more broad population. During the 1990s, the U.S. Congress authorized more devolution of authority for spending decisions to states and localities, opening the door for more decategorizing opportunities in programs such as TANF and the Child Care and Development Fund (CCDF) (Flynn & Hayes, 2003). In some states, TANF dollars are being used to support mental health consultation. The rationale for this is parents are able to stay productive members of the work force if their young child is not being expelled from their child care program because of challenging behaviors. In other states, CCDF dollars are being used to fund the same service as a quality improvement strategy.

There are several other strategies that states can use to enhance the availability of federal funding streams as part of their comprehensive financing plan, such as leveraging federal funds in those programs where matching funds are required and administrative claiming that allows states to get federal reimbursement for certain activities for targeted groups (Fisher, Cohen, & Flynn, 2000). One of the most important issues that advocates of children's services need to attend to when approaching either of these strategies is securing the upfront commitment to reinvesting these new federal dollars into programs and services for young children and their families.

Leveraging federal funds relies on strategically increasing the amount of state-level matching funds that can be used to draw down additional federal dollars. This can occur in one of two ways—with entitlement programs or block grants. There are a few open-ended entitlement programs still left at the federal level; the most notable examples relevant to young children are Medicaid (Title XIX) and Foster Care (Title IV-E). In this type of program, the federal government agrees to pay a certain percentage of any and all of the allowable expenses the states incur for eligible recipients. There is no limit to how much the federal government will pay these states each year. This is in sharp contrast to most formula grants in which there is a finite amount of federal money allocated each year, which is distributed to states based on a set of factors. This entitlement relationship provides a unique opportunity for states to maximize the amount of federal money they draw down for these activities. Matching funds can be provided from localities, and in some specific cases private dollars can be used as match (Fisher, Cohen, & Flynn, 2000). For example, Vermont leveraged its Medicaid dollars by matching them with state child care dollars and then targeting the funds for early childhood mental health services. These strategies are particularly advantageous for those states where the federal percentage exceeds 50% of the allowable costs for Medicaid expenditures. In addition, many block grants require states provide matching money to draw down their federal share. In those cases where a state has not put up their full amount of match, shifts in program priorities can free up other state funds to ensure the maximum federal participation.

Another strategy that is relevant to the open-ended entitlement programs is referred to as administrative claiming. Essentially, this approach generates additional federal revenue to support the essential administrative activities states undertake to efficiently administer Medicaid and Title IV-E. The federal government will pay 50% of allowable administrative expenditures; however, what qualifies in this category has been interpreted quite broadly by some states. Often these decisions are made on a regional basis in collaboration with officials in the federal administrative offices. Disallowances result when states have been too creative in their administrative claiming, serving as a counterweight to aggressively pursuing these federal funds. The Finance Project has a helpful description of some of the nuances of administrative claiming as well as some examples of how states and communities have used this strategy (Fisher, Cohen, & Flynn, 2000).

Reliance only on federal funding to support a continuum of mental health services for young children and their families is unrealistic and unwise. Whereas federal funds can be an important component of a comprehensive financing strategy, ultimately states will need to harness their own resources and those of the private sector. One strategy for expanding services is to create new sources of funding to support early childhood populations. This can be accomplished through a variety of mechanisms, including designating a new line item in the governor's budget (similar to Maryland's experience; see the Evaluation Data Matter in Maryland case study, this chapter). In California, legislation passed in 1998 that added a 50-cent per pack tax to cigarettes, which created *First 5 California* and generated more than $600 million per year in new money to support young children and their families (see Chapter 6 for more details about the First 5 initiative). One of the biggest advantages of this strategy is that the populations to be served, scope of services, and use of funds can all be aligned with the vision of comprehensive systems in each jurisdiction.

Evaluation Data Matter in Maryland

In Maryland, one of the five goals adopted by the Early Childhood Mental Health Steering Committee was to make mental health consultation available in more jurisdictions. Through an interagency partnership between the state mental health and child care agencies, funding was made available for two pilot projects using the Child Care and Development Fund. One urban and one rural site were funded for $200,000 per year for 2 years. In addition, money was designated for an independent evaluation by Georgetown University. Legislation was passed that required these projects to report their results to the legislative and executive branches following their initial implementation (Perry, 2005). Strong positive findings contributed to the decision by the governor to include $1.87 million in new funding for replicating these projects in additional areas of the state. This money was approved by the 2006 legislature.

■ ■ ■

Philanthropic foundations and the business community are also essential partners in building a comprehensive financing system. Often foundations are eager partners in jointly funding innovations in service delivery, especially as pilot and demonstration projects establish which services are providing the best outcomes (see the Partnering with Philanthropic Foundations in Colorado case study, this chapter). The private sector also has a stake in healthy children and their families; employers are seeking a productive work force now and for future generations. A leading group of economists at the Federal Reserve Bank in Minneapolis, including Rob Grunewald, Art Rolnick, and James Heckman, articulated the business case for investing in early childhood development. There work has galvanized new energy by the private sector in partnering with others seeking to capitalize on the unique opportunities for shifting developmental trajectories in the early childhood period. As recognition grows about the foundational role of early social-emotional development in increasing the odds that young low-income children will succeed in school, states may consider targeting or setting aside some proportion of prekindergarten funding to support intentional strategies to improve social-emotional outcomes in the context of early education initiatives.

Partnering with Philanthropic Foundations in Colorado

Colorado has relied on state and community philanthropic foundations to provide the glue dollars that sustain their early childhood mental health efforts. Since 2000, a grass roots effort has expanded to create an early childhood mental health system in Colorado. Early on, Colorado foundations supported the coordination of Harambi, a group of committed providers, administrators, and family members who wanted to infuse social-emotional support into early childhood programs across the state. Building on that effort, foundations participated in funding a statewide conference on early childhood mental health that brought together a variety of stakeholders to learn about the importance of identifying emotional disorders early and developing services and supports to meet those emotional needs. Foundation members were part of a Colorado team who participated in a Policy Academy sponsored by the National Technical Assistance Center for Children's Mental Health at Georgetown University. The goal of the academy was the development of a strategic plan and policy initiative to promote early childhood mental health. Using the strategic plan and other data Colorado gathered, a SAMHSA system of care grant funded Project BLOOM, which is a four-county project that is building integrated and sustained services and supports for young children with and at risk for mental health problems. Once again the foundation community has supported the development of a sustainability tool kit for Colorado communities to use as they expand mental health consultation services across the state.

Indiana's Central Reimbursement Office

As part of their efforts to implement an interagency financing system for their Part C program—First Steps—state officials in Indiana created an innovative system for coordinating an array of federal and state funding streams. At the core of this effort is the establishment of a Central Reimbursement Office. This electronic system uses the Individualized Family Service Plan as the authorizing document for the payment of individualized services recommended by the multidisciplinary team. As part of this system redesign, the state generated uniform rates for each category of service, regardless of the funding source that will be tapped. This replaced the former system of unequal payments to individual vendors and inequalities across funding sources. It also resulted in providers and families being blind to the source of payment. All reimbursements are settled using a *pay and chase* method, which means the state pays the providers and then seeks reimbursement based on a funding hierarchy individualized to the eligible child. This new financing system pools state and federal resources across program lines. For example, First Steps spending comes from a pool of combined state and federal dollars from state appropriations for early intervention services, federal Part C allocations, Title V Maternal and Child Health Services Block Grant, including their program for children's special health care services, the Social Services Block Grant, Medicaid, and TANF. Medicaid and private health insurance are mobilized for therapeutic services provided to enrolled children and families (Johnson, Knitzer, & Kaufmann, 2002).

MOVING FORWARD WITH FINANCING

In the current policy and fiscal climate, the onus is on states and communities to create a comprehensive financing plan to support a continuum of early childhood mental health services and supports as well as the infrastructure to support and sustain this continuum. In part, this reflects the need for each jurisdiction to implement a customized approach to mobilizing resources to support their unique service array based on their system's strengths, history, and local culture. There is no one way to achieve the right blend of public and/or private funds; however, there are some significant policy and fiscal issues listed here that, if addressed, could make the job of building a comprehensive fiscal plan more straightforward for states and communities:

1. There is a need to infuse screening and social-emotional and developmental monitoring into a broad array of early childhood programs and environments. In the current policy and fiscal climate, there are several programmatic vehicles at the federal level that should be major resources for states in early identification of young children with or at risk for social-emotional difficulties—The Early Periodic Screening Diagnosis and Treatment (EPSDT) program, which is part of Medicaid, and the Infants and Toddlers with Disabilities Education program (IDEA, Part C). The former is targeted to low-income families, and the latter is linked to state Child Find efforts designed to identify children from birth through age 21 who have an array of disabilities. Unfortunately, most states are not taking advantage of the broad mandate embodied by the amendments to EPSDT nearly 2 decades ago through OBRA 1989 (see Johnson, 2006, for a discussion of the current opportunities for maximizing Medicaid). Likewise, the promise to identify children who may have emotional or behavioral disorders during early childhood remains largely unfulfilled by states and communities. This is an example in which the federal framework does not need to be altered; rather, the states need to maximize their use of these existing mechanisms to include and pay for screening for social-emotional development using age-appropriate and validated tools.

There, however, is a need for federal leadership on how screening and assessment can be supported across other early childhood programs and environments, such as home visiting, child care, and the WIC program.

2. There is a need to align current eligibility criteria for programs that support mental health promotion, prevent, and early intervention with scientific knowledge of the most prevalent conditions affecting young children and their caregivers. Right now, there is a mismatch between the knowledge base about the kinds of risk factors that increase the odds of poor social-emotional development in young children and the eligibility for early intervention services for them, their families, and their other caregivers. The demographic, familial, and environmental risk factors that put young children in harm's way for poor social-emotional development are not typically included in the eligibility criteria for mental health and related services; only a diagnosis is included. There are no major *categorical* federal programs providing resources for young children and their families to prevent early school failure and promote early school readiness related to social-emotional and behavioral functioning. (A very small grant program, *Foundations for Learning*, uses a multiple risk factor framework to define eligible young children, but it now funds four programs across the country.) This underscores the need to craft a more responsive legislative framework at the federal level that states and communities can capitalize on as they build their early childhood mental health systems.

3. There is a need to expand the definition of the range of services that can be reimbursed under Medicaid and private insurance. The current system of health care reimbursement is designed to pay for services provided directly to an *identified patient*. This means that it is very difficult to pay for services that help children by helping their family and other caregivers, as well as consultation provided to other professionals, such as pediatricians or child care providers. This problem extends to challenges faced by states as they try to provide mental health services to the family members of a young child, which is often critical because the very risk factors that place many infants and young children in jeopardy are their parent's depression or substance abuse. Therefore, aligning the reimbursement system with what we know as best practices for mental health services and supports for young children would allow states and communities to make better use of these fiscal resources.

4. There is a need to expand the funding to support the system's infrastructure. In the current policy and fiscal climate, there are more resources that can be mobilized to pay for direct services for young chil-

dren and their families, but fewer that can support system-level infra-structure. These include *enabling services* (e.g., bilingual translation, outreach, case management) and functions (e.g., needs assessment, evaluation, planning, policy development, coordination, quality assurance, standards development, information systems, mechanisms to disseminate and increase information about emerging evidence-based practices effectively to the work force). Each federal grant comes with its own administrative requirements and accountability standards and these do not often lend themselves to cross-agency infrastructure building. One exception to this is the Early Childhood Comprehensive Systems program, administered by the federal Maternal and Child Health Bureau. This initiative is notable in its explicit focus on early childhood mental health as one of five key target areas, as well as its emphasis on cross-system planning and coordination. Increased funding for this innovative systems-building program would allow states to leverage these federal dollars as they move from planning to implementation.

As states move forward with their efforts to create systems that infuse a continuum of early childhood mental health services and supports into a range of early childhood environments, they will need to be creative, tenacious, and active in securing financing to support and sustain their work. The lives of young children and their families, especially those at risk for developing emotional and behavioral disorders, will benefit from these labors, and the investments will yield great returns in the future.

REFERENCES

Aber, J.L., Pedersen, S., Brown, J.L., Jones, S.M., & Gershoff, E.T. (2003). *Changing children's trajectories of development.* New York: National Center for Children in Poverty.

Conduct Problems Prevention Research Group. (1992). A developmental and clinical model for the prevention of conduct disorders. *Development and Psychopathology, 4,* 509–527.

Dunlap, G., Conroy, M., Kern, L., DuPaul, G., VanBrakle, J., Strain, P., et al. (2003). *Research synthesis of effective intervention procedures.* Tampa, FL: Center for Evidence-Based Practice.

Fisher, H., Cohen, C., & Flynn, M. (2000). *Federal funding for early childhood supports and services: A guide to sources and strategies.* Washington, DC: The Finance Project.

Flynn, M., & Hayes, C.D. (2003). *Blending and braiding funds to support early care and education initiatives.* Washington DC: The Finance Project.

Individuals with Disabilities Education Improvement Act of 2004, PL 108-446, 20 U.S.C. §§ 1400 *et seq.*

Johnson, K. (2006). *Maximizing the use of EPSDT to improve the health and development of young children.* New York: National Center for Children in Poverty.

Johnson, K., & Knitzer, J. (2005). *Spending smarter: A funding guide for policymakers and advocates to promote social and emotional health and school readiness.* New York: National Center for Children in Poverty.

Johnson, K., & Knitzer, J. (2006). *Early childhood comprehensive systems that spend smarter: Maximizing resources to serve vulnerable children.* New York: National Center for Children in Poverty.

Johnson, K., Knitzer, J., & Kaufmann, R. (2002). *Making dollars follow sense: Financing early childhood mental health services to promote healthy social and emotional development in young children.* New York: National Center for Children in Poverty.

Knitzer, J. (2002). *Building services and systems to support the healthy emotional development of young children: An action guide for policymakers.* New York: National Center for Children in Poverty.

Office of Special Education Programs. (2002). *Twenty-fourth annual report to Congress on the implementation of the Individuals with Disabilities Education Act (IDEA).* Washington, DC: U.S. Department of Education.

Perry, D.F. (2003). *Report on the early childhood mental capacity assessment.* Washington, DC: Georgetown University, Center for Child and Human Development.

Perry, D.F. (2005). *Evaluation results for the early childhood mental health consultation pilot sites.* Washington, DC: Georgetown University, Center for Child and Human Development.

Shonkoff, J.P., & Phillips, D.A. (Eds.). (2000). *From neurons to neighborhoods: The science of early childhood development.* Washington, DC: National Academies Press.

State of Vermont. (2006, May 12). *Training provided for the State Medical Agency by the Children's Upstream Project (CUPS).* Burlington, VT: Unpublished manuscript.

Striffler, N., Perry, D., & Kates, D. (1997). Planning and implementing a finance system for early intervention services. *Infants and Young Children, 10,* 57–65.

Wischman, A., Kates, D., & Kaufmann, R. (2001). *Funding early childhood mental health services and supports.* Washington, DC: Georgetown University Center for Child and Human Development.

ZERO TO THREE. (2005). *Diagnostic classification of mental health and developmental disorders of infancy and early childhood (DC:0–3R).* (Rev. ed.). Washington, DC: ZERO TO THREE.

III

Infusing Mental Health Promotion, Prevention, and Intervention into Early Childhood Services and Supports

■ ■ ■

11

Infusing Mental Health Supports and Services into Pediatric Primary Care

Margot Kaplan-Sanoff

■ ■ ■

Sara's parents carefully carry their sleeping baby daughter into the pediatrician's office for her 2-month checkup. They turn eagerly as the doctor enters the exam room; they are ready to learn about their baby who often seems to be fussy and inconsolable. As first-time parents, they have a lot of questions to ask, but they wait for the doctor to start the exam.

The pediatrician notes that the baby is sleeping comfortably in her father's arms, whereas the mother stares vacantly into space. Is she tired from having been up all night attending to her daughter, or is she as disengaged as she seems? The doctor reviews the chart to see if the family has called the practice between visits.

"So, tell me about Sara," begins the pediatrician. "She certainly looks peaceful sleeping in her father's arms." Both parents nod warily as they exchange uneasy glances. "Is this what she is usually like?" continues the pediatrician.

That question opens the floodgates for the parents. They report that she is usually fussing. They cannot stop the crying and cannot understand what they might be doing wrong. They are at their wit's end explains the father, as the mother looks away and starts to cry. This is their long awaited baby, but no one is having much fun. They feel confused and saddened that they cannot comfort their baby, and they report that they "walk on eggshells" at home so as not to interrupt her all too short naps.

As if on cue, Sara awakens and starts squirming and fussing, waving her arms about, and turning her head frantically from side to side.

■ ■ ■

When new parents bring their baby to their pediatric clinician (pediatrician, family physician, or pediatric or family nurse practitioner), they often feel unsure about the quality of their parenting and the decisions they are making regarding their infant. Dr. T. Berry Brazelton (Osborn & Reiff, 1983; Reisinger & Bires, 1980) finds that parents are passionate for the answers to two questions when they come for their child's checkup. The first question, "How is my baby doing?" is usually adequately addressed, but the second, "How am I doing as a parent?" is frequently unheard, unanswered, or ignored. After the birth of a new baby, the infant and family are in such a dynamic state of flux that parents are often receptive to professional information, guidance, and support to help them cope with the demands of new parenthood. Traditionally, the health care system is the first institution that parents encounter with their newborn. Although pediatric practices may not recognize or feel the potential power they have to influence a child's outcome, they have an enormous window of opportunity to offer families child development information and family support in the nonstigmatizing environment of pediatric primary care.

CONTEXT AND RESEARCH BASE

The American Academy of Pediatrics recommends 10 regularly scheduled well-child visits before the age of 3 years. Starting at birth, these visits are, for many parents, the only opportunity for professionals to observe and interact consistently with families with very young children. These visits are meant to focus on the health and development of the child; however, historically pediatric clinicians have focused only a small portion of the average well-child visit on behavior or development (Osborn & Reiff, 1983; Reisinger & Bires, 1980). Lack of time, inadequate training, and staffing shortages are often cited as obstacles to devoting more time to behavioral issues (Camp, Gitterman, Headley, & Ball, 1997; Minkovitz, Mathew, & Strobino, 1998). Furthermore, in this era of managed care, most well-child visits have been reduced to 12–15 minutes. This barely gives the clinician time to ask the parents' opinion of how their baby is developing, conduct the physical examination, provide some anticipatory guidance, and give the immunizations.

This is not, however, what parents want. In a national survey conducted by The Commonwealth Fund in 1996, almost 80% of parents of young children reported that they felt unsure about how to care for their newborns and wanted more information from their pediatric clinicians in at least one of the following six areas: 1) newborn care, 2) sleep patterns, 3) appropriate response to crying, 4) toilet training, 5) discipline, and 6) encouragement of learning (Young, Davis, Schoen, & Parker, 1998). Less than half reported that they had talked with their pediatric clinicians about how to deal with their children's sleep problems and what to do when their children cried. Less than 25% reported talking with their children's health professional about how to discipline their children or how to encourage them to learn. Parents reported that they were frequently frustrated by their toddlers' behavior on a typical day, with 60% reporting that they yelled at their children. Not only did parents report feeling aggravated and angry, they also were not reading or playing with their infants and toddlers, thus missing important opportunities to help their children learn. Approximately half of the parents said they were having difficulty coping, and 40% said that they felt frustrated by their children's behavior or that their children "got on their nerves" at least once a day. Not surprisingly, these parents were also more likely to report negative disciplinary practices, such as spanking, hitting, and yelling. Finally, 40% of mothers and 30% of fathers reported experiencing one or more of five depressive symptoms during the week prior to the interview, including feeling depressed, feeling sad, believing that people disliked them, crying, or not enjoying life most or at least some of the time.

Another survey conducted in 1997 by ZERO TO THREE (1997) found that parental understanding of young children based on their developmental stages was to some extent limited or inappropriate. Specifically, two important child development concepts are not well understood by parents. First, more than half of the parents in the survey thought that the more caregivers a child has before the age of 3 years, the better the child will be at adapting and coping with change. Second, parents believed that the more stimulation a baby receives, the better the baby will develop. Neither is true. Infants need continuity with a limited number of caregivers to develop relationships, and too much stimulation can be overwhelming. Finally, parents did not fully understand the connections between healthy child development and their own parenting practices.

Beyond basic child rearing, many parents express feeling insecure and worried about how to raise their children in a world that bears little resemblance to that of their own childhood. Should they try to raise children who are friendly and cooperative? Or should their focus be on fostering academic skills, such as early reading? How should they respond to a toddler's unwillingness to share toys? Is cognitive development or emotional development more important?

In addition, the litany of potential threats to children's well-being seems to be expanding (e.g., media portrayals of violence and sex, community violence, short maternity leaves, effects of potentially inadequate child care, threat of living in an unhealthy home or community environment). As society grapples with new values and new challenges to children, the media and internet present an increasing array of *experts* to advise parents, each of whom has a different message and a different agenda. It is not surprising that many mothers and fathers have become confused and would like to rely on their pediatric clinicians to help them make sense of the cacophony of mixed messages.

Parents want help with their infants and toddlers, and the pediatric clinician is often the only professional with whom they consistently interact. Yet, it has been reported that in 60% of all routine well-child visits, the physician ignored parental concerns or provided no developmental or behavioral information or guidance (Hickson, Altemeler, & O'Connor, 1983). Similarly, pediatric clinicians frequently spend less than 1 minute on anticipatory guidance during a visit (Osborn & Reiff, 1983); therefore, pediatric clinicians are missing opportunities to provide critical information about child development, reframe child behavior, and support families as they struggle with both the demands of caring for young children and their own feelings of self-esteem.

When parents bring their babies to a pediatric office, they offer clinicians a window of opportunity to see into their lives and the lives of their children. Pediatric clinicians are in a unique position to offer families consistent, long-term relationships based on the care and support of their children. They can also offer a nonstigmatizing environment in which parents can ask about their worries and concerns. Questions that a parent dares not ask a mother-in-law, such as "Is my baby normal?," are less intimidating if asked to an understanding pediatric clinician. Pediatric care for young children offers a powerful vehicle to infuse mental health services into an ongoing system of care if the clinicians recognize the influence that they bring to daily interactions with families.

MODELS OF CARE

Despite the best of intentions, pediatric clinicians do not always choose effective strategies for supporting parents. Perhaps the biggest offender may be the clinician who gives advice, such as instructions on toilet training, strategies for feeding, assurance that everything is going well (even if parents do not think so), brief explanations of discipline techniques, and so forth. For some parents who are simply seeking concrete information, giving advice can work well if it meets the parents' specific needs. Strategies for fever control or management of a diaper rash usually require little more than information; however, advice that is unsolicited, such as anticipatory guidance about something for which a parent has not expressed interest (e.g., weaning from the breast or bottle) can be overwhelming to parents, many of whom cannot process all the information and advice they are being given within a 12-minute period (during which time they are anticipating the stress of an impending immunization). In addition, advice is typically one-sided; that is, the pediatric clinician lectures and the parent listens.

Teachable Moments

Almost every well-child visit offers shared experiences in the office between pediatric clinicians and parents around the behavior or development of the child. These shared experiences or *teachable moments* (Zuckerman & Parker, 1997) provide an opportunity for the pediatric clinician and the parents to comment about something they have observed about the child or the parents in the moment, to ask a specific question, or to share a concern. Teachable moments take advantage of a shared attentiveness to the child's health and behavior, the enormous interest of the parents in their child, and a heightened parental desire to learn. For some parents, implicit worries about what the pediatric clinician might discover, fears about how the pediatric clinician might judge their competence as parents, or a particular concern that they bring to the visit contribute to parents' heightened emotion and interest in the interactions during the visits. For example, a pediatric clinician might comment on a young toddler's somewhat frenetic exploration of the exam room ("He certainly likes to explore his surroundings."), which provides an opportunity for the parents to see their child's behavior with pride or to ask about a concern ("He's always getting into everything, and we worry about his safety.") or to focus the discussion ("We noticed that when he's busy exploring or playing at home, he ignores our requests and just keeps playing."). By commenting on the toddler's behavior, the pediatric clinician creates a teachable moment in which to help the parents better understand their child's behavior and their own response to that behavior. It may also be an opportunity to reframe a behavior from being considered *bad* or *annoying* to *expected and positive*. The behavior may still annoy the parent, and that should be acknowledged, but by positively reframing it the pediatric clinician may help the parents see the behavior and their response to it from a different perspective.

Although a child's behavior often initiates a teachable moment, it is up to the pediatric clinician to capitalize on it. First, the clinician *reads* the child's behavior together with the parent by describing it and offering a constructive interpretation of its significance. Second, the clinician may model possible responses to the child's behavior as it occurs, such as setting a limit to jumping off the exam table. This modeling may consist of a behavioral response without a verbal comment (e.g., taking the child off the exam table) or it may be delivered indirectly to the parents by talking to the child ("Do you want to get down? Is that what you're trying to tell us by jumping?"). Although young children may not understand the words, they are particularly sensitive to an adult's response, tone of voice, and facial expression. Third, the clinician elicits parental responses directly by using their reactions to the behavior to explore potential concerns ("How does she tell you when she wants something? It must be hard for you to not know what she wants"). Chances are that if the clinician finds the child's behavior challenging, so do the parents. These three steps—1) reading the child's behavioral cues, 2) modeling possible responses, and 3) engaging parents in dialogue about the behavior—create a spontaneous, unforced conversation about a specific behavior without the parents becoming defensive and by allowing for a blend of action, observation, and information sharing.

The goals of creating teachable moments during a well-child visit are to 1) enhance parental understanding of the child's needs and the parents' responses to those needs, 2) promote a *goodness of fit* (Thomas, Chess, & Birch, 1968) between the parents and the child, 3) model constructive interactions with the child, and 4) enhance the relationship between the pediatric clinician and the parents. Teachable moments are always present during visits; it is the clinical judgment of the pediatric clinician as to how those moments should be used. Pointing out a child's strengths may help the parents feel better about their parenting. Asking parents how they understand a confusing aspect of the child's behavior (e.g., "Why do you think he comes into bed with you every night?") both acknowledges their role as experts on their child and supports them in making informed decisions about how they might set limits with their child. Any advice or information that the pediatric clinician wishes to give may fall on deaf ears if the clinician fails to pay attention to the implicit context of a parent's question or request. In addition to patiently listening to a new parent's concerns, a clinician must also praise their parenting skills. Parents pay close attention to what their clinician says about their child and their parenting. Because child-rearing decisions are often met with criticism and expectations from relatives and friends, any perceived negative comment, whether implicit or explicit, stays with parents and can erode the parent–clinician relationship. Often, how a comment is said can be even more important than what is actually said (e.g., seemingly unimportant comments can easily wound or uplift a parent). It is this window of opportunity that makes the pediatric visit an excellent vehicle for supporting a child's social-emotional development, the parent–child relationship and the parent–clinician relationship. Table 11.1 provides examples of how to create teachable moments during well-child visits.

Temperament as a Vehicle for Understanding Child Behavior

Popular parenting books often imply that parents will quickly learn to recognize their baby's cries and, therefore, understand the meaning of their child's distress. Yet, many new parents are bewildered by their infant's seemingly random behavior. Early pediatric visits offer an opportunity to

Table 11.1. How to create teachable moments

Ask an evocative question.

"What is the worst that could happen?"

"What are you worried about?"

Turn a parent's statement or observation about his or her child into a question.

"Are you concerned that she's always on the go and will never be able to sit down and learn?"

Elicit a behavior from a child that points to a general developmental process.

Give a young child a board book and comment on how he puts it in his mouth, looks at the pictures, or turns the pages.

Describe the child's behavior and explore the parents' understanding of that behavior.

"What do you and his father think about his crying at night?"

Point out a discrepancy between what parents assume about their child and something they have just observed about the child.

"You are worried that she is so impatient and gets frustrated so easily. Did you see how carefully she is stacking these blocks"?

explore with parents the meaning of their baby's behavior. By exploring the child's behavior together, the pediatric clinician can model how to think about a child's behavior and to derive possible meaning from it. One way to conceptualize the notion that behavior has meaning is to explore the baby's temperament, that is, the "how" of their behavior, with parents. Children are born with a unique combination of temperamental characteristics, such as intensity, distractibility, and activity level that define their particular temperamental style. These temperamental characteristics are derived from genetic, intrauterine, central nervous system, and postnatal environmental factors (Gunnar, Tout, deHaan, Pierce, & Stansbury, 1997). Temperament is likely to stay relatively constant as long as the interplay between the individual and the environment is stable, but it is susceptible to change. Researchers (Thomas, Chess, & Birch, 1968) have identified nine temperamental characteristics that can be used in combination to describe temperamental constellations, such as the *easy baby* (about 40% of the population), the *slow-to-warm baby* (about 15% of the population), the *difficult baby* (10% of the population), or a combination of constellations (the remaining population). The nine temperament characteristics are described on a rating scale in Table 11.2. Easy babies are characterized by their high adaptability, positive mood, low intensity of reaction, and rhythmicity. These babies make parenting fairly easy for their mothers and fathers—they sleep and eat on a regular schedule, can adapt to changes in their schedule, and react to new situations with enthusiasm. Slow-to-warm babies are less quick to adapt to new stimuli; demonstrate mildly intense negative responses; and require frequent exposure to new foods, objects, and situations before they adapt and feel comfortable with these new experiences. For parents who are always on the go and spontaneous,

Table 11.2. Temperament scale of the nine temperament characteristics

After each characteristic, rate your child on a scale of 1–10 with 10 being the most active, intense, rhythmic, and so forth.

1. **Activity level:** Some children are active. They kicked a lot in the uterus before they were born, they moved around in their bassinets, and were always on the run as toddlers and preschoolers. They can grow up to be people who just need a lot of activity and movement to be happy. Other children and people are content with much less activity.

   1 _____10

   Not very active   Active   Very active

2. **Rhythmicity:** Some people have regular cycles of needs. They eat, sleep, and have bowel movements on schedule almost from birth. Others are more sporadic and much less predictable.

   1 _____10

   Not very regular   Regular   Rhythmic

3. **Approach–withdrawal:** Some children delight in everything new; others withdraw from new situations. The first bath makes some babies laugh and others cry. There are children and adults who love to try new experiences and are eager to jump right in. There are also those that need to take a lot of time to warm up to new people, places, foods, and so forth.

   1 _____10

   Slow to warm   Approaches   Enthusiastic

4. **Adaptability:** Some children and adults adjust quickly to change; others are unhappy at every disruption of their normal routine.

   1 _____10

   Dislikes changes   Adjusts slowly   Quickly adjusts to new experiences

5. **Intensity of reaction:** There are those that react to things with great joy or great frustration and those that respond to life in a milder, less intense way.

   1 _____10

   Low key reactions   Some reaction   Intense reaction

6. **Threshold of responsiveness:** Some children seem to react to every sight, sound, and touch. For instance, they awaken at a slight noise or become overwhelmed by visual clutter or pungent smells. They may turn into adults who have difficulty screening out the world and are easily overstimulated. Others seem unaware of bright lights, loud street noises, wet diapers, or crowded rooms.

   1 _____10

   Low tolerance for sensory input   Moderate tolerance for sensory input   High tolerance for sensory input

7. **Quality of mood:** Some people's moods switch rapidly from happy to upset. Others can stay in one emotional state for what may seem like a very long time.

   1 _____10

   Even tempered   Moods change quickly

8. **Distractibility:** Most people get fussy when they are hungry or tired or upset, but some can be easily distracted by activities, people, television, or interruptions in routine. Similarly, when children want to do something dangerous or prohibited, some of them can be distracted by another, safer idea, whereas others are more single-minded, persistent, and focused on what is desired.

   1 _____10

   Stays very focused   Usually focused   Easily distracted

9. **Attention span:** Some people stay happily focused with one task for a long time. Others quickly move from one activity to another.

   1 _____10

   Moves often from one activity to another   Stays with one task for long periods

Reprinted from the Healthy Steps Training Institute. (1996). *Healthy Steps Multimedia Kit.* Boston: Boston University School of Medicine. © Boston University School of Medicine; reprinted with permission from Margot Kaplan-Sanoff.

slow-to-warm babies can present a poor fit between the parents' expectations and lifestyle and the baby's needs. Finally, difficult children have
irregular biological functions, experience negative moods, are highly persistent, and display intense reactions to new experiences. Not surprisingly,
these children present the most problems for parents and are more often
referred later for behavioral and mental health therapies.

The pediatric clinician's role in helping parents better understand
their children's temperamental styles is critical to supporting parental decision making and their sense of self-understanding and confidence. Temperamental characteristics alone may not cause problems; however, the fit
between the demands and expectations of parents and the characteristics
of the child can cause a struggle. Some practices use a temperament scale
(as in Table 11.2) that is filled out with the parents when a child is 4
months old and repeated at appropriate intervals to help parents obtain a
clearer notion of how their child copes with change and expresses himself.
Teaching parents how to read their child's behavioral cues to get a better
understanding of the child's temperamental style can greatly enhance the
parent–child relationship and create a goodness-of-fit between child temperament and parental expectation and behavior. Talking with parents
about the type of opportunities and environments that best support their
child lays the foundation for increased parental competence and a better
understanding of how their child's style might fit with a proposed child
care or other socialization experience. For example, knowing that a slow-
to-warm child might need a parent to stay at a birthday party when the
other parents have left helps parents' plan their behavior to support their
child's further development without embarrassing the child or feeling
ashamed about their child's unwillingness to mingle with the other children at the party.

Reach Out and Read

Pediatric clinicians can have an impact on a child's readiness for kindergarten starting very early in infancy. Pediatricians have a unique professional opportunity to encourage early language and literacy behaviors in
very young children well before they enter formal education. Early literacy is a developmental process similar to learning to talk. It is dependent
on several factors, including cognitive abilities, curiosity, brain development, and exposure to literacy related experiences. One factor which consistently correlates with successfully learning to read is a history of being
read to as a young child. Developed by the Department of Pediatrics at
Boston Medical Center, Reach Out and Read (ROR) (http://www.
reachoutandread.org) provides an efficient and evidence-based approach
to increasing the amount of time that parents spend looking at books with

their very young children (Mendelsohn et al., 2001). This approach recommends that starting at the 6-month well-child visit and at every well-
child visit thereafter, the pediatric clinician should give the child a new developmentally and culturally appropriate book. Using this as a teachable
moment, the clinician and parent talk about what the baby is learning from
the book and how early experiential book handling can build the child's
early literacy skills. In time, children often ask the clinician for their new
book and parents anticipate watching their child enjoy books. ROR operates in more than 4,000 pediatric sites around the country with parents reporting that they are more likely to engage in book related behaviors with
their children if they participated in ROR.

ROR not only supports specific early literacy skills, such as letter recognition and book handling behaviors, it also enhances social-emotional development by supporting *emotional literacy*. Sharing books with very young babies by holding them and talking about the pictures in the book instills a love
of books, print, and language. Books about feelings help children learn the
words to express their emotions, such as scared, angry, sad, or frustrated.
(The ZERO TO THREE web site at http://www.zerotothree.org/
brainwonders/earlyliteracy includes a current list of books for very young
children that supports social-emotional development and emotional literacy.)

Adult Health Risks

Adult behavior can also have a profound effect on child development and
behavior. Data from the Adverse Childhood Experiences study (ACE)
strongly suggests that children are affected in a variety of ways by exposure
to such adult risk factors as mental illness (especially depression), alcohol
and/or drug abuse, and domestic violence (Feletti, et al., 1998). These
adult risk factors have been linked to childhood depression and other
childhood mental health concerns, risk-taking behaviors that have an impact on school and peer relations, and self-regulatory behavior problems.
Because several of these adult risk factors are comorbid, children are likely
to grow up in homes with multiple risk factors. For example, a child may
grow up with a depressed mother who is using drugs to self-medicate or
live in a family where alcohol use exacerbates an abusive relationship between the parents. The ACE data indicate a correlation rather than causation between adult risk factors and child behavior, providing evidence that
each child's genetic makeup, temperament, and environmental factors
have an effect on their individual outcomes. Identifying and intervening
early in the lives of children living with such significant adult risk factors
is critical to child development. In any given year, approximately 22% of
the adult population has a diagnosis of some form of mental health disorder, with rates of depression particularly high among mothers of young

children (Nitzin & Smith, 2004). The 2002 evaluation of Early Head Start reports that 48% of mothers of 1-year-old children enrolled in the program reported multiple depressive symptoms (Administration on Children, Youth, and Families, 2002). The effects of maternal depression on young children have been well documented. Infants of depressed mothers show difficulties engaging in social interactions and regulating their affect and arousal (Weinberg & Tronick, 1998), whereas preschoolers engage in dangerous and/or provocative challenging behaviors. Maternal depression can also affect parenting behaviors, such as the ability to establish routines for sleeping, eating, or reading to children, and the use of such prevention practices as car seat use or baby proofing the house for safety.

Pediatric care has the potential to be a two-generational model of care by considering adult risk behavior as a critical component of the pediatric clinician's responsibility in addressing the health and development of children. As Zuckerman (1995) describes it as, "The best way to help children is to help their parents, and the best way of reaching parents is through their children" (p. 759).

The pediatric visit can be used as a vehicle for engaging families in discussions of their own health and behavioral risks by routinely conducting family health screenings and providing follow-up support and referrals for mental health, smoking cessation, and counseling. In fact, Kahn and his colleagues (1999) report that 85% of women in their research said they would welcome or not mind being asked about such adult risk factors as alcohol problems, depression symptoms, or abuse, and 90% said they would welcome or not mind an offer of help with making related appointments. Clearly, the *captive* nature of the pediatric visit lends itself to supporting parental mental health within the context of a nonstigmatizing pediatric relationship.

Integrated Models of Care

How can a pediatric clinician accomplish all that is expected? Several new approaches to pediatric care embrace the medical home model that focuses attention on the need for an ongoing source of primary care that is, "accessible, continuous, comprehensive, coordinated, compassionate, and culturally effective" (American Academy of Pediatrics, Committee on Children with Disabilities, 2001, p. 184).

These approaches combine the strategies discussed previously in this chapter into an integrated service delivery system by supporting a relationship-based practice model that addresses young children's physical, intellectual, and emotional growth and development. In a traditional medical practice, one pediatric clinician typically tries to address all of children's health-related needs. These programs expand this model of a solo practitioner to a team approach to primary health care for very young children with care coordination from outside the medical staff.

Healthy Steps for Young Children: Promoting Child Health and Development

Healthy Steps, which was developed by the Division of Developmental and Behavioral Pediatrics at Boston University School of Medicine and funded by The Commonwealth Fund, the Robert Wood Johnson Foundation, and more than 100 funding partners, cross-walked services with the Bright Future initiative to ensure comprehensive service delivery for children birth-to-3 years and their families. Healthy Steps incorporates a child development specialist, called a Healthy Steps Specialist, into the medical team as the primary child development and family support resource for families who brings to the practice an expertise in child and family development. Healthy Steps Specialists have backgrounds and training in child development, early intervention, child care, social work, counseling and nursing. The roles of the Healthy Steps Specialist include

- Conducting office visits jointly with the pediatric clinician during regular well-child appointments

- Conducting home visits to support and enhance parent–child interactions and to promote home safety

- Preventing and helping parents manage common behavioral concerns related to early learning, fussiness, sleep, feeding, toilet training, temper tantrums, and so forth

- Checking on children's developmental progress and family health and behavior as part of an office or home visit

- Facilitating parent groups

- Staffing the child development telephone information line

- Providing referrals and follow-up, as appropriate, to help families make connections within the community

Healthy Steps serves more than 11,000 children in 46 sites across the United States in HMOs, PPOs, clinics, and private practices. More than 400 pediatric clinicians, family physicians, and pediatric and family residents are participating in Healthy Steps. The Johns Hopkins Bloomberg School of Public Health is rigorously evaluating Healthy Steps using medical record review, parent and provider satisfaction and knowledge questionnaires, telephone interviews, and contact logs. Initial 3-year data reported in the Journal of the American Medical Association (JAMA) indicate that for all children, not just those at high risk, the quality of pediatric care in the first 3 years of life was dramatically improved because of Healthy Steps. By changing the structure and process of pediatric care, Healthy Steps has significantly improved the delivery of pediatric developmental services (Minkovitz, Hughart, Strobino, et al., 2003). The evaluation found that, among other results, families involved in the Healthy Steps program were more likely than nonparticipating families to

- Discuss concerns with someone in the practice about a variety of issues, such as the importance of routines, discipline, language development, temperament, and sleeping patterns

- Receive a developmental screening (eight times more likely)

- Be highly satisfied with care because someone in the practice went out of his or her way for them (twice as likely)

- Discuss their *sadness* with someone in the practice (3.3 times more likely)

- Ensure that infants sleep on their backs to help reduce the risk of sudden infant death syndrome (SIDS)

- Receive timely well-child visits and vaccinations (1.5 times more likely)

- Remain with the practice beyond 20 months of age

Healthy Steps helped parents better understand their children's behavior and development, thereby producing more favorable disciplinary practices. Healthy Steps mothers were 30% less likely to use severe physical discipline and 22% less likely to rely on yelling or slapping. Furthermore, Healthy Steps mothers were 22% more likely to show picture books to their infants and 24% more likely to play with their babies every day. Physicians were five times more satisfied with the ability of their clinical staff to meet the developmental needs of their patients than physicians without a Healthy Steps Specialist. They viewed Healthy Steps as a valuable service that helped children receive more timely visits and maintained families in their practices.

Healthy Steps augments standard medical care through a delivery system that represents a significant transformation of pediatric care for children birth-to-3 years. It offers a core set of services that, taken together, restructure the way health care is delivered. Although the precise mix and intensity of services is determined by the individual sites, Healthy Steps practices extend services beyond the supervision of physical health to include enhanced well-child visits, home visits by the Healthy Steps Specialist, parent groups, a child development telephone information line, child development and family checkups, links to community resources for children and families, written materials for parents that emphasize prevention, and communication among team members. Each of these practices is explained later in this section.

Healthy Steps practices accomplish these integrated strategies by using a team approach, allowing both the pediatric clinician and the Healthy Steps Specialist to interact together in the same exam room with the family during well-child visits. As a team, clinician and specialist build on each other's knowledge and resources, responding to parents' questions and concerns with both a medical focus and a developmental perspective. For example, if a family voices concern about their child's eating, the pediatric clinician might use the growth chart to reassure the family about their baby's weight gain, and then the Healthy Steps Specialist might ask about the family's routines for feeding, their expectations about the baby's eating, and whether this concern is based on feedback from other family members or friends. As one father enrolled in Healthy Steps said, "We hear so much conflicting information about her eating that we don't know what to think."

In truth, there is no common wisdom about child-rearing to which all parents can subscribe. For example, every pediatric practice has different guidelines for when to start solid foods. On a larger scale, every culture has different behavioral expectations for children. By focusing the content of pediatric care on infant health, development, and behavior within the context of children's families and communities, Healthy Steps offers parents a vehicle through which to make their own informed decisions about what they want for their children and their families. This begins by encouraging parents to set the agenda for each visit and be active participants in their children's care. The establishment of a trusting relationship between the practice and the family allows the parents to consider multiple views of child behavior. Healthy Steps practices assume that relationships are the key to development—relationships between parents and children, mothers and fathers, parents and extended family, and the family and the practice. Healthy Steps services are delivered with deliberate thought as to how to nurture and support these multiple relationships with the goal of emotional well-being for the child and the family.

It is the Healthy Steps Specialist who most often nurtures those relationships by addressing the social-emotional health issues of the child and family. The Healthy Steps Specialist has the opportunity to observe the parents and child during the physical exam and to comment on the affect of the baby and the parents. By addressing what the child and family might be feeling or thinking during the visit, the Healthy Steps Specialist becomes a very tangible symbol for the social-emotional issues of development and parenting that can surface within the context of pediatric care. It is most often the Healthy Steps Specialist who remarks on the baby's curiosity or perhaps fearful expression. It is the Healthy Steps Specialist who comments on the parents' affective state and perhaps their concealed anxiety or anger. The Healthy Steps Specialist models how to use strong emotional language within the context of the visit, and she or he becomes the concrete representation for mental health—the reminder to consider the emotional well-being of children and families. One Healthy Steps pediatrician remarked, "Now when I hear a mother's voice crack with emotion, I don't ignore it. I think, what would Cathy (the Healthy Steps Specialist) say to the mother? And I say those words—Cathy's words—out loud. She has taught me to pay attention to emotional expressions, not to dismiss them" (W. Findlay, personal communication, 1999). Pediatric clinicians report that they rely on their Healthy Steps Specialists to keep them in the emotional moment of an interaction rather than focusing on all the other patients they need to see that session. They also report that their patient visits, although not lasting longer than before, are more fulfilling and elucidating. The following sections explain the individual services offered by Healthy Steps (http://www.healthysteps.org).

Enhanced Well-Child Visits

The pediatric clinician and Healthy Steps Specialist function as a team. They both are present to conduct each well-child visit together in the same room with the family, offering continuity of care for children and families. The visits are structured to answer questions about the child's upcoming developmental stages, as well as to administer the physical examination and developmental tools to gauge the child's growth and development. Early learning and literacy activities are offered as part of the Reach Out and Read program. The team uses teachable moments to help parents understand their child's temperament and behavior through observation and discussion of shared experiences in the office. In addition, parental health risks, such as depression, household smoking, substance abuse, and domestic violence, are identified and addressed by asking direct questions about parental conflict; use of cigarettes, alcohol, and/or drugs; and depressive symptoms, such as a lack of appetite or loss of interest in activities.

Home Visits by the Healthy Steps Specialist

A sequence of home visits by the Healthy Steps Specialist is offered to parents during the first 3 years of a child's life at predictable junctures in the child's development, such as between 9 and 12 months when most infants become increasingly mobile and active. Because parents are more comfortable in their own homes, they will often share concerns about their child's development or their own issues that they may be hesitant to bring up in the pediatric office. Home visits also give Healthy Steps Specialists the opportunity to observe safety measures in the home, conduct developmental checkups, and discuss anticipatory guidance in more detail.

Parent Groups

Group sessions run by the Healthy Steps Specialist provide information and opportunities for social support from other parents in the practice who have children of similar ages. Sessions might include discussions on infant behavior, cardiopulmonary resuscitation, toilet training, and early learning activities.

Child Development Telephone Information Line

Healthy Steps Specialists staff a child development information line that complements the medical information and emergency line. Parents can call at any time with questions about their child's behavior, such as crying, sleeping difficulties, discipline, or family disagreements concerning child-rearing decisions. These calls are answered within 24 hours and followed up in the next well-child visit or by a home visit.

Child Development and Family Checkups

Developmental checkups are conducted during office or home visits to detect early signs of developmental or behavior problems using specifically designed screening and assessment tools. Check-ups also create teachable moments to help both parents and the pediatric practice learn more about the child's learning and coping style, temperament, and problem-solving skills. Finally, they provide opportunities to ask parents about their own health risks, such as smoking or depression, as they relate to the baby.

Links to Community Resources for Children and Families

Both the Healthy Steps Specialist and the pediatric clinician make referrals for families for such services as early intervention, speech and language assessment, WIC, smoking cessation, child care, adult mental health, or housing.

Written Materials for Parents that Emphasize Prevention

Parents receive a variety of materials designed to involve them more fully in their child's health care visits. They are given handouts at age-appropriate visits with information on medical care (e.g., "What should I do when my baby has an ear infection?"); developmental and behavioral issues (e.g., "Why is my toddler fearful?"); and practical issues (e.g., "Good Nights— Solutions for Bedtime Battles"). They also receive age-specific newletters, *Linkletters*, 2 weeks before their next scheduled appointment, which address issues frequently asked during the visit and include a self-help questionnaire for parents to respond to before the visit. When they arrive for the visit, parents are given a Parent Prompt Sheet. These prompt sheets, which are timed to the specific issues of the upcoming well-child visit, suggest a series of questions that the parents might want to ask the pediatric team. They encourage parents to become active participants in their child's health care by setting the agenda for each well-child visit.

Communication Among Team Members

Healthy Steps practices hold regular team meetings so that all members of the pediatric team can share information learned during home visits, on the telephone line, in parent groups, or during developmental checkups. Healthy Steps Specialists also make notes in the medical record to facilitate follow-up and referral.

Assuring Better Child Health and Development: Improving Access to Preventive Services

Assuring Better Child Health and Development (ABCD) was initiated by The Commonwealth Fund to examine systems change efforts in key states (i.e., North Carolina, Vermont, Washington, and Utah, and joined in Phase II by California, Illinois, Minnesota, and Iowa) led by the state Medicaid offices. These statewide initiatives examined strategies for funding developmental screening, surveillance, assessment, and care coordination services for children through changes to Medicaid billing and reimbursement policies. Although the American Academy of Pediatrics (AAP), Bright Futures, and the Future of Pediatric Education II (FOPE II) all support the importance of screening very young children in primary care for prevention of school failure and for the possible prevention of extensive intervention services as children get older, various financial, staffing, and access barriers continue to prevent many busy pediatric practices from instituting universal screening for infants and young children.

Starting Early, Starting Smart: Pediatric Primary Care as Intervention

Starting Early, Starting Smart (SESS) is a national public–private partnership between the private Casey Foundation and the Substance Abuse and Mental Health Services Administration (SAMHSA) in the U.S. Department of Health and Human Services to support the integration of substance abuse and mental health services into pediatric primary care (as well as early childhood environments, such as Head Start). SESS has identified two critical objectives. The first is to improve access to and use of a comprehensive set of needed services for families and their young children. The second is to improve parental behavioral health, family functioning, and child social-emotional development. SESS utilizes the infrastructure of pediatric primary care to provide services to families in familiar environments where they already bring their children for care; to integrate comprehensive services into these environments through collaboration with relevant providers; to increase access to and use of basic services for families, such as nutritional services, housing, and child care; and to increase access and continued utilization of needed intervention services, such as parenting education, adult mental health, substance abuse treatment, and child mental health treatment (EMT Associates, 2003). SESS programs put the family at the center of the service delivery system, involving them in the identification of needs and development of solutions. This is accomplished by blending service delivery of a broad range of environmental and individual supports for children and families, facilitating referrals to the community, and making each environment where families are seen more sensitive and responsive to the importance of strong familial and institutional support of the healthy social-emotional development of infants and young children. Initial data on SESS programs indicates that many were successful at decreasing drug use among family members who were problem users, reducing verbal aggression among caregivers, decreasing indicators of parental stress among parents experiencing high levels of such stress, increasing positive interactions between parents and children, and improving language development in children (EMT Associates, 2003).

Successful SESS programs have much in common with other comprehensive pediatric approaches by creating medical homes for infants and young children that are family centered and deliver a wide range of services within a cultural context that supports family decision making. The programs create multiple opportunities for both formal and informal interactions between families using a mix of paraprofessional staff who typically work directly with families and professional staff who meet specific health and developmental service needs.

CHALLENGES

While there are many challenges to the integration of social-emotional issues into pediatric primary care, the most critical ones are training of clinicians, changing the structure of pediatric practice, and reimbursement for services.

Training of Pediatric Clinicians

Although there are certainly highly qualified pediatric clinicians practicing today, many of them have focused their training on disease prevention and management with less emphasis on early childhood behavior and development, especially social-emotional development. Yet, behavior and development have become the new morbidity in pediatric primary care. Developmental and behavioral pediatrics only became a board certified subspecialty in 2002; therefore, there are few senior clinicians available who can mentor younger pediatricians and residents on child behavior and mental health, particularly in infants and toddlers. Training for all pediatric clinicians in social-emotional and mental health issues for very young children and their families represents a significant barrier to using pediatric primary care as a vehicle to support childhood mental health. In 2005, The Duke Endowment funded the Healthy Steps program at the University of North Carolina at Chapel Hill to implement the Healthy Steps North Carolina Residency Initiative, establishing Healthy Steps practices at all pediatric residency training programs in North Carolina.

Transforming Pediatric Practice

To implement an integrated, comprehensive program requires that the pediatric practice transform itself by including a focus on child development and mental health as a routine part of the well-child visit. This is not business as usual; rather, it changes the practice into one that considers multiple viewpoints. Although the primary emphasis of the visit is still on health, this family-centered approach to a medical home brings a focused child development and mental health lens to the interaction in the office. Other members of the team may ask questions about parental concerns that the pediatric clinician had not considered. For example, if the parent of a young preschool-age child expresses worry that her child is gaining too much weight, the clinician might use the growth chart to illustrate the child's obesity risk. Other members of the team might consider a different viewpoint to discern if this is perhaps a cultural view of weight; an issue of control or concern within the extended family; or a problem of limited, healthy food resources that the family might not think to disclose to the pediatric clinician. During visits in which the child development specialists and pediatric clinician see the family together, clinicians and specialists gradually develop a system of interacting with each other and *sharing* patients. For some solo practitioners who are accustomed to seeing families by themselves, the idea of sharing a family's attention might be challenging to their professional sense. As most admit, however, the relief of having someone with whom to share difficult cases quickly overshadows their initial concern about sharing.

Being a member of a team rather than a solo practitioner requires many clinicians to rethink how they conduct their office visits and to leave space (literally and figuratively) for other team members to add insight to the visit.

Often another team member will have information from a home visit or phone conversation that can add to the discussion of how to help a baby to sleep through the night or how to set appropriate limits for a toddler, for example. Then, at the end of a visit, the clinician can move on to the next patient, leaving the child development specialist in the room with the family to review the suggestions made, to clarify options for the family, to review their concerns about the child or family, and to facilitate successful referrals.

Pediatric clinicians also report feeling more equipped to sit with parents who have a difficult story to tell because they no longer feel as though they have to provide all the answers to solve the sometimes overwhelming problems with which some parents are faced. Clinicians now have allies as they work with families, that is, someone who can stay in touch with the family until the next well-child visit and explore such mental health constructs as those unconcious "ghosts in the nursery" (Fraiberg, Shapiro, & Cherriss, 1980) that might be influencing parents' decision-making about their children. Finally, many clinicians who had previously defined their role as working exclusively with children rather than families (with the obvious exception of family medicine or med/peds clinicians) are forced to think about how to listen to and to talk with adults about such serious risk factors as domestic violence. Although there was some initial resistance to attending to adult health and behavioral risks, having the back-up support of other team members to help with a facilitated referral makes it easier for pediatric clinicians to explore these sensitive issues.

Reimbursement

The major barrier to increasing expanded health service delivery systems is financial. The long-term solution to this constraint is to gain reimbursement for developmental services within the standard health care reimbursement systems (i.e., HMOs, private health insurance, Medicaid). The Centers for Medicare and Medicaid Services (2003) have published a final rule effective January 1, 2004, that allows payers in the health care system to reimburse for Current Procedural Terminology (CPT) codes 96110 and 96111. These codes cover developmental screening as performed by nurses and physicians, respectively. Yet, the health care field seeks to reduce outlays unless they pay for themselves during the same period in which the outlays are made. As a result, a long-term preventive program, such as Healthy Steps, garners great interest but little reimbursement. Strategies to address this challenge have included substituting Healthy Steps Specialist time for that of physicians, which allows the physician to see additional patients or more chronically ill children, using Healthy Steps as a marketing device, presenting data for increased reimbursement for this expanded service from public or private insurers, advocating to have employers require insurers to support this level of high quality care as part of work and family issues, and charging an additional fee for Healthy Steps services.

PRACTICE AND POLICY RECOMMENDATIONS

Lessons learned from implementation of these new models of care suggest that to be successful, programs first need a local champion within the health care organization. That champion is usually one of the senior physicians in the practice who can rally the support of others. Second, and equally important, is to have a strong clinic administrator or nurse manager who has the authority to implement changes within the system. For example, the administrator might need to institute a computerized booking system or facilitate a system for team members other than clinicians to write notes in the medical record. A third necessary strategy to ensure success is to hold regularly scheduled team meetings. These meetings ensure that all members of the pediatric team are familiar with the approaches used and that there is a forum to air concerns and grievances. This last strategy is, in many cases, the hardest to achieve. Pediatric practices tend not to have regularly scheduled clinic meetings, in part because the time is not reimbursable. Those sites that have an identified champion, an administrator who is able to institute the changes needed to successfully implement a medical home, and regularly scheduled team meetings are most able to sustain themselves over time, increase their case load, and secure institutional support for their approach.

In several key Healthy Steps sites, the Healthy Steps Specialist emerged as the champion who was able to diffuse Healthy Steps throughout the organization. For example, at Advocate Healthcare in Chicago, the energy, enthusiasm, and commitment of a senior Healthy Steps Specialist helped spread Healthy Steps to several other sites within the health care organization and to several other sites in Chicago. Similarly, a pediatric practice in Grand Junction, Colorado diffused the Healthy Steps model into a family practice in their community using their Healthy Steps Specialists as models and trainers.

CONCLUSION

The birth of a new baby often stirs up old conflicts, longings, losses, and fantasies that propel families into rethinking how they make decisions about their lives and their futures. Primary care pediatrics can provide a nonstigmatizing venue in which to support and address their questions and concerns. By responding to the needs of parents with young children who want more from their primary care visits than just immunizations and height and weight checks, these expanded models of care offer a window of opportunity for families to explore their child-rearing decisions by examining those issues that have an impact on their mental health and that of their young children. In addition, for families who might otherwise refuse or lack access to mental health care, these pediatric practices offer them entrance into the system of care by encouraging families to consider their own mental health as important to the development of their young children. Adults who might not seek intervention for themselves will often consider it for the sake of their children with the support of a pediatric practice.

Expanded models of pediatric care help parents to focus not only on their babies, but also on how they are doing as parents. One Healthy Steps family explained that "Healthy Steps is like having access to a grandparent with credentials; the practice knows about you and your baby, but they also know the research and the resources you need to help you figure things out" (S. Governo, personal communcation, 1999).

REFERENCES

Administration on Children, Youth, and Families, Head Start Bureau, Department of Health and Human Services. (2002). *Making a difference in the lives of infants and toddlers and their families: The impacts of Early Head Start: Executive Summary.* Washington, DC: Department of Health and Human Services.

American Academy of Pediatrics, Committee on Children with Disabilities. (2001). Developmental surveillance and screening of infants and young children. *Pediatrics, 108,* 192–195.

Camp B.W., Gitterman, B., Headley, R., & Ball, V. (1997). Pediatric residency as preparation for primary care practice. *Arch Pediatric Adolescent Medicine, 151,* 78–83.

Centers for Medicare and Medicaid Services. (2003, April 1). *Updated skilled nursing facility (SNF) no pay file for April 2005.* Retrieved on October 1, 2006, from http://www.cms.hhs.gov/MLNMattersArticles/downloads/MM3642.pdf

EMT Associates, Inc. (2003). *Starting Early Starting Smart final report: Summary of findings.* Washington, DC: Casey Family Programs and the U.S. Department of Health and Human Services, Substance Abuse and Mental Health Administration.

Fraiberg, S., Shaprio, V., Cerniss, D.S. (1980). Treatment modalities. In S. Fraiberg (Ed.), *Clinical studies in infant mental health: The first year of life.* (pp. 49–77). New York: Basic Books.

Feletti, V., Anda, R., Nordenburg, D., Williamson, D.F., Spitz, A.M., Edwards, V. (1998). Relationship of childhood abuse and household dysfunction to many of the leading causes of death in adults. *American Journal of Preventive Medicine, 14*(4), 245–258.

Gunnar, M.R., Tout, K., deHaan, M., Pierce, S., & Stansbury, K. (1997). Temperament, social competence, and adrenocortical activity in preschoolers. *Developmental Psychobiology, 31,* 65–85.

Healthy Steps Training Institute. (1996). *Healthy Steps multimedia kit.* Boston: Boston University School of Medicine.

Hickson, G.B., Altemeler, W.A., & O'Connor, S. (1983). Concerns of mothers seeking care in private pediatric offices: Opportunities for expanding services. *Pediatrics, 72,* 619–624.

Kahn R.S., Wise, P.H., Finkelstein, J.A., Bernstein, H.H., Lowe, J.A., & Homer, C.J. (1999). The scope of unmet maternal health needs in pediatric settings. *Pediatrics, 103,* 576–581.

Mendelsohn, A., Mogilner, L., Dreyer, B., Forman, J., Weinstein, S., Broderick, M., et al. (2001). The impact of a clinic-based literacy intervention on preschool children. *Pediatrics, 107,* 130–134.

Minkovitz, C., Hughart, N., Strobino, D., Scharfstein, D., Grason, H., Hou, W., et al. (2003). A practice-based intervention to enhance quality of care in the first 3 years of life: The Healthy Steps for Young Children Program. *Journal of the American Medical Association, 290*(23), 3081–3091.

Minkovitz, C., Mathew, B., & Strobino, D. (1998). Have professional recommendations and consumer demand altered pediatric practice regarding child development? *Journal of Urban Health: Bulletin of the New York Academy of Medicine, 75*(4), 739–750.

Nitzin, J., & Smith, S.A. (2004). *Clinical preventive services in substance abuse and mental health update: From science to services.* Rockville, MD: Center for Mental Health Services, Substance Abuse and Mental Health Services Administration.

Osborn, L.M., & Reiff, M.I. (1983). Teaching and well child care. *Clinical Pediatrics, 22*(7), 505–508.

Reisinger, K.S., & Bires, J.A. (1980). Anticipatory guidance in pediatric practice. *Pediatrics, 55,* 889–892.

Thomas, A., Chess, S., & Birch, H. (1968). *Temperament and behavior disorders in children.* New York: University Press.

Weinberg, M.K., & Tronick, E.Z. (1998). Emotional characteristics of infants associated with maternal depression and anxiety. *Pediatrics, 102,* 1298–1304.

Young, K.T., Davis, K., Schoen, C., & Parker, S. (1998). Listening to parents: A national survey of parents with young children. *Arch Pediatric Adolescent Medicine, 152,* 255–262.

ZERO TO THREE. (1997). *Key Findings from a nationwide survey among parents of zero to three year olds.* (Conducted by Peter D. Hart Research Associates.) Washington, DC: ZERO TO THREE.

Zuckerman, B. (1995). Preventive pediatrics—New models of providing needed health services. *Pediatrics, 95,* 758–762.

Zuckerman, B., & Parker, S. (1997). Teachable moments: Making the most out of the office visit. *Contemporary Pediatrics,14*(2), 20–25.

12

Infusing Mental Health Supports and Services into Infant and Toddler Environments

Tammy L. Mann, Stefanie Powers, Jennifer Boss, and Lynette M. Fraga

■ ■ ■

The science of early childhood development has firmly established that the first 3 years of life represent a remarkable period of development with great opportunities and equally great vulnerabilities (National Research Council and Institute of Medicine, 2000). The foundation for a child's ability to think, feel, speak, and make sense of their world is established during these early years. Although it is true that all aspects of development (social-emotional, cognitive, and linguistic) unfold in the context of the relationships that infants experience with adults in their environment, healthy social-emotional development is especially dependent on the quality of these early relationships (National Scientific Council on the Developing Child, 2004; Shonkoff & Phillips, 2000).

Infants and toddlers who experience nurturing and responsive relationships are much more likely to form attachments with adults that encourage confidence, curiosity, and the drive to explore their environment. Young children who have trouble managing their emotions can have difficulty in problem solving and other related cognitive functions. These children are also more likely to have difficulty relating and getting along with peers and other adults as they mature and develop (National Scientific Council on the Developing Child, 2004). This chapter defines infant mental health and what professionals and parents in a variety of environments can do to support mental wellness in very young children. It also explores the challenges that must be overcome and the important policy recommendations that support needed capacity in the field of early childhood development.

DEFINING INFANT MENTAL HEALTH

Infant mental health is the developing capacity of the birth-to-3 year old child to experience, regulate, and express emotions; form close and secure interpersonal relationships; and explore the environment and learn—all in the context of family, community, and cultural expectations for young children. Infant mental health is synonymous with healthy social-emotional development (ZERO TO THREE, 2001).

Babies learn to experience, regulate, and express emotions in the context of supportive relationships with adults who are able to read and respond to their cues. Babies who are having difficulty coping with external stimulation (e.g., as evidenced by crying, gaze aversion, distressed facial expression) need adults who notice their discomfort and are able to support them by making the adjustments that help them regain a calm state. Furthermore, when adults provide sensitive and responsive care, babies form trusting relationships that in turn foster their ability to explore their environment and engage with others. Regardless of where care is provided— at home, in child care, or with relatives or friends—babies need adults who understand and are in tune with their needs and know how to respond to those needs by creating a warm, responsive, and nurturing environment.

CHALLENGES TO THE HEALTHY SOCIAL-EMOTIONAL DEVELOPMENT OF VERY YOUNG CHILDREN

> Infant mental health disorders are emotional and behavioral patterns that interfere significantly with very young children's capacity to meet age-appropriate, cultural, and community expectations for managing emotions, forming close and secure interpersonal relationships, and exploring the environment. Very young children's healthy social and emotional development may be disrupted, or begin to deviate significantly from typical patterns because of constitutionally based individual differences, problems in the infant or toddler's primary caregiving relationships, or the interaction between the child and aspects of the caregiving environments. Infants and toddlers with mental health disorders experience suffering, pain, and disorganization. (Emde, 2001)

Although biological factors can have an impact on social-emotional development, it is also clear that challenges in caregiving relationships and environments can have a negative impact on social-emotional development. A variety of factors may interfere with the ability of parents or other caregivers to be emotionally available and responsive. In some cases, these challenges may stem from parents who are experiencing their own mental health concerns. Considerable research has documented the negative impact of maternal depression on the parent–child relationship (Carter, Garrity-Rokous, Chazen-Cohen, Little, & Briggs-Gowan, 2001; Field, 1997; Goodman & Gottlieb, 1999). Problems can also occur when parents feel overwhelmed with economic issues, such as inadequate housing, limited financial resources, lack of employment, limited or no access to health care due to employment status, all of which further compromise their ability to manage the demands of highly dependent infants or active toddlers. Finally, having a parental history of abuse and/or neglect can impede a parent's ability to meet the needs of their infants and toddlers if they have not benefited from mental health services to address those issues. A lack of sensitive and responsive caregiving often yields unmet emotional needs that can result in developmental challenges for the infant who is very much dependent on trusting adults to make necessary adaptations as they interact and experience their environment. Brain development research points to the amazing capacities of the young child, as well as their vulnerability to adverse environmental circumstances. The more risk factors present, regardless of whether they are constitutional or environmental, the greater the likelihood of a negative impact on healthy development in all areas of functioning.

ZERO TO THREE published *Diagnostic Classification of Mental Health and Developmental Disorders of Infancy and Early Childhood (DC:0–3)* in 1994 to address the need for a systematic developmentally based approach to the classification of mental health and developmental disorders in the first 4 years of life. The popularity of the tool has grown considerably since that time, with many states, communities, programs, and clinicians using it to best diagnose infants and very young children. DC:0–3 has been revised (DC:0–3R [2005]) to incorporate the new knowledge and clinical experiences from the past decade. It is used as a complement to the *Diagnostic and Statistical Manual of Mental Disorders*, and some states use a crosswalk between the two instruments for billing purposes.

THE INFANT MENTAL HEALTH SERVICE CONTINUUM: PROMOTION, PREVENTION, AND INTERVENTION

The definition of social-emotional wellness and mental health disorders in very young children suggests that one must consider mental health from a promotion, prevention, and intervention (also referred by some as *treatment*) perspective. Because babies simultaneously have amazing capabilities and vulnerabilities, families must have access to services and needed supports throughout their development. Table 12.1 notes general definitions associated with each concept on this infant mental health service continuum.

Efforts to promote social-emotional wellness in young children should be targeted at adults who are directly responsible for caring for

Table 12.1. Definitions of each concept on the infant mental health service continuum

Promotion strategies are aimed at enhancing and supporting the social-emotional well-being of very young children by responding to cues and providing a safe and nurturing environment.

Prevention strategies ensure that young children at risk for mental health difficulties are screened early on and provided necessary supports to address early symptoms before they develop into more significant mental health disturbances.

Intervention strategies focus on providing needed mental health intervention to very young children in the context of relationships with parents (e.g., dyadic parent-child psychotherapy) that address persistent symptoms indicative of mental health disorders.

young children (e.g., parents; child care providers, including family, friends, and neighbors). Helping adults understand the importance of responsive care embedded in nurturing relationships is key to promoting emotional health and wellness for young children. In instances where children are at risk for emotional difficulties, service providers should have proper procedures to identify and address signs and symptoms that may be suggestive of an early onset of social-emotional difficulties. Should intervention for emotional difficulties become necessary, mental health professionals must have the training and support required to address such issues. The issue of promotion, prevention, and intervention strategies will be addressed further later in this chapter.

INFUSING MENTAL HEALTH INTO ENVIRONMENTS THAT PROVIDE SERVICES TO INFANTS AND TODDLERS

To best address the social-emotional needs of infants and toddlers it is important to ensure that the environments where babies spend many hours a day are adequately equipped with trained staff and have the necessary resources to meet their needs. Through anticipatory guidance and careful questioning, health care providers can support parents to understand and respond to their babies' cues, unique temperament, and cope with any regulatory or behavior challenges. Also, in response to a growing body of research about the negative impact of maternal depression on babies, pediatricians are beginning to screen for depression or inquire about it during well-baby checkups (Rosman, Perry, & Hepburn, 2005). Kaplan-Sanoff (see Chapter 11) provides examples of practices used by primary care providers to support optimal social-emotional development in young children.

The needs of families have changed over the years, and the environments and types of individuals providing support to infants and toddlers have also changed. As more parents work, many more very young children are being cared for by relatives and child care providers than in previous years. In addition, as the science of early childhood development continues to evolve, there has been a growth in early childhood programs aimed at both supporting parents and ensuring that very young children are in environments that support all aspects of their development—social-emotional, cognitive, and linguistic. The following sections briefly describe the environments in which many infants and toddlers are now spending a considerable amount of time and later discuss strategies that professionals in these environments can use to address social-emotional needs from a promotion, prevention, and intervention perspective.

Center-Based and Family Child Care

Much has changed since the 1970s regarding the variety and quantity of programs and services available to families with infants and toddlers, largely as a result of increased numbers of women in the work force. In 1975, only 34% of women in the work force had children under 3 years compared to 61% in 2000 (Oser & Cohen, 2003). Figure 12.1 depicts the arrangements that families have come to rely on for infant and toddler child care.

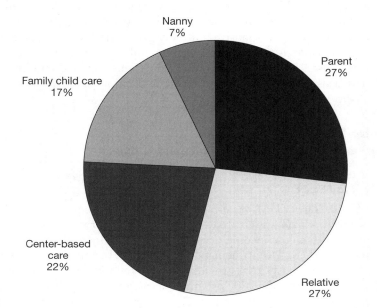

Figure 12.1. Child care arrangements for children under 3 years with employed mothers. (Adapted from Ehrle, J., Adams, G., & Tout, T. [2001]. *Who's caring for our youngest children: Child care patterns of infants and toddlers?* Washington, DC: The Urban Institute; adapted with permission.)

With more than 70% of infants and toddlers receiving care from someone other than a parent, child care environments are an important focal point for supporting early development. Evidence suggests that more than 6 million infants and toddlers are presently receiving some form of regular, nonparental care (The Future of Children, 2001). Looking across a variety of studies (e.g., NICHD,1994, 2002, 2003a, 2003b), it is now clear that child care has the ability to both support development by providing high-quality responsive care with well-trained caregivers or undermine it by putting young children at risk for developmental problems when that care is substandard. To the extent that caregiving is responsive, warm, and sensitive, beneficial outcomes for young children emerge. When care is inconsistent, harsh, and unsupportive, developmental problems occur, especially if an infant's experiences are further complicated by his or her parent's inability to meet the infant's needs due to poverty and/or its many corollaries (e.g., mental health issues, substance abuse, domestic violence, inadequate housing). Unfortunately, far too many child care environments (home and center based) are unable to consistently offer high-quality care that benefits development. Variations in quality are most often related to adult–child ratios, teacher qualifications and training, and staff turnover rates, for both center and family child care environments. Phillips and Adams (2001) note that in most large-scale studies of child care, roughly 20% of the centers studied fall below the minimal thresholds for adequate care. Much of what makes these environments inadequate include nonresponsive and unengaged teachers and caregivers, inadequate materials to support learning, and far too many health and safety hazards. A lack of adequate state regulations, minimal requirements and standards, and a lack of monitoring and enforcement contribute to low-quality care.

Center-Based and Home-Based Intervention Programs for Infants and Toddlers

Early Head Start

Early Head Start (EHS) was established in 1994 through the Head Start Reauthorization and was created as a comprehensive, two-generation program that targets low-income pregnant women and families with infants and toddlers (U.S. Department of Health and Human Services, 1994). Since its inception, EHS has provided services to more than 71,000 infants and toddlers in more than 700 programs across the country. EHS provides a comprehensive array of services that targets the health (physical and social-emotional), education (cognitive and language), and nutritional needs of very young children. Parents are also able to access services that meet their needs (e.g., prenatal, health, educational, vocational) directly from the program or through referral to community-based providers.

EHS programs are funded to provide services in environments that meet the needs of participating families. Some programs offer center-based services, others provide services in the home, and still others offer a combination of center- and home-based services. The programs are governed by a comprehensive set of performance standards that articulate the scope of services that each program is expected to provide. The Head Start program performance standards cover services in three broad programmatic areas: 1) child health and development, 2) early childhood education, and 3) family and community partnerships. EHS programs (and Head Start programs because they are governed by the same set of regulations) are given flexibility in determining how to best provide those services required by the performance standards.

At the program's inception, congress mandated that an experimental study test the impact of the program. Data collected when children were 24 and 36 months suggests that EHS programs are having a positive impact on children and parents (Administration on Children, Youth, and Families, 2002). EHS participants performed significantly better than non–EHS participants on measures of cognitive, language, and social-emotional development. Parents who participated in EHS also experienced a variety of positive benefits, including more emotionally supportive interactions with their children, more support for language and learning, a greater tendency to read to their children, and less inclination to spank. Furthermore, those EHS programs that implemented the Head Start program performance standards earlier in their program development experienced a higher rate of significant outcomes. To date, EHS continues to represent the federal government's largest investment in a comprehensive program aimed at meeting the needs of low-income families expecting or nurturing children, prenatally to age 3 years.

Nurse Home Visiting Program

Among the many home visiting programs that now exist, the Nurse Home Visiting program has been among the most extensively tested using an experimental research design. This program began in 1977 as a research demonstration program that provided home visits to first-time, low-income mothers during pregnancy and through their child's second year of life (Olds et al., 1999). Home visits were provided by nurse practitioners to address the following goals: 1) improve pregnancy outcomes for mothers by reducing health-related behaviors that lead to poor birth outcomes for infants; 2) improve child health and development by supporting parents to provide competent care for their children; and 3) improve economic self-sufficiency of families by helping parents with family planning, education, and employment. Results of a randomized clinical trial with the first cohort of participants in Elmira, New York identified a number of significant intervention benefits. These benefits included positive outcomes across all three goal areas, especially for those participants who were young, unmarried, and poor.

Rather than push for program expansion with these early findings, Olds and his colleagues (1999) elected to replicate the research to learn more about how long benefits would last once the intervention ended; whether the benefits might apply to other cultural groups (e.g., African Americans, Hispanics); whether benefits emerge if paraprofessionals are used instead of nurses; and whether it would be possible to create a standard intervention protocol such that other nurses could be trained and new programs established to effectively implement this intervention. Subsequent research in Memphis and Denver provided important answers to these questions. Olds (2002) found that it was possible to replicate the findings with other culturally diverse groups and yield similar benefits for mothers and their young children, and benefits from the program lasted well beyond the early childhood period of development. They also found that nurses were more effective than paraprofessionals and that it was possible to create an intervention protocol that would support training others nurses and establishing new programs. The research documenting the effectiveness of the Nurse Home Visiting program, both short term and long term, has been documented in a number of published studies (see Kitzman et al., 2000; Korfmacher, O'Brien, Hiatt, & Olds, 1999; Olds et al., 1999; Olds et al., 2002; Olds & Kitzman, 1993).

The program exists in 91 sites across the country and has been named the Nurse–Family Partnership program (Nurse–Family Partnerships, 2005). Programs are financed through a variety of public (federal and state) and private funding sources. A national office is now available to support all facets of program implementation, including start-up planning and on-going training and support. The model of services offered through the Nurse–Family Partnership program continue to reflect the basic tenants of the intervention established through research on program efficacy. Home visits begin during the second trimester of a mother's pregnancy and continue through the child's second birthday. The frequency and intensity of visits change over time as specified in the standard intervention protocol. The content of visits are organized around challenges that mothers encounter during pregnancy and as the infant develops. Regular assessments are conducted to address issues that surface during a family's participation. These assessments are standard across all sites implementing this program model. Nurses must have a bachelor's degree and must participate in a 2-week training program during their first year to learn about the program model and intervention protocol. In addition, nurses must also obtain 46 hours of continuing education units focusing on assessing parent–infant interaction. These nurses carry a caseload of 20–25 families and receive regular clinical supervision from a senior nurse. Communities that implement this model must do so in a manner that reflects what the research has shown to be effective. Longitudinal research across each of the sites (Elmira, Memphis, and Denver) continues pioneering the widespread implementation of this home visiting program model.

Parents as Teachers

Parents as Teachers (PAT) was initially launched in 1981 as a pilot program by the Missouri Department of Elementary and Secondary Education in collaboration with four school districts as a result of concern about preschoolers from disadvantaged backgrounds starting school without the skills that many of their peers from more affluent communities would bring to kindergarten. The program was designed to decrease the number of children entering school in need of special assistance (Wagner & Clayton, 1999). The program expanded quickly in Missouri following an evaluation when the children reached third grade that suggested the initial pilot program had been successful. Since 1985, PAT has expanded to more than 2,800 sites across the country, including U.S. territories, and more than 140 international program sites (Parents as Teachers, 2005). Programs are implemented by a host of agencies, including school districts, hospitals, churches, social service agencies, Head Start, Even Start, and family resource centers. Funding for program services are generated through federal, state, local, and private funding streams.

The major goals of the current program include 1) empowering parents to give their child the best possible start in life through increased knowledge of child development and appropriate ways to foster growth and learning, 2) giving children a solid foundation for school success, 3) preventing and reducing child abuse and neglect, 4) increasing parents' feelings of competence and confidence, and 5) developing true home–school community partnerships. Although the program was initially established for parents with children birth-to–3 years, the program now provides services to families during the first 5 years of life. Parent educators, although hired by the local agency implementing the program, must be trained and credentialed by the Parents as Teachers (2005) National Training Center at the time of hire and on an annual basis thereafter.

The PAT model includes the following four key elements: 1) personal visits, 2) developmental screenings, 3) group meetings, and 4) resource networking. When the program was initiated, personal visits were offered monthly but have changed under the current model to match the needs of the families served. Parent educators offer more frequent visits to families that have more intense needs. Parent educators use a standard curriculum and conduct developmental screenings on an annual basis to ensure that any delays are detected early on and are addressed by an appropriate early intervention professional. Parents have the opportunity to participate in monthly parent group meetings that provide information about parenting, offer an opportunity for parents to share with one another, and participate in community outings and events. Finally, parent educators provide resource networking to ensure that they gain access to health, employment, job training, and related resources that have an impact on their ability to meet the needs of their children and family. A number of evaluations (e.g., randomized, quasi-experimental, single group designs) conducted since the program's inception suggest that PAT has had a positive impact on both parenting and child outcomes.

Healthy Families America

Established in 1992 by Prevent Child Abuse America, the Healthy Families America program aims to promote positive parenting and child development in an effort to prevent child abuse and neglect by providing home visiting services to families at high risk. More than 450 communities across the country are providing services through this program (Prevent Child Abuse America, 2005a). Healthy Families America home visitors work with families to address issues related to fostering positive parent–child interaction, understanding child development, and providing assistance in meeting family needs. A unique feature of the program involves performing systematic assessments for all families in a given geographic area. Results from this assessment are then used to decide which subset of families (e.g., first-time parents, adolescent parents) will be offered home visitation services.

Healthy Families America services are supported through a combination of public and private funding. Private foundation funds are used to support critical activities that include training, quality assurance, state systems development, and research. More than 70% of the program's federal funding support comes from Temporary Assistance to Needy Families (TANF) and the Social Security Act and is combined with state funding streams (e.g., general revenue, tobacco, TANF Maintenance of Effort) to support service delivery activities (Prevent Child Abuse America, 2005b).

Agencies designated as Healthy Family America sites must apply for affiliation and subsequent credentialing by agreeing to implement 12 critical elements that serve as the framework for implementing and delivering services. These elements are grouped into three areas. They are 1) service initiative, 2) service content, and 3) staff characteristics (Prevent Child Abuse America, 2005a). Service initiation elements address the intensity and duration of services provided to participants. Service content elements include the kinds of issues each program must be prepared to address when visiting families, such as providing culturally relevant services and materials; focusing on the comprehensive needs of the child and parent; and involving related professionals, such as medical providers, when appropriate. Staff characteristics speak to the skills, training, and qualification of the home visitors.

Since the program's inception in 1992, more than 15 studies to date have been conducted to determine the efficacy of the program model. The studies vary widely in terms of population studied (e.g., single parents, teen parents, parents with many risk factors); design (e.g., single group, comparison, randomized); and number of sites included in the study (single versus multi-site). Results from these studies suggest that the program is having a positive impact on parenting, family health, school readiness, and self-sufficiency.

INFUSING MENTAL HEALTH PROMOTION, PREVENTION, AND INTERVENTION STRATEGIES INTO PROGRAMS FOR INFANTS AND TODDLERS

Programs for infants, toddlers, and their families can intervene at each of the three points on the continuum of mental health services to create a comprehensive approach to infant mental health. Program staff members may already do many of these strategies without recognizing them as experiences or activities that support infant mental health. All staff members in a program for families with very young children play a role in the healthy social-emotional development of infants and toddlers. A parallel process mirrors healthy relationships among all who come into contact with infants and young children–relationships between parents and their children, between staff and children and staff and families, and among staff members themselves.

Partnerships with local service providers play a key role in providing comprehensive mental health services at all points on the continuum. Partnerships are vital to both the depth and breadth of the services available to families and can also be a source of professional development for staff members. Evidence from the national evaluation of Early Head Start noted significant benefits for child care agencies who partnered with Early Head Start programs to provide services (Love, Raikes, Paulsell, & Kisker, 2004).

Strategies to Promote Healthy Social-Emotional Development

The promotion of infant mental health happens in the daily interactions between staff members and families and in the program policies and procedures regarding all facets of program implementation, such as parent involvement, communication, staff development, and health and safety. The promotion of infant mental health begins with the quality of the relationships at all levels of the program—between program administrators and service providers, between staff members and families, and between children and their parents. The strategies that can be used to promote the healthy social-emotional development of infants and toddlers, such as focusing on relationships, using daily routines, and creating safe and nurturing environments, are discussed in the following sections.

Focus on Relationships

The quality of the relationships between young children and their adult caregivers (parents, grandparents, child care professionals) has a direct impact on social-emotional health and well-being in infants and toddlers, and helps caregivers understand infant development and the powerful role they play in fostering healthy emotional functioning. As the architects of Early Head Start noted,

> The child–caregiver relationships with the mother, father, grandparent and other caregivers are critical for providing infants and toddlers support, engagement, continuity and emotional nourishment necessary for health development, and the development of healthy attachments. Within the context of caregiving relationships, the infant builds a sense of what is expected, what feels right with the world, as well as skills and incentives for social turn-taking, reciprocity and cooperation. (U.S. Department of Health & Human Services, 1994)

The work with parents must first begin by developing relationships that are respectful and collaborative. Program staff members convey respect by seeking to understand what parents want for their children and how parents view their strategies and approaches to child rearing. Parents' goals for their children and their approach to child rearing are heavily influenced by culture. For example, some parents might find the idea of *responding to infant cues* akin to *spoiling* an infant. In this case, staff members might introduce the idea that acknowledging and meeting an infant's emotional needs helps children learn to regulate and manage their own emotions and behaviors. This work with parents takes time and must take into consideration the cultural expectations that drive parenting behavior. Respectful and trusting relationships with parents allow families to see staff members as resources when they encounter difficulties in meeting their children's needs. The extent to which parents are comfortable reaching out to child care teachers or home visitors to discuss parenting challenges or other concerns depends a great deal on how proactive staff are in forging relationships that communicate to parents that their thoughts and ideas about how to best support their child's development are welcomed and desired.

Program administrators play an important role in establishing the overall tone and environment that characterizes the program. To the extent that directors and other program leaders understand, respect, and value relationships in their program, they are better able to support staff in establishing respectful and meaningful relationships with children and parents. Program policies that honor the significance of relationships are reflected in staffing practices, such as teacher–child ratios and group size. Infants and toddlers should be cared for in small groups to allow caregivers the opportunity to read and respond to infant cues. Large staff–child ratios and group sizes undermine a teacher's ability to provide responsive care in a timely fashion and impede the child's ability to develop close, trusting relationships with a consistent caregiver.

The practices of *primary caregiving* and *continuity of care* further support strong early relationships. Primary caregiving refers to the practice of assigning a primary caregiver to be responsible for the care of a child during the day. Although other caregivers may be in the classroom providing care, the primary caregiver takes the lead and provides consistency for the child and family. Continuity of care is the practice of keeping children with the same caregiver throughout their early years rather then the customary practice of moving children to a different classroom based on chronological age or developmental skills. The frequent change in classrooms during a child's first 3 years creates ongoing disruptions in routines and the repeated loss of significant relationships.

Use Daily Routines

Both center- and home-based early care and education programs provide rich opportunities to support social-emotional development through the daily caregiving routines in which staff and family members engage each day. Home visitors are able to observe firsthand how family interactions and the home environment can be used to support infant development. They are able to point out the many ways that ordinary experiences, such as taking a bath, eating meals, or going for a walk, support their child's growth and development in significant ways. These *teachable moments* (see Chapter 11) offer some of the best opportunities for learning and have a lasting impact because they are rooted in real-life experiences.

In center-based environments, program directors must support teachers in their efforts to use daily routines with infants and toddlers as an important opportunity to build relationships and understand individual children in their care. Teachers can gain valuable information about individual children's temperament, coping abilities, and what it takes to successfully engage with infants and toddlers by carefully observing their behavior as they address basic needs through their day. This information is a critical component in individualizing the curriculum and in providing high-quality early learning experiences.

Create Safe and Nurturing Environments

Environments for infants and toddlers need to be safe, comfortable, and support active exploration with attentive adults nearby to respond to needs and support their learning. Sensitive caregivers help children understand and make sense of experiences in their environment. When children are exposed to environments that are unsafe, unpredictable, and provide limited support, their growing sense of competence and willingness to reach out and explore is compromised.

Health and safety issues are key infant mental health promotion strategies. Safety concerns have a direct impact on the interactions between caregivers and children. If an environment is unsafe for children to freely explore, much time and energy is spent on behavior management rather than quality caregiving and play experiences. Home visitors can help parents identify safety hazards in the home and create *safe zones* for free exploration. Safety regulations for licensed center-based and family child care are minimum standards, and program directors should take special care to ensure that all staff know and follow established guidelines.

Another important aspect of the environment is the amount of sensory stimulation. Although there is a great deal of individual variation, infants, especially, can be easily overstimulated. Overstimulation can be caused by too much noise, activity, or movement; too many lights or brightly contrasting colors; too much handling; or too many interactions with others. When stressed by too much stimulation, infants may become irritable, inconsolable, or so disengaged that they go to sleep to tune out the environment. Caregivers play a crucial role in early emotional regulation by watching for the baby's cues regarding how much stimulation is too much and helping the infant maintain a quiet and alert state of arousal, which is when he or she is most available to engage with others and with the surrounding world.

Strategies to Prevent Infant Mental Health Problems

Programs such as Early Head Start, Healthy Families America, and the Nurse Home Visiting program that focus on very young children who are at risk for adverse outcomes in social-emotional and other domains of development are ideal for buffering against adverse outcomes by providing targeted intervention services. Some prevention strategies to consider, such as identifying warning signs, conducting developmental screening and assessment, and offering mental health consultation, are discussed in the following sections.

Identify Warning Signs

One of the ways these programs can make a difference is to ensure that staff who are working with families are aware of warning signals that might require additional evaluation. These signs might include chronic feeding or sleep difficulties; inconsolable fussiness or irritability; incessant crying with little ability to be consoled; inability to adapt to new situations; inability to establish relationships with other children or adults; excessive hitting, biting, or pushing of other children; or very withdrawn behavior (ZERO TO THREE, 2005).

It is important to recognize as well that when a parent suffers from emotional distress, his or her ability to be emotionally available and responsive to an infant can be compromised. Thus, programs that are able to provide supports and services for parents to meet their own needs as individuals are also providing important preventive strategies to buffer the negative effect of parental distress on children.

The variety of backgrounds, languages, and customs of participating families is also important to consider when trying to understand the meaning of behavior. Practices that might be considered *red flags* for problems in American culture may be perfectly acceptable in another culture. Bed sharing, for example, is a hotly debated topic and customs vary widely from one culture to another on if, when, and how long children should be allowed to share a bed with their parents.

Conduct Developmental Screening and Assessment

The screening process is used to determine whether social-emotional as well as other developmental skills are progressing as expected or whether there is cause for concern and further evaluation. Fortunately, with increased attention focused on social-emotional development, there has been an increase in the number of screening tools and assessments—Squires, Bricker, and Twombly's (2002) *Ages & Stages Questionnaire®: Social-Emotional (ASQ:SE)* and Briggs-Gowan and Carter's (2002) *Brief Infant–Toddler Social and Emotional Assessment (BITSEA)*—available to support progress.

Screening alone is not indicative of a mental health diagnosis. It is the first step in an evaluation process designed to help determine whether an in-depth evaluation is necessary. Subsequent assessment activities to determine eligibility for early intervention services or make diagnoses must be completed by trained professionals with experience in the diagnostic assessment of infants and toddlers.

Parents should be full, voluntary participants in the screening and assessment process and any follow-up evaluations. The family context provides opportunities to identify early problems (e.g., screening for maternal depression). Screening procedures should be culturally sensitive and include multiple sources of information to both identify challenges and build on existing child and family strengths and resources.

Offer Mental Health Consultation

Many intervention programs have found it useful to employ the services of mental health consultants on a regular basis to work with their staff (see Chapter 13). For example, Head Start performance standards require that Head Start and Early Head Start programs offer a regular schedule of on-site mental health consultation that supports both staff and parents. These consultations might include classroom observations, individual consultations with parents regarding difficulties their child might be experiencing, sessions with staff about typical and atypical behavior, and workshops that address issues related to social-emotional development. The frequency and intensity of consultation services provided by mental health programs vary. Some child care programs, through creative community partnerships and support from state agencies interested in enhancing capacities, are providing resources to create and maintain mental health consultation activities in child care environments.

Strategies for Intervention for Social-Emotional Problems in Infants and Toddlers

Infusing intervention strategies in environments that serve infants and toddlers is challenging due to the fact that so few mental health professionals have been trained to provide these kinds of services. The following strategies of using a relationship-based approach and collaborating with community providers help build a system of support for treating infant mental health disturbances.

Use a Relationship-Based Approach

Infant mental health intervention is never approached by looking at the infant or toddler in isolation from his or her relationships and experiences with caregivers. This approach may differ from how mental health issues are addressed with older children and adults. Intervention for social-emotional problems should take into consideration the important people in the child's life, the quality of those relationships, and how the caregiving environment supports the child's capacities.

A relationship-based approach necessitates that all staff members view themselves as part of the intervention in the sense that all the interactions children and families have with the program have an impact on and may make a difference in how fully a family engages in the program and benefits from the services offered. It also recognizes that staff members are individuals; that is, their temperaments, past experiences, and family and cultural values influence how they respond to families. Supportive or reflective supervision can help staff members understand their own reactions to the children and families with whom they work and develop strategies that use this self-awareness to enrich their work. Thus, supervisory strategies must include time for regular opportunities to reflect with staff members on their work in an open and supportive environment.

Collaborate with Community Providers

Intervention for social-emotional disturbances can involve a variety of disciplines, such as early intervention providers, psychologists and psychiatrists, special educators, or occupational therapists, and may take place in a variety of environments. Depending on the problem and the age of the child, intervention could involve, for example, a therapeutic play group at a local gym with an occupational therapist, intervention with a special educator in the child's home, or parent–child psychotherapy in the office of a child psychologist.

Having a network of supports and services through community-based providers can facilitate how quickly families are able or willing to access services and how comfortable they are engaging with community providers. If, for example, staff members from an early care and education program invite service providers to use space at their center to meet with the parents or to provide direct services to the child in the classroom, family members may feel more open to the intervention.

BEYOND INDIVIDUAL PROGRAM STRATEGIES: THE NEED FOR A SYSTEMIC APPROACH TO INFUSING INFANT MENTAL HEALTH INTO ENVIRONMENTS THAT SERVE INFANTS AND TODDLERS

The extent to which staff members in programs that serve very young children feel equipped to address mental health issues is worth deep exploration. In October 2000, the Head Start Bureau convened an Infant Mental Health Forum to better understand the unique challenges confronting EHS programs across the country in meeting the social-emotional needs of infants and toddlers. As noted earlier, the Head Start Program Performance Standards specify the type of services EHS programs are required to provide at each point along the mental health service continuum. As a result of convening this forum, which included program staff, researchers, clinicians, and technical assistance providers, it was clear that many programs were struggling to address service needs at the prevention and intervention ends of the continuum, largely due to limited access to mental health professionals who understood and had experience providing services to very young children.

The Head Start Bureau responded to this need by funding the Early Head Start National Resource Center at ZERO TO THREE to implement the Pathways to Prevention Training Initiative. This effort was a multifaceted strategy that included materials development and ongoing intervention and consultation support. To address the acute needs for intervention and capacity building, 24 programs from around the country were selected to participate in this initiative through a competitive application process. Although programs had flexibility in determining activities based on local community needs, all had to agree that their efforts would focus on one of the following three goals: 1) increasing staff skills and knowledge in infant mental health; 2) strengthening critical program supports (e.g., a system for supervision); and 3) building the community's capacity to address the mental health needs of infants and toddlers. Programs were paired with infant mental health consultants to help them with one or more of these goals. These consultants worked with team leaders from each program site, along with their local mental health consultant to create a plan they would implement during their participation in Pathways to Prevention. (Additional details about the core elements of the model and lessons learned from evaluation activities are described in Boss, Mann, and Randolph [2004]). The results of this work have been shared broadly with the national network of the EHS program through print materials, audio conference calls, and presentations at national conferences in an effort to support greater attention to the mental health needs of young children and appropriate strategies for addressing those needs.

PART C OF THE INDIVIDUALS
WITH DISABILITIES EDUCATION IMPROVEMENT ACT

In 1986, Congress passed PL 99–457 amending the Education of the Handicapped Act by creating a new program focused on building comprehensive systems of early intervention services for infants and toddlers with disabilities and their families. In 1991, PL 99–457 was reauthorized as the Individuals with Disabilities Act Amendments (PL 102-119). The Infants and Toddlers program was later renamed "Part C" based on other amendments to this act, the most recent being the Individuals with Disabilities Education Improvement Act (IDEA) of 2004 (PL 108-446). The U.S. Department of Education provides formula grants to states and jurisdictions to provide early intervention (EI) services to all children below the age of 3 years who are experiencing a developmental delay or have a diagnosed physical or mental disability that has a high probability of resulting in delay. States may also choose to provide services to infants and toddlers who are biologically or environmentally at risk for developmental problems. Many states are currently taking a closer look at their EI system to ensure that infants and toddlers with mental health problems are identified and served by expanding the screening and assessment tools they use, providing intervention on typical and atypical social-emotional development to early intervention providers, and working more closely with mental health agencies.

CHALLENGES

Identifying and addressing the mental health needs of infants and toddlers, especially at the intervention end of the continuum, is fraught with challenges. Some challenges clearly reflect long-standing issues confronting mental health, regardless of the child's age, whereas others are related to work force issues, especially in child care, that makes providing consistent care by familiar caregivers a considerable challenge. Some of these challenges include

- The stigma associated with mental health problems

- Staff turnover in group care environments

- The shortage of mental health professionals trained to work with infants and toddlers

- Limited training opportunities for mental health professionals interested in infant mental health specialization

Unfortunately, mental health has long been considered a taboo topic with considerable stigma attached to it. The idea that very young children can and do suffer emotional pain is still one that many are unwilling to acknowledge. Whether acknowledged or not, however, clinical evidence is mounting that demonstrates the reality of such experiences for very young children. To ignore these problems makes it considerably more difficult for families because of a lack of validation that difficulties warranting attention do exist and that there is an absence of resources to support them. Emde (2001) emphasizes the importance of recognizing pain and suffering in young children, "It's difficult—but essential—to recognize pain and suffering in young children."

Acknowledging that such difficulties exist is the first step toward helping to put development back on track. That is, of course, assuming that communities have mental health professionals trained and able to provide such services.

The high rate of staff turnover in child care environments means that even children exhibiting no mental health difficulties are in jeopardy due to the risk of not having their basic social-emotional needs met due to a lack of consistent relationships. Much of the instability is associated with poor pay, low status, and lack of employment security. The need for a stabilized work force in child care is not a new concept. Advocates for quality child care have sounded this alarm for years because they know that all children, but especially infants and toddlers, benefit from having familiar and consistently available caregivers and teachers. Although some gains have been made with the advent of quality rating systems and programs, such as Teacher Education and Compensation Helps (TEACH) that reward teachers with monetary bonuses for gaining additional training and certifications, these strategies alone are inadequate to stem the rate of turnover. For more permanent gains to be made and sustained, many believe that child care requires a significant level of subsidization from public funds that parallels what military child care environments received once the federal government made a commitment to enhance the quality and availability of child care to ensure that armed services professionals were able to focus on mission-related responsibilities (Lombardi, 2003). Similar attention needs to be paid at all levels of government if these long-standing quality and work force issues are to be adequately addressed.

In many states, the absence of reimbursement policies through public and insurance programs for infant mental health intervention services means that few incentives exist for mental health professionals to specialize in this area of practice. A few states (e.g., Texas, Michigan, Florida) made some progress in this area, but in most states such services are not reimbursable. Limited opportunities to be gainfully employed as an infant mental health clinician has a direct impact on the number of training and professional development programs at the pre-service level. The Harris Professional Development Network and Infant Mental Health certificate programs provide rich training opportunities to a multidisciplinary cadre of professionals interested in specializing in this area of practice. They provide a foundation that must be expanded over time to see increases in the number of mental health professionals able to provide consultation and intervention-related services. Beyond preservice training, frontline providers who work with infants and toddlers (in both homes and center environments) require supervision that is relationship based, reflective, and consistently available. Working with infants and toddlers is emotionally intensive work. Parents often have strong feelings about what they want for their children and how to best address issues that relate to toileting, feeding, sleeping, guidance, and discipline. Teachers and caregivers bring their own professional and personal values and beliefs to their work. Staff members need support from supervisors who understand how relationships have an impact on a child's developmental experience. The Harris programs and Infant Mental Health certificate programs provide an important avenue for gaining training and experience needed to provide this form of supervision (see Chapter 5). More opportunities are needed given the number of environments and diverse array of professionals working with very young children and their families.

PRACTICE AND POLICY RECOMMENDATIONS

As continued interest in early social-emotional development for infants and toddlers grows, there are a number of strategies that would support capacity building in services across the promotion, prevention, and intervention continuum. Recently, ZERO TO THREE, in partnership with the National Conference of State Legislators (Cohen, Onunaku, Clothier, & Poppe, 2005), articulated several recommendations in a publication that speaks to strategies that must be implemented along the promotion, prevention, and intervention continuum.

- Promotion

  - Increase general public's awareness and understanding of early childhood mental health.

  - Integrate social-emotional development into existing services.

- Prevention

  - Expand early screening and early identification activities.

  - Provide mental health consultation to child care programs.

  - Invest in family mental heath services and supports.

- Intervention

  - Change Medicaid reimbursement policies for infant mental health services.

  - Expand the number of early childhood mental health clinicians that understand and are able to address mental health issues in very young children.

  - Address the distinct needs of young children affected by maltreatment, substance abuse, and domestic violence.

Gains are being made in select states across the country committed to creating and improving systems and services that address the mental health needs of very young children. Continued growth will require commitment from all levels of government, institutions of higher education, media outlets, service providers, and parents to increase awareness and build the capacity required to address mental health needs of very young children. Mental health clinicians, advocates, researchers, and policy experts have a responsibility to continue educating, informing, and supporting capacity-building activities that result in more families gaining access to comprehensive systems of care that can adequately address such problems. The potential for children's optimal development depends on it, and research makes it clear that intervening at the earliest possible point to enrich and sustain the most important relationships in the lives of very young children does make a lasting and significant difference.

REFERENCES

Administration on Children, Youth, and Families. (2002). *Making a difference in the lives of infants and toddlers and their families: The impact of Early Head Start. (Executive summary).* Washington, DC: Author.

Boss, J., Mann, T., & Randolph, S. (2004). Building infant mental health capacity through consultation: Early Head Start's approach. *ZERO TO THREE, 24*(6), 4–9.

Briggs-Gowan, M.J., & Carter, A.S. (2002). *Brief-Infant–Toddler Social and Emotional Assessment (BITSEA): Manual (Version 2.0).* New Haven, CT: Yale University.

Carter, A., Garrity-Rokous, F., Chazen-Cohen, R., Little, C., & Briggs-Gowan, M. (2001). Maternal depression and comorbidity: Predicting early parenting, attachment security, and toddler social-emotional problems and competencies. *Journal of the Academy of Child and Adolescent Psychiatry, 40*(1), 18–26.

Cohen, J., Onunaku, N., Clothier, S., & Poppe, J. (2005). Helping young children to succeed: Strategies to promote early childhood social and emotional development. Washington, DC: ZERO TO THREE & National Conference of State Legislators.

Education of the Handicapped Act Amendments of 1986, PL 99-457, 20 U.S.C. §§ 1400 *et seq.*

Ehrle, J., Adams, G., & Tout, T. (2001). *Who's caring for our youngest children: Child care patterns of infants and toddlers?* Washington, DC: The Urban Institute.

Emde, R. (2001). A developmental psychiatrist looks at infant mental health challenges for Early Head Start: Understanding context and overcoming avoidance. *ZERO TO THREE, 22*(1), 21–24.

Field, T. (1997). The treatment of depressed mothers and their infants. In L. Murray & P.J. Cooper (Eds.), *Postpartum depression and child development* (pp. 221–235). New York: The Guilford Press.

The Future of Children. (2001). Caring for infants and toddlers: Analysis. *The Future of Children, 11*(1), 2–5.

Goodman, S.H., & Gottlieb, I.H. (1999). Risk factors for psychopathology in children of depressed mothers: A developmental model for understanding mechanisms of transmission. *Psychological Review, 106*, 458–490.

Individuals with Disabilities Education Act Amendments of 1991, PL 102-119, 20 U.S.C. §§ 1400 *et seq.*

Individuals with Disabilities Education Improvement Act of 2004, PL 108-446, 20 U.S.C. §§ 1400 *et seq.*

Kitzman, H., Olds, D.L., Sidora, K., Henderson, C.R., Hanks, C., Cole, R., et al. (2000). Enduring effects of nurse home visitation on maternal life course: A 3-year follow-up of a randomized trial. *Journal of the American Medical Association, 283*(12), 1983–1989.

Korfmacher, J., O'Brien, R., Hiatt, S., & Olds, D.L. (1999). Differences in program implementation between nurses and paraprofessionals providing home visits during pregnancy and infancy: A randomized trial. *American Journal of Pubic Health, 89*(12), 1847–1851.

Lombardi, J. (2003). *Time to care: Redesigning child care to promote education, support families, and build communities.* Philadelphia: Temple University Press.

Love, J.M., Raikes, H.H., Paulsell, D., & Kisker, E.E. (2004). Early Head Start's role in promoting good quality child care for low-income families. In J. Lombardi & M.M. Bogel (Eds.), *Beacon of hope: The promise of Early Head Start for America's youngest children* (pp. 44–62). Washington, DC: ZERO TO THREE.

National Research Council and Institute of Medicine. (2000). From neurons to neighborhoods: The science of early childhood development. In J.P. Shonkoff & D.A. Phillips, (Eds.), *Committee on Integrating the Science of early childhood development: Board on children, youth and families, commissions on behavioral and social sciences education.* Washington, DC: National Academies Press.

National Scientific Council on the Developing Child. (2004). Young children develop in an environment of relationships. Working Paper No. 1. Retrieved August 30, 2005 from http://www.developingchild.net/reports.shtml

NICHD Early Child Care Research Network. (1994). Child care and child development: The NICHD study of early child care. In S.L. Friedman & H.C. Haywood (Eds.), *Developmental follow-up: Concepts, domains, and methods* (pp. 377–396). New York: Academic Press.

NICHD Early Child Care Research Network. (2002). Early child care and children's development prior to school entry: Results from the NICHD study of early child care. *American Educational Research Journal, 39,* 133–164.

NICHD Early Child Care Research Network. (2003a). Does quality of child care affect child outcomes at age 4 1/4? *Developmental Psychology, 39,* 451–469.

NICHD Early Child Care Research Network. (2003b). The NICHD study of early child care: Contexts of development and developmental outcomes over the first seven years of life. In J. Brooks-Gunn, A.S. Fuligni, & L.J. Berlin (Eds)., *Early child development in the 21st century* (pp. 181–201). New York: Teachers College Press.

Nurse–Family Partnerships. (nd) Retrieved September 5, 2005, from http://www.nursefamilypartnership.org

Olds, D.L. (2002). Prenatal and infancy home visiting by nurses: From randomized trials to community replication. *Prevention Science, 3*(3), 153–172.

Olds, D.L., Henderson, C.R., Kitzman, H.J., Eckenrode, J.F., Cole, R.E., & Tatelbaum, R.C. (1999). Prenatal and infancy home visitation by nurses: Recent findings. *The Future of Children, 9*(1), 44–65.

Olds, D.L., & Kitzman, H. (1993). Review of research on home visiting for pregnant women and parents of young children. *The Future of Children, 3*(3), 53–92.

Olds, D.L., Robinson, J., O'Brien, R., Luckey, D.W., Pettitt, L.M., & Henderson, C.R. (2002). Home visiting by paraprofessionals and by nurses: A randomized controlled trial. *Pediatrics, 110*(3), 486–496.

Oser, C., & Cohen, J. (2003). *America's Babies: The ZERO TO THREE Policy Center Data Book.* Washington, DC: ZERO TO THREE.

Parents as Teachers. (nd). *What is Parents as Teachers?* Retrieved August 31, 2005, from http://www.patnc.org

Phillips, D., & Adams, G. (2001). Child care and our youngest children. *The Future of Children, 11*(1), 35–52.

Prevent Child Abuse America. (nda). Healthy families America: A distinctive approach to home visiting. Retrieved August 30, 2005, from http://www.healthyfamiliesamerica.org.

Prevent Child Abuse America. (ndb). How are Healthy Families America programs funded? Retrieved August 30, 2005, from http://www. healthfamiliesamerica.org

Rosman, E., Perry, D., & Hepburn, K. (2005). *The best beginning: Partnerships between primary care and mental health and substance abuse services for young children and their families.* Washington, DC: Georgetown University, National Technical Assistance Center for Children's Mental Health.

Shonkoff, J.P., & Phillips, D.A. (Eds.). (2000). *From neurons to neighborhoods: The science of early childhood development.* Washington, DC: National Academies Press.

Squires, J., Bricker, D., & Twombly, E. (2002). *Ages & Stages Questionnaires®: Social-Emotional (ASQ:SE): A parent–completed, child-monitoring system for social-emotional behaviors.* Baltimore: Paul H. Brookes Publishing Co.

U.S. Department of Health and Human Services. (1994). *The statement of the advisory committee on services for families with infants and toddlers.* Washington, DC: Author.

Wagner, M.M., & Clayton, S.L. (1999). The Parents as Teachers program: Results from two demonstrations. *The Future of Children, 9*(1), 91–115.

ZERO TO THREE. (1994). *Diagnostic classification of mental health and developmental disorders of infancy and early childhood* (DC:0–3). Washington, DC: ZERO TO THREE.

ZERO TO THREE. (2005). *Diagnostic classification of mental health and developmental disorders of infancy and early childhood (DC:0–3R).* (rev. ed.). Washington, DC: ZERO TO THREE.

ZERO TO THREE Infant Mental Health Task Force. (2001, December). *Definition of infant mental health.* Unpublished manuscript.

ZERO TO THREE Infant Mental Health Task Force (2002, May). *Definition of infant mental health disorder.* Unpublished manuscript.

13

Promoting Social-Emotional Development in Young Children

Mental Health Supports in Early Childhood Centers

Paul J. Donahue, Beth Falk, and Anne Gersony Provet

■ ■ ■

Raising young children in this country has become an increasingly challenging endeavor. Many families across the economic spectrum do not live in communities with established child-rearing networks. The mobility of families, which often reduces access to extended kin, and the financial realities, which often require both parents to work outside the home, are just two of the factors that have limited the transfer of child-rearing techniques and strategies across generations and across town. In many places, the pressures to focus on achievement-oriented activities at a young age have limited parents' time and desire to attend to more basic developmental concerns. Early academic expectations have intensified, such that parents often feel compelled to teach letters, colors, and numbers to their preschoolers at home, sometimes at the expense of fostering children's independence, listening skills, or imagination. The gap between early childhood *experts* and parents appears to be widening, and the *conventional wisdom* can be hard to identify. Conflicting ideas about sleep arrangements, toileting, and discipline are just a few of the issues on which there seems to be less agreement or commonly followed advice. Furthermore, there is a lack of shared understanding of how to respond to tragedy, whether it is a death or separation in the family or a trauma in the local community or the nation, and there are often few places for parents to turn for help.

Early childhood centers are in a unique position to bridge this gap. Once viewed as playful and optional additions to family life, preschools and child care centers fill important educational and economic demands in this country. With the advances in the study of brain development in infants and toddlers and research on the early acquisition of learning skills, preschool education has taken on a new significance. Early childhood programs also meet the needs of working families who require out-of-home child care. Nearly 60% of women with children younger than age 6 are in the labor force and need child care for at least part of the work week (Zigler, Finn-Stevenson, & Stern, 1997). Recent changes in welfare and workfare legislation have also increased the demands for child care, and more young children are now spending extended days in center-based care. It is now widely accepted that early childhood educators play a major role in shaping children's emotional, social, and cognitive development, and they help to lay the foundation for future academic success (Shonkoff & Phillips, 2000). Many early childhood centers have also become cornerstones of their community, offering parenting workshops, recreational programs, and health and education classes.

With their increasing prominence, early childhood programs are typically the first to feel the impact of family stresses. In many urban and some rural communities, Head Start centers and childcare programs serve large numbers of disadvantaged families. Many of these children are affected by their parents' struggle to provide for their families' basic needs and to maintain adequate housing and employment; they come to their centers bringing their worries with them. Fewer young children now live in two-parent households than at any point in recent times. Across all socioeconomic groups, a large percentage of marriages that have produced children now end in divorce, and 40%–50% of children born in this country in the last decade will reside in single-parent homes at some point in their childhood (Dubow, Roecker & D'Imperio 1997). With these developments, early childhood education programs are often implicitly or explicitly asked to take on a more primary role in child rearing.

The increase in the reported incidence of trauma in families has raised new concerns about the psychological development and educational needs of young children. Violence, both within the home in the form of domestic violence and child abuse and in the community, has been shown to have a profound impact on children's emotional adjustment and cognitive development (Cohen & Walthall, 2003; Pynoos & Eth, 1986; ZERO TO THREE, 1994). In families affected by substance abuse, HIV/AIDS, mental illness, and other debilitating diseases, children have been forced to deal with the loss or potential loss of parenting figures, often forcing young children to take on caregiving responsibilities. Research has shown that children with many risk factors and those exposed to multiple traumas are far more likely to show signs of emotional maladjustment or behavior problems (Breslau, Chilcoat, Kessler, & Davis, 1999; Rutter & Quintin, 1977).

Young children are especially vulnerable to the disruptions caused by traumatic events because they do not have well-developed physical or psychological resources to defend against them. They depend on adults to help them make sense of the trauma, heighten their resilience, and shield them from its ill effects. When their primary caregivers are also affected, they are less available to provide reassurance to their young children and to help them re-establish their sense of safety and security. As a result, the burden of care for these children often shifts, at least in part, to caregivers outside their home. The child care center often takes on added significance for children affected by trauma who crave consistency and nurturance and are looking for a safe haven where they can play and learn and focus on more age-appropriate tasks of development.

CHALLENGES IN THE CLASSROOM

Many of the children who have had disruptions in their early development and attachments present with challenging behaviors in the classroom. They may appear to be fearful, disorganized, inattentive, and unresponsive to learning (Koplow, 1996). Head Start teachers have reported that their students are displaying more symptoms of emotional distress, including withdrawal, depression, acting out, and aggressive behaviors (Yoshikawa & Knitzer, 1997). This trend mirrors findings from epidemiological research suggesting an increased prevalence of psychiatric disorder in children with onset at younger ages (Cohen, Provet, & Jones, 1996). Many of the disturbances that emerge in older children can be traced to risk factors present in infancy and early childhood (Werner, 1989).

Many early childhood programs are struggling to adapt to this added responsibility. Teachers and other preschool staff are often overwhelmed by the extent of their children's disturbance or distress, and they do not feel they have received adequate training to respond to their needs (Knitzer, 1996). They fear that opening up discussion of traumatic or stressful events might lead to unpredictable emotional reactions in the children that they cannot control. Teachers also often feel pressured to maintain a formal academic curriculum with an emphasis on the mastery of cognitive concepts, and they do not feel it is appropriate to use classroom time to deal with children's emotional turmoil (Hyson, 1994).

In addition to coping with an increase in family stresses and childhood trauma, many early childhood programs are struggling to maintain developmentally appropriate curriculum in the face of external pressure to focus more directly on early academic tasks. This trend is seen frequently but not exclusively in middle class communities where pressure to compete with peers and stay ahead of age expectancies can add undue stress to children and their families. Preschools that emphasize social-emotional development more than teaching pre-academic skills often feel at odds with the parents they serve and, not infrequently, with local school districts whose expectations for kindergarten children are often at the far end of a developmental continuum. As one teacher described the situation in Westchester County, New York, "Kindergarten is now equivalent to second grade just 15 years ago" (G.M., personal communication, October 17, 2002). As a result, some preschools feel they must move forward with learning tasks before many children have the developmental skills to succeed, including the ability to separate and work independently, to tolerate frustration and persevere, and to remain attentive and delay gratification.

INTEGRATING MENTAL HEALTH AND EARLY CHILDHOOD EDUCATION

Moving Beyond Traditional Interventions

As preschools have had to adapt to this changing climate, so too have mental health practitioners. Drawing from work pioneered with older children and adolescents, researchers and clinicians working with young children are now recommending that mental health providers expand their focus beyond the traditional model of office or clinic-based services (Knitzer, 1996). High-risk children and families are often unresponsive to these services because intervention can be derailed by logistical difficulties (e.g., transportation, child care), financial constraints, or psychological factors (e.g., family disorganization, fear or mistrust of mental health agencies). In a typical clinic model, intervention occurs only when a child's behavior or emotional distress reaches clinically significant levels. Symptoms often escalate and behavior becomes more entrenched in the intervening period between first detection of emotional problems and referral for intervention. It is also not uncommon for educational and mental health agencies to have an *all or none* threshold for psychological intervention in which children who do not qualify for a diagnosable mental illness receive few or no services. In the process, opportunities for prevention or early intervention are often lost.

Traditional therapies are also usually not well integrated with the rest of children's lives, as other professionals involved rarely get or give regular feedback on their progress. Nor do they have a chance to plan interventions together. Instead, young children tend to be segmented into functional parts (speech and language, cognitive, emotional, and so forth), with each specialist devising his or her own intervention plan and sometimes ignoring the underlying developmental struggles and stressors that a more holistic approach might uncover. Mental health services often still emanate from a child-focused rather than a family or systems approach. In this framework, clinicians spend much time and energy on the specific presenting difficulty in the child and relatively little examination of the family as a key contributor to the problem as well as a central player in its resolution. As young children are so dependent and emotionally engaged with their caregivers, clinicians who fail to involve parents, teachers, and other significant adults during intervention can miss critical opportunities for change.

A Collaborative Model: Mental Health Consultation

Given the changes in early childhood education and mental health, the preschool has become, in many ways, the ideal environment for integrating the work of professionals in both disciplines. Forging a partnership between mental health professionals and teachers allows schools to provide a comprehensive approach to the emotional and cognitive development of the children they serve. The preschool is also a logical place for clinicians to reach out and involve parents in their children's development and to support them in developing their own coping strategies. Unlike the clinic or office, the school provides ample opportunities for more informal and brief interactions between a mental health consultant and parents. In this way, parents and other family members can come to know the clinicians at their own pace in a familiar environment often before any concerns regarding developmental delays or emotional distress in the children have been noted.

Early childhood programs are often mainstays in their neighborhoods, respected and trusted by the local population. Joining together with these programs gives clinicians the imprimatur to practice without the same stigma or skepticism that might be applied in the less familiar office environment. The experienced mental health consultant will also seek to learn more about the ethnic and cultural traditions of the families, the program, and the local community. The preschool–mental health partnership presents the opportunity to provide interventions that respond to the needs of all the children in the center, not just those with identifiable symptoms of emotional disturbance or those deemed most at risk. Clinicians can be available to consult on issues of any magnitude as their primary role is to foster the behavioral, emotional, and cognitive development of all children. This prevention model includes *check-ups* of all the classrooms through observations, participation in team meetings, and *wellness* visits with those children who are responding well to the school environment. This allows the clinician to not only respond to crises and dire situations, but in some instances to anticipate them and provide early intervention to children at risk. In addition, the consultant has the opportunity to acknowledge and enhance the everyday workings of the teachers and staff in the school that create a welcoming environment and foster the social-emotional competence of all the children.

PRECURSORS TO AN EFFECTIVE COLLABORATION: SKILLS AND COMPETENCIES

Developing an effective collaboration between mental health providers and preschools requires a good deal of enthusiasm, respect, and support from both parties. The mental health consultant must be careful to develop a set of shared assumptions and goals with the school and not assume a rigid *expert* stance regarding the ways to enhance the children's development. The process of defining goals should result from a mutual examination that draws on the expertise of both teachers and clinical staff. Consultants must also recognize and appreciate the opportunities available in this environment to have an impact on many children, parents, and educators. Although clinicians of diverse backgrounds and experience can function in this role, the effective consultant must be flexible and team oriented, enjoy community-based environments, and be comfortable working autonomously. The consultant must also be adept at handling multiple roles and responsibilities, including crisis intervention, parent workshops, child observations and assessments, teacher training, and systems work. Perhaps most importantly, consultants should acknowledge their own limitations as sole agents of change and seek to share their knowledge and training with teachers and parents who will have the greatest impact on the young children in their community.

The partnership is enhanced when teachers are willing to consider their educational role in broad terms that encompass the social-emotional development of children. The mental health collaboration will also be strengthened if teachers are open to new ideas and disciplines and are willing to integrate these in the classroom. Ideally, they are willing to undertake new challenges with the consultant, focus on feelings and social skills, confront difficult realities of children's lives, and reflect on and discuss their own feelings and reactions elicited in their work with the children.

Entering the Preschool System

The early days of the collaboration are often marked by wariness and confusion on each side. Most consultants report some degrees of discomfort in the new, unfamiliar terrain of nursery school, particularly those trained in traditional mental health environments. Although not often met with overt resistance or hostility by the early childhood staff, they may not feel particularly welcome, supported, and at ease. Typically, consultants are unsure of the staff's feelings about them and may be unclear about their role in the program. In the following scenario, a consultant's initial meeting took an unexpected turn.

It was the consultant's first visit to the small nursery school to which she had been assigned. After being warmly greeted by the director, the consultant then expected to learn more about the center and talk with the director about her role. Instead, the director immediately launched into a story about the illness of a friend. Throughout the lengthy exposition, the director described her friend's ordeal in great detail and included a complex description of the multiple interconnections of the people in her life and in the community. At first, the consultant felt confused and off-balance. What was going on here? As she listened, she wondered why the director was telling her, a stranger, all of this. Was she desperately in need of someone to talk to and saw the consultant as a therapist? It did not appear so. She was telling a good story, her pain contained and secondary.

It gradually became clear as the story unfolded and the consultant relaxed that the purpose of the story was to introduce the consultant to the life of the community of which the director was an intimate part. Behind the evident poverty and decaying buildings was a vital community and an extensively connected and caring group of people to which the center was inextricably linked. The director was introducing all of this to the consultant and also closely observing her response. She wondered if this outsider would be able to appreciate the many facets of the community—the strengths as well as the weaknesses. Will she enter and become a part of it, or will she remain outside, seeing it as dangerous, foreign, and something to be kept at a distance and judged?

■ ■ ■

This example illustrates the complexity of entering an early childhood program, particularly when both consultant and program are new to the work. For the program, it is opening a door to the outside, showing strengths, vulnerabilities, hopes, and fears. It can be a threatening experience as well as a hopeful one. For the consultant, who is often trained in very different ways of intervening, it means entering a complex system as an outsider whose role is not clearly defined. This ambiguity can create many opportunities, but it can also cause the consultant to feel ungrounded and struggling to define his or her role. For the child care staff, the first task is observing the consultant. Will this person understand the difficulties they are facing? Will the consultant be compassionate or harsh and undermining? How can he or she help? How much should they tell the consultant? Whose side is he or she on? It is critical for the consultant to be sensitive and responsive to the feelings and perceptions of the staff as they evaluate each other in the early stages of their work together. This involves spending time together, listening to staff, and establishing a dialogue with them. Openness, flexibility, a desire to listen, and the ability to empathize with the various staff members are all important tools that the consultant can use to begin this dialogue.

Not only should the consultant address any preconceptions the staff has about a consultant's role, but he or she should also step back from any preconceived ideas about the way the entry process should proceed. Although the consultant will have an agenda for this early phase of entry, he or she should avoid developing fixed notions regarding the sequence and pacing of this process. For example, in the previous vignette, the consultant had to relinquish her expectations about the purpose of the first meeting with the director. In particular, she had to let go of her initial impulse to learn more concrete information about the center up front and, instead, allow the process to unfold in a less controlled manner. She could then respond to the director's underlying desire to introduce the consultant to the life of the community.

Although openness and the need for flexibility are essential, there are some general guidelines to consider when entering into a preschool child care program. First is the need to work closely with the director of the program, particularly in the beginning of the partnership. The director is often in the best position to report on the program's strengths and assess its needs. The consultant and director will initially establish a list of priorities and rough schedule for the consultant and a schedule of how much time will be spent in the classroom, meeting with teachers, and engaging parents. A solid working relationship will develop over time and with input from both director and consultant. The director may not have formal mental health training, but he or she should nonetheless feel a certain degree of comfort with the consultant's clinical judgment, finding it compatible with her expertise in early childhood as well as the dictates of common sense. It should be understood that the mental health professional operates within certain confidentiality guidelines that place some limits on sharing clinical material, particularly if therapy is conducted on site. The director, however, should feel that the consultant provides relevant information to the director and the staff in an appropriate and timely manner and is able to invite the participation of involved teachers, social workers, and specialists throughout the various stages of this process.

The consultant must next consider how to introduce his or her work to the staff, which can be a sensitive process. Clearly, the consultant's usefulness to the program must be clear. The consultant should acknowledge expertise in relevant areas, such as child development, the effect of stress and trauma on young children, classroom management of acting out behaviors, and how and when to intervene when children show signs of emotional distress or developmental delays. The consultant, however, wants to avoid being narrowly defined as the *expert* or the *problem fixer.* The consultant can work toward this goal by communicating a genuine collaborative mind-set by welcoming the professional expertise of the center's staff and openly sharing his or her assessments of the program's strengths and areas where he or she might be of help. The consultant can do this in a formal way by structuring time to spend with the teachers in each classroom and making appointments for contact outside the room. Typically, however, the process unfolds in a more natural and informal way. The consultant may be asked to observe a child and, in the process, spend time with all the teachers and children in the classroom. During this process, the consultant gets to know the teachers and hopefully establishes the reputation of an interested, nonjudgmental, and supportive professional.

This process evolves over time and occurs in many contexts. Spending time in the staff room and drinking coffee and chatting with staff is a way to establish a more relaxed tone. Providing needed help by covering the classroom when a teacher steps out, helping on the playground or with a special project, or joining mealtime preparations and clean up is another way to establish spirited collaboration with the staff. The goal is to let staff get to know the consultant at the same time that the consultant is getting to know the center.

Many consultants find that the environment is more like a large family than a formal and rigidly hierarchical agency or company. As a result, exchanges with staff may be more casual and intimate. For example, a consultant may share more personal information than typically shared in other professional environments. Depending on the style of the consultant, this may be a pleasure or a disconcerting ambiguity that shifts the usual professional stance. In either case, the consultant is likely to develop new and more broadly defined professional relationships that require an adjustment period for both sides.

This early stage of relationship building lays the foundation for the nature of possible interventions that the consultant can offer the center. In a typical clinic environment, the therapist relationship is more narrowly defined and tends to focus on an individual, a family, and those individuals directly involved. The preschool consultant is most effective when he or she views potential clients as the children (individually and as a group), the teacher (as an individual and a conduit to the children, the director, and staff), and the system as a whole. The entry period, therefore, sets the stage for building a multitude of relationships, including those less typically involved in traditional environments.

As the consultant becomes familiar with the director and staff and discusses possible roles he or she may have in the program, he or she must be careful to build in time for the entry process. As much as possible, he or she should present and reiterate, if necessary, the need to develop relationships with the staff, children, and parents through observations, helping out in class, and meeting with parents informally before being asked to commit to specific interventions or goals. Often this entails holding back on responding actively to calls for help, which can be very difficult for a consultant looking to prove his or her worth to staff or wanting to actively try out interventions with children. Similarly, the consultant may feel pressured to respond quickly when the center's needs appear to be intense. Although issues of safety always require immediate action, the consultant must nonetheless strive to act thoughtfully and appropriately, avoiding hasty interventions. It may be difficult for some of the involved individuals to wait out this seemingly slow and unstructured entry; however, the consultant must recognize that a restrained, thoughtful, and gradual beginning helps establish appropriate and effective relationships that lay the foundation for the success of future interventions.

Collaboration with Teachers

The mental health consultant working with early childhood teachers is more effective when working to develop an open and respectful relationship with them—one that encourages a free flow of information back and forth. The degree of warmth and trust in the relationship will further influence a teacher's acceptance of this *outsider's* presence and will have an impact on the children's willingness to relate to the consultant and share their feelings and concerns. At some point, the consultant must prove his or her worth to the teacher by actively helping in the classroom, dealing with difficult children, or being available to discuss personal issues. The consultant should also recognize that the teachers are the key agents of change within the program and that the work in the classroom has the most far-reaching impact on the children. It is also important for the consultant to gain an appreciation for the fact that early childhood teachers are often firmly embedded in the communities they serve and frequently have long-standing relationships with the families that they will refer to the consultant.

Interventions in the classroom often emanate from teachers who seek to try out or obtain approval for their ideas from the mental health consultant. For example, a suggestion to use more transitional objects with Andre, a 4-year-old boy from Brazil with severe separation anxiety, or to provide more special time to 3-year-old Anna, whose father recently died after a long illness, are but two examples of strategies proposed and carried out by teachers with the consulting psychologist's encouragement.

This team approach can demystify notions of *promoting mental health* and reassure teachers that the consultant is there to support their work and help the children feel more comfortable. During this process, the teachers often come to realize that their goals in the classroom of helping children feel secure, teaching them to share and work cooperatively, working with them to overcome frustration, and helping them to focus and learn self-control are in fact the *cornerstones* of social-emotional competence in young children.

Classroom management techniques often require more intense and joint planning, but they generally begin with the teacher's request for help with difficult-to-manage children. The following is an example of such a scenario.

Andrew, a 3½-year-old boy, was an overly energetic child in the classroom. Impulsive and somewhat aggressive, he would frequently run about the room crashing into other children or toys and disturb free play as well as story time. Early attempts to contain his aggression were fairly successful. Dr. Jones, the consulting psychologist, and Andrew's teacher, Ms. Winn, designed a behavior plan for school and home that his parents gladly adopted. His impulsiveness and hyperactivity continued to wreak havoc, however, especially during circle time. Finally Ms. Winn decided to have Andrew sit in an adult-size chair with a cushion by her side at circle time—a chair in which no other children were allowed to sit. Andrew readily took to this idea, and although fidgety and often inattentive, he began to sit through most circle times. Few other children complained about Andrew's special chair as they seemed to recognize that his sitting there allowed them to enjoy the teacher's stories. In fact many became protective of Andrew's new position and would mildly scold each other if they tried to usurp his place.

In this case, the consultant helped to design a behavior rewards system, but played a more critical role in supporting the teacher's ideas for how to contain and manage her student. Together they charted his progress, looking for changes in the frequency, intensity, and duration of the targeted behaviors. This process is often critical with more active or impulsive preschoolers, as it highlights that attention, impulse control, and inhibition are developmental processes not fixed entities. Seeing progress toward more self-control and focus is often the key to teachers being more receptive to these children and less likely to want to label them or, in more severe cases, to ask that they be medicated or removed from their classrooms.

In a well-functioning partnership, even the most traumatic events can be jointly addressed by teacher and consultant, as shown in the following example.

Ms. Marano, an experienced head teacher, and Ms. Andrews, a consulting social worker, had been working closely together at St. Joseph's Head Start for 2 years. Although initially quite anxious when discussing her children's emotional concerns, Ms. Marano had gained considerable confidence in this area and knew she could call on Ms. Andrews for support as needed. One Monday morning, 4-year-old Charles announced to the class that his mother had been stabbed over the weekend. Ms. Andrews was immediately called into the classroom to speak with Charles and his teacher and lead a brief circle time in which she clarified what had happened, elicited the children's concerns regarding their own and Charles's safety, and offered them the opportunity to discuss things further with her or Ms. Marano whenever they desired. Ms. Marano did not shy away from this event and continued to report on Charles's and the other children's progress in team meetings and to call Ms. Andrews back for check-ups with the class over the next several weeks.

In this case, Charles undoubtedly would have benefited from having an insightful, experienced, and psychologically minded teacher. Yet, the teacher's ability to call the consultant to share the burden of processing this trauma and to follow the mental health professional's lead added a further dimension to her classroom repertoire and allowed her to explore new emotional territory without major trepidation.

Engaging Parents

Becoming familiar with parents in early childhood centers is much different than in traditional mental health environments. As mentioned, there are many opportunities for informal contact—at drop-off and pick-up times when parents often gather to have coffee or chat, in the classroom with parent volunteers, and at parent gatherings or workshops. The consultants may be expected to join in local debates and share some details of their own family and personal life with staff members and parents. Similar to therapy, each consultant needs to come to his or her own limits of disclosure and to assess how these limits have an impact on the relationship with the center. Yet, for many mental health professionals, this less confined role can be a welcome break from the more formal structure of traditional psychotherapy and gives them the opportunity to support social-emotional development in a more typical context.

Often interventions with parents involve brief targeted interventions aimed at remediating specific fears or anxieties of children in the preschool. In some cases, the consultant may maintain a relationship with a parent, and the intervention may focus on helping the child indirectly through parent contact and *checking in* with the teacher:

The Rosens, whose daughter Nancy attended preschool in their suburban town, had watched their home burn to the ground after some faulty wiring ignited a massive fire. The consultant at the preschool, Dr. Douglas, had heard about the fire, but the teacher and school director reported that Nancy, who was a friendly and confident 4-year-old child, was doing well and did not appear to need the consultant's help at school. The family had found a suitable house to rent while their home was being rebuilt, and they all seemed to be coping well. About 1 month after the fire, Mrs. Rosen called the consultant and explained that although Nancy seemed fine during the daytime, she was having a difficult time falling asleep, insisted on sleeping in her parents' bed, and woke up many times during the night. Everyone was exhausted, and Mrs. Rosen felt a mixture of sympathy and anger toward her young daughter.

Mrs. Rosen did not want the consultant to see Nancy directly, but she was extremely eager to talk about how to handle the sleep problem. They spoke extensively for the next 2 weeks, and during these conversations the consultant primarily provided a sounding board for Mrs. Rosen, as well as made some concrete recommendations. These included having Mrs. Rosen and Nancy play out fire scenarios using dollhouse figures and puppets, attempt relaxation techniques at bedtime, and have one of Nancy's parents sit in her bedroom while she fell asleep. Mrs. Rosen used some of the recommendations and chose not to try others, and she remained in phone contact with the consultant over the next several weeks. Nancy's sleep disturbance gradually improved, and she was also able to talk about the experience of the fire with more ease. The consultant did not hear from Mrs. Rosen again until later in the spring when she called to let him know how much better things were going at home.

In this example, the parents made use of the consultant in a spontaneous, circumscribed manner; however, such brief interventions often carry meaning that goes beyond the immediate situation. Many parents report a sense of reassurance and relief in knowing that a mental health professional is on-hand just in case to answer questions, listen, and provide an informed opinion when necessary. Just as teachers test the waters with the consultant during the entry period, parents also may try out the consultant to see if this is a person who can be trusted and is approachable and helpful. Even when their encounters are brief, parents' positive experiences with a consultant are likely to encourage them to support the notion of on-site mental health services, to feel more comfortable with mental health professionals in general, and to spread the word to other parents.

Once they become a familiar presence, consultants need to be aware of boundary issues in presenting education or intervention recommendations to parents, as they may not always be eager to participate and may be confused by the on-site presence of a mental health specialist. Children who display signs of behavior or emotional problems in early childhood centers have usually not been previously identified as needing services. Parents who enroll their children in nursery schools or child care are not necessarily seeking support or advice with these issues as they would if, for instance, they voluntarily came to a mental health provider. Often the need for more parental input arises when a child's functioning is compromised in the classroom or when his or her behavior is disruptive and has an impact on other children. In these instances, the centers typically ask parents to come in and discuss the situation. Parents are more likely to comply with this request and react less defensively if they have had a previous relationship with the center and if the staff and the consultant assume a nonthreatening tone in presenting the areas of concern. If there is a healthy rapport, calling parents in for a discussion can be a relatively simple process, and the consultant may well be welcomed as another potential problem solver.

When Ms. Boudreau was asked to come into the Little Tots Center to discuss her son's separation difficulty, she was not surprised. Ben, a 3-year-old boy who had recently immigrated with his family from Europe, was tearful and clingy throughout much of each morning and seemed to be reacting in part to his mother's inconsistency during drop-off times. She would sometimes stay briefly and reassure him, but at other times she would stay for extended periods as he began to cry or show other signs of distress. During their meeting, the consultant suggested that Ben bring classroom books home that she could translate into French, her native language, to help him feel more comfortable and more connected with his peers. The consulting psychologist advised her to stick to a more consistent pattern in the morning, staying for 10–15 minutes to help him settle and then leaving him in the care of his teachers. Within 2 weeks, this combination of a fixed routine and using books as transitional objects greatly eased Ben's partings with his mother, and he began to more actively join in classroom activities.

The mother in this example was already well disposed toward the school, acknowledged her son's problems, and was not threatened or alarmed by the notion of psychological intervention. The consultant and teacher also had time to discuss the issues in advance and were hopeful that they could work together with the child and his mother. At times, children's classroom difficulties are presented in a less coordinated and timely manner and to parents who are less prepared to hear about them. The consultant may be asked to intervene when there are strains in the relationship between the parents and the preschool. Often, the goal in these cases is to improve communication and foster a mutual understanding between parents and staff, as well as respond to the current problem.

Ms. Gonzalez worked as an administrator at a public school prekindergarten, and her 4-year-old son, Manny, was enrolled in the program. Manny was an active and rambunctious boy who was prone to accidents at home and in school. Previous incidents at the school in which he had sustained minor cuts and bruises had left his parents angry and suspicious, and they believed that Manny's teachers were not providing adequate supervision and did not particularly care for him. In classroom visits, the consultant, Dr. Monroe, did not find that supervision was a problem, but he did observe that the teachers were not comfortable with Manny and the three or four other active boys in the class. They ranged from being tentative to sometimes being harsh and overbearing with them. To help the situation, Dr. Monroe encouraged the teachers to have more active outdoor playtime, and then he organized ball games for these boys. During one of these, Manny was tackled by two other boys and received a fairly serious gash above his lip. He was brought to the nurse who administered first aid and contacted Manny's mother, whose office was just down the hall. Ms. Gonzalez was furious that she had not been contacted directly by the teachers and by what she again perceived to be a lack of supervision because nobody could tell her exactly what had happened.

Dr. Monroe was informed by the director of Ms. Gonzalez's reaction and so he stopped by her office at lunch that day. He explained that he had in fact been supervising Manny, and that the teachers had not been remiss in their duty. He also talked at length with Ms. Gonzalez about Manny's high activity level and shared ideas about how to help Manny channel some of his energy and organize himself both at home and in school. He also encouraged Ms. Gonzalez to sit down with Manny's teachers and raise her concerns directly with them. She scheduled a meeting for the following week and seemed to feel that the teachers heard her concerns. The remainder of the school year passed without any major incident, and the consultant observed that the teachers seemed more attentive and more comfortable with Manny.

In this example, a moment of crisis turned into an opportunity for a parent and staff to take stock of their relationship and openly air their disagreements. Rather than contribute to a lingering resentment by both parties, it forced open the issues between them, helped along by some coaxing from the consultant. The fact that the consultant was involved in the incident placed him squarely in the center of the dispute for a brief time. Although this was an awkward position, he worked hard not to be defensive with the child's mother and not to shy away from her anger. Being in this position also allowed him to share some of the *blame* with the teachers and to further empathize with their dilemmas in dealing with active preschool boys.

Observation and Assessment of Children

Federal mandates regarding services for children with disabilities have spawned a large system of assessment centers and service providers, regulated through the Individuals with Disabilities Education Improvement Act (IDEA) of 2004 (PL 180-446). Preschool-age children who present with clear developmental problems are frequently referred to agencies and/or school districts for evaluations to determine whether a disability exists and, when appropriate, are directed to services or special preschool programs. Mental health consultants in clinical environments are often asked to work with children and families who have already gone through an extensive and standardized evaluation process. In contrast, mental health professionals in early childhood environments are able to approach assessment from a much broader and more flexible perspective.

For on-site consultants, referrals represent a wide continuum of cognitive, behavioral, and emotional issues and often require only informal assessments. Consultants can be helpful in differentiating where on this spectrum an initial referral may reside. Sometimes all that may be necessary is for the consultant to observe and offer reassurance about a child.

The consultant and teacher met to talk about Lorenzo, a boy whom the teacher described as "hyper" and inattentive. The consultant observed Lorenzo and noticed several things that he shared with the teacher. Lorenzo was an exuberant, and extremely physically active 3-year-old. He did not join the class during circle time on the day the consultant observed; instead, he quietly played with puzzles in another part of the room, but he did not appear to disrupt the rest of the group. Although his attention span was limited, Lorenzo was able to respond when called upon in group time.

What really struck the consultant was Lorenzo's affection for his teacher. Lorenzo took every opportunity to fling his arms around the teacher, giving her giant bear hugs. The embrace was always returned, and the teacher generally seemed to enjoy having this active independent boy in her class. She was usually able to cajole him into following the routines and rules of the classroom without engaging in prolonged power struggles. As the consultant and teacher talked, it became clear to both that Lorenzo was still adjusting to his first structured group experience. It was too soon to form conclusions about his activity level or attention span, and the conversation ended with an agreement to keep in touch about Lorenzo, but not to refer him for any other intervention at this time. The teacher seemed satisfied and somewhat relieved by this decision. The consultant did suggest that the teacher keep Lorenzo right next to her during group time to prevent him from wandering away.

In this instance, the consultant was able to offer a simple and pragmatic suggestion that was useful for the child and supportive of the teacher. Such recommendations are more readily offered when the consultant is on-site on a regular basis and able to participate in the ongoing monitoring and evaluation of the child's needs.

In other situations, these preliminary observations will be only the beginning of a multifaceted plan. Assessment is intertwined with the ongoing collaboration process, and consultants are able to use the many resources available within the preschool—teachers, administrative staff, the family worker, even the bus driver—to gather information and insight about the child. Parents are always contacted and consulted prior to any individual meeting with a child and always need to be part of planning any ongoing interventions. On-site consultants offer their professional perspective and expertise when trying to understand a child, and they also have easy access to those who know the child best, an opportunity that is rarely afforded in traditional clinical practice. When children need to be referred outside the center for evaluations and/or special services, the consultant can provide information about the special education process and talk with teachers and parents from the vantage of someone who is an ongoing partner within the preschool community. In addition, the referral process can be approached in a sensitive manner as the consultant and teacher use their respective skills and strengths to guide families through the process.

4-year-old Juanita, a sweet, quiet child from a Spanish speaking home, seemed to fade into the background of her busy classroom. Midway through the school year, the consultant, Ms. Cooper, talked with the child's teacher, Ms. Hernandez, about Juanita's slow pace in learning letters and numbers and her limited ability to listen to stories and answer questions about them. Ms. Hernandez commented that Juanita did not converse in either Spanish or English, and although she was playful and friendly, she often seemed "spacey" and "out of it." The child would be starting kindergarten in the fall, and Ms. Cooper thought she might need special education support. The consultant recommended a full developmental evaluation, which would include a speech-language assessment, a psychological evaluation, and educational testing. Ms. Cooper and Ms. Hernandez then discussed how to broach the subject with Juanita's mother, a single parent from Central America with limited education and knowledge of English. They decided that Ms. Hernandez, who spoke Spanish, would invite the mother into school to talk about Juanita. Ms. Cooper would join them to explore the idea of testing with the support and translating expertise of the teacher.

■ ■ ■

The on-site model of assessment allows the mental health professional to formulate a richer understanding of the transactional nature of the child and his or her environment. There is greater room for flexibility and creativity in tailoring recommendations and collaborating with teachers to devise interventions. The consultant is in a position to make more meaningful and nuanced suggestions by using his or her understanding of the range of developmental abilities, helping school staff distinguish between delays and atypical development, and having a grasp of the child's school and family environment and expectations. When the consultant is a consistent presence in the preschool, it is more likely that the staff will raise both serious problems and less significant concerns, making it possible to address children's difficulties when they are milder and less entrenched. Rather than removing a child from an everyday environment for the purposes of evaluation, the on-site consultant is often able to bring the assessment process to the child. When appropriate, the consultant can also provide information and guidance about referrals for special education and related services or for therapeutic interventions.

Interventions with Children

The mental health consultant works with children in diverse ways. At times, he or she observes or intervenes with a particular child, a small group of children, or the children in the classroom as a whole. Although less frequent, the consultant may even have the opportunity to address all the children of the program as a group during special assemblies or school events; however, most group work occurs within each classroom. After becoming a more familiar presence in the classroom, the consultant may work with the class as a group to support their general emotional development or to address specific psychological concerns. The effective consultant–teacher team finds opportunities to address these issues during free play, mealtimes, and unplanned interactions.

Some teachers express the understandable concern that the unstructured nature of more free flowing conversation will contribute to disorder in the classroom. Indeed, depending on the content, this can occur. Although verbal expression of more negative feelings can, at times, lead to a more expressive, less controlled atmosphere, this short-term consequence is usually outweighed by the gains in understanding and support that occur when such themes are opened for discussion. Children are, in fact, more likely to become unruly and disruptive when their feelings remain unspoken but continue to lurk beneath the surface. Whereas they are often notably calmed when given the opportunity to express themselves to adults who listen to them. These group discussions are not, however, meant to be biased toward more difficult or painful emotional content— the children are free to express both negative and positive thoughts and feelings. The open sharing of joy, excitement, and other warm feelings is an equally important part of establishing an emotionally supportive environment in the classroom, especially for children who live in more difficult or deprived home environments.

Consultants and teachers collaborate to build a therapeutic emotional environment during informal group discussions as well as through planned special activities, such as storytelling, the use of personalized books, and dramatic and creative arts. These activities can be particularly relevant when issues of special concern are addressed.

In a classroom for children from homeless families, the consultant joined the teacher in using puppets and fairy tales to address important themes. Two puppets, one with a sad face and the other with a happy face, were used to introduce *talking time* and became central figures for the class as the children recognized and expressed their own feelings. In addition, enactment of fairy tales became favorite activities designed to address key issues and worries. The children repeatedly enacted *The Three Little Pigs* as a means of communicating their experiences with residential instability. In this way, they were able to articulate their worries about lack of shelter and their fears about the dangers they faced in their daily lives.

Through such dramatic play, as well as through art and music, children can identify, lend voice to, and strive toward mastery of painful feelings and experiences.

The typical classroom is well structured to provide this healing group process for most children, but there are some children who benefit from a more therapeutic or targeted group experience within the school. Preschool groups can serve a variety of purposes, such as socialization, development of empathy, and growth of interpersonal skills through play and group discussions. Groups provide another way to reach young children whose development may be negatively affected by stressful life events and reflected in maladaptive behaviors such as withdrawal, aggression, or hyperactivity. By observing and working with children's issues in the small group environment, the therapist can observe and further assess social-emotional problems identified in the classroom, interpret and address problems in peer relationships, and intervene to improve adjustments to transitions, listening, and turn-taking.

Seven boys from 4 to 5 years of age were referred to a group in a preschool program for homeless children. The intensity of the boys' distress quickly became apparent in the therapeutic group. Although engaging, the boys were extremely active and impulsive, displaying hostility and sadistic behavior toward the therapist and each other. The boys often pretended they were dogs, with one as the master who brutalized the others. They often wanted to be turned into monsters, lest they be eaten by one. As the group evolved, hostility gradually gave way to more varied and positive play. For example, *good dogs* could be differentiated from *bad dogs* by their behavior, a *good drink* could turn the monsters back into normal boys, and the therapist was seen as a *superhero* who could protect everyone.

Sometimes children respond to the consultant's words by elaborating the play or making a revelation about their lives. At other times, words seem to fall on deaf ears and the children do not necessarily respond to what is said. Even when children are not yet able to make use of interpretations or even simple invitations to talk about their lives, however, they benefit from the opportunity to play out their feelings and issues in the supportive group milieu.

Conducting therapeutic groups within the preschool environment requires sensitivity and attunement to how the group experience affects the children once they return to the classroom. Transitions can be difficult despite adequate time, thoughtfulness, and the inclusion of structures and rituals for ending the group. As in any therapeutic encounter, the consultant must use his or her creativity and clinical knowledge to get through the critical moments. Communicating with teachers and acknowledging the annoyance of classroom interruptions while also emphasizing the important of helping children re-enter the classroom are vital to the success of therapeutic groups in early childhood environments.

In addition to group interventions, whether with the class as a whole or in small groups, consultants can sometimes provide individual therapy for children when indicated. Some centers are set up to allow the consultants to provide on-site intervention either with individual work within the classroom or through pull-out services outside the rooms. There are times when demands of privacy, classroom disruption, or parent participation require a separate space for therapeutic intervention. Whether sessions are held within the classroom or in a separate dedicated space, there are instances when individual intervention is a useful addition to the classroom's educational and psychological curriculum.

Early childhood teachers often identify children who could benefit from brief, preventive intervention. The most frequent referrals are for children with behavior problems or those with symptoms of depression or anxiety. Parents are always contacted and consulted prior to any individual meeting with a child, and they always need to be part of planning any ongoing interventions. Ideally, both parent and child receive support that strengthens their resilience and improves their relationship with each other, as in the following example.

Four-year-old Philip was referred for brief intervention after his teachers became more aware of his isolation and self-deprecating remarks and behaviors. Philip's mother was depressed and overburdened, and at the time she was unable to offer much support to him. She frequently referred to him as *bad* and compared him negatively to his younger brother. In the early phase of intervention, Philip repeatedly depicted a mother rejecting and killing her son and then running off with her younger child.

Philip's therapist openly discussed his mother's difficulties, but also attempted to engage his strengths and skills, particularly his keen intelligence. She supported and facilitated Philip's creative use of materials and his dramatic and symbolic play. She also helped his teachers to identify and support his strengths and need for nurturance. They readily accepted these suggestions and applied them to their interactions with Philip as well as the other children in the class, focusing on how each was a *special person*.

Work with Philip's mother was initially difficult because her depression had left her detached from his feelings as well as her own. She did, however, support his intervention and the classroom interventions, and she gradually began to identify with a more positive view of Philip. After leaving his nursery school, Philip was granted a scholarship to a local parochial school. Proud of his achievement, Philip's mother was an enthusiastic participant at his graduation and became more actively involved with his education the following year.

■ ■ ■

Individual and group therapy, although not possible in all environments, can expand the benefits of mental health consultation, offering services to children and families who may not be available or eligible for such interventions in traditional clinic environments.

The on-site consultant may also be helpful in determining which children may require interventions that exceed what the preschool is able to offer. At this writing, most early childhood centers follow a mandate to include children with special needs in the typical classroom. For young children, this goal is particularly salient given the fluidity of development as well as the opportunity for modeling offered by children within the behavioral norm. In a classroom where children with diverse backgrounds, skills, and developmental levels can interact and be taught on a variety of levels, there is an opportunity for a rich educational, social, and behavioral cross-pollination. Nonetheless, those children with severely compromised emotional, cognitive, and relational capacities often require a smaller adult–child ratio with teachers and clinicians specially trained to meet their needs.

There are also children without severe neurological or psychiatric pathology who nonetheless express their difficulties with aggressive and potentially dangerous behavior that poses a risk to teachers and peers and cannot be adequately addressed in the typical classroom. Children whose behavior difficulties emerge from having endured multiple family stressors or chronic trauma may benefit from a therapeutic environment in which specially trained teachers and mental health staff have the opportunity for early intervention with children as well as their families. The stated goal of these programs is usually to increase children's coping skills and resiliency so that they may enter a mainstream educational environment in the future.

Alternative environments work best when the goal of least restrictive placement is carefully monitored and where there is fluid and unhindered opportunity for children to move from therapeutic environments to typical ones. Although true for all children, it is particularly the case for preschoolers that even the most behaviorally challenged and emotionally stressed child can shift rapidly to higher levels of functioning and should have the opportunity to readily move to typical class rooms that match their gains. There are children who are vulnerable to severe emotional disorganization and who become, for example, psychotic or thought disordered under stress, but who can ultimately function in a normal environment when the stressors are identified and removed. Any system should have the structure to carefully diagnose children without gender, race, or class bias and to enable children to shift out of therapeutic environments without stigma or other administrative barriers.

WORKING WITH CHILDREN AFFECTED BY TRAUMA

Consultants in preschool environments often have the unique opportunity to strengthen supports and build resilience in young children exposed to trauma, often before they present worrisome symptoms. They are also in a position to intervene at an early stage when children have begun to display signs of distress. Researchers have described a common pattern of symptoms in traumatized children of all ages that include visualization, specific fears, and repeated memories of the events, as well as repetitive play and reenactments of the trauma and diminished expectations about the future (Pfefferbaum, 1997; Terr, 1991). Children exposed to chronic stress also tend to engage in denial about their experiences, and in extreme cases withdraw into a *psychic numbness* in which they avoid all emotional interactions and responses. These children are also prone to rage reactions, and their anger can be turned against themselves in the form of self-abuse or risk-taking behaviors.

Although covering a range of behaviors, these symptoms can be a useful starting point for the consultant and teacher who are observing children who may have been exposed to one or more traumatic events or chronic stressors, including separation from a parent, foster care placement, being a witness or victim of violence, abuse or neglect, death of a family member, hospitalization or illness, mental illness in a parent, or loss of a family home through fire or eviction. It is particularly worth identifying children who display more than one of these symptoms and do so consistently over time. Of course, not every child who is angry and plays roughly with dolls or other toys has been the victim of abuse or other trauma, but these behaviors do warrant careful attention and monitoring over time, and the preschool staff should strive to listen closely to their stories. When participating in the daily activities of the center, the consultant can help the staff to differentiate the more normative behaviors and play from those that suggest more serious concerns.

The trauma model also draws attention to behaviors that may be easily overlooked. The withdrawn child may be seen as shy or quiet and indeed may be a welcome presence in a classroom of otherwise active children; however, when this behavior persists for several weeks or months, after most children in the room are comfortably engaged with each other, further observation and assessment is necessary. Severely limited responsiveness in the classroom can be a symptom of intensive and long-term trauma. Likewise the overly active child who enjoys jumping and climbing, for example, is commonly viewed as exuberant or perhaps hyperactive. Although these are plausible explanations, repeated instances of children putting themselves at risk by climbing on tables, jumping from high places, or darting in the street all warrant closer observation and a more careful review of the children's history. If these behaviors continue or escalate after appropriate limit setting in the classroom, the mental health consultant should begin a more formal assessment process, including a discussion with parents about possible exposure to trauma. Self-abusive behaviors, including head banging, tearing at one's skin, and hair pulling deserve immediate attention, as do apparent life-threatening behaviors.

Although it is important that early childhood professionals recognize the symptom clusters and isolated behaviors associated with trauma, they should also understand that the impact of trauma on young children often expresses itself in a more global manner that affects their ability to achieve age-appropriate developmental tasks. Young children under chronic stress, especially maltreated children and those exposed to violence, have often failed to develop a secure attachment to their caregivers and do not have a sense of basic security or trust in the world (Cohen & Walthall, 2003; Osofsky, 1995). They may be wary of strangers and hypervigilant; that is, they notice any minor deviations in their immediate environment that could portend danger. These children often have extreme difficulty separating from their parents when coming to preschool and cannot readily carry an image of their caregivers through the school day. They may be exceptionally clingy and appear anxious when their caregivers are absent. Children with a history of trauma often fear and expect rejection, especially from adults. To limit their exposure to this further insult, they may avoid establishing connection to their teachers or forming meaningful relationships with other children. Others may act out aggressively and actively push people away from them, fulfilling their own prophecy of their unworthiness and protecting them from the potential loss of affection from a significant adult figure.

Young children exposed to violence at home or in their community are particularly vulnerable and can come into the classroom looking frightened, angry, or out of control. More than anything else, they need to feel that their school is a predictable environment in which they can safely play and learn. Consistent, caring teachers who treat these children as individuals and value their ideas and imagination can do much to reduce the impact of the violent events they have witnessed or endured. Often the consultant's role is to remind these teachers of the value of their role in creating this warm and secure environment, particularly when they are confronted with difficult to manage and seemingly incorrigible children. For some of these children, school is the only place they feel safe, particularly if their families are unstable or threatening or if they live in dangerous neighborhoods or shelters.

This background of safety and security can allow children to begin to reach out to their teachers and to develop hope in relationships, often after first testing adults. In most cases, timid and withdrawn children with patient teachers can eventually feel comfortable enough to try out new toys and to explore the room enough to expand their repertoire of cognitive activities. Children who are angry and aggressive present different challenges. It is often the consultants' role to help teachers maintain a sense of optimism with aggressive children and to plan concrete interventions to help them maintain their self-control, as well as to work with the class as a whole so that the aggressive child does not become disdained or feared. Practical suggestions regarding limit setting, appropriate consequences for classroom outbursts, and behavioral planning are an essential part of any early childhood consultant's repertoire. The consultant must also recognize, however, that these interventions are emotionally and physically draining for teachers and often the most difficult part of their jobs.

Creating a reparative milieu for children living with violence involves an acceptance of their experiences and a willingness to talk about what they have seen or heard. Affirming their perceptions and feelings about the events that they have witnessed can go a long way toward reducing their symptoms and helping them to feel less isolated and alone with this knowledge. Yet, many teachers shy away from these discussions because they fear that they will open a Pandora's box of feelings and private family details that should not be discussed in the classroom. As a start, however, most teachers are willing to let a mental health consultant talk to the child privately as in the following example.

On arriving at the Rainbow Center on Monday, Dr. Edwards learned that Alan's mother had been murdered the previous week, apparently by her boyfriend. Although he lived with his grandmother, Alan saw his mother frequently and had a fairly good relationship with her. The school had reached out to the grandmother immediately by sending food and offering to help in any way they could. Alan told his teachers what had happened when he arrived at school the next day, but he had not discussed it since then. His demeanor, however, had changed markedly. He looked wan and tired and appeared noticeably upset and sad. He complained frequently of headaches and stomach pains and asked that his grandmother be called to take him home.

Dr. Edwards had known Alan for 2 years, and they had a good rapport despite infrequent contact during that academic year. He explained to Alan that he had heard about the news and was sorry and wondered if Alan wanted to talk about it. Although reluctant at first, Alan told Dr. Edwards that nobody at home was talking about his mother. He related some details about the funeral, most notably that he was surprised to see all the adults crying but that he and his brother Andre, 1 year older, were two of the few people who did not cry. Dr. Edwards talked to Alan about feeling mixed up, not knowing if he should cry, or where crying was allowed. He also told Alan that sometimes bodies hurt when feelings are hurt. Alan's eyes slowly welled with tears while they were talking, and he seemed visibly relieved to have someone with whom he could talk about this tragic loss.

In the subsequent weeks, Dr. Edwards visited with Alan on a regular basis. He also encouraged a young male teacher in his class to spend time with Alan each morning and to check in regarding how he was feeling. Dr Edwards encouraged all the teachers to be aware of his grief symptoms, including his body pains and his increasing oppositional behavior in the classroom. When one teacher suggested that he should be *getting over* her death and was now using it as an excuse to act out in class, Dr. Edwards offered to meet with the classroom team to discuss Alan's behavior and to provide some instruction on the normal grieving process for young children. After the meeting, the teachers seemed more compassionate toward Alan. They began to remind him that he could talk about his feelings and that he did not have to act out to call attention to his plight.

■ ■ ■

There are times when an entire community is affected by a catastrophic event, whether manmade or natural. Reports of victims of hurricanes, floods, earthquakes, and other natural disasters have stressed the psychological impact of these events on children and families that can persist long after the devastation has passed and the restoration process has concluded. Recent incidents of school violence have shattered the calm and security of some suburban and rural communities and have led many residents to question long held beliefs and values. It is now common practice to dispatch crisis response teams to schools and communities affected by violence or disaster, but there is often much more confusion about how to handle public traumatic events with young children. There is a common misperception both in families and in preschools that young children are not aware of what has occurred around them.

Young children pose more of a quandary because they often do not speak directly about their fears or worries related to recent events. They often do, however, play out these concerns and frequently need help from adults to articulate what they are experiencing. In most instances, preschoolers need some details about what they have heard of or witnessed; they need an opportunity to express their feelings about the event and they need reassurance that they and those close to them will remain unharmed and safe in the future. Few events brought these needs to the forefront more than the tragic occurrences of September 11, 2001.

Trauma and 9/11

The catastrophe of the September 11, 2001, terrorist attacks in the United States created unprecedented challenges for mental health professionals working with young children. Even those consultants who had prior knowledge and experience working with children exposed to trauma were challenged by the scope and nature of the demands that unfolded in the days, weeks, and months after 9/11. The impact of the attacks struck the entire nation with reverberations that resounded well beyond New York, Washington, and Pennsylvania—sites of the actual disasters. Many people living in the northeast knew colleagues, friends, and family members who lived or worked in New York or Washington, and nearly everyone was affected, either directly or indirectly, by this national tragedy.

Consultants working in early childhood environments were involved in a set of decisions and actions, many of which had to be made on the spot. For consultants working in the New York metropolitan area, the questions were immediate and urgent. Are we in imminent danger? Should school be closed and the children sent home? Should the children be told about what was happening? How could staff be kept informed without causing panic or chaos? In the days that followed, most preschools remained open, but it was far from business as usual. In one suburban district, many fathers who worked in downtown New York were suddenly omnipresent—dropping off and picking up their children. Everyone, school staff and families alike, were dealing with the immediate aftermath; some were faced with terrible news, others with the relief that they and their loved ones were spared. Many programs in the affected areas focused on crisis action plans that involved planning for emergency evacuations and simulating responses to chemical, biological, and nuclear attacks.

Within this atmosphere of intense loss, apprehension, and confusion, those working in early childhood programs did their best to maintain a positive, predictable, and calm atmosphere for young children. Mental health consultants trained to work with children who had experienced traumatic events were guided by their prior experiences; however, there were aspects of the 9/11 attacks that were new. In contrast to traumas that affect individuals or a relatively small group, the 9/11 attacks triggered a national emergency. Most children were aware of the attacks, and many saw the devastating photographs and televised images of the planes crashing into the World Trade Center. For those who worked with young children, the question was not "Should the children be told?" but instead "How do we talk about this with young children?" The urge to protect children from terrible events was tempered by the knowledge that it was impossible to fully shield them from the situation. Consultants who had established close working relationships within early childhood programs

were in a vital position to work collaboratively with other school personnel to make decisions about how to respond to the unfolding events; to
closely monitor the reactions of the children; and to provide immediate
support to children, families, and staff.

On September 12, 2001, the consultant and school director in one
suburban preschool close to New York City recommended that teachers in
all the classrooms give the children an open-ended suggestion to draw a
picture about *what happened yesterday*, with no preconceived notion of
whether their pictures would pertain to the attack. What followed was a
moving outpouring of pictures and words dramatically confirming that
most of these children were highly aware of the attacks and were trying to
understand the events through the young child's blend of knowledge,
wishes, and imagination. Vivid pictures of airplanes crashing into buildings, buildings on fire, and even stick figures dropping from buildings were
accompanied by words, such as

- "Yesterday I watched the tower falling."

- "The gray stuff is smoke, the red is fire in the buildings and windows,
  and daddy was safe."

- "I'm sad because the workers work hard and the building fell down because the hijackers shot the person who was driving and he fell over-
  board and he crashed into the building to steal all the money."

- "This is the fire and these are the people jumping out the windows.
  They almost died."

- "This is the earth, falling buildings, and the bad guys are all confused
  because there are whirlwinds in the middle."

- "This is a picture of the zigzag fireballs. No people were there because
  they all died. All the people are now home and safe."

- "I felt sad when I saw it because I liked those buildings and I saw it on
  TV with mom and dad and lots of people got hurt."

- "My uncle is fine."

- "At first they thought it was an accident. Then they realized it was bad
  guys."

This straightforward intervention—asking children to share their perceptions, feelings, and thoughts through an open-ended drawing and/or dictation activity—served several important purposes. The staff felt reassured
that a unified approach was being taken in the school during a national
emergency. This led to a greater sense of shared experience and support as

teachers from several classrooms looked at the children's pictures together, a process that inevitably led them to discuss their own situations and reactions. The consultant and teachers were able to quickly identify which children seemed most disturbed or confused by the attacks and needed extra attention from the teacher and more frequent home–school communication. Given their pre-existing knowledge of the students, the consultant and staff at this preschool were also able to observe children who were more vulnerable because of their own histories of trauma or loss, offering additional support as needed.

During the next few weeks, the consultant and classroom teachers also talked with the children about the many ways people were helping each other in the wake of the attacks. Talking about firefighters, policemen, doctors, and other helpers was one way to mitigate feelings of helplessness that often accompany trauma and to retain an atmosphere of safety. Another schoolwide drawing and dictation activity was initiated in late September, and the children were asked to write to anyone who had helped during the past 2 weeks. The consultant and teachers again examined and discussed what the children spontaneously produced. As before, the children's responses varied widely. Some of the children's dictated words reflected their first-hand experiences with the events; others were the blend of fantasy and reality that is a hallmark of the preschool mind:

- "Thank you for trying to save my dad's friends. I was scared when the elevator fell. I'm happy my dad is still alive."

- "Thank you for cleaning up New York City. That was a mean thing to wreck the twin towers. Is it hard cleaning up all those big pieces of cement? It is probably very hard."

- "Thank you for saving all the people at the World Trade Center. You must be very nice and good."

- "Are you going to come back if another building falls?"

- "Thank you for cleaning up after the bad people. Why did they hijack the plane and hit the World Trade Center?"

- "Thank you for keeping us safe."

Throughout the school year, the consultant had many conversations with parents, school staff, and mental health professionals who were dealing with the aftermath of 9/11 in other environments. The consultant also kept a notebook with copies of the pictures created immediately after September 11, as well as drawings that were produced over the entire school year. This helped the school staff monitor the long-term emotional reactions and adjustment of the children, and it also became a lasting document of an extraordinarily stressful time. The on-site collaborative model of consultation and intervention proved to be an especially meaningful and beneficial model during a national trauma that affected even our youngest children.

CONCLUSION

A strong preschool–mental health partnership can lead to decisive change and can leave programs with more effective tools to meet their children's needs (Donahue, 1996; Donahue, Falk & Provet, 2000; Goldman, Botkin, Tokunaga, & Kuklinski, 1997). The shared vision of professionals can give staff new hope that they can confront difficult behaviors and emotionally charged material in the classroom. Children and families also benefit from the combined focus on children's social-emotional development and early intervention efforts aimed at preventing more serious problems from developing later on in childhood. In addition, an effective mental health collaboration can enhance a program's resilience and reduce the stress of staff as they join together to face the day-to-day challenges of meeting the educational and emotional needs of the young children they serve.

Despite increasing recognition of the value of these partnerships, obtaining the necessary resources to initiate and support ongoing mental health collaborations remains a daunting challenge for most early childhood programs. Efforts by Head Start to include consultation as part their program mandates have made funds more available in some districts, but still does not address the needs of most centers. Publicly funded prekindergarten programs also give more children access to mental health professionals when they allow families to utilize the resources of the local school district. State initiatives to provide some funding for consultation have been approved in a number of regions, including Connecticut, Ohio, and Arkansas. The more comprehensive of these programs also offer training for both early childhood and mental health professionals to learn more about development and trauma in early childhood and to understand how to develop effective and stable partnerships. As these early intervention and prevention models gain credibility and as research on the effectiveness of consultation models expands, it is to be hoped that more specifically tailored funding will allow most early childhood centers to have a mental health consultant to help them work toward their primary goals of fostering the development of young children and keeping them on track toward future emotional health and academic success.

REFERENCES

Breslau, N., Chilcoat, H.D., Kessler, R.C., & Davis, G.C. (1999). Previous exposure to trauma and PTSD effects of subsequent trauma: Results from the Detroit Area Survey of Trauma. *American Journal of Psychiatry, 156,* 902–907.

Cohen, P., Provet, A., & Jones, M. (1996). The prevalence of emotional and behavioral disorders in childhood and adolescence. In B. Levin & J. Petrila (Eds.), *Mental health services: A public health perspective.* (pp. 193–209). New York: Oxford University Press.

Cohen, E., & Walthall, B. (2003). *Silent realities: Supporting young children and their families who experience violence.* Washington DC: The National Child Welfare Resource Center for Family-Centered Practice.

Donahue, P. J. (1996). The treatment of homeless children and families: Integrating mental health services into a Head Start model. In Zelman, A. (Ed.), *Early intervention with high-risk children* (pp. 151–170). Northvale, NJ: Jason Aronson.

Donahue, P.J., Falk, B., & Gersony Provet, A. (2000). *Mental health consultation in early childhood.* Baltimore: Paul H. Brookes Publishing Co.

Dubow, E.F., Roecker, C.E., & D'Imperio, R. (1997). Mental health. In R.T. Ammerman & M. Hershon (Ed.), *Handbook of prevention and treatment with children and adolescents: Intervention in the real world context* (pp. 259–286). New York: John Wiley & Sons.

Goldman, R.K., Botkin, M.J., Tokunaga, H., & Kuklinski, M. (1997). Teacher consultation: Impact on teachers' effectiveness and students' cognitive competence and achievement. *American Journal of Orthopsychiatry, 67,* 374–384.

Hyson, M.C. (1994). *The emotional development of young children: Building an emotion-centered curriculum.* New York: Teachers College Press.

Individuals with Disabilities Education Improvement Act of 2004, PL 108-446, 20 U.S.C. §§ 1400 *et seq.*

Knitzer, J. (1996). Meeting the mental health needs of young children and their families. In Stroul, B.A. (Ed.), *Children's mental health: Creating systems of care in a changing society.* Baltimore: Paul H. Brookes Publishing Co.

Koplow, L. (1996). *Unsmiling faces: How preschools can heal.* New York: Teachers College Press.

National Center for Children in Poverty. (1998). *Five million children.* New York: Author.

Osofsky, J.D. (1995). The effects of exposure to violence on your children. *American Psychologist, 50,* 782–788.

Pfefferbaum, B. (1997). Post-traumatic stress disorder in children: A review of the past 10 years. *Journal of the American Academy of Child Psychiatry, 36,* 1503–1511.

Pynoos, R.S., & Eth, S. (1986). Witness to violence: The child interview. *Journal of the American Academy of Child Psychiatry, 25,* 306–319.

Rutter, M., & Quintin, D. (1977). Psychiatric disorder: Ecological factors and concepts in causation. In H. McGurk, (Ed.), *Ecological factors in human development.* Ampsterdam: North Holland.

Shonkoff, J.P., & Phillips, D.A. (Eds.). (2000). *From neurons to neighborhoods: The science of early childhood development.* Washington, DC: National Academies Press.

Terr, L.C. (1991). Childhood traumas: An outline and overview. *American Journal of Psychiatry, 30* 138–143.

Werner, E. (1989). High-risk children in young adulthood: A longitudinal study from birth to 32 years. *American Journal of Orthopsychiatry, 59,* 72–81.

Yoshikawa, Y., & Knitzer, J. (1997). *Lessons from the field: Head Start mental health strategies to meet changing needs.* New York: National Center for Children in Poverty.

ZERO TO THREE. (1994). *Caring for infants and toddlers in violent environments: Hurt, healing, and hope.* Arlington, VA: Author.

Zigler, E.F., Finn-Stevenson, M., & Stern, B.M. (1997). Supporting children and families in the schools: The school of the 21st century. *American Journal of Orthopsychiatry, 67*, 396–407.

14

Evidence-Based Practices for Young Children with and at Risk for Social-Emotional or Behavior Problems

Lise Fox and Glen Dunlap

Anna leaves the pediatrician's office with a sense of frustration. She has become increasingly concerned about her 20-month-old toddler, Adam. She tried to explain to her doctor that Adam seems to have more difficult behavior than other children. Although she is a first-time parent, she sees that her friends do not experience similar challenges with their young children. Adam tantrums every day, for long periods of time, and seems impossible to soothe. He has also started biting himself and Anna when she tries to pick him up or redirect him. The pediatrician thinks that it is just the *terrible twos*; however, Anna thinks it is something more serious.

Emma, a 4-year-old, has been asked to leave three child care programs because of her behavior. The last preschool worked diligently to support her, but finally gave up when she caused another child to break her arm by pushing her off the slide. Her parents have sought help for Emma but without much success. They attended a parenting class, but did not learn any strate-

Preparation of this chapter was supported by the Center for Evidence-Based Practice: Young Children with Challenging Behavior, funded by the Office of Special Education Programs, U.S. Department of Education (H324Z010001), and the Center on the Social and Emotional Foundations for Early Learning, funded by the Administration for Children and Families, Department of Health and Human Services (PHS 90YD0119).

gies that helped them address Emma's increasingly difficult aggression and noncompliance.

Since the mid-1990s, research on the outcomes for children with severe problem behavior and behavior disorders has demonstrated that "early childhood is a critical period for the onset of emotional and behavioral impairments" (The President's New Freedom Commission on Mental Health, 2003, p. 57). Behavior problems identified during the preschool years often persist into adolescence and beyond, and data have shown that teenagers described as emotionally disturbed have a history of problem behavior as far back as the preschool years (Campbell & Ewing, 1990; Loeber et al., 1993; Moffitt, 1993). Indeed, longitudinal studies have confirmed that severe problem behaviors identified in preschool have stability over time and continue to be evident 3–7 years later (Campbell & Ewing, 1990; Egeland, Kalkoske, Gottesman, & Erickson, 1990; Fischer, Rolf, Hasazi, & Cummings, 1984; Richman, Stevenson, & Graham, 1982). For preschoolers identified with clinical levels of disruptive disorders, 50% or more have been found to display problematic levels of challenging behaviors both 4 years later and well into the upper elementary school years (Campbell, 1995; Lavigne et al., 1998: Shaw, Gilliom, & Giovannelli, 2000). About 6 % of all boys appear to follow an *early starter* or *life-course-persistent* developmental pathway for conduct problems characterized by violence and serious anti-social behavior in adolescence (Moffitt, Caspi, Dickson, Silva, & Stanton, 1996; Nagin & Tremblay, 1999).

The outcomes for children who continue on a developmental pathway to a diagnosis of emotional and behavioral disorders are bleak. Students who are identified under the Individuals with Disabilities Education Improvement Act (IDEA) (2004) as having emotional and behavior disorders (EBD) have about a 50% chance of dropping out of school (Wagner et al., 1991). Post-school outcomes include low employment levels, poor work histories, and low wages (Bullis & Gaylord-Ross, 1991; Bullis, Nishoika-Evans, Fredericks, & Davis, 1993; Frank & Sitlington, 1997). These children with EBD are also at risk for a number of social problems, including school bullying, gang-related activity, substance abuse, juvenile offenses, and acts of violence (Batsche & Knoff, 1994; Patterson, DeBaryshe, & Ramsey, 1989; Sprague & Walker, 2000; Tolan, Guerra, & Kendall, 1995). Considering the fact that these outcomes have been found to act as accelerators and predictors for adult violence and criminal behavior (American Psychological Association, 1993), the conclusion is grim—a direct connection exists between preschool disruptive behavior and adolescent and/or adult antisocial behavior.

Fortunately, since the mid-1990s, there has been a great escalation of awareness regarding the impact of untreated social-emotional and behavior problems and the need for effective early interventions designed to prevent and resolve problems and redirect the trajectories of destructive developmental pathways (e.g., Shonkoff & Phillips, 2000). In concert with the burgeoning national trend in fields such as medicine and education, much of this new awareness has been manifested as a call for *evidence-based practices* that can be used to prevent problems from emerging and/or to intervene when problems are already apparent. The definition of evidence-based practices has been a source of some contention, and different standards have been proposed depending on the questions, populations, and practices that are the topics of concern. In a laudable effort to address the issue using a functional approach with broad applicability, Dunst, Trivette, and Cutspec (2002) advanced the following definition of evidence-based practice.

> Practices that are informed by research, in which the characteristics and consequences of environmental variables are empirically established and the relationship directly informs what a practitioner can do to produce a desired outcome. (2002, p. 3)

This definition provides room for diverse sources of data and accommodates information from a variety of research strategies. In this sense, it provides a framework with which to describe a foundational understanding of strategies, techniques, programs, and practices relevant to prevention and intervention with social-emotional and behavior challenges of young children.

The purpose of this chapter is to summarize knowledge pertinent to prevention and intervention for young children's social-emotional and behavior problems. The discussion is organized in the context of a model that encompasses primary, secondary, and tertiary prevention strategies (Fox, Dunlap, Hemmeter, Joseph, & Strain, 2003). Within each level, practices are described that have empirical support and represent evidence-based approaches. The model that is presented in this chapter is supported by evidence at each level, although some of the practices have a more extensive research base than others. Thus, this model provides an empirically supported framework for program development and the organization of program practices within early childhood and early intervention programs.

A MODEL FOR PREVENTION AND INTERVENTION

There is substantial research identifying the risk factors that are associated with the later development of intractable problem behavior. Primary risk factors include variables related to child health and behavior, family demographics and functioning, and economic circumstances (Huffman,

Mehlinger, & Kerivan, 2000). More specifically, identified risk factors include low birth weight and neurodevelopmental delays; difficult temperament; early behavior and adjustment problems; family composition and instability; low levels of maternal education; parental substance abuse; parental psychological problems (e.g., maternal depression); poor parenting practices; immigrant status; minority status; low socioeconomic status; maltreatment; and insecure attachment. In addition, there is research that provides information on the factors that may prevent or protect children who are at risk for these problems from developing problem behavior. Resilience factors include child's self-confidence, higher cognitive functioning, easy temperament, residence with both parents, positive parental relationship with child, higher level of maternal education, stable and predictable family environment, secure attachment, and high-quality early education and care.

Although there is limited research on exactly how these factors contribute or protect children from developing future problem behavior, a consideration of these factors is warranted in the design of prevention and intervention programs. Knowledge of factors that place children at risk for problem behavior and factors that contribute to positive outcomes has led to the design of programs that can address factors that may be amenable to change (e.g., parenting practice, child adjustment, child relationship with others) and include factors that may contribute to child resilience (e.g., high-quality early education practices).

A helpful approach for conceptualizing the range of prevention and intervention practices that may be employed to support children's social development is based on the public health model of prevention. In this model, the forms of prevention and intervention are differentiated based on risk status of segments of a population (Gordon, 1983, 1987; Simeonsson, 1991). The goal of the public health model is to reduce disease or a condition by implementing a hierarchy of prevention and intervention efforts within a whole population. The public health model considers interventions at three levels: 1) universal or primary efforts are the application of primary prevention initiatives that are designed to reduce the incidence of a disorder within the entire population; 2) secondary practices are those designed to reduce the prevalence (i.e., old and new cases) of a condition or disease; and 3) tertiary efforts are designed to reduce the complications of the disorder once it is manifested. When the public health model is applied to early intervention for young children's social and behavioral competence, the model takes on a slightly different focus. The traditional conceptualization of the model is predicated on knowledge of causal pathways that lead to the disorder or disease. If the causal pathway is identified (e.g., the source of a disease), then it is possible to develop relatively simple interventions that may affect the entire population that is at risk (e.g., immunization).

As the public health model is applied to promoting children's social competence and reducing problem behavior, the application of the public health model must be adjusted in consideration of the complex risk factors that are related to poor child social and behavioral outcomes. In the application to children's social and behavioral health, the levels of intervention may be defined differently. Universal or primary intervention efforts are designed to reduce the risk that young children will develop problem behavior. Secondary or selective interventions are provided to children who are at increased risk of problem behavior and delayed social development and are designed to reduce the potential severity of the problem. Tertiary or indicated interventions describe interventions that are used to address the most severe manifestations of the problem.

The model is presented as a triangle with universal interventions at the base. Universal interventions are provided to all young children. As you move up the triangle, the number of children who may be in need of the subsequent intervention practices grows smaller.

The application of the public health model to promoting the social-emotional development of young children in the context of early childhood classrooms has been described for the field (Fox et al., 2003). The model includes the provision of high-quality programs as the universal prevention strategies. Research indicates that children who attend programs judged to be high quality are significantly less likely to have problem behavior (Helburn et al., 1995; National Research Council, 2001; NICHD, 1999). A high-quality program includes well-planned environments, the development of nurturing relationships with children, and the use of developmentally appropriate practices to foster and support children's engagement in the program. At the secondary (selective intervention) level, the model for young children includes a focus on the instruction of social skills and the support of social-emotional development in a planned, systematic, and intensive fashion. At the tertiary (indicated level), early educators and intervention personnel are guided to implement intensive individualized interventions for young children with persistent challenging behavior using a team-facilitated behavior support process.

This chapter broadens the application of the model to include both home and community environments and discuss evidence-based practices that would be included at each level of the model (see Figure 14.1). Note that the figure includes four components, with the universal or primary level being divided into 1) positive relationships and responsive parenting; and 2) predictable, high-quality environments for early care and education. Both of these components are vital for primary prevention, and they are distinguished here only because of their distinct and essential contributions to healthy child development. As the four levels are reviewed, the

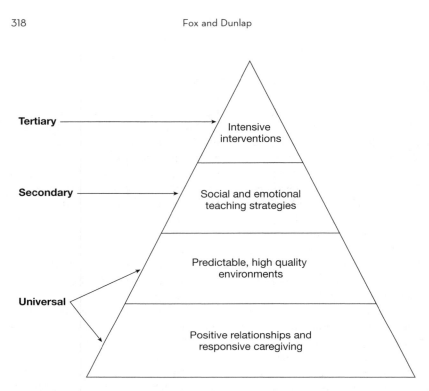

Figure 14.1. An example of promotion, prevention, and intervention model for supporting young children's social development and addressing challenging behavior.

emphasis is to provide the reader with practical strategies that are focused on enhancing the social and behavioral outcomes of young children.

Universal Intervention

Universal intervention strategies are essential and foundational to the development of a young child's social competence. The research on factors that contribute to children's risk and resilience in the area of social competence provides support to the importance of these practices for all children. At the core of these strategies is the importance of establishing a positive relationship with the child. Although one may question why this must be articulated as a strategy (as it is assumed to be widely accepted as integral to the development of mental health), it is important to point out that if the child does not have a positive relationship with primary caregivers then intervention should begin with a focus on establishing one. It is within the relationship with a primary caregiver that the infant begins learning interpersonal and emotional skills that serve as the foundation for the development of communication and social competence (Bronson, 2000; Landy, 2002).

The development of a positive relationship between the child and caregiver can be negatively affected by maternal depression. There is a highly predictive relationship between maternal depression and the development of behavior problems in young children (Black et al., 2002; Gross, Sambrook, & Fogg, 1999; Harden et al., 2000; Leadbeater & Bishop, 1994; Shaw, Winslow, Owens, & Hood, 1998; Spieker, Larson, Lewis, Keller, & Gilchrist, 1999). In addition to the neurological vulnerability that may be genetically passed from mother to infant, interventionists should be aware of the difficulties mothers who are depressed may have when developing a relationship with their infant. Imagine the mother who finds little joy in parenting, does not have the energy to play with her infant, and has very low levels of affect when teaching her child social skills and language. The development of a young child's social competence is highly reliant on the responsive input the child receives from the caregiver. If the caregiver is unable to fill that role, it is not surprising that delays would occur with her child.

In addition to a positive relationship, the following are important practices for universal prevention: responsive parenting, predictable environments, and high-quality early education. Responsive parenting describes parenting skills that are necessary to guide the child's social, communication, and behavioral development. There is evidence that when parents are lacking these skills, children are more likely to have problem behavior and delays in social development. Programs that provide parent education and training to parents with parenting risk factors, such as Early Head Start (Love et al., 2002) and the Nurse Home Visiting program (Olds et al., 1998), have been successful in supporting parents in the development of parenting skills which result in better outcomes for children's social development.

A related factor that is linked to positive social development is the provision of predictable environments. The literature has been clear about the importance of predictable and stable environments for the development of social competence. Young children who experience instability in residence and changes in caregivers (e.g., two-parent home to one-parent home) are more likely to demonstrate problem behavior (Ackerman, Kogos, Youngstrom, Schoff, & Izard, 1999). When families are unable to provide a predictable and stable environment, intervention programs are challenged to provide the types of family supports that are needed. Family supports, such as informal social supports, respite care, or housing assistance, may seem to bear little relationship to the promotion of a child's social development; however, there is some evidence that when more comprehensive supports are provided to families (e.g., counseling, employment assistance, housing assistance, economic assistance, substance abuse assistance), children will fare better than those whose families did not have access to supports (Singer et al., 1989).

About 61% of young children (birth-to-6 years) spend part of their day in some kind of out-of-home care or early education environment (Federal

Interagency Forum on Child and Family Statistics, 2002). Research has demonstrated that when these programs meet the definition of high quality (i.e., quality environments, caregiving interactions, and child–adult ratios), the child's social and behavioral development is supported (Howes, Phillips, & Whitebrook, 1992; Love, Meckstroth, & Sprachman, 1997; Peisner-Feinberg et al., 1999). Thus, it is important that intervention programs consider the nature of the child's early education and care environments and ensure that quality practices are implemented.

Providing Universal Strategies

The universal strategies described may be readily available for some children. For example, children generally do well when they are favored with parents who are skilled at parenting, when they attend high-quality early education programs, and when they have predictable and stable caregiving. Unfortunately, there are many children who do not readily access these supports and who require the assistance of programs that can facilitate access to and implementation of these supports. Intervention programs (e.g., early intervention, family support programs, home visiting programs, child health care programs) may be needed to provide families with parent education and family support that is focused on building positive relationships, promoting responsive parenting, and providing a stable environment. In addition, intervention programs (e.g., mental health consultation, child care resource teams, early intervention) are needed to ensure that all early education and care environments (from formal early childhood programs to family child care) are able to develop positive relationships with children and provide a high-quality early education program.

The provision of universal strategies to support families may occur through home visiting programs by a visiting nurse or practitioner skilled in child development. In a home visiting model, parents are provided with instruction, information, and social support. Parents may also be provided with information during routine health care visits, instructional video-tapes, or written materials. Another mechanism used to support families includes parent education and support groups that may be offered in the community to all families or offered to a targeted number of families who receive services through a particular agency.

The adoption of universal strategies by child care and early education programs may also require a focused effort. There are many community child care and early education programs that may need the assistance of a resource agency, technical assistance provider, or mental health consultant to understand and implement the early childhood education practices that offer universal prevention strategies. In early education programs, universal practices begin with the development of positive relationships between the child and caregivers and the design of predictable, developmentally appropriate classroom environments.

The following scenarios demonstrate how two different community programs deliver services that include universal prevention strategies.

The Kristoff family is receiving early intervention for Emily, their toddler with developmental delays, through a local provider of Part C services (IDEA). A need that the family identified for support was to receive help in learning how to guide their child's development. Mrs. Kristoff expressed that she was often frustrated by Emily's behavior and found her to be difficult to manage. The Part C program offered to enroll Mrs. Kristoff in a parenting class or to provide parent training through home visiting. Mrs. Kristoff chose to have a home visitor work with her. The home visitor set up weekly meetings with her. Each week the home visitor introduced a new parenting concept to Mrs. Kristoff, provided some guidance on ways to use the strategies with Emily, observed their interaction, provided feedback, and addressed any concerns that Mrs. Kristoff shared with her.

The Director of Wee Ones Child Care contacted the community mental health agency. She was seeking assistance for supporting the staff of her child care program. Her staff had become increasingly concerned about their ability to meet the needs of children who were exhibiting problem behavior. The mental health consultant visited the program and observed in the classroom. He met with the director and shared that the first area he would like to address was to help the program design the physical environment and classroom routines in ways that would support children's appropriate behavior. In the following months, he conducted two workshops and provided teachers with individual technical assistance in translating the concepts shared in the training to their classrooms. After the classroom modifications were made, the teachers uniformly reported that they felt as if classroom behavior management had become less of a problem, although they still had concerns about individual children.

Secondary Intervention

The secondary level of the model is focused on teaching social-emotional skills to young children who are at risk for social developmental delays or problem behavior. A highly successful approach to supporting children at this level of the model is through the use of a targeted social-emotional instructional curriculum (Joseph & Strain, 2003). Parents and/or early educators who have daily contact with the child may implement curricula that provide instruction on social competence. Curricula that are designed for home implementation by parents or primary caregivers are delivered through parent training programs where the family member learns strategies for teaching the child.

The Triple P (Positive Parenting Program) is a parent training curriculum that includes multiple levels ranging from universal prevention to a more intensive program for parents whose children are exhibiting serious challenging behavior. The universal program includes parenting tip sheets, parenting videotapes, and materials for conducting a coordinated promotional campaign to provide information on common parenting issues and solutions. The Triple P continuum becomes more targeted with subsequent levels ranging from level 2, which offers a script to provide parenting advice, to level 5, which offers behavioral family intervention for families whose children have persistent problem behavior. The program is based on 1) a recognition of the importance of providing parents with positive child management skills to break the cycle of coercive or ineffective parenting; 2) the efficacy of applied behavior analysis; 3) the importance of teaching children social and communication skills within everyday contexts; and 4) the merits of addressing parental beliefs, self-efficacy, and problem solving (Sanders, Markie-Dadds, & Turner, 2003).

Triple P was developed in Australia and has been extensively evaluated with studies that include randomized trials (Sanders, Markie-Dadds, Tully, & Bor, 2000; Sanders & McFarland, 2000). In a randomized study of the effects of three conditions of Triple P compared to a wait list control group of 3-year-old children with disruptive behavior, the program resulted in significant changes in parenting behavior and child disruptive behavior for all of the Triple P intervention conditions. The three conditions of Triple P that were evaluated were 1) standard Triple P (parent training with a therapist who guided the intervention); 2) enhanced Triple P (a more intensive curriculum that includes parent communication and coping skills instruction); and 3) self-directed Triple P (where families used a workbook and written materials on their own). Changes in child behavior, parenting competence, and consumer satisfaction were higher for families in the therapist-supported variants of the model (Sanders et al., 2000).

There are also models for supporting the development of children's social competence that can be applied within the early childhood classroom environment. One of these models, *The Incredible Years* training series, offers both a classroom and parent training component (Webster-Stratton, 1992; Webster-Stratton & Hammond, 1997; Webster-Stratton & Reid, 1999; Webster-Stratton & Taylor, 2001). *The Incredible Years Basic* program parenting course for young children (ages 2–7) is a 12-week program for parents that is focused on teaching parents how to play with their child; positive reinforcement strategies; the use of logical and natural consequences; problem-solving strategies; and the use of positive discipline strategies, including ignoring and time-out. This program may be followed by the advance program that provides training on effective communication with children and other adults and problem-solving strategies for adults and children. The advance program was designed to provide parents who have multiple risk factors, including depression, marital discord, poor coping skills, and lack of support. *The Incredible Years* training series also offers a teacher training program designed to provide early educators with instruction on using attention, praise, and encouragement; motivating children through incentives; using prevention strategies; responding to disruptive behavior; building positive relationships with students; and teaching social skills. The early childhood component of the program that is used with children is called the Dina Dinosaur Social Skills and Problem-Solving Curriculum (Webster-Stratton, 1990). It was designed to promote children's social competence and can be delivered to children within a clinical environment offered to small groups of children who have conduct problems or as a classroomwide curriculum for all children. The classroom application involves circle time discussion scripts, practice activities, and strategies for promoting skill use throughout the child's day.

Studies that have examined the efficacy of *The Incredible Years* training series have documented impressive outcomes. Randomized studies of the effects of the Basic parenting course for parents of 4–8-year-old children with conduct disorders have shown a reduction in the child's aggressive and destructive behavior and increases in children's pro-social skills (Webster-Stratton, 1984; Webster-Stratton & Hammond, 1997; Webster-Stratton, Hollinsworth, & Kolpacoff, 1989). Parents who receive the training show a reduction in the use of spanking and negative parenting behavior and increases in the use of praise and effective discipline techniques (Webster-Stratton, 1984; Webster-Stratton et al., 1989; Webster-Stratton & Hammond, 1997). Children who participated in the clinical application of the Dina Dinosaur Curriculum showed significant decreases in aggression and increases in problem solving (Webster-Stratton & Hammond, 1997; Webster-Stratton & Reid, 1999). Research that examined the combination of the parent training with the clinical program for children showed greater results than parent training alone (Webster-Stratton & Hammond, 1997; Webster-Stratton & Reid, 1999).

Providing Secondary Interventions

Parent education efforts including a targeted social-emotional curriculum can provide parents with essential skills in how to give their child instructions, set limits, use praise, and use natural and logical consequences. Group training efforts often include parent discussion, viewing videotapes, role-plays, and at-home assignments. Another format for delivering this information is through a one-to-one intervention visit that occurs in the home environment where the interventionist may work with the parent, observe parent-child interactions, and provide the parent with feedback on the implementation of the instructional content.

In early education and care environments, a social-emotional curriculum is adopted for classroom implementation. The curricular focus areas typically include making friends, resolving conflicts, identifying feelings, and solving problems. These curricula involve the presentation of a lesson to a small or whole group with planned extension activities to ensure that the key concepts of lessons are taught and reinforced within other classroom activities. There is some evidence that the most effective implementation of a social-emotional curriculum is when there is both a parent education and teacher implementation component.

The following scenarios describe a parent training curriculum offered to a parent and the implementation of a social skills curriculum that includes a parent training and early education component.

Ms. Martinez was worried about her child's behavior problems. Her 4-year-old son, Jorge, has difficulty when playing with other children his own age. He hits to gain access to toys, has long tantrums when children do not play "his way," and is not able to play with other children without very close supervision. She expressed her concern to her pediatrician who provided her with a pamphlet on a parent education program offered by the community parent resource center. Ms. Martinez began attending the program where she was taught strategies she could use to teach Jorge how to express his emotions appropriately and play with others. Ms. Martinez enjoyed the sessions that included videotapes, role-plays, and discussions with other families who had similar concerns. Each week she was provided with take-home activities to implement with Jorge.

In the Lakeview Head Start program the teachers have been trained to implement the Dina Dinosaur Treatment Program (Webster-Stratton & Reid, 2003). In addition, the parent liaison with the program has been trained to provide parents with *The Incredible Years* BASIC and ADVANCE program. The teachers are pleased with the lesson scripts they use within circle time and excited to see how the children respond to the puppets that are used to teach many of the skills. They have noticed that the implementation of the curriculum has been helpful for several of the children who have difficulty with anger management and peer conflict. Many of the parents have enrolled in the BASIC parent training component and a few have also taken the ADVANCE course. The teachers in the program have commented that since implementing *The Incredible Years* program they find it easier to work with families in discussing and addressing the social skills needs of the children enrolled in the program. Although there has not been a formal evaluation of the adoption of the program, the staff of Lakeview Head Start feel that the implementation of the program has reduced child problem behavior and increased parent competence.

■ ■ ■

Indicated Intervention

At the top of the triangle is the relatively small percentage of children and families who are in need of interventions that will address a child's serious and persistent challenging behavior. When children have persistent challenging behavior that is not responsive to parent management strategies or social skills promotion efforts, a more focused and intensive approach may be needed. This section describes three different intervention models that have unique applications and strengths: 1) Parent–Child Interaction Therapy, 2) Regional Intervention Program, and 3) Positive Behavior Support.

Parent–Child Interaction Therapy offers a clinically based parent training program for parents of children with conduct disorders that provides parents with instruction on how to play with the child, develop a positive relationship with the child, and gain child compliance (Brestan & Eyberg, 1998; Eyberg, Boggs, & Algina, 1995). The program typically involves 12–14 weekly intervention sessions that last 1–2 hours each. The sessions are divided into two distinct phases—child-directed interaction and parent-directed interaction. The first phase, child-directed interaction, is focused on teaching parents how to play with their child while using praise, imitation, descriptive commenting, and enthusiasm. Once the parent demonstrates criteria for the use of these skills during an observation, intervention begins on parent-directed interaction. The focus of the parent-directed interaction phase is to teach the parent how to give clearly stated instructions and deliver consequences for child compliance. Each session with the parent and child involves parent-alone instruction time, observation of the parent with the child to assess progress in learning the skills, and live coaching during parent–child interactions. In addition, parents are provided with homework on how to practice the skills within the home.

A synthesis of 17 research studies evaluating Parent–Child Interaction Therapy provides evidence that the intervention results in significant improvements in child behavior functioning (Gallagher, 2003). Behavior changes were noted in parent and teacher rated behavior problems and observation of child compliance rates within observation sessions. Further results showed a decrease in child and teacher ratings of hyperactivity and inattention, a decrease in whining and/or crying during clinic sessions, and a reduction in children who would qualify for a diagnosis of disruptive behavior disorder (Gallagher, 2003). Changes in social-emotional competence were measured in several studies showing improvement in social competence. Longitudinal follow-up assessments, however, have not shown that those posttreatment gains were maintained over time (Eyberg et al., 2001; Funderburk et al., 1998; Nixon, 2001).

The Regional Intervention Program (RIP) provides a unique model of parent and child intervention for children who have challenging behaviors. In this program, experienced parents (i.e., parents who have completed the program) provide training to incoming parents in strategies of positive behavior management (Timm, 1993). The RIP program takes place within a preschool environment where children are taught the social skills necessary to be successful in group care and school environments and parents are taught strategies to manage their children's behavior and promote their children's social competence and positive peer interactions. In continuous operation since 1969, RIP has been replicated extensively in the United States and several other countries. Evaluation data have indicated that parents readily learn improved patterns of parent–child interactions and that the children show rapid improvements in compliance and adaptive behavior (Strain & Timm, 2001). In addition, ongoing long-term follow-up data indicate high levels of maintenance for both the children and the parents, along with high levels of consumer satisfaction (Strain & Timm, 2001). Although no direct comparison data are available, the favorable outcomes seen in RIP participants is in stark contrast to the dire projections suggested by other studies of similar populations (e.g., Dodge, 1993; McCord, 1978).

Positive Behavior Support (PBS) is an intervention approach that shows promise for providing effective, comprehensive, and individualized interventions for young children with severe and persistent challenging behavior (Blair, Umbreit, & Bos, 1999; Dunlap & Fox, 1999; Frea & Hepburn, 1999; Galensky, Miltenberger, Stricker, & Garlinghouse, 2001; Moes & Frea, 2000, Reeve & Carr, 2000). Although PBS is a relatively new approach, it is based on a rich foundation of research in applied behavior analysis, family support, team processes, and person-centered values (Carr et al., 2002; Kincaid & Fox, 2002; Lucyshyn, Dunlap, & Albin, 2002). In applications with young children, the PBS model emphasizes a family centered, team-based strategy of assessment and comprehensive support that takes place in the natural contexts of the child's and family's ongoing activities (Dunlap & Fox, 1996; Fox, Dunlap, & Cushing, 2002; Fox, Dunlap, & Powell, 2002). Although specific applications vary, the general PBS model for young children includes three main phases. Phase 1 includes the development of a trusting rapport with the family and child, person-centered planning and goal setting, functional assessment of challenging behavior, ecological assessment of resources available in home and community contexts, and development of a comprehensive behavior support plan. Phase 2 involves home- and community-based implementation of the plan with the initial stages usually involving direct guidance and support from the PBS consultant and the level of support being gradually faded over a number of weeks of implementation. Phase 3 involves ongoing evaluation and transition to long-term follow-up, typically with additional planning and individualized family assistance. The objectives of PBS for young children are to 1) enhance the family's competence and confidence in problem solving, preventing, and intervening with challenging behaviors and enhance self-advocacy; and 2) develop the child's social and communication skills while reducing serious challenging behaviors (Dunlap & Fox, 1996; Powell, Dunlap, & Fox, 2006).

Because the PBS process, as currently defined, is relatively new, there are few data to directly attest to its effectiveness in achieving comprehensive family and child outcomes. The empirical foundations of PBS, however, are extensive. Data indicate gains in parent competencies (e.g., Robbins & Dunlap, 1992; Robbins, Dunlap, & Plienis, 1991) and child progress (e.g., Dunlap & Fox, 1999; Robbins et al., 1991). In addition, a large number of single-subject experimental studies show that the elements of PBS support plans are efficacious in reducing challenging behaviors and increasing adaptive responding of young children (Conroy, Dunlap, Clarke, & Alter, 2005).

Blake is a 22-month old toddler with mild developmental delays. During the past 6 months, his behavior has become increasingly more difficult. At home, he clings to his parents and refuses to be independent. When asked to transition to an activity that he does not prefer, he cries, extends his body, and bites the adult. He is enrolled in an early childhood program where he is experiencing similar challenges. Blake will tantrum and bite adults when he does not want to do an activity. More frequently, he will bite peers if they are playing with a toy that he wants or if they seek to share a toy with which he is playing.

The teachers and the family sought the assistance of a community psychologist who recommended that Blake be placed in a playpen for a time-out whenever he bit. This addressed the need to isolate Blake from children he had hurt and to provide the adults with a strategy to demonstrate to Blake that biting was not going to be tolerated. It did not, however, help in reducing his biting and he was spending much of the day in the playpen isolated from peers or family activities. In response to the preschool's growing frustration with Blake's lack of progress, the director contacted a mental health consultant who had expertise in Positive Behavior Support (PBS).

The mental health consultant gathered together the parents, teacher, classroom assistant, and program director to form a behavior support team for Blake. She taught the team how to gather data on Blake's behavior in a manner that would shed light on the triggers and maintaining consequences of his biting (i.e., functional behavioral assessment). The team analyzed the data they collected with the assistance of the mental health consultant and learned that Blake was biting to get out of difficult activities, to access preferred toys, and to keep other children from touching the toys he was using. Once the team understood the purpose of the behavior, they were able to develop a support plan to prevent the behavior from occurring and to help Blake learn new skills. They worked together to teach Blake to ask for a break from an activity and to ask for toys or objects he preferred. In addition, they systematically taught Blake peer interaction strategies and how to share or take turns with a peer. In addition to teaching Blake replacement skills, the team identified strategies that they could use to make activities less difficult for Blake and ways to ensure that Blake knew when he could have preferred toys and objects. They also agreed on how they would respond to Blake to ensure that his behavior did not result in a *pay-off* or reinforcement.

The plan was implemented at school and the team was pleased with the results. The mental health consultant helped the team develop a similar plan for the behaviors that Blake was having at home and in the community. Blake's biting and resistance behavior completely stopped.

CONCLUSION

Addressing social-emotional and behavioral disruptions in the development of young children requires attention and effective action at all levels of prevention. At the level of primary prevention, it is known that serious problems can be minimized if children have access to positive, nurturing, stable relationships with caregiving adults. It is also known that high-quality early education environments can be important in setting the stage for positive interactions with peers and for the development of a range of critical social competencies. These primary prevention factors can effectively reduce the number of children in need of more directed strategies at the secondary and tertiary levels.

For those children who are seriously at-risk for social-emotional problems or who are beginning to demonstrate maladaptive behavioral tendencies, evidence indicates that a number of social-emotional teaching programs and curricula can be effective in guiding the children to more prosocial patterns of interaction (Joseph & Strain, 2003). Such secondary prevention programs are usually conducted in small groups and can be effective and relatively cost-efficient strategies for resolving early inclinations toward more serious behavioral disorders. Inevitably, however, there will be young children who have already developed severe social-emotional and behavioral challenges. For these children, the more intensive and individualized strategies at the tertiary level are indicated. A number of programs, including RIP and PBS, have been demonstrated to be effective or to be highly promising for these children and their families.

As discussed in this chapter, there is some evidence to support quality practices at each of these levels of prevention. Still, in some cases, the evidence is not overwhelming. The data that exist are still largely of a piecemeal nature. The studies that have contributed important findings have tended to be relatively small scale, and essentially no studies have included large numbers of participants such that the replicability and generality of the practices or programs could be thoroughly examined. It is hoped that, concurrent with the rising appreciation of the seriousness of the issue, more resources will be invested in research to aid our understanding of evidence-based practices and the methods that will be needed to implement those practices to benefit the largest numbers of children and families.

REFERENCES

Ackerman, B., Kogos, J., Youngstrom, E., Schoff, K., & Izard, C. (1999). Family instability and the problem behaviors of children from economically disadvantaged families. *Developmental Psychology, 35*, 258–268.

American Psychological Association. (1993). *Violence and youth: Psychology's response.* Washington, DC: Author.

Batsche, G.M., & Knoff, H.M. (1994). Bullies and their victims: Understanding a pervasive problem in the schools. *School Psychology Review, 23*(2), 165–174.

Black, M.M., Papas, M.A., Hussy, J.M., Dubowitz, H., Kotch, J.B., & Starr, R.H. (2002). Behavior problems among preschool children born to adolescent mothers: Effects of maternal depression and perceptions of partner relationship. *Journal of Clinical Child and Adolescent Psychology, 31*(1), 16–26.

Blair, K.C., Umbreit, J., & Bos, C.S. (1999). Using functional assessment and children's preferences to improve the behavior of young children with behavioral disorders. *Behavioral Disorders, 24*, 151–166.

Bowman, B.T., Donovan, M.S., & Burns, M.S. (Eds.). (2001). *Eager to learn: Educating our preschoolers.* National Research Council, Committee on Early Childhood Pedagogy, Commission on Behavioral and Social Sciences and Education. Washington, DC: National Academies Press.

Brestan, E.V., & Eyberg, S.M. (1998). Effective psychosocial treatments of conduct-disordered children and adolescents: 29 years, 82 studies, and 5,272 kids. *Journal of Clinical Child Psychology, 27*, 180–189.

Bronson, M.B. (2000). *Self-regulation in early childhood: Nature and nurture.* New York: The Guilford Press.

Bullis, M., Nishoika-Evans, V., Fredericks, H.D. & Davis, C. (1993). Identifying and assessing the job-related social skills of adolescents and young adults with emotional and behavioral disorders. *Journal of Emotional and Behavioral Disorders, 1,* 236–250.

Bullis, M., & Gaylord-Ross, R. (1991). Transitions for youth with behavioral disorders. In L. Bullock & R.B. Rutherford, Jr. (Eds), *CEC mini-library: Working with behavioral disorders.* Reston, VA: Council for Exceptional Children.

Campbell, S.B. (1995). Behavior problems in preschool children: A review of recent research. *Journal of Child Psychology and Psychiatry, 36*(1), 113–149.

Campbell, S.B., & Ewing, L.J. (1990). Hard-to-manage preschoolers: Adjustment at age nine and predictors of continuing symptoms. *Journal of Child Psychology and Psychiatry, 31,* 871–889.

Carr, E.G., Dunlap, G., Horner, R.H., Koegel, R.L., Turnbull, A.P., & Sailor, W., et al. (2002). Positive behavior support: Evolution of an applied science. *Journal of Positive Behavior Interventions, 4*(1), 4–16.

Conroy, M.S., Dunlap, G., Clarke, S., & Alter, P.J. (2005). A descriptive analysis of behavioral intervention research with young children with challenging behavior. *Topics in Early Childhood Special Education, 25,* 157–166.

Dodge, K. (1993). The future of research on conduct disorder. *Development and Psychopathology, 5,* 311–320.

Dunlap, G. & Fox, L. (1996). Early intervention and serious problem behaviors: A comprehensive approach. In L.K. Koegel, R.L. Koegel, & G. Dunlap (Eds.), *Positive behavioral support: Including people with difficult behavior in the community.* (pp. 31–50). Baltimore: Paul H. Brookes Publishing Co.

Dunlap, G., & Fox, L. (1999). A demonstration of behavioral support for young children with autism. *Journal of Positive Behavior Interventions, 1,* 77–87.

Dunst, C.J., Trivette, C.M., & Cutspec, P.A. (2002). Toward an operational definition of evidence-based practices. *Centerscope, 1*(1), 1–10.

Egeland, B., Kalkoske, M., Gottesman, N., & Erickson, M.F. (1990). Preschool behavior problems: Stability and factors accounting for change. *Journal of Child Psychology and Psychiatry, 31,* 891–909.

Eyberg, S.M., Boggs, S.R., & Algina, J. (1995). Parent–child interaction therapy: A psychosocial model for the treatment of young children with conduct problem behavior and their families. *Psychopharmacology Bulletin, 31,* 83–91.

Eyberg, S.M., Funderburk, B.W., Hembree-Kigin, T.L., McNeil, C.B., Querido, J.G., & Hood, K.K. (2001). Parent-child interaction therapy with behavior problem children: One and two year maintenance of treatment effects in the family. *Child and Family Behavior Therapy, 23,* 1–20.

Federal Interagency Forum on Child and Family Statistics. (2002). *America's children: Key national indicators of well-being.* Washington, DC: U.S. Government Printing Office.

Fischer, M., Rolf, J.E., Hasazi, J.E., & Cummings, L. (1984). Follow-up of a preschool epidemiological sample: Cross-age continuities and predication of later adjustment with internalizing and externalizing dimensions of behavior. *Child Development, 55,* 137–150.

Fox, L., Benito, N., & Dunlap, G. (2002). Early intervention with families of young children with autism and behavior problems. In J.M. Lucyshyn, G. Dunlap, & R.W. Albin (Eds.), *Families and positive behavior support: Addressing problem behaviors in family contexts* (pp. 251–269). Baltimore: Paul H. Brookes Publishing Co..

Fox, L., Dunlap, G., & Cushing, L. (2002). Early intervention, positive behavior support, and transition to school. *Journal of Emotional and Behavioral Disorders*, *10*, 149–157.

Fox, L., Dunlap, G., Hemmeter, M.L., Joseph, G.E., & Strain, P.S. (2003). The teaching pyramid: A model for supporting social competence and preventing challenging behavior in young children. *Young Children*, *58*, 48–52.

Fox, L., Dunlap, G., & Powell, D. (2002). Young children and challenging behavior: Issues and considerations for behavior support. *Journal of Positive Behavior Interventions*, *4*, 208–217.

Frank, A.R., & Sitlington, P.L. (1997). Young adults with behavioral disorders— before and after IDEA. *Behavioral Disorders*, *23*, 40–56.

Frea, W.D., & Hepburn, S.L. (1999). Teaching parents of children with autism to perform functional assessments to plan interventions for extremely disruptive behaviors. *Journal of Positive Behavior Interventions*, *1*, 112–116.

Funderburk, B.W., Eyberg, S.M., Newcomb, K., McNeil, C.B., Hembree-Kigin, T., & Capage, L. (1998). Parent-child interaction therapy with behavior problem children: Maintenance of treatment effects in the school setting. *Child and Family Behavior Therapy*, *20*(2), 17–38.

Galensky, T.L., Miltenberger, R.G., Stricker, J.M., & Garlinghouse, M.A. (2001). Functional assessment and the treatment of mealtime behavior problems. *Journal of Positive Behavior Intervention*, *3*, 211–224.

Gallagher, N. (2003). Effects of parent-child interaction therapy on young children with disruptive behavior disorders. *Bridges*, *1*(4), 1–16.

Gordon, R. (1983). An operational classification of disease prevention. *Public Health Reports*, *98*, 107–109.

Gordon, R. (1987). An operational classification of disease prevention. In J.A. Steinberg & M.M. Silverman (Eds.), *Preventing mental disorders* (pp. 20–26). Rockville, MD: Department of Health and Human Services.

Gross, D., Sambrook, A., & Fogg, L. (1999). Behavior problems among young children in low-income urban day care centers. *Research in Nursing & Health*, *22*(1), 15–25.

Harden, B.J., Winslow, M.B., Kendziora, K.T., Shahinfar, A., Rubin, K.H., Fox, N.A., et al. (2000). Externalizing problems in Head Start children: An ecological exploration. *Early Education and Development*, *11*, 357–385.

Helburn, S., Culkin, M.I., Morris, J., Mocan, N., Howes, C., Phillipsen, L. et al. (1995). *Cost, quality, and child outcomes in child care centers (2nd ed.).* Denver: University of Colorado at Denver, Economics Department.

Howes, C., Phillips, D., & Whitebrook, M. (1992). Thresholds of quality: Implications for the social development of children in center-based child care. *Child Development*, *63*, 449–460.

Huffman, L.C., Mehlinger, S.L., & Kerivan, A.S. (2000). Risk factors for academic and behavioral problems at the beginning of school. In *Off to a good start: Research on the risk factors for early school problems and selected federal policies affecting children's social and emotional development and their readiness for school* (pp. 1–93). Chapel Hill: University of North Carolina, FPG Child Development Center.

Individuals with Disabilities Education Improvement Act of 2004, PL 108–446, 20 U.S.C. §§ 1400 *et seq.*

Joseph, B.E., & Strain, P.S. (2003). Comprehensive evidence-based social-emotional curricula for young children: An analysis of efficacious adoption potential. *Topics in Early Childhood Special Education*, *23*, 65–76.

Kincaid, D., & Fox, L. (2002). Person-centered planning and positive behavior support. In S. Holburn & P. M. Vietze (Eds.), *Person-centered planning: Research, practice, and future directions* (pp. 29–50). Baltimore: Paul H. Brookes Publishing Co.

Landy, S. (2002). *Pathways to competence: Encouraging healthy social and emotional development in young children.* Baltimore: Paul H. Brookes Publishing Co.

Lavigne, J.V., Arend, R., Rosenbaum, D., Binns, H., Christoffel, K.K., Kaufer, K., et al. (1998). Psychiatric disorders with onset in the preschool years: I. Stability of diagnoses. *Journal of the American Academy of Child and Adolescent Psychiatry, 37*(12), 1246–1254.

Lavigne, J.V., Gibbons, R.D., Christoffel, K.K., Arend, R., Rosenbaum, D., Binns, H.J., et al. (1996). Prevalence rates and correlates of psychiatric disorders among preschool children. *Journal of the American Academy of Child and Adolescent Psychiatry, 35,* 889–897.

Leadbeater, B.J., & Bishop, S.J. (1994). Predictors of behavior problems in preschool children of inner-city Afro-American and Puerto Rican adolescent mothers. *Child Development, 65,* 638–648.

Loeber, R., Wung, P., Keenan, K., Giroux, B., Stouthamer-Loeber, M., Van Kammen, W.B., et al. (1993). Developmental pathways in disruptive child behavior. *Development Psychopathology, 5,* 103–133.

Love, J.M., Kisker, E.E., Ross, C.M., Schochet, P.Z., Brooks-Gunn, J., Paulsell, D. et al. (2002). *Making a difference in the lives of infants and toddlers and their families: The impacts of early Head Start, executive summary.* Washington, DC: U.S. Department of Health and Human Services, Administration for Children and Families.

Love, J.M., Meckstroth, A., & Sprachman, S. (1997). *Measuring the quality of program environments in Head Start and other early childhood programs: A review and recommendations for future research.* Washington, DC: U.S. Department of Education, National Center for Education Statistics. Working Paper No. 97-36.

Lucyshyn, J.M., Dunlap, G., & Albin, R.W. (Eds.). (2002). *Families and positive behavior support: Addressing problem behaviors in family contexts.* Baltimore: Paul H. Brookes Publishing Co.

McCord, J. (1978). A thirty year follow-up of treatment effects. *American Psychologist, 33,* 284–289.

Moes, D.R., & Frea, W.D. (2000). Using family context to inform intervention planning for the treatment of a child with autism. *Journal of Positive Behavior Interventions, 2,* 40–46.

Moffit, T.E. (1993). Adolescence-limited and life-course-persistent antisocial behavior: A developmental taxonomy. *Psychological Review, 100,* 674–701.

Moffitt, T.E., Caspi, A., Dickson, N., Silva, P., & Stanton, W. (1996). Childhood-onset versus adolescent-onset antisocial conduct problems in males: Natural history from ages 3 to 18 years. *Development and Psychopathology, 8,* 399–424.

Nagin, D., & Tremblay, R.E. (1999). Trajectories of boys' physical aggression, opposition, and hyperactivity on the path to physically violent and nonviolent juvenile delinquency. *Child Development, 70*(5), 1181–1196.

National Research Council. (2001). Eager to learn: Educating our preschoolers. In B.T. Bowman, M.S. Donovan, & M.S. Burns (Eds.), *Committee on Early Childhood Pedagogy, Commission on Behavioral and Social Sciences and Education.* Washington, DC: National Academies Press.

NICHD Early Child Care Research Network. (July, 1999). Child outcomes when child care center classes meet recommended standards for quality. *American Journal of Public Health, 89*(7), 1072–1077.

Nixon, R.D.V. (2001). Changes in hyperactivity and temperament in behaviourally disturbed preschoolers after parent-child interaction therapy (PCIT). *Behaviour Change, 18,* 168–176.

Olds, D., Henderson, C., Cole, R., Eckenrode, J., Kitzman, H., & Luckey, D. (1998). Long-term effects of nurse home visitation on children's criminal and antisocial behavior: 15-year follow up of a randomized trial. *Journal of the American Medical Association, 280*(14), 1238–1244.

Patterson, G.R., DeBaryshe, B.D., & Ramsey, E. (1989). A development perspective on antisocial behavior. *American Psychologist, 44,* 329–335.

Peisner-Feinberg, E.S., Burchinal, M.R., Clifford, R.M., Culkin, M.L., Howes, C., Kagan, S.L., et al. (1999). *The children of the cost, quality, and outcomes study go to school: Executive summary.* Chapel Hill: University of North Carolina at Chapel Hill, Frank Porter Graham Child Development Center.

Powell, D., Dunlap, G., & Fox, L. (2006). Prevention and intervention for the challenging behaviors of toddlers and preschoolers. *Infants and Young Children, 19*(1), 25–35.

The President's New Freedom Commission on Mental Health. (2003). *Achieving the promise: Transforming mental health care in America. Final report.* (DHHS Publication No. SMA 03-3832). Rockville, MD: U.S. Department of Health and Human Services.

Qi, C.H., & Kaiser, A.P. (2003). Behavior problems of preschool children from low-income families: Review of the literature. *Topics in Early Childhood Special Education, 23,* 188–216.

Reeve, C.E., & Carr, E.G. (2000). Prevention of severe behavior problems in children with developmental disorders. *Journal of Positive Behavior Interventions, 2,* 144–160.

Richman, N., Stevenson, J., & Graham, P.J. (1982). *Preschool to school: A behavioral study.* London: Academic Press.

Robbins, F.R., & Dunlap, G. (1992). Effects of task difficulty on parent teaching skills and behavior problems of young children with autism. *American Journal on Mental Retardation, 96,* 631–643.

Robbins, F.R., Dunlap, G., & Plienis, A.J. (1991). Family characteristics, family training, and the progress of young children with autism. *Journal of Early Intervention, 15,* 173–184.

Sanders, M.R., Markie-Dadds, C., Tully, L., & Bor, B. (2000). The Triple P—Positive Parenting Program: A comparison of enhanced, standard, and self-directed behavioural family intervention for parents of children with early onset conduct problems. *Journal of Consulting and Clinical Psychology, 68,* 624–640.

Sanders, M.R., Markie-Dadds, C., & Turner, K.M.T. (2003). Theoretical, scientific, and clinical foundations of the Triple-P Positive Parenting Program: A population approach to the promotion of parenting competence. *Parenting Research and Practice Monograph, 1,* 1–24.

Sanders, M.R., & McFarland, M.L. (2000). The treatment of depressed mothers with disruptive children: A controlled evaluation of cognitive behavioural family intervention. *Behaviour Therapy, 31,* 89–112.

Shaw, D., Gilliom, M., & Giovannelli, J. (2000). Aggressive behavior disorders. In C.H. Zeanah (Ed.), *Handbook of infant mental health.* New York: The Guilford Press.

Shaw, D.S., Winslow, E.B., Owens, E.B., & Hood, N. (1998). Young children's adjustment to chronic family adversity: A longitudinal study of low-income families. *Journal of the American Academy of Child and Adolescent Psychiatry, 37,* 545–553.

Shonkoff, J.P., & Phillips, D.A. (Eds.). (2000). *From neurons to neighborhoods: The science of early childhood development.* Washington, DC: National Academies Press.

Simeonsson, R.J. (1991). Primary, secondary, and tertiary prevention in early intervention. *Journal of Early Intervention, 15,* 124–134.

Singer, G.H.S., Irvin, L.K., Irvine, B., Hawkins, N.J., & Cooley, E. (1989). Evaluation of community-based support services for families of persons with developmental disabilities. *The Journal of The Association for Persons with Severe Handicaps, 14*, 312–323.

Spieker, S.J., Larson, N.C., Lewis, S.M., Keller, T.E., & Gilchrist, L. (1999). Developmental trajectories of disruptive behavior problems in preschool children of adolescent mothers. *Child Development, 70*, 443–458.

Sprague, J., & Walker, H. (2000). Early identification and intervention for youth with antisocial and violent behavior. *Exceptional Children, 66*(3), 367–379.

Strain, P.S., & Timm, M.A. (2001). Remediation and prevention of aggression: An evaluation of the Regional Intervention Program over a quarter century. *Behavioral Disorders, 26*, 297–313.

Timm, M.A. (1993). The Regional Intervention Program. *Behavioral Disorders, 19*, 34–43.

Tolan, P.H., Guerra, N.G., & Kendall, P.C. (1995). A developmental-ecological perspective on antisocial behavior in children and adolescents: Toward a unified risk and intervention framework. *Journal of Consulting and Clinical Psychology, 63*(4), 579–584.

Wagner, M., Newman, L., D'Amico, R., Jay, E.D., Butler-Nalin, P., & Marder, C. (Eds.). (1991). *Youth with disabilities: How are they doing? The first comprehensive report from the National Longitudinal Transition Study of Special Education Students.* Menlo Park, CA: SRI International.

Webster-Stratton, C. (Ed.). (1984). *The Incredible Years Parent Training Manual: BASIC Program.* (Available from *Incredible Years*, 1411 8th Avenue West, Seattle, WA 98119).

Webster-Stratton, C. (1990). *The teacher's and children's videotape series: Dina Dinosaur's social skills and problem-solving curriculum.* Seattle: University of Washington Press.

Webster-Stratton, C. (1992). *The Incredible Years: A trouble-shooting guide for parents of children ages 3-8 years.* Toronto: Umbrella Press.

Webster-Stratton, C. (1994). Advancing Videotape Parent Training: A comparison study. *Journal of Consulting and Clinical Psychology, 62*, 583–593.

Webster-Stratton, C, & Hammond, M. (1997). Treating children with early-onset conduct problems: A comparison of child and parent training interventions. *Journal of Consulting and Clinical Psychology, 65*, 93–109.

Webster-Stratton, C., Hollinsworth, T., & Kolpacoff, M. (1989). The long-term effectiveness and clinical significance of three cost-effective training programs for families with conduct-problem children. *Journal of Consulting and Clinical Psychology, 57*(4), 550–553.

Webster-Stratton, C., & Reid, M. J. (1999). *Effects of teacher training in Head Start classrooms. Results of a randomized controlled evaluation.* Paper presented at the Society for Prevention Research, New Orleans.

Webster-Stratton, C., & Reid, M. J. (2003). Treating conduct problems and strengthening social and emotional competence in young children: The Dina Dinosaur Treatment Program. *Journal of Emotional and Behavioral Disorders, 11*, 130–143.

Webster-Stratton, C., & Taylor, T. (2001). Nipping early risk factors in the bud: Preventing substance abuse, delinquency, and violence in adolescence through interventions targeted at young children (0-8 years). *Prevention Science, 2*, 165–192.

15

Promoting Resilience in Young Children and Families at the Highest Risk

The Challenge for Early Childhood Mental Health

Jane Knitzer and Elena P. Cohen

■ ■ ■

4-year-old Maria Martinez lives with her father and her mother who are both immigrants from Honduras. For 2 years, they, along with their 6-year-old son and 4-month-old daughter, have been living in the basement of their church. With the support of church members, Ms. Martinez was able to get prenatal care and well-baby care for her three children, but Maria has always been challenging. At 2 years old, much to Ms. Martinez's concern, Maria was not talking, appeared to be deaf, banged her head on walls and on her crib, and screamed loudly, especially at night. Her pediatrician ruled out a hearing problem and told Ms. Martinez that Maria's behavior was probably the result of a language delay related to hearing Spanish from her parents and English from others. The doctor did not refer Maria to an early intervention program, but he recommended limiting the use of Spanish and enrolling her in a child care program. Despite concerted attempts to follow up on these recommendations, it took the family almost 2 more years to get subsidized space in a family child care home. Then, within 3 weeks, the child care provider told Ms. Martinez that she could not bring Maria back because other parents had complained about Maria's hitting and biting. At home, Maria's behavior became less and less manageable. Ms. Martinez had even stopped the sporadic cleaning work she was doing because nobody would take care of Maria. When Ms. Martinez did errands outside the house, she waited until Maria was asleep, strapped her firmly in the stroller, and came back home when she woke up. Finally, after a visit to the emergency room, the hospital assigned a home visitor to Ms. Martinez. The home visitor discovered that Maria was always in her crib, which was positioned so she could not possibly climb out because Ms. Martinez feared that she would hurt the baby and did not know what else to do. Mr. Martinez tried to discipline Maria by hitting her, but it never worked. The home visitor referred Maria for an evaluation. Six months later Maria was diagnosed with an autistic spectrum disorder and the family was linked to Early Intervention.

■ ■ ■

Sandy was born full-term at a large, urban university hospital to Mary, a physical therapist, and Mitch, a journalist. They had been married for 5 years and eagerly awaited the birth of their first child. As a baby, Sandy slept a lot, but was very fussy and hard to soothe when she was awake. As she grew, her temperament continued to be difficult. She rarely looked her parents directly in the eyes, smiled infrequently, and cried for long stretches while awake. When the pediatrician heard these symptoms, he put Sandy on a special formula. Although Sandy seemed to have no limits or boundaries, was not verbally expressive, and hit and bit her parents, they believed she would outgrow the problems and refused relatives' suggestions that they see a specialist. After the birth of a sibling, Sandy was enrolled in a child care center. Mitch and Mary were shocked when, during the first parent–teacher conference, they were told that a teacher's aide was assigned to watch Sandy most of the day to prevent her from hurting other children in the class. The preschool staff believed that a speech delay might account for Sandy's behavior problems and suggested an evaluation by the early intervention program. The initial assessment showed that Sandy had a delay in expressive language, and once a week speech therapy was provided. At home, however, Sandy's difficult behavior was escalating and causing Mary and Mitch to constantly argue over how best to manage her. When the preschool asked that Sandy be removed from the 4-year-old group, both parents sought the advice of a child psychiatrist. The psychiatrist recommended family therapy, a behavioral *star chart*, and an antidepressant for Sandy. The early intervention program found that Sandy no longer qualified for services, so the family used their own resources for a private speech therapist but stopped family therapy because it was too expensive. By the time Sandy entered public kindergarten, she was taking three psychotropic medications, seeing a private speech therapist 2 days a week, and seeing an occupational therapist once a week. Twice during Sandy's fifth year, Mary called the police because she found Sandy's behavior unsafe. On one occasion Sandy ran away from home, and on the other she locked her brother in a closet after hitting him on the head. The psychiatrist hospitalized Sandy a week after her sixth birthday.

John, soon to be 5 years of age, was in a psychiatric hospital for the second time in 3 months because of his very aggressive and dangerous behaviors. He had already been expelled from several child care environments. His mother, Deborah, has struggled with her own frequent psychiatric hospitalizations throughout her life, and, more recently, had been dealing with her conflict-ridden relationship with John's father, with whom there was a history of severe domestic violence. Deborah receives services from the adult mental health system (including individual therapy, medication monitoring, and supportive housing), but no help with parenting. The county they live in has an early childhood system of care in place. Within a few days, with Deborah's help, the system of care coordinator pulled together a team meeting, including both of Deborah's parents, who were very supportive; John's preschool program teacher; John's intervention team at the hospital; representatives from the child and the adult serving systems; and a family advocate from Family Ties, the county family advocacy group. After a discussion of Deborah's goals (including wanting to learn to drive because of her fear of using public transportation, going to school, and having her son succeed in school), a preliminary service plan was developed. Two weeks later, at the follow-up support circle meeting, Deborah proudly reported that she will be learning how to drive as an outcome of her vocational program meeting. John is doing well in school and at home, and Deborah and John are spending more time with her parents. Deborah has been in regular contact with Family Ties, and she has been in touch with a program in the community to help her deal with her former partner and the domestic violence. She is feeling more in control of her life. The support team created around Deborah and John will continue to meet on a regular basis.

Since the mid-1990s, there has been increasing recognition of the need to develop an early childhood mental health system to help families and caregivers promote positive, social-emotional, and behavioral competence in young children (Donahue, Falk, & Gersony Provet, 2000; Johnson, Knitzer, & Kaufmann, 2002; Knitzer, 2002). Much of the focus of these efforts has been on strengthening promotion and prevention strategies to support parents and other caregivers in community environments (e.g., pediatric practices, child care, Early Head Start and Head Start, family support programs); however, children such as Maria, Sandy, and John need more, yet often get nothing. In the family stories described here, only John and his family received meaningful help. The clinical knowledge base about the kinds of interventions that can help infants, toddlers, preschoolers, and families facing greater risks of poor social-emotional, behavioral, and school outcomes is growing (Boggs et al., 2004; Hood & Eyberg, 2003, Shonkoff & Phillips, 2000; Zeanah, 2000). Yet, making sure that this knowledge is used more widely remains a challenge. This chapter explores the ways in which communities and states are beginning to organize to provide the kind of integrated family focused interventions that these higher risk young children and families need. The first section highlights the scope of the challenge, the second section highlights lessons from research that can inform community efforts, and the third section offers examples of what programs and communities are doing to integrate these very seriously troubled young children into system of care efforts. Throughout, the focus is on building capacity, not on the specifics of clinical interventions.

THE SCOPE OF THE CHALLENGE

Although there has been no national epidemiological study of the prevalence of young children with or at risk of diagnosable emotional and behavioral disorders, recent research suggests that in fact the prevalence rates are not different from that of older children. Thus, in a study of a large pediatric practice, researchers reported that 17% of the young children seen had identifiable disorders that vary by specific diagnosis (Angold, Egger, Erkanli, & Keefer, 2005). It is also known that problems vary by income. Overall, according to a national sample of children in kindergarten, 10% of children showed behavior problems (West, Denton, & Reaney, 2001). Analyses of low-income samples consistently show rates that are two or three times as high (Qi & Kaiser, 2003; Raver & Knitzer, 2002).

From a service delivery perspective, understanding the context in which these problems emerge is critical to tailoring the right mix of services and supports to respond to what families want and need. The roots of the problems facing the most high-risk young children and families are complex and varied, often involving some combination of temperament, genetic, and, sometimes, multigenerational family and community factors. Through a broad lens, research and experience suggest that there are two pathways to significant social-emotional and behavior problems in young children. The first pathway affects infants, toddlers, and preschoolers whose earliest experiences fail to provide them with the kind of nurturing, consistent care and stimulation that are the basic ingredients of healthy early brain development. Many of these young children have been exposed to trauma (e.g., domestic violence, placement in foster care). Often their parents are unable to protect them from actual or psychological harm; for a small group of them, parents or other relatives may inflict the harm. Young children, especially babies and toddlers, exposed to this level of stress experience what scientists are calling *toxic stress* (National Scientific Council on the Developing Child, 2005). In terms of crafting service and policy responses, it is also important to recognize that the parents of these young children are typically in highly stressed economic and psychological circumstances, facing risks above and beyond poverty and low education that include domestic violence, maternal depression, or other mental health challenges and/or addiction. Often, they also have long histories of exposure to trauma and/or the experience of poor parenting (Bower-Russa, Knutson, & Winebarger, 2001. These risks can be seen as barriers to effective parenting in the same way that they are typically seen as barriers to employment. They have repeatedly been linked with poor social-emotional development in young children (Qi & Kaiser, 2003; Shonkoff & Phillips, 2000) and increased risk of social-emotional disorders in older children (Edleson, 1999; Weissman et al., 2006).

The second group of young children with or at risk for serious emotional and behavioral disorders is made up of young children similar to Sandy, who was described earlier, who show significant problems even in the face of nurturing parenting and appropriate stimulation. Many of these young children are in families where parents have successfully reared other children and, except for the stresses related to having a young child with serious problems, do not experience the other types of risk factors just highlighted. Often these parents report that they were aware from the beginning that there was something wrong with their children, but no one would listen.

Whatever the family circumstances or the pathways leading to the problems, all of these young children have a developmentally rocky start in life. As babies, many show serious problems in their ability to relate to others, or they may exhibit symptoms of depression and/or regulatory, sleep, eating, and communication disorders. As preschoolers, they have problems regulating their own emotions and may *misread* the cues of others or disconnect with learning. Some are angry and aggressive; others are withdrawn and unable to communicate. Some are both. Typically, and euphemistically, they are described as children with the most challenging behaviors. Similar to John, Maria, and Sandy, many of these young children are being expelled from child care and preschool environments. A national study found that young children are expelled at about three times the rate of children in kindergarten through high school, with substantial variation in rates by state, race, and gender (Gilliam, 2005). Although most of these expulsions are of young children who are 3 and 4 years old, a Chicago study found that 42% of programs surveyed had actually asked at least one family with a baby to leave (Cutler & Gilkerson, 2002).

INVESTING IN HIGH-RISK YOUNG CHILDREN AND FAMILIES

The research case for investing in sufficiently intensive early intervention and treatment on behalf of these babies, toddlers, and preschoolers, and often their families, is compelling. The research on the impact of toxic stress on early brain development supports the urgent need to invest in parent–child relationship-based interventions that can help parents shift the developmental trajectory for young children showing early signs of serious problems (Gunnar & Davis, 2003; National Scientific Council on the Developing Child, 2005). Similarly, research on adult barriers to effective parenting (one of the most enduring protective factors of all) (Luthar, 2006) compels attention to the urgency of addressing parental challenges related to mental illness, especially depression, and parents' histories of trauma (Knitzer, 2002; Knitzer & Lefkowitz, 2006, Van DeMark et al., 2005). It is also becoming clear that the roots of mental illness start earlier in children than previously understood. For example, whereas early onset conduct disorder has long been recognized, evidence is mounting that depression, anxiety, and other disorders also start earlier (see Chapter 2). Although it is beyond the scope of this chapter to review this research in detail, collectively the research has important implications for interventions and systems building on behalf of the most vulnerable young children and families.

First, and of the utmost importance, the research challenges the prevailing mental health paradigm that focuses on the child, not the child in context with the family. In this paradigm, parents are *collateral*. Collateral refers to playing an accompanying or secondary role. For young children (and older children), parents are not secondary. Therefore, when developmental risks are related to significant familial factors, it is clear that there is a need not just for supporting families, but for a *family intervention approach*. A family intervention approach has four aspects. First, it involves intervention for parental risk factors that interfere with effective parenting. Parental risk factors include, for example, depression, substance abuse, and domestic violence. Second, it couples the intervention with relationship-based parenting supports or training (e.g., recall how John's mother received lots of help with her mental health issues, but none with parenting until the team plan). Third, it includes targeted prevention and early intervention for the child. Fourth, it calls for continued attention to a family's basic needs (e.g., health care, food, housing). The group of young children who might benefit from a multigenerational family intervention approach is significant, primarily because the prevalence rates of risk factors associated with impaired parenting are significant. Research on women enrolled in Early Head Start, for example, finds that a stunning 48% of the sample showed symptoms of depression, 12% at clinical levels (Early Head Start Research and Evaluation Project, 2003). Research is also showing high rates of depression symptoms in fathers—20% of fathers enrolled in Early Head Start. Although the impact of parental depression on young children will depend on the timing and severity of the depression, negative consequences are well-documented (Ramchandani, Stein, Evans, & O'Connor, 2005). Prevalence rates of other adult risk factors are also of concern. Estimates show that 10% of all children, including young children, are in homes with one or more parent involved with substance abuse. Similarly, rates of exposure of young children to domestic violence are also high, although specific data are lacking (Knitzer & Lefkowitz, 2006).

Organizing Systems of Care to Address Multiple Family Needs

One way to begin to move toward a family intervention approach is to organize existing services within and across programs by the extent and complexity of the risks the families face. There is clear theoretical support for this. Social and mental health problems, often seen in isolation, actually share fundamental risk factors (Masten & Wright, 1998; Olds, Robinson, Song, Little, & Hill,1999). Moreover, the more risk factors a child experiences, the greater the odds of poor outcomes, whatever the specific risks. Early Head Start researchers, for example, found that families with infants and toddlers enrolled in the program who had two to three risk factors (deemed moderate levels of risk) benefited the most from the program, whereas families experiencing four or more risk factors did not (Love et al., 2002). Follow-up reports after the children entered kindergarten, however, found that even for these most at-risk young children, outcomes improved over time, perhaps building on the foundation that Early Head Start provided (R. Cohen, personal communication, March 28, 2006). Ensuring access to early and intensive family-based interventions organized around type of risk can give higher-risk parents a fair shot at effective parenting. Such interventions can also help others make informed decisions about when the children have to be removed from their parents.

Interventions Targeting Barriers to Effective Parenting

Organizing systems of care to incorporate the first prong of a family intervention—addressing adult barriers that get in the way of effective parenting—takes boldness and courage. The problem is that the way services are organized lags behind the knowledge base. Thus, it is known that adult barriers often have significant negative impacts on young children

(Fantuzzo & Mohr, 1999; Gewirtz & Edleson, 2004; Hair, McGroder, Zaslow, Ahluwalia, & Moore, 2002). Moreover, the knowledge base about how to treat mental health and addiction disorders in adults is growing daily (Institute of Medicine, 2006). This is especially true with respect to depression, where it is clear that effective intervention can be delivered in the context of primary care (e.g., in early childhood environments such as Head Start or through home visiting programs) and adapted to meet the needs of low-income women (Miranda & Green, 1999). It is also known that concern about their young children can motivate parents facing depression, substance abuse, and domestic violence to seek and accept intervention, often overcoming the fear that their children will be taken from them, or especially motivated to seek help by the threat of losing their children. But putting the infrastructure in place to support attention to both young children and their parents is complex and challenges how systems are now organized (Biebel, Nicholson, Williams & Hinden, 2004).

Interventions to Address the Parent-Child Relationship

The second prong of a family intervention approach—relationship-based parenting—aims to repair or prevent damaged parent–child relationships and help parents meet their children's basic needs for physical sustenance and protection, emotional security, and social interactions. Parents with identified mental illness, advocates, and other family members speak of the stresses related to parenting that these adults experience, such as not knowing how to talk about mental illness, not knowing how to help their children, fearing the loss of custody, and fearing for their children's own mental health status (Mowbray, Nicholson, & Bellamy, 2003). Mothers who experience domestic violence try valiantly to make the best decisions they can to protect their children, weighing, for example, the consequences of leaving an abuser or not leaving (Schechter, 2004). Often, however, they are treated as if they do not care about their children. Some parents cannot help their young children unless they can re-establish the attachment bonds with their children, and they need support to do so (Moore & Finkelstein, 2001).

Beyond targeting internal family factors that impact parenting, resilience research also suggests the importance of broadening the reach to include community interventions to support caregivers in their parenting roles. The goal is to mobilize resources to wrap a protective web around a child (Luthar & Zelazo, 2003; Masten, 2001; Werner, 2000). One way to do this is through teams that bring together both formal and informal caregivers, as highlighted in John's story. Another way is to build on community assets that can directly influence parents and indirectly influence their children. Cleaning up parks, reducing community violence, and diminishing drug dealing are examples of steps community groups can take to make it possible for parents to allow their young children to play outside in their neighborhood. These activities may have an impact on not only a child's sense of competence and safety, but also a parent's.

At the same time, it is also important to recognize that many families with young children with challenging behaviors will not need intensive intervention for their own issues. Rather, families such as John's and Sandy's need family support and the opportunity to help determine what services they and their children most need.

Interventions Focused on the Young Child

The third prong of a family intervention early childhood mental health approach puts the child in the center and focuses on prevention and early intervention strategies. Such a focus includes ongoing screening of young children in highest-risk circumstances and mechanisms to ensure that if necessary the children have access to early intervention services. It also requires explicit efforts to ensure that the children have access to ongoing health care because data suggest that many of them have undiagnosed health conditions (Knitzer, 2002).

Interventions Addressing Basic Family Needs

Finally, the fourth prong must be ongoing attention to the family's needs for concrete services, such as help to purchase and prepare food, provide heat, and obtain appropriate housing. No mental health intervention for families facing material hardship will be effective without also attending to their basic needs.

WORKING WITH THE MOST VULNERABLE FAMILIES IN EARLY CHILDHOOD SYSTEMS OF CARE

Goals and Strategies

For young children facing the most serious threats to healthy emotional outcomes, as for all young children, the aim of intentional early childhood mental health interventions should be to promote positive, age-appropriate behaviors and regulatory capacity. For young children and families experiencing more severe risks, however, achieving these goals requires specific systems-building goals and implementation strategies. This section highlights six organizing goals that emerge from the review of the current field-based perspectives as well as from research. It also provides some examples of how these principles are being translated into practical strategies while recognizing that there are many routes to implementing the goals.

Goal 1: Ensure that all Higher-Risk Young Children Have Access to High-Quality, Comprehensive, and Continuous Early Care, Learning Experiences, and Medical Homes

Strategy: Engage in Special Outreach Efforts to Connect Young Children Facing Higher Risks with Quality Early Childhood Programs   Priority enrollment in Head Start or Early Head Start to children who are experiencing violence, have been maltreated, or are in foster care is an important strategy. Recognizing this, the Child Care and Development Block Grant permits states to identify young children in foster care as having priority status for child care subsidy slots. It is also important that all early childhood environments serving these young children make sure that the children are connected to a medical home and that they and their families have access to health insurance through Medicaid or the State Children's Health Insurance Program (SCHIP).

Strategy: Ensure That All Vulnerable Children Have Access to High-Quality, Ongoing, Early Childhood Experiences with Staff Trained to Help Higher-Risk Young Children   Quality early childhood programs play a critical role in providing a stable, nonstigmatizing environment for children at risk for physical, cognitive, and social delays as a result of their home environment or other psychosocial stressors. As such, these programs can help prevent or reverse early harm to young children (see the Center for the Study of Social Policy project: Strengthening Families Through Early Care and Education, as described at http://www.cssp.org/doris_duke/indext.html). For the children and families fortunate enough to be in quality early childhood programs, the staff are often the first to see the impact of family stressors and the consequences in the behavior and development of the children. Thus they are in a position to provide rapid early intervention as well as a safe zone for young children experiencing highly stressful times in their lives (Cohen & Knitzer, 2004). Home visiting programs, comprehensive early childhood programs, family support, and community-based health clinics also provide information, connection to resources (e.g., legal help), and opportunities for more intensive family support.

Strategy: Invest State and Local Funds in Comprehensive Programs for Infants and Toddlers, such as Early Head Start or Evidence-Based Home Visiting Programs   Given the importance of the earliest experiences and relationships in setting the stage for lifelong problems or competencies, investing in research-informed programs with higher-risk populations represents a wise investment of local and state dollars.

Strategy: Ensure That All Young Children Have Access to a Medical Home
A medical home means that not only do children have access to an ongoing and familiar source of pediatric care, but that the care offers compre-

hensive physical and developmental services. Strategies to implement medical homes not just for children with special health care needs but for all children are growing (Rosman, Perry, & Hepburn, 2006), and although some highly vulnerable young children are deemed children with special health care needs, many are not. Coordination of services for these children can make a significant difference for them and their primary caregivers. Some pediatric environments also support parents by helping them anticipate developmental stages and even screen for maternal depression.

Goal 2: Promote Early Identification and Access to Appropriate Interventions and Treatment, Especially in the Context of Normalizing Environments

Strategy: Build Consultation Capacity to Help Pediatric Staff, Child Care Providers, Teachers, and Home Visitors Respond More Appropriately to the Highest-Risk Young Children and Families in their Care   The experience of both Maria's and Sandy's (described earlier) pediatricians failing to recognize the level of need in the family and losing important time and opportunities to provide meaningful help is not at all atypical. Therefore, strategies targeted to improve the capacity of the pediatric community to recognize and respond to signs of serious early problems is crucial. Community partnerships through links with the local pediatric society and the early childhood mental health community represent one pathway, but there are also emerging models based in pediatric practice that reflect the use of formal screening tools for young children and, in some instances, parents to capture issues related to parental risk factors as well (Rosman, Perry, & Hepburn, 2006).

Similarly, consultation strategies in early childhood environments are emerging in response to widespread staff concern. Young children in the most high-risk circumstances often seem fearful, disorganized, inattentive, and unresponsive to learning (Koplow, 1996). Staff report not knowing how to help, and, as noted above, many of these children have been expelled or are at risk of expulsion because of their challenging behaviors. Although still limited, some research on the positive benefits of early childhood mental health consultation is beginning to emerge (Brennan, Bradley, Allen, Perry, & Tsega, 2005). National data, for example, suggest that when child care providers have access to behavioral consultation, it can reduce the incidence of expulsions (Gilliam, 2005). States and communities are responding. For example, seeking to reduce such expulsions on a statewide basis, Michigan has organized its early childhood mental health consultation strategy around preventing expulsion. Consultants can also help staff sort out when a problem requires a referral and when it can be addressed within the context of the early childhood program. Others are using consultation more broadly. For example, Colorado is building a network of early childhood specialists linked to community mental health centers, and San Francisco has developed culturally responsive networks of consultants to child care programs. Although much more needs to be learned about models and strategies, particularly for the highest-risk children (see Chapter 13), consultation clearly represents an important linchpin in the effort to build systems of supports to promote healthy social-emotional outcomes for more troubled young children, as well as those facing moderate risks.

Strategy: Ensure Access to Specialized Intervention for Young Children with Identified Social-Emotional Disorders The knowledge base about how to help the most troubled young children is growing (see Chapter 14). A recent estimate suggests that 120,000 young children, many of them identified as Seriously Emotionally Disturbed (SED), were receiving services through community mental health centers—about 9% of all children seen (Pottick et al., 2002). In addition, communities are using behavioral aides and wrap-around teams in child care environments in much the same way that they are used for older children, although there is no research reported on the effects of these services with young children. Some programs are using combinations of effective approaches, sometimes in the context of therapeutic nurseries. For example, the River Oak Program for Children in Sacramento, California combines a structured early childhood curriculum with an evidence-based parenting support practice known as *The Incredible Years* (Webster-Stratton, 1998); families needing more intensive help receive a version of Parent Management Therapy. There are also models of family driven programs. For example, the Early Childhood Centers (ECC) of the Positive Education Program (PEP) in Cleveland and the Regional Intervention Program (RIP) in Tennessee (Strain & Timm, 2001) help parents learn new behavior skills and use parents who have been through the program as coaches for other parents. Research from both RIP and ECC report findings showing the positive long-term effects of early intervention. Taking these and other clinically validated practices to scale, however, remains a major challenge.

Strategy: Make Sure that Both In-Service and Preservice Professional Development Strategies Prepare Teachers to Deal with Young Children and Families Facing Higher Risks States and communities are rethinking the kind of training that those who work with young children at higher risk need to have to be able to help the children and their families. For example, Colorado's Office of Professional Development is exploring not just staff competencies related to early literacy and math, but also to health and mental health issues. Research shows, there is an opportunity to teach the social-emotional skills needed to succeed in the early school years in the context of effective early learning strategies (Klein & Knitzer, 2006).

Goal 3: Implement Family Intervention and Family Support Strategies Tailored to Family Circumstances, Culture, and Developmental Stages

Strategy: Nest Intensive Interventions for High-Risk Children and Their Families in the Context of Comprehensive Early Childhood Programs Early childhood programs that have at their core providing relationship-based child development and family support experiences provide a powerful context in which to embed more intensive family focused intervention strategies. Because families trust these environments, they are more likely to accept interventions than if they are referred elsewhere, particularly to what many perceive as stigmatizing mental health agencies. Early Head Start, with its strong evidence of efficacy in improving parent and child outcomes, coupled with indications that it is not as effective for higher-risk babies, toddlers, and families, is already becoming a laboratory for these kinds of efforts. For example, in Syracuse, New York, the People's Equal Action and Community Effort (PEACE), Inc., Early Head Start program has developed a partnership with the local correctional facility and with the substance abuse agencies in the community to help young children and their mothers who are either in prison or coming out of prison for drug abuse convictions (Knitzer & Lefkowitz, 2006). In Boston, Massachusetts, efforts are in progress to design and evaluate Family Connections, a program to address depression in the lives of Head Start staff, families, and children (W. Beardslee, personal communication, March 18, 2006). Home visiting programs are also exploring new ways of embedding more intensive services into their models. For example, Every Child Succeeds, a multicounty home visiting program in Ohio and Kentucky is integrating in-home cognitive behavior therapy for depressed mothers into the core home visiting program, which is based either on the Healthy Families America or the Nurse–Family Partnership model. Preliminary results from a randomized control trial are impressive. At the beginning of the intervention, 44% of the mothers showed elevated symptoms of depression. At the end of the Health Families Program intervention, 70% of the group no longer met criteria for major depression, and an additional 15% exhibited partial recovery. The mothers also reported greater acceptance of and a closer bond with their children. The children also benefited; some dramatically. For example, based on an evaluation of the overall program, 64% of children who were delayed in language during the first year of life were developing normally at the end of the program. Babies with delayed social and interpersonal abilities during the first year of life were doing even better—92% were developing normally (Ammerman et al., 2005).

Strategy: Tailor and Individualize Parenting Supports For many of the most vulnerable families, the usual and customary parent training and support strategies may not be enough. Families confronting multiple psychological, social, and educational barriers need extended therapeutic support to make use of any parenting education provided to them (Daro, 2002), including the opportunity to reflect on their own childhood experiences as a means of developing empathy for their children (Frazier, McPherson, MacLeod, Scott, & Johnson, 1996). Parents also need a *safe* context in which to address their own guilt and anxiety about their children, along with fears that they will lose custody. Sometimes these efforts are integrated into parent–child therapy (Van Horn, Best & Lieberman, 1998). Other experts are testing out curricula and approaches that are especially targeted to high-risk parents (Clark, Keller, Fedderly, & Paulson, 1993; Knitzer & Lefkowitz, 2006; Luthar & Walsh, 1995; Moore & Finkelstein, 2001). In general, these curricula, such as the Nurturing Fathers curricula, help parents to

- Reflect on how they were parented and how they want their children parented

- Understand not just what to expect from young children, but also how to manage their own issues in relation to children (e.g., developing safety plans)

- Learn how to nurture, discipline, and maintain ties with their children.

Luthar and Walsh (1995) recommend that treatment for substance-abusing parents include a group parenting support component that focuses on

- How to deal with children's responses to parental drug abuse behavior

- Management and support strategies related to parenting and to maternal self-management skills

- Ensuring the safety of the children

- Preventing and treating negative child outcomes

For parents with serious mental illness, a recent review concludes that the two essential services are 1) parent education and 2) support and case management that is delivered through a strength promoting, family centered orientation (Hinden, Kiebe, Nicholson, Henry & Katz-Leavy, 2006). Promoting resilience and recovery in the adults means helping them to become connected with new social networks, such as informal support groups, facilitated by other parents or community leaders. Parents who themselves are in recovery can be powerful role models of hope (Knitzer, 2000). At the same time, it must be noted that careful evaluations, particularly using randomized control designs of these more informal strategies, are virtually nonexistent.

Strategy: Organize Program and Community Services for Young Children by Type of Family Risk   Given the powerful evidence about the negative impacts of multiple risk and chronic trauma, both individual programs and communities are beginning to organize services according to the levels of risk that families experience, similar to a promotion, prevention, and intervention framework. For example, the California River Oak Center for Children, based on an assessment of the child, the caregiver's emotional well-being, parenting philosophy, and a videotaped play interaction, offers two home visiting programs organized to respond to different intensities of family need and risk. One program, the Black Infant Program, is a statewide home visiting service designed to reduce health disparities and prevent child abuse in medium- to high-risk African American families. Higher-risk families participate in a home visiting model in which the home visitor has access to a multidisciplinary team of specialized consultants. Families, including foster families, with babies facing the most serious relationship problems are offered an intensive mental health intervention.

Similarly, on a countywide scale, in San Mateo County, California, through the countywide Pre-to-Three Initiative, a collaboration of public and private agencies target all pregnant women and newborns covered by MediCal as well as any high-risk children up to age 5 years. Through Touchpoints, a program to help parents and staff learn to *read* babies' cues more effectively, staff from multiple agencies working with infants and toddlers receive cross-disciplinary training. Prevention and general parenting support strategies include parenting classes that use multicultural curricula and drop-in parent support groups. Babies are screened using the *Ages & Stages Questionnaires® (ASQ)* (Bricker & Squires, 1999), and depending on the level of risk, families are assigned to one of three home visiting teams that are designed to provide and manage services depending on a family's level of risk for mental health problems or substance abuse. An evaluation (reported in Knitzer & Lefkowitz, 2006) suggests the overall approach is effective, finding improvements in parental confidence, behaviors related to early school success (e.g., reading), and health-related behaviors (e.g., up-to-date immunizations, greater use of car seats).

Goal 4: Implement Timely Interventions to Stop the Negative Chain Reaction Following Exposure to Significant Trauma in Young Children and the Effects of Historical Trauma in Their Parents

Strategy: Reduce the Impact and Facilitate the Recovery of Children Who Have Been Exposed to Trauma   Experiencing neglect and abuse and witnessing community and family violence put young children at significant risk for developmental failures and emotional disturbances, as well as the risk of additional victimization or perpetration of violence later in life. The children may also face long-term negative consequences, ultimately affecting their adult functioning, including parenting (McAlister Groves, 1999, 2002). Interventions to reduce the negative consequences of the trauma are being implemented in a range of environments, including hospitals, battered women shelters, and Early Head Start programs (Schechter, 2004). Interventions aiming to help young children understand and cope with their emotional responses to the violence—according to their age and developmental stage—while promoting their acquisition of positive behavior patterns vary in intensity and type. Some strategies include working with parents and other caregivers to build their capacity to be sensitive to the needs of traumatized young children in their care (Cohen & Walthall, 2003). One well known program is the Child Witness to Violence Project (CWVP) at Boston Medical Center. Founded in 1992 it now provides counseling and other support services to children to help them heal from the trauma of exposure to violence and to help parents help their children. The program also provides consultation and training to the network of caregivers.

Although many of these services are not viewed as *traditional* mental health therapy, they are essential in helping women and children affected by domestic violence (Groves, Roberts, & Weinreb, 2000). Other programs that are responsive to the compelling evidence of trauma in the histories of parents (Bassuk, Buckner, Perloff, & Bassuk, 1998; Miranda & Green, 1999) involve family intervention. For example, the San Francisco General Hospital program (Van Horn, Best, & Lieberman, 1998) approaches the mother–child relationship as critical to the success of the child's adjustment in the aftermath of violence. The federally funded National Child Traumatic Stress Network (NCTSN) continues to build partnerships to explore new clinical approaches, including for young children (http://www.nctsnet.org).

Goal 5: Develop Targeted Screening, Outreach, and Trauma-Informed Intervention Strategies for Groups of High-Risk Young Children

Strategy: Use Environments Where Young Children and Families Facing Significant Risks Are Concentrated as the Entry Point for Services   Environments such as shelters, courts, and prisons where high-risk families are concentrated provide important entry points for beginning the healing and helping process. For example, New York established a network of Children's Centers tied to the courts to not only provide drop-in child care, but also to try to connect the children and families with programs, such as Head Start. This is especially important given research suggesting that for the most part these young children were not enrolled in any early childhood programs. In Dade County, Miami, the juvenile court sees that young children involved in abuse, neglect, and family violence are evaluated using Prevention and Evaluation of Early Neglect and Trauma (PREVENT), which is an assessment protocol that includes evaluation of reciprocal bonding and attachment between parent and child through videotaped interactions to determine the extent to which parental bonds can be repaired. The court has also supported efforts to engage some of the families in dyadic therapy, as well as provide the young children with a program similar to Early Head Start. Findings have been very promising (Lederman, Osofsky, Katz, 2001). In San Francisco, an early childhood mental health initiative for homeless children and families brought early childhood mental health consultants to the shelters. About half of the children ages 2–5 years had great difficulty controlling their aggression, and about 45% had behaviors consistent with depression and withdrawal.

Strategy: Implement Evidence-Based Interventions for Caregivers of Young Children Who Must Be Removed from Their Families   Young children who must be removed from their homes are clearly one of the most vulnerable groups of young children. Before the Adoption and Safe Families Act (ASFA) of 1997, child welfare agencies focused primarily on the safety and permanence of children. ASFA however has expanded the focus of child welfare systems to children's developmental well-being. This provides an important opportunity to engage in early intervention. Recent changes in the Child Abuse Prevention and Treatment Act further reinforce this concern for child well-being. Although no new resources are provided, the legislation requires that children from birth to 3 years in substantiated abuse and neglect cases be referred for developmental screening. Other interventions such as the Multidimensional Treatment Foster-Care Preschool Program (Fisher, Burraston, & Pears, 2005) are currently being tested to determine their effectiveness.

Strategy: Target Community Planning and Capacity-Building to Highest-Risk Young Children   A challenge of focusing more attention on the most vulnerable young children is how best to craft a response without derailing the appropriate emphasis on prevention and early intervention for less stressed and distressed families. One way to do this is to make sure that broad cross-system planning and systems design efforts include stakeholders from the adult mental health and substance abuse agencies, child welfare, and shelters, and also include other representatives who come into contact with these families on a regular basis, including core early childhood stakeholders. Bringing those who see their mission as primarily adult focused to the table opens up the possibility of better cross-system collaboration, for example, between the adult mental health system and those involved with early childhood mental health. (Currently, only in special circumstances do those involved with adult mental health even determine if an adult client is a parent.) Similar challenges apply to substance abuse, although there has been a greater focus on parents and children together in that system.

A second approach is to target special planning efforts to vulnerable groups of young children. For example, the Juvenile Services Coordinating County of Tucson, Arizona spearheaded a comprehensive planning process (the Pima County Prevention Partnership) to prevent juvenile delinquency by focusing on children from birth to 6 years. The council identified children involved in dependency proceedings, preschool-age children showing high levels of violence and aggressiveness, children of incarcerated parents, children in families with substance abuse problems, children in families experiencing domestic violence, and children in families with older siblings who are chronic truants. They also identified nationally effective preventive programs for them. Although implementation resources are limited, they have already started a mandatory trauma screening program for young children exposed to family trauma and have trained police in what to do when entering homes with young children (Knitzer & Lefkowitz, 2006).

Goal 6: Track Parental and Child Outcomes for Higher Risk Young Children as Part of a Larger Accountability System for Early Childhood

Although there has been an increased emphasis on tracking outcomes, particularly those related to school readiness, there are few planned systemwide efforts to disaggregate outcome data by level or risk, or link it with early intervention experiences. As noted elsewhere (see Chapter 6), however, research and measures that provide the framework for building more effective data systems are expanding and perhaps will be a catalyst to integrate some of the measures into administrative data sets.

TOWARD THE FUTURE: ADDRESSING THE POLICY, CLINICAL, AND RESEARCH CHALLENGES

There is a relatively large population of young children who are at risk for serious social-emotional, behavioral, and academic outcomes as they transition to school and beyond. It is clear that with concerted efforts, a significant percentage of these potential higher-risk families might successfully respond to carefully designed interventions. Some of the approaches and strategies to make this happen are natural extensions of the current efforts to strengthen mental health consultation and other prevention and early intervention strategies. Others will require considerable strategic planning and reorganizing. Five core challenges are highlighted here.

One of the most daunting challenges will come from trying to implement an early childhood *family mental health system* designed to reduce threats to effective parenting and improve outcomes for young children. Neither the mental health nor the substance abuse treatment systems pay much attention to the fact that their clients are parents, including parents of young children (Beardslee & Knitzer, 2003). Nor have domestic violence agencies been well integrated into the early childhood intervention framework (Schechter, 2004). The reality is that providing integrated adult services that address adult risks to parenting and the realities of parenting in these circumstances is still a far cry from the usual and customary practice. Changing not just the regulations and fiscal practices, but the culture of these adult-focused systems will require new policy incentives. Yet, as the larger mental health system moves toward *transformation* (The President's New Freedom Commission on Mental Health, 2003), helping parents recover their parenting capacity provides a powerful hook that holds the promise of significant payoff for the next generation.

Another major challenge is the urgent need to strengthen the policy capacity within each state to promote effective early childhood mental health services. In the face of compelling research and pressing needs, the mental health and early childhood systems increasingly recognize that even very young children can experience serious mental health problems and suffer from emotional pain, anxiety, and depression. Yet, even for the most troubled young children, the policy response lags behind. For example, some state mental health agencies still do not permit children under 6 years access to services, nor do some permit reimbursement for family therapy. Moreover, although it is known that typically the best way to help young children is to help those who are closest to them, the mental health system is still organized as if the only way to help children, even infants and toddlers, is to focus directly on them. The fact that the policy paradigm simply has not caught up with the state of knowledge regarding the nature of therapeutic interventions for young children and families means that families and providers have to struggle needlessly to make the best use of the knowledge that is now available, causing a tragic waste of both human and fiscal resources. Guidelines to spend existing funds in a *smarter* manner (Johnson & Knitzer, 2005) are emerging, but the disconnect between the clinical and developmental knowledge base and the fiscal and policy infrastructure needs to be proactively addressed.

A third challenge is a clinical one, which is to refine the clinical strategies that can be used to help young children and families, particularly trauma-informed strategies that can be mobilized to respond to immediate trauma as well as prior trauma that interfere with parenting and with healthy child development. Pima County, which requires screening of young children experiencing family violence, exemplifies one approach.

Similarly, efforts from within the health community to promote screening and intervention of pregnant and parenting women for depression, as well as substance abuse and domestic violence, are vitally important. The evidence, however, that one generation's (i.e., the parent's) intervention is another generation's prevention and early intervention (Weissman, Pilowsky, Wickramaratne, Talati, Wisniewski, & Fava, 2006) is not embedded into the still highly individualistic paradigm that guides so many human services agencies. Given the indisputable negative effects of depression and related *adversities* on young children, screening and help for parents is central to a preventive early childhood strategy.

The fourth challenge is a research challenge. There is an urgent need to develop a focused research agenda to design and test complex interventions for the most vulnerable young children and families and track the longer-term pay-off, particularly in terms of early school performance. The risk factors and their consequences are widely known and are routinely used in describing both research and programs. Too often, however, they are accepted as givens, not as opportunities for intervention. The sad truth is that far more is invested in research to understand the consequences of risk factors for young children and parents than in designing, testing, and taking to scale interventions that might change the all too predictable negative trajectories. A thoughtful preventive science research agenda focused on the most vulnerable young children and families is long overdue. Similarly, it is necessary to expand the knowledge base about effective parenting supports for parents experiencing grave threats to their nurturing ability, particularly strategies that can repair damaged early parent–child relationships, and put the parent–child relationship on a new trajectory. The field of infant mental health continues to make strides in understanding early intervention (Clark, Keller, Fedderly, & Paulson, 1993; Zeanah, 2000), but emerging best practices are not widespread, and fiscal barriers are considerable.

Furthermore, although a great deal is known about the consequences of risk factors for young children's mental health and development, more research is needed on evidence-based interventions and on the cost efficacy of intensive early childhood mental health investments. Research studies clearly support the *return on investment* for comprehensive interventions for young children in general, but systematic research addressing intervention strategies to improve the developmental trajectory for the most high-risk young children is still limited. Organizing services by level of risk and, indeed, recognizing differential levels of risk in young children, however, opens up new opportunities for this kind of research. There is a long way to go, however, before understanding that which children and parents will benefit significantly. Some research, for example, suggests that it is difficult to predict which parents will benefit from intensive interventions and that even parents who appear to look like they will never be *good enough* parents to care for their children can benefit from them (Lederman, Osofsky, & Katz, 2001).

Finally, the fifth challenge is to mobilize the political will and resources needed to fully implement the vision that every child will enter school ready to succeed, regardless of the level of individual and family risk. A family-focused early childhood mental health support system can be one important tool in this effort.

REFERENCES

Ammerman, R.T., Putnam, F.W., Stevens, J., Holleb, L.J., Novak, A.L., & Van Ginkel, J.B. (2005). In-home cognitive behavior therapy for depression: An adapted treatment for first-time mothers in home visitation. *Best Practices in Mental Health*, *I*(1), 1–14.

Angold, A., Egger, H.L., Erkanli, A., & Keefer, G. (2005) *Prevalence and comorbidity of psychiatric disorder in preschoolers attending a large pediatric services*. Manuscript submitted for publication.

Bassuk, E.L., Buckner, J.C., Perloff, J.N., & Bassuk, S.S. (1998). Prevalence of mental health and substance use disorders among homeless and low-income housed mothers. *American Journal of Psychiatry*, *155*(11), 1561–1564.

Beardslee, W.R., & Knitzer, J. (2003). Strengths-based family mental health services: A family systems approach. In K. Maton, C. Schellenbach, B. Leadbeater, & A. Solarz (Eds.), *Investing in children, youth, families, and communities: Strengths-based research and policy* (pp. 157–171). Washington, DC: American Psychological Association.

Biebel, K., Nicholson, J., Williams, V., & Hinden, B.R. (2004). The responsiveness of state mental health authorities to parents with mental illness. *Administration and Policy in Mental Health*, *32*(1), 31–48.

Boggs, S.R., Eyberg, S.M., Edwards, D.L., Rayfield, A., Jacobs, J., Bagner, D., et al. (2004). Outcomes of parent–child interaction therapy: A comparison of treatment completers and study dropouts one to three years later. *Child & Family Behavior Therapy*, *26*(4), 1–21.

Bower-Russa, M., Knutson, J., & Winebarger, A. (2001). Disciplinary history, adult disciplinary attitudes, and risk for abusive parenting. *Journal of Community Psychology*, *29*(3), 219–240.

Brennan, E.M., Bradley, J.R., Allen, M.D., Perry, D.F., & Tsega, A. (2005). *The evidence base for mental health consultation in early childhood settings: Research synthesis and review*. Washington, DC: Georgetown University, National Technical Assistance Center for Children's Mental Health.

Bricker, D., & Squires, J. (1999). *Ages & Stages Questionnaires® (ASQ): A parent-completed, child-monitoring system* (2nd ed.). Baltimore: Paul H. Brookes Publishing Co.

Center for the Study of Social Policy. (nd). *Strengthening Families Through Early Care and Education Project*. Retrieved October 1, 2006, from http://www.cssp.org/doris_duke/index.html

Clark, R., Keller, A.D., Fedderly, S.S., & Paulson, A.W. (1993). Treating the relationships affected by postpartum depression: A group therapy model. *Zero to Three*, *13*(5), 16–23.

Cohen, E., & Knitzer, J. (2004). Young children living with domestic violence:The role of early childhood programs. In S. Schechter (Ed.), *Early childhood, domestic violence and poverty: Taking the new steps to help young children* (series paper 2). Iowa City, Iowa: University of Iowa, School of Social Work.

Cohen, E., & Walthall, B. (2003). *Silent realities: Helping parents and other caregivers respond to young children who witness violence.* Washington, DC: National Child Welfare Resource Center for Family-Centered Practice.

Cutler, A., & Gilkerson, L. (2002). *Unmet needs project: A research, coalition building, and policy initiative on the unmet needs of infants, toddlers and families.* Chicago: University of Illinois at Chicago and Erikson Institute.

Daro, D. (2002). Educating and changing parents: Strengthening the primary safety net for children. In K. Browne, H. Hanks, P. Stratton, & C. Hamilton-Giachritsis (Eds.), *Early prediction and prevention of child abuse: A handbook.* New York, NY: John Wiley & Sons.

Donahue, P.J., Falk, B., & Gersony Provet, A. (2000). *Mental health consultation in early childhood.* Baltimore: Paul H. Brookes Publishing Co.

Early Head Start Research and Evaluation Project. (2003). *Research to practice: Depression in the lives of Early Head Start families.* Washington, DC: U.S. Department of Health and Human Services, Administration for Children, Youth and Families.

Edleson, J. (1999). Children's witnessing of adult domestic violence. *Journal of Interpersonal Violence, 14*(8), 839–870.

Fantuzzo, J.W., & Mohr, W.K. (1999). Prevalence and effects of child exposure to domestic violence. *The Future of Children, 9*(3), 21–32.

Fisher, P., Burraston, B., & Pears, K. (2005). The early intervention foster care program: Permanent placement outcomes from a randomized trial. *Child Maltreatment, 10*(1), 61–71.

Frazier, B., McPherson, A., MacLeod, S., Scott, S., & Johnson, C. (1996). Revisiting parenting groups: A psychosocial approach. *ZERO TO THREE, 16*(6), 19–24.

Gewirtz, A., & Edleson, J.L. (2004). *Young children's exposure to adult domestic violence: Toward a developmental risk and resilience framework for research intervention.* Iowa City: The University of Iowa, School of Social Work.

Gilliam, W. (2005). *Prekindergarteners left behind: Expulsion rates in state prekindergarten systems.* New Haven, CT: Yale University Child Study Center.

Groves, B.M., Roberts, E., & Weinreb, M. (2000). *Shelter from the storm: Clinical intervention with children affected by domestic violence.* Boston: Boston Medical Center.

Gunnar, M.R., & Davis, E.P. (2003). Stress and emotion in early childhood. In R.M. Lerner & M.A. Easterbrooks (Eds.), *Handbook of psychology: Developmental psychology* (Vol. 6) (pp.113–134). New York: John Wiley & Sons.

Hair, E.C., McGroder, S.M., Zaslow, M.J., Ahluwalia, S.K., & Moore, K.A. (2002). How do maternal risk factors affect children in low-income families? Further evidence of two-generational implications. *Journal of Prevention and Intervention in the Community, 23*(12), 65–94.

Hinden, B, Kiebe, K, Nicholson, J., Henry, A., & Katz-Leavy, J. (2006) A survey of programs for parents with mental illness and their families: Identifying common elements to build the evidence base. *Journal of Behavioral Health Services and Research, 33*(1), 1-20.

Hood, K.K., & Eyberg, S.M. (2003). Outcomes of parent-child interaction therapy: Mothers' reports of maintenance three to six years after treatment. *Journal of Clinical Child and Adolescent Psychology, 32*(3), 419–429.

Institute of Medicine, Committee on Crossing the Quality Chasm: Adaptation to Mental Health and Addictive Disorders. (2006). *Improving the quality of health care for mental and substance abuse conditions.* Washington, DC: The National Academies Press.

Johnson, K., & Knitzer, J. (2005). *Spending smarter: A funding guide for policymakers to promote social and emotional health and school readiness.* New York: National Center for Children in Poverty, Columbia University, Mailman School of Public Health.

Johnson, K., Knitzer, J., & Kaufmann, R. (2002). *Making dollars follow sense: Financing early childhood mental health services to promote healthy social and emotional development in young children.* New York: National Center for Children in Poverty, Columbia University, Mailman School of Public Health.

Klein, L., & Knitzer, J. (2006). *Effective preschool curricula and teaching strategies.* New York: National Center for Children in Poverty, Columbia University, Mailman School of Public Health.

Knitzer, J. (2000). *Promoting resilience: Helping young children and parents affected by substance abuse, domestic violence, and depression in the context of welfare reform.* New York: National Center for Children in Poverty, Columbia University, Mailman School of Public Health.

Knitzer, J. (2002). *Building services and systems to support the healthy emotional development of young children: An action guide for policymakers.* New York: National Center for Children in Poverty, Columbia University, Mailman School of Public Health.

Knitzer, J., & Lefkowitz, J. (2006). *Helping the most vulnerable infants, toddlers, and their families.* New York: National Center for Children in Poverty, Columbia University, Mailman School of Public Health.

Koplow, L. (Ed.). (1996). *Unsmiling faces: How preschoolers can heal.* New York: Teachers College Press.

Lederman, C.S., Osofsky, J.D., & Katz, L. (2001). When the bough breaks the cradle will fall: Promoting the health and well being of infants and toddlers in juvenile court. *Juvenile and Family Court Journal, 52*(4), 33–38.

Love, J.M., Kisker, E.E., Ross, C.M., Schochet, P.Z., Brooks-Gunn, J., Pausell, D., et al. (2002). *Making a difference in the lives of infants and toddlers and their families: The impacts of Early Head Start.* Washington, DC: U.S. Department of Health and Human Services, Administration for Children and Families.

Luthar, S.S. (2006). Resilience in development: A synthesis of research across five decades. In D. Cicchetti & D.J. Cohen (Eds.), *Developmental psychopathology: Risk, disorder and adaptation* (2nd ed.). New York: John Wiley & Sons.

Luthar, S.S., & Walsh, K.G. (1995). Treatment needs of drug-addicted mothers: Integrated parenting psychotherapy interventions. *Journal of Substance Abuse Treatment, 12*(5), 341–348.

Luthar, S.S., & Zelazo, L.B. (2003) Research on resilience: An integrative review. In S.S. Luthar (Ed.), *Resilience and vulnerability: Adaptation in the context of childhood adversities* (pp. 510–550). New York: Cambridge University Press.

Masten, A.S. (2001). Ordinary magic: Resilience process in development. *American Psychologist, 56*(3), 227–238.

Masten, A.S., & Wright, M.O.D. (1998). Cumulative risk and protection models of child maltreatment. In B.B.R. Rossman & M.S. Rosenberg (Eds.), *Multiple victimization of children: Conceptual, developmental, research and treatment issues* (pp. 7–30). Binghamton, NY: Haworth.

McAlister Groves, B. (1999). Mental health services for children exposed to domestic violence. *The Future of Children, 9*(3), 122–132.

McAlister Groves, B. (2002). *Children who see too much: Lessons from the Child Witness to Violence Project.* Boston: Beacon Press.

Miranda, J., & Green, B.L. (1999). The need for mental health services research focusing on poor young women. *Journal of Mental Health Policy and Economics, 2,* 73–80.

Moore, J., & Finkelstein, N. (2001). Parenting services for families affected by substance abuse. *Child Welfare, 80*(2), 221–238.

Mowbray, C.T., Nicholson, J., & Bellamy, C.D. (2003). Psychosocial rehabilitation service needs of women. *Psychiatric Rehabilitation Journal, 27*(2), 104–113.

National Scientific Council on the Developing Child. (2005). *Excessive stress disrupts the architecture of the developing brain.* Waltham, MA: Brandeis University, Heller School for Social Policy and Management. Retrieved January 11, 2005, from http://www.developingchild.net/papers/excessive_stress.pdf

Olds, D., Robinson, J., Song, N., Little, C., & Hill, P. (1999). *Reducing risks for mental disorders during the first five years of life: A review of preventive interventions.* Alexandria, VA: Center for Mental Health Services, Substance Abuse and Mental Health Services Administration.

Pottick, K.J., Warner, L.A., Isaacs, M., Henderson, M.J., Milazzo Sayre, B.A., & Manderscheid, R.W. (2002). Children and adolescents admitted to specialty mental health care programs in the United States, 1986 and 1997. In R.W. Manderscheid & M.J. Henderson (Eds.), *Mental health United States, 2002* (pp. 314–326). (DHHS Publication No. SMA04-3938). Washington, DC: U.S. Government Printing Office.

The President's New Freedom Commission on Mental Health. (2003). *Achieving the promise: Transforming mental health care in America. Final report.* Rockville, MD: U.S. Department of Health and Human Services, Substance Abuse and Mental Health Services Administration.

Qi, C.H., & Kaiser, A.P. (2003). Behavior problems of preschool children from low income families: Review of the literature. *Topics in Early Childhood Special Education, 23*(4),188–216.

Ramchandani, P., Stein, A., Evans, J., & O'Connor, T.G. (2005). Paternal depression in the postnatal period and child development: A prospective population study. *The Lancet, 365,* 2201–2205.

Raver, C., & Knitzer, J. (2002). *Ready to enter: What research tells policymakers about strategies to promote social and emotional school readiness among three- and four-year-old children.* New York: National Center for Children in Poverty, Columbia University, Mailman School of Public Health.

Rosman, E., Perry, D., & Hepburn, K. (2006). *The best beginning: Partnerships between primary health care and mental health and substance abuse services.* Washington, DC: Georgetown University, National Technical Assistance Center for Children's Mental Health.

Schechter, S. (Ed.). (2004). *Early childhood, domestic violence and poverty: Helping young children and their families.* Iowa City: University of Iowa, School of Social Work.

Shonkoff, J.P., & Phillips, D.A. (Eds.). National Research Council & Institute of Medicine, Board on Children, Youth, and Families, Committee on Integrating the Science of Early Childhood Development (2000). *From neurons to neighborhoods: The science of early childhood development.* Washington, DC: National Academies Press.

Strain, P., & Timm, M. (2001). Remediation and prevention of aggression: An evaluation of the Regional Intervention Program over a quarter century. *Behavioral Disorders, 26*(4), 297–313.

Van DeMark, N.R., Russell, L.A., O'Keefe, M., Finkelstein, N., Noether, N., & Gampel, J. (2005). Children of mothers with histories of substance abuse, mental illness, and trauma. *Journal of Community Psychology, 33*(4), 445–459.

Van Horn, P., Best, S., & Lieberman, A.F. (1998, November). *Breaking the chain: Preventing transmission of trauma in children through parent-child psychotherapy.* Paper presented at the International Society for Traumatic Stress Studies Annual Meeting, Washington, DC.

Webster-Stratton, C. (1998). Preventing conduct problems in Head Start children: Strengthening parenting competencies. *Journal of Consulting and Clinical Psychology, 66*(5), 715–730.

Weissman, M.M., Pilowsky, D.J., Wickramaratne, P.J., Talati, A., Wisniewski, S.R., & Fava, M. (2006). Remissions in maternal depression and child psychopathology: A STAR*D-child report. *JAMA: Journal of the American Medical Association, 295*(12), 1389–1398.

Werner, E.E. (2000). Protective factors and individual resilience. In J.P. Shonkoff & S.J. Meisels (Eds.), *Handbook of early childhood intervention* (2nd ed.). Cambridge, UK: Cambridge University Press.

West, J., Denton, K., & Reaney, L.M. (2001). *The kindergarten year: Findings from the Early Childhood Longitudinal Study, kindergarten class of 1998–1999* (Publication No. NCES 2001-023). Washington, DC: U.S. Department of Education, National Center for Education Statistics.

Zeanah, Jr., C.H. (2000). *Handbook of infant mental health* (2nd ed.). New York: The Guilford Press.

Appendix A

Self-Assessment Guide

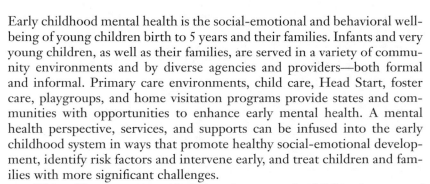

Early childhood mental health is the social-emotional and behavioral well-being of young children birth to 5 years and their families. Infants and very young children, as well as their families, are served in a variety of community environments and by diverse agencies and providers—both formal and informal. Primary care environments, child care, Head Start, foster care, playgroups, and home visitation programs provide states and communities with opportunities to enhance early mental health. A mental health perspective, services, and supports can be infused into the early childhood system in ways that promote healthy social-emotional development, identify risk factors and intervene early, and treat children and families with more significant challenges.

This self-assessment guide is based on an early childhood system of care framework (see Figure A.1) developed to help states and communities conceptualize, organize, and integrate services and supports to meet the mental health needs of young children and their families. Because every state and community is unique with differing needs and capacities, this system of care construct is meant to be used flexibly by your state or community. It provides an illustration of the interdependence and complexity of a system, the need for multiple stakeholders and partners, and the building blocks (infrastructure development) that underpin services and supports. An early childhood system of care approach can be built on existing collaboration efforts with services and supports delivered in environments where young children and families are already served. Early childhood providers and mental health agencies are often unfamiliar partners that may not have worked closely together; yet, each offer specific skills, expertise, and access to services and environments that when combined meet

Developed by Roxane K. Kaufmann in association with the National Technical Assistance Center for Children's Mental Health. Washington, DC: Georgetown University, Center for Child and Human Development.

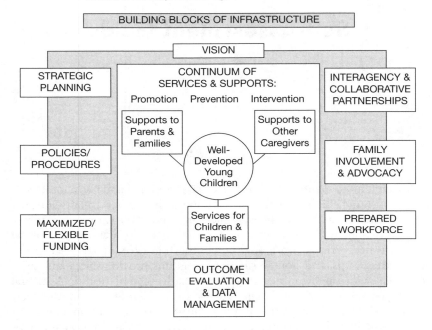

A Framework for Early Childhood Mental Health in A System of Care

Fosters the social and emotional well-being of all
infants, toddlers, preschool-age children and their families

BUILDING BLOCKS OF INFRASTRUCTURE

VISION

STRATEGIC PLANNING

CONTINUUM OF SERVICES & SUPPORTS:

Promotion   Prevention   Intervention

INTERAGENCY & COLLABORATIVE PARTNERSHIPS

Supports to Parents & Families

Well-Developed Young Children

Supports to Other Caregivers

POLICIES/ PROCEDURES

FAMILY INVOLVEMENT & ADVOCACY

Services for Children & Families

MAXIMIZED/ FLEXIBLE FUNDING

PREPARED WORKFORCE

OUTCOME EVALUATION & DATA MANAGEMENT

Figure A.1.   Diagram of early childhood mental health in a system of care.

the increasingly prevalent needs for preventive and early behavioral health interventions for children birth to 5 years and their families.

VISION, VALUES, AND GUIDELINES

- Has your state or community developed a vision, values, and/or guidelines for early childhood mental health? Who was involved in the process?

- Have you determined the population(s) to be served? Be very specific with regard to age of children, how at-risk is defined, and whether a diagnosis is needed to serve children.

POLITICAL AND BUDGET ENVIRONMENT

- Has your state or community experienced changes to the budget that have an impact on early childhood, mental health, or related programs?

- Has the political will to address these early childhood issues changed recently?

STRATEGIC PLANNING AND/OR POLICY DEVELOPMENT

- Are there formal or informal planning processes in your state or community related to early childhood mental health? What is the focus of the initiative(s), which agencies and partners are participating, and which agency is the "lead agency" (if appropriate)?

- What, if any, key legislative or policy initiatives existed prior to your state's early childhood mental health planning? What, if any, key legislative or policy action has occurred as a result of your initiative (e.g., legislation on serving children with multiple risk indicators, a governor's order, changes in Medicaid reimbursement)?

INTERAGENCY PARTNERSHIPS

- Has your state or community developed formal interagency agreements or Memorandum of Understanding (MOU) between early childhood agencies, mental health, and other agencies that guide the planning or delivery of services?

- Has your state developed strong informal interagency partnerships?

- How are state and community partnerships cultivated and maintained?

- What are the interagency issues that you are struggling with currently, if any?

FAMILY INVOLVEMENT AND ADVOCACY

- What family advocacy groups are involved in the planning of your initiative, and what roles have they played in the development and implementation of system-building efforts?

- Are you including families of young children in your planning efforts?

- How are you reaching out to a diverse representation of families— families of color, non-English speakers, and different income groups and families served by different service sectors?

- What supports are provided to facilitate family involvement (e.g., transportation costs, child care, stipends, training)?

- Have you had difficulty in identifying and approaching families of young children with mental health needs? If yes, how are you addressing this issue?

SERVICES AND SUPPORTS

- To what extent does your state or community have a comprehensive array of services and supports for young children and their families? What are the major services and supports for children and for families? Are they available statewide or communitywide?

- How do families and children access early childhood mental health services? Are there multiple points of entry for early childhood mental health services?

- What family supports, such as respite, parent-to-parent support, and family resource centers, are available? How are families informed about these?

- What services and supports are available to other caregivers (e.g., mental health consultation, mentoring, training, reflective supervision, crisis support)?

- Is your state or community funding pilot or demonstration projects? Are they being evaluated?

- What is your state's or community's current service capacity in the areas of 1) promotion, such as the use of mental health screening in physician's offices and library corners with social-emotional health information; 2) preventive services, such as prenatal screening for high-risk mothers, home visiting, and mental health consultation; and 3) intervention services, such as play therapy or dyadic intervention?

CULTURAL COMPETENCE

- Do you have a plan or initiative to address cultural competence in your state or community?

- Is cultural competence being addressed at multiple levels, including policy, system planning, and service delivery?

- What are the major ethnic and racial groups in your state or community?

- Are different ethnic and racial groups involved in your planning efforts?

- Is training available to providers and families on cultural and linguistic competence?

PREPARED WORK FORCE

- How is your state or community addressing the need for well-trained providers (e.g., early childhood mental health in-service and pre-service training, preparation for early childhood and mental health professionals, certification requirements)?

- Do service providers include nontraditional as well as credentialed professionals?

MAXIMIZED AND/OR FLEXIBLE FUNDING AND SUSTAINABILITY

- Is there an inventory of the major federal, state, and local funding being used for early childhood mental health services and supports, noting eligibility criteria?

- How are you organizing funding (e.g., blended, braided, or pooled funding), and are any of the funds flexible?

- Have you been able to redeploy or reinvest funds from restrictive environments (hospitals, residential intervention)?

- Does your state have a managed care initiative, and, if so, are mental health services carved out? Are developmental services bundled?

- Do you have a sustainability plan? If so, please specify.

- Is Early Periodic Screening, Diagnosis, and Treatment being used in your state or community? How?

- Have you reached out to include multiple agencies, foundations, and community organizations to gain broad ownership in your system?

MONITORING AND EVALUATION

- How do you evaluate the progress and effectiveness of your system development and implementation?

- How do you ensure quality services and supports and measure outcomes for children and families?

- How are you using data to advocate for system change?

- Does your state or community have a cross-system data collection mechanism?

Appendix B

Self-Assessment Checklist for Personnel Providing Services and Supports for Children with Disabilities and Special Health Care Needs and Their Families

■ ■ ■

This checklist is intended to heighten the awareness and sensitivity of personnel to the importance of cultural diversity and cultural competence in human service environments. It provides concrete examples of the kinds of values and practices that foster such an environment. There is no answer key with correct responses, however, if you frequently respond "C," you may not necessarily demonstrate values and engage in practices that promote a culturally diverse and culturally competent service delivery system for children with disabilities or special health care needs and their families.

DIRECTIONS

Please select A, B, or C for each item listed following.

A = Things I do frequently

B = Things I do occasionally

C = Things I do rarely or never

Adapted from Goode, T.D. (1989). *Promoting cultural competence and cultural diversity in early intervention and early childhood settings.* Washington, DC: Georgetown University, Center for Child and Human Development.

PHYSICAL ENVIROMENT, MATERIALS, AND RESOURCES

1. I display pictures, posters and other materials that reflect the cultures and ethnic backgrounds of children and families served by my program or agency.

2. I ensure that magazines, brochures, and other printed materials in reception areas are of interest to and reflect the different cultures of children and families served by my program or agency.

3. When using videos, film, or other media resources for health education, treatment, or other interventions, I ensure that they reflect the cultures of children and families served by my program or agency.

4. When using food during an assessment, I ensure that meals provided include foods that are unique to the cultural and ethnic backgrounds of children and families served by my program or agency.

5. I ensure that toys and other play accessories in reception areas, as well as those used during assessment, are representative of the various cultural and ethnic groups in the local community and the society in general.

COMMUNICATION STYLES

6. For children who speak languages or dialects other than English, I attempt to learn and use key words in their language so that I am better able to communicate with them during assessment, treatment, or other interventions.

7. I attempt to determine any familial colloquialisms used by children and families that may have an impact on assessment, treatment, or other interventions.

8. I use visual aids, gestures, and physical prompts in my interactions with children who have limited English proficiency.

9. I use bilingual staff or trained and/or certified interpreters for assessment, treatment, and other interventions with children who have limited English proficiency.

10. I use bilingual staff or trained and/or certified interpreters during assessments, treatment sessions, meetings, and other events for families who would require this level of assistance.

11. When interacting with parents who have limited English proficiency, I always keep in mind that

  • Limitations in English proficiency are in no way a reflection of their level of intellectual functioning

  • Their limited ability to speak the language of the dominant culture has no bearing on their ability to communicate effectively in their language of origin

  • They may or may not be literate in their language of origin or English

12. When possible, I ensure that all notices and communications to parents are written in their language of origin.

13. I understand that it may be necessary to use alternatives to written communications for some families. For example, verbal communication may be a preferred method of receiving information.

14. I understand the principles and practices of linguistic competency, and I

  • Apply them within my program or agency

  • Advocate for them within my program or agency

15. I use alternative formats and varied approaches to communicate and share information with children and/or their family members with disabilities.

VALUES AND ATTITUDES

16. I avoid imposing values that may conflict or be inconsistent with those of cultures or ethnic groups other than my own.

17. In group therapy or intervention situations, I discourage children from using racial and ethnic slurs by helping them understand that certain words can hurt other people.

18. I screen books, movies, and other media resources for negative cultural, ethnic, or racial stereotypes before sharing them with children and their parents or agency.

19. I intervene in an appropriate manner when I observe other staff or parents within my program or agency engaging in behaviors that show cultural insensitivity, bias, or prejudice.

20. I understand and accept that family is defined differently by different cultures (e.g., extended family members, fictive kin, godparents).

21. I recognize and accept that individuals from culturally diverse backgrounds may desire varying degrees of acculturation into the dominant culture.

22. I accept and respect that male–female roles in families may vary significantly among different cultures (e.g., family decisions, play, and social interactions with children).

23. I understand that age and life cycle factors must be considered in interactions with individuals and families (e.g., high value placed on the decisions of elders or the role of the eldest male in a family).

24. Even though my professional or moral viewpoints may differ, I accept the family/parents as the ultimate decision makers for services and supports for their children.

25. I recognize that the meaning or value of medical treatment, health care, and health education may vary greatly among cultures.

26. I recognize and understand that beliefs and concepts of emotional well-being vary significantly from culture to culture.

27. I understand that beliefs about mental illness and emotional disability are culturally based. I accept that responses to these conditions and related interventions are heavily influenced by culture.

28. I accept that religion and other beliefs may influence how families respond to illness, disease, disability, and death.

29. I recognize and accept that familial folklore, religious, or spiritual beliefs may influence a family's reaction and approach to a child born with a disability or later diagnosed with a physical and/or emotional disability or special health care needs.

30. I understand that traditional approaches to disciplining children are influenced by culture.

31. I understand that families from different cultures will have different expectations of their children for acquiring toileting, dressing, feeding, and other self-help skills.

32. I accept and respect that customs and beliefs about food and its value, preparation, and use are different from culture to culture.

33. Before visiting or providing services in the home environment, I seek information on acceptable behaviors, courtesies, customs, and expec-

tations that are unique to families of specific cultures and ethnic groups served by my program or agency.

34. I seek information from family members or other key community informants that will assist in service adaptation to respond to the needs and preferences of culturally and ethnically diverse children and families served by my program or agency.

35. I advocate for the review of my program's or agency's mission statement, goals, policies, and procedures to ensure that they incorporate principles and practices that promote cultural diversity and cultural competence.

Appendix C

Self-Assessment Checklist for Personnel Providing Services and Supports in Early Intervention and Early Childhood Environments

■ ■ ■

This checklist is intended to heighten the awareness and sensitivity of personnel to the importance of cultural diversity, cultural competence, and linguistic competence in early childhood environments. It provides concrete examples of the kinds of practices that foster such an environment. There is no answer key with correct responses, however, if you frequently responded "C," you may not necessarily demonstrate practices that promote a culturally diverse and culturally competent learning environment for children and families within your classroom, program, or agency.

DIRECTIONS

Please select A, B, or C for each item listed following.

A = Things I do frequently

B = Things I do occasionally

C = Things I do rarely or never

Adapted from Goode, T.D. (1989). *Promoting cultural competence and cultural diversity in early intervention and early childhood settings.* Washington, DC: Georgetown University, Center for Child and Human Development.

PHYSICAL ENVIRONMENTS, MATERIALS, AND RESOURCES

1. I display pictures, posters, and other materials that reflect the cultures and ethnic backgrounds of children and families served in my early childhood program or environment.

2. I select props for the dramatic play and housekeeping area that are culturally diverse (e.g. dolls, clothing, cooking utensils, household articles, furniture).

3. I ensure that the book/literacy area has pictures and storybooks that reflect the different cultures of children and families served in my early childhood program or environment.

4. I ensure that toys and other play accessories (that depict people) are representative of the various cultural and ethnic groups both in my community and the society in general.

5. I read a variety of books exposing children in my early childhood program or environment to various life experiences of cultures and ethnic groups other than their own.

6. When diverse books are not available, I provide opportunities for children and their families to create their own books and include them among the resources and materials in my early childhood program or environment.

7. I encourage and provide opportunities for children and their families to share experiences through storytelling, puppets, marionettes, or other props to support the oral tradition common among many cultures.

8. I plan trips and community outings to places where children and their families can learn about their own cultural or ethnic history as well as the history of others.

9. I select videos, films, or other media resources reflective of diverse cultures to share with children and families served in my early childhood program or environment.

10. I play a variety of music and introduce musical instruments from many cultures.

11. I ensure that meals provided include foods that are unique to the cultural and ethnic backgrounds of children and families served in my early childhood program or environment.

12. I provide opportunities for children to cook or sample a variety of foods typically served by cultural and ethnic groups other than their own.

13.   If my early childhood program or environment consists entirely of children and families from the same cultural or ethnic group, I feel it is important to plan an environment and implement activities that reflect the cultural diversity in the society at large.

14.   I am cognizant of and ensure that the curricula I use include traditional holidays celebrated by the majority culture, as well as those holidays that are unique to the culturally diverse children and families served in my early childhood program or environment.

COMMUNICATION STYLES

15.   For children who speak languages or dialects other than English, I attempt to learn and use key words in their language so that I am better able to communicate with them.

16.   I attempt to determine any familial colloquialisms used by children and families that will assist and/or enhance the delivery of services and supports.

17.   I use visual aids, gestures, and physical prompts in my interactions with children who have limited English proficiency.

18.   When interacting with parents and other family members who have limited English proficiency, I always keep in mind that

   • Limitation in English proficiency is in no way a reflection of their level of intellectual functioning

   • Their limited ability to speak the language of the dominant culture has no bearing on their ability to communicate effectively in their language of origin

   • They may be neither literate in their language of origin nor English

19.   I ensure that all notices and communication to parents are written in their language of origin.

20.   I understand that it may be necessary to use alternatives to written communications for some families. For example, verbal communication may be a preferred method of receiving information.

21.   I understand the principles and practices of linguistic competency, and I

   • Apply them within my early childhood program or environment

   • Advocate for them within my program or agency

22. I use bilingual or multilingual staff and/or trained and/or certified foreign language interpreters for meetings, conferences, or other events for parents and family members who may require this level of assistance.

23. I encourage and invite parents and family members to volunteer and assist with activities regardless of their ability to speak English.

24. I use alternative formats and varied approaches to communicate with children and/or their family members with disabilities.

25. I arrange accommodations for parents and family members who may require communication assistance to ensure their full participation in all aspects of the early childhood program (e.g., hearing impaired, physical disability, visually impaired, illiterate or low literacy).

26. I accept and recognize that there are often differences between language used in early childhood and/or early intervention environments, or at school, and in the home environment.

VALUES AND ATTITUDES

27. I avoid imposing values that may conflict or be inconsistent with those of cultures or ethnic groups other than my own.

28. I discourage children from using racial and ethnic slurs by helping them understand that certain words can hurt other people.

29. I screen books, movies, and other media resources for negative cultural, ethnic, racial, or religious stereotypes before sharing them with children and their families served in my early childhood program or environment.

30. I provide activities to help children learn about and accept the differences and similarities in all people as an ongoing component of program curricula.

31. I intervene in an appropriate manner when I observe other staff or parents in my program or agency engaging in behaviors that show cultural insensitivity, bias, or prejudice.

32. I recognize and accept that individuals from culturally diverse backgrounds may desire varying degrees of acculturation into the dominant culture.

33. I understand and accept that family is defined differently by different cultures (e.g., extended family members, fictive kin, godparents).

34. I accept and respect that male–female roles in families may vary significantly among different cultures (e.g., family decision-maker, play and social interactions expected of children).

35. I understand that age and life cycle factors must be considered in interactions with families (e.g., high value placed on the decisions or child-rearing practices of older family members, the role of the oldest female in the family).

36. Even though my professional or moral viewpoints may differ, I accept the family and/or parents as the ultimate decision makers for services and supports for their children.

37. I accept that religion, spirituality, and other beliefs may influence how families respond to illness, disease, and death.

38. I recognize and understand that beliefs and concepts of mental health or emotional well-being, particularly for infants and young children, vary significantly from culture to culture.

39. I recognize and accept that familial folklore, religious, or spiritual beliefs may influence a family's reaction and approach to a child born with a disability or later diagnosed with a disability or special health care needs.

40. I understand that beliefs about mental illness and emotional disability are culturally based. I accept that responses to these conditions and related interventions are heavily influenced by culture.

41. I understand that the health care practices of families served in my early childhood program or environment may be rooted in cultural traditions.

42. I recognize that the meaning or value of early childhood education or early intervention may vary greatly among cultures.

43. I understand that traditional approaches to disciplining children are influenced by culture.

44. I understand that families from different cultures will have different expectations of their children for acquiring toileting, dressing, feeding, and other self-help skills.

45. I accept and respect that customs and beliefs about food and its value, preparation, and use are different from culture to culture.

46. Before visiting or providing services in the home environment, I seek information on acceptable behaviors, courtesies, customs, and expectations that are unique to families of specific cultural groups served in my early childhood program or environment.

47. I advocate for the review of my program's or agency's mission statement, goals, policies, and procedures to ensure that they incorporate principles and practices that promote cultural diversity, cultural competence, and linguistic competence.

48. I seek information from family members or other key community informants that will assist me to respond effectively to the needs and preferences of culturally and linguistically diverse children and families served in my early childhood program or environment.

Appendix D

Spending Smarter

*A Funding Guide for Policy Makers and
Advocates to Promote Social-Emotional
Health and School Readiness*

THE SPENDING SMARTER CHECKLIST: A GUIDE FOR POLICY MAKERS, FAMILIES, ADVOCATES, AND SERVICE PROVIDERS

Following are a set of questions for state officials, families, advocates, and practitioners that can help drive a strategic approach to strengthening social and emotional school readiness and building early childhood mental health capacity. No state has implemented all of these recommendations, but together they provide a framework for prioritizing state and local action.

☐ Yes, done
☐ Under development
☐ Needs effort

1. Does your state have a cross-agency strategic planning group to build strategic early childhood mental health capacity? Does the planning group

    • Include families? Providers?

    • Link to a larger early childhood/school readiness planning process?

    • Include a dedicated fiscal planning group?

This checklist is adapted from *Spending Smarter: A Funding Guide for Policymakers and Advocates to Promote Social and Emotional Health and School Readiness*, (2005) by Kay Johnson and Jane Knitzer. *Spending Smarter* is designed to help state legislators, agency officials, families, and other advocates think strategically and take steps to meet the challenge of utilizing existing funding streams to promote the social and emotional health and school readiness of young children. The framework and content of Spending Smarter is designed to help state and local leaders maximize the effect of federal funding and feel confident that they are using existing resources in the most effective way. (Full copies of the report and other resources to help promote school readiness are available from the web site of the National Center for Children in Poverty, http://www.nccp.org)

☐ Yes, done
☐ Under
   development
☐ Needs effort

2. Does the state cross-agency strategic agenda include explicit efforts to build overall system capacity? Does your state

- Map how each system currently supports prevention, early intervention, and intervention services?

- Map gaps in existing community-based programs or early childhood mental health initiatives across the state?

- Create incentives for community-based, cross-agency training initiatives?

- Implement targeted collaborations across Individuals with Disabilities Education Improvement Act (IDEA) of 2004 (PL 108-446) Part C, child welfare, and early childhood programs?

- Build common definitions across programs for young children at risk of early school failure and/or developing social and emotional disorders?

- Ensure family/two-generation intervention for the most vulnerable (e.g., promoting collaboration across child and adult mental health, substance abuse, and domestic violence programs)?

- Pay for intervention for adults in the context of home visiting programs and comprehensive early childhood programs?

- Use smaller grant programs strategically to promote system-building capacity (e.g., Foundations for Learning, Safe and Drug Free Schools, Early Learning Opportunities, and Good Start, Grow Smart)?

☐ Yes, done
☐ Under development
☐ Needs effort

3. Is your state maximizing the effect of Medicaid and/or the State Children's Health Insurance Program (SCHIP)? Does your state

- Require/permit Early & Periodic Screening, Diagnostic, and Treatment age-appropriate screening and diagnostic tools for infants, toddlers, and preschoolers that are sensitive to social, emotional, and behavioral issues?

- Pay for covered services delivered in a range of community-based settings?

- Include separate definitions and billing codes for developmental assessment/screening and diagnostic evaluations?

- Use state matching funds strategically with Medicaid to support behavioral and mental health consultation in child care and home visiting programs?

- Provide reimbursement for parent-child therapy?

- Cover necessary services for social and emotional needs under the SCHIP benefits package?

☐ Yes, done
☐ Under development
☐ Needs effort

4. Is your state maximizing the effect of Title V Maternal and Child Health Services Block Grant? Does your state

- Use Title V's flexible funding strategically to cover services and supports for families and other caregivers that cannot be provided through Medicaid (e.g., cross-training)?

- Explicitly include children who are at increased risk for developmental, behavioral, or emotional challenges according to the state definition of Children with Special Health Care Needs (CSHCN)?

- Maximize the potential of the Early Childhood Comprehensive Systems (ECCS) planning grants, including a focus on the most vulnerable?

- Use the flexibility under Title V to develop and/or finance programs for maternal depression or other two-generation intervention strategies?

☐ Yes, done
☐ Under development
☐ Needs effort

5. Is your state maximizing the effect of the Child Care and Development Fund (CCDF) to promote social and emotional health and school readiness? Does your state

- Define explicit strategies to promote social and emotional health and school readiness competencies in children and improve the skills of caregivers in the state's CCDF plan?

- Use CCDF funds to support training for the early childhood community on social, emotional, and school readiness issues?

- Ensure that the highest-risk young children are in high-quality child care settings?

- Use CCDF funds to support early childhood mental health consultation through the quality set-aside? Use other funds?

☐ Yes, done
☐ Under development
☐ Needs effort

6. Is your state maximizing the potential of special education programs on behalf of infants and toddlers at risk of developmental delays and on behalf of preschoolers with identified disabilities? Does your state

- Ensure appropriate social and emotional assessments in IDEA Part C Child Find screening activities, as well as in comprehensive, developmental, multidisciplinary evaluations?

- Use the option to extend IDEA Part C eligibility to at-risk infants and toddlers, with emphasis on social, emotional, and environmental risk factors?

- Identify infants and toddlers exposed to substance abuse, domestic violence, and maternal depression as a high-risk group? Extend eligibility for Part C services?

□ Yes, done
□ Under develop-
  ment
□ Needs effort

7. Is your state maximizing the effect of the Child Abuse Prevention, Adoption and Family Services Act of 1988 (PL 100-294)? Does your state

   • Require collaboration across public health agencies, child protection systems, and community-based programs to provide child abuse and neglect prevention as well as intervention services?

   • Have a mechanism to ensure that screenings of young children at risk who have experienced abuse or neglect and/or witnessed domestic violence lead to interperiodic reviews, assessments, and/or referrals for early intervention?

   • Require that all children from birth to age 3 entering the foster care system be assessed through the IDEA Part C Early Intervention program?

□ Yes, done
□ Under develop-
  ment
□ Needs effort

8. Does your state maximize the effect of programs serving the most vulnerable families with young children? Does your state

   • Use Title IV-B funding to create two-generation child mental health and behavioral interventions for families with young children in or at risk for foster care placement?

   • Use Temporary Assistance for Needy Families (TANF) grant dollars for family counseling, service coordination, substance abuse intervention, family support, and training activities?

   • Transfer TANF funds to the CCDF to jump-start behavioral and mental health early childhood consultation strategies?

- Strategically use funds from family violence/domestic violence, substance abuse, prevention, intervention, and community-based family resource and support to promote intervention and two-generation strategies targeted to families with young children?

REFERENCES

Child Abuse Prevention, Adoption and Family Services Act of 1988, PL 100-294, 42 U.S.C. §§ 5101 *et seq.*

Individuals with Disabilities Education Improvement Act (IDEA) of 2004, PL 108-446, 20 U.S.C. §§ 1400 *et seq.*